## MODERN AMERICAN CRITICISM
Walter Sutton

## MUSICOLOGY
Frank Ll. Harrison     Mantle Hood
Claude V. Palisca

## THE ORIGINS OF AMERICAN HUMANISTIC SCHOLARS
Robert H. Knapp

## PHILOSOPHY
Roderick M. Chisholm     Herbert Feigl
William K. Frankena     John Passmore
Manley Thompson

## RELIGION
Paul Ramsey, ed.
Philip H. Ashby     Robert M. Grant
James M. Gustafson     J. H. Nichols
Harry M. Orlinsky     John E. Smith
Claude Welch

## RELIGION, A HUMANISTIC FIELD
Clyde A. Holbrook

*The aim of these volumes is to present a critical account of American humanistic scholarship in recent decades. They have been commissioned by the Council of the Humanities, Whitney J. Oates, Chairman, of Princeton University and were made possible by a grant from the Ford Foundation.*

—Richard Schlatter, General Editor.

RICHARD SCHLATTER, GENERAL EDITOR

*Humanistic Scholarship in America*

❧ THE PRINCETON STUDIES ☙

THE COUNCIL OF THE HUMANITIES
WHITNEY J. OATES, CHAIRMAN
PRINCETON UNIVERSITY

ANTHROPOLOGY

Eric R. Wolf

ART AND ARCHAEOLOGY

James S. Ackerman     Rhys Carpenter

CHINESE PAINTING

Wen Fong

CLASSICS

Eric A. Havelock

ENGLISH LITERATURE

David Daiches

FOREIGN LITERATURE

Henri Peyre

HISTORY

John Higham
Leonard Krieger     Felix Gilbert

LINGUISTICS

Eric P. Hamp     Karl D. Uitti
Rulon Wells

# HISTORY

ﻉ§ §ﻉ

## JOHN HIGHAM

WITH

## LEONARD KRIEGER
and
## FELIX GILBERT

PRENTICE-HALL, INC.    ENGLEWOOD CLIFFS    NEW JERSEY

# FOREWORD

When we first planned the volumes for the Ford Humanities Project at Princeton we set as our goal a series of essays that would be "contributions to that part of American intellectual history which has to do with humanistic scholarship." The present volume is such a contribution and more too. For it appears that historical scholarship occupies so central and commanding a position in America today that a volume describing that scholarship inevitably comes near to being a full history of the American mind.

In an earlier volume of this series (*The Origins of American Humanistic Scholars*), Robert Knapp remarks that "of all the disciplines reviewed in this study . . . history is in the most fortunate circumstances"; "historians have a surer confidence both in their mission and their effectiveness than scholars in other humanistic disciplines . . . and they less often complain of their isolation from the mainstream of the intellectual life of their times." The essays in this volume show in detail how this has come about. John Higham describes the "renewal" in historical studies in recent decades and points to the happy circumstance that the "academic schism between history and the humanities [has] largely healed."

The philosopher of our era has vacated the chair of speculative thought and no longer talks about the big questions that interest all thinking men. The literary critic has a hard job filling the role of universal pundit because so much of the best literature of our time is esoteric: he inevitably talks mostly about books and poems that the educated public has not read. The historian, however, whose method is rigorous and intellectually exacting, but whose work is interesting and intelligible to amateurs as well as professionals, to generalists as well as specialists, is both scientist and humanist and has taken over the roles abandoned by the philosopher and the critic.

In the final essay in this volume, Professor Gilbert indicates the centrality of the historian's task:

The foremost task of the historian is to regain an image of the past in which history emerges as the conceptualization of a unified process. For the existence of history as a profession and as an independent field depends on the conception of the past as a totality. But the need for reconstructing a historical consciousness that integrates the present with the past is much more than the professional interest of the historian. It is rooted in the general need of our time. Because history is the study of man in his social conditions, the establishment of the relation of the past to the present reasserts the role of man in a world that appears to slide out of human control. And justification for the concern with history is the conviction that "there is no future without a past and there is no past without a future."

Because I was once a historian myself, I have had a special interest in this volume. My hopes that it would be a superlative study have, I think, been fulfilled. Nothing could be a more apt illustration of the excellent state of historical scholarship in this country than these learned, graceful, and illuminating essays.

RICHARD SCHLATTER
General Editor

# PREFACE

History is one of the oldest and most protean forms of intellectual activity. Any story about human experience that tries to exclude fable and error in the interest of truth has a claim to the name of history. Our constant need to remember the jumble of experience in orderly sequence makes everyone a historian. In daily life historical thinking engages each of us, just as we must all be moralists in making decisions, actors in playing roles, and artists in arranging materials. The reconstruction of the past not only resembles such stubbornly practical occupations but also incorporates them: it involves commitment, enactment, and design. History is common; but it is also complex.

Accordingly, it has always resisted codification. Historical thinking proceeds with a minimum of rules, lending itself to all the cross-purposes of life. Historians have never elaborated a special language, a consistent theoretical system, or uniform criteria for evaluating their performance. Until fairly recent times, history had no distinctive place in educational curriculums, and few men gave their whole careers to writing it. In Samuel Johnson's rude opinion,

> Great parts were not requisite for a historian, as in that kind of composition all the greatest powers of the human mind are quiescent. He has facts ready to his hand, so he has no exercise of invention. Imagination is not required in any high degree; only about as much as is used in the lower parts of poetry. Some penetration, accuracy, and coloring will fit a man for such a task, who can give the application which is necessary.[1]

Yet the development of historical understanding, during the century following Johnson's summary verdict, was one of the most striking features of Western culture. Both historiography and historical thinking in a larger sense advanced as never before. We have come to realize that the historical movement of the nineteenth century was perhaps second only to the scientific revolution of the

[1] *Boswell's London Journal, 1762-1763*, ed. Frederick A. Pottle (1950), p. 293.

seventeenth century in transforming Western thought and shaping our modern mentality.[2] One consequence was extensive organization and professionalization of research. Another consequence was penetration of a historical point of view into art, literature, philosophy, theology, and the new sciences of man. Herder, Marx, Darwin, Tolstoy, and Weber, to name just a few, were all historical thinkers. Henceforth no cultivated person could feel that history left the greatest powers of the mind quiescent.

An adequate account of the historical movement is yet to be written, and we have not aspired to so large an undertaking in this volume. Our interest centers on the American professional historian. We have tried, however, to understand his involvement in the whole historical movement and in the difficulties it has encountered. While scholarship progressed in refinement and comprehensiveness, history seemed to lose in the intellectual life of the early twentieth century some of the importance it had in the nineteenth. How historians responded under the particular conditions of American culture is one of our chief concerns.

In order to speak to such large questions, we have had to be selective in coverage. Of the eight thousand historians employed in colleges and universities in the United States in 1962, nearly half specialize in American history. Another quarter interest themselves primarily in modern Europe.[3] The remainder are scattered among a great variety of other fields. To have analyzed the internal development of these many fields would have meant assigning chapters to a large number of specialists. Rather than fragment our report, we have confined our discussion of historical literature to the two fields of widest contemporary interest after giving an over-all view of the historical profession from the point of view of institutions and assumptions. Thus the book begins by examining the social and institutional situation of American historians, moves on to their general conceptions about the study of history, then specifies the patterns of meaning they have found close at hand in their own national past and a little more distantly in Europe. Finally, the view widens to permit a summation of the characteristics of American

[2] Herbert Butterfield, *Man on His Past* (1960), p. vii.
[3] U.S. Department of Labor, *Occupational Outlook Handbook, 1963-64*, p. 169, gives total figures. The estimate by fields is from Dexter Perkins and John L. Snell's *The Education of Historians in the United States* (1961), pp. 30-32.

scholarship against a background of historical thought and activity in other countries.

This book was originally conceived in more modest terms. We set out simply to report on the state of historical scholarship in America today. As historians, we soon discovered that we could not make sense of the present apart from the past. To find ourselves we needed to look back; the book became a history. Each author went back as far as he thought necessary to establish a firm base. Professor Krieger, in asking how Americans comprehend European history, reaches all the way back to our earliest historical writing. Professor Gilbert, in asking how the historical enterprise in modern America compares with the study of history in Europe, starts from the crystallization of history as an academic discipline in the early nineteenth century. The main body of the book begins with the transformation of American universities in the 1870's and 1880's and the establishment of historical study therein. Although we have tried not to be superficial, we are fully conscious of having realized no more than a first approximation of a complicated story.

In analyzing themselves and their antecedents as honestly as men can, the authors have enjoyed a most fruitful congeniality. After agreeing to a general plan of attack, each went his own way. Each is alone responsible for the faults of his part of the job. But we have profited from reading and criticizing one another's work, and we have drawn much encouragement from learning that our individual paths led in a common direction. The first three sections of the book also benefited greatly from the generous response many colleagues at home and abroad made to impertinent inquiries. Thanks are owing especially to Miriam and Alfred Vagts, Arthur M. Schlesinger, Allan Nevins, and Roy F. Nichols for supplying certain manuscripts and memories; to Boyd C. Shafer of the American Historical Association, and Paul Webbink and Eleanor C. Isbell of the Social Science Research Council, for facilitating access to the files of their respective organizations; to Bradford Perkins, Boyd C. Shafer, Trygve Tholfsen, and W. Stull Holt for a critical reading of various chapters; and to Stuart Samuels, Raymond Detter, and Susan Brimm for strengthening parts of the research.

JOHN HIGHAM
Professor of History
University of Michigan

# CONTENTS

## CONTENTS

## ⋙ I ⋘

# THE HISTORICAL PROFESSION

‰ॐๆ‱

From the time of the earliest English settlements in America, men and women of many sorts have been writing history. No one group has ever had a monopoly of the production of competent histories. Leadership in setting standards, however, has usually belonged to a particular class. Twice this leadership has changed hands.

During the seventeenth century the best history was written by Puritan clergymen and by lay officials associated with them in creating a new Zion in the wilderness. They wrote hastily, in whatever moments they could spare from active labors in behalf of the Puritan cause. Their history was a further extension of scripture: a chronicle of God's inscrutable will working within their own community. Clergymen long remained one of the most numerous species of historical writers, but their importance diminished as the church ceased to form the cultural center of American life.

In the eighteenth century, patrician historians came to the fore. The growth of private wealth allowed a margin of leisure time for their studies. The weightiness of history appealed to the strong sense of social responsibility that characterized many American gentlemen; to them the historian was the ultimate human judge of men and events. They strove—without always succeeding, of course—to play a judicial role fairly and impartially, for the patrician, untrammeled by religious orthodoxy, prided himself on his independence of mind. He participated in a wide, transatlantic literary culture and wrote for an unspecialized, cultivated audience.[1] During the greater part of the eighteenth and nineteenth centuries the patrician historian held the center of the stage, and in the works of Thomas Hutchinson, Charles Gayarré, Francis Parkman, Henry C. Lea, and others, his history reached a high level of accuracy and distinction.

After 1870 a new social type appeared, and by the end of the cen-

[1] The most detailed studies are Michael Kraus's *The Writing of American History*, rev. ed. (1953); David D. Van Tassel's *Recording America's Past, 1607-1884* (1960); Kenneth Murdock's *Literature and Theology in Colonial New England* (1949), pp. 67-97; Richard S. Dunn's "Seventeenth-Century English Historians of America," in *Seventeenth-Century America*, ed. James Morton Smith (1959), pp. 195-225. For social origins see also George H. Callcott's "Historians in Early Nineteenth-Century America," *New England Quarterly*, XXXII (1959), 496-520.

tury it was becoming the dominant figure in American historiography. As the Puritan gave way to the patrician, so the patrician at length yielded leadership to the professional historian. Unlike any of his predecessors, the professional historian devoted substantially his entire career to teaching and writing. Earlier scholars, largely self-taught, usually turned to serious historical studies in their mature years. The professional learned his skills and fixed his course as a student at a university, there imbibing precept and example from established scholars.

Two signal developments in higher education made this possible. First, the breakdown of the old classical curriculum and the rise of the elective system created a new need for college teachers of history. College curriculums until the 1870's had room for very few history courses, and these were generally taught by professors primarily interested in the classics or in philosophy. As late as 1884 the four hundred American institutions of higher education had about twenty full-time teachers of history. At Princeton the sole professor of history also taught political science.[2] A decade later nearly a hundred college teachers devoted full time to history, and the demand was growing steadily.[3] Meanwhile the modern university, conceived as a center for research and graduate training, became at last, after many abortive antebellum attempts, the capstone of the educational system. The opening of The Johns Hopkins University in 1876 and the transformation of Harvard during the same decade pointed the way. The university supplied an institutional setting for professional scholarship, and, by the requirements for its Ph.D. degree, transmitted an incentive for research to the college teachers whom it trained. The professional historian materialized in the guise of a teacher-specialist. After a long intervening period of free-lance scholarship, historians again became, as they had been in Puritan New England, servants of an institution.

Although the university provided a new institutional basis for historical scholarship, it could not alone supply the discipline and esprit de corps a profession requires. A profession is, among other

[2] Charles W. Eliot, *Educational Reform: Essays and Addresses* (1909), pp. 105-106; G. Stanley Hall, ed., *Methods of Teaching and Studying History* (1886), pp. 49-50; J. F. Jameson, "The American Historical Association, 1884-1909," *American Historical Review*, XV (1909), 2.

[3] J. F. Jameson, "The American Historical Review, 1895-1920," *American Historical Review*, XXVI (1920), 2.

things, a body of individuals with a particular skill, who by cooperative action establish and maintain their own standards of achievement instead of obeying some external authority. While universities furnished professional training and opportunity, the new type of scholar also needed his own nationwide organization for the promotion of his collective interests and the regulation of his work. This he secured through the American Historical Association, founded in 1884. The reciprocal relations between this emerging Association and the existing world of amateur scholarship constitute the central theme in the formation of a historical profession.

# FORMATIVE YEARS

It is clear in retrospect that amateur and professional historians operate very differently, and that the shift from one kind of leadership to the other has not been all clear gain. The most conspicuous advantage of professionalism inhered in the coordination of many individuals' efforts. "Scholars and students can no longer afford to live in isolation," insisted the chairman at the organizing session of the American Historical Association.[1] By working together, professionals pooled their knowledge and collaborated with more or less success in assembling materials, facilitating research, organizing collective projects, disseminating ideas, criticizing results, and multiplying the number of historians. One result was an enormous quantitative increase in sound historical writing. Moreover, the professional spirit of coordination required, in theory at least, that every individual investigation should reach outward toward a larger organization of historical knowledge; every local inquiry should relate itself to a general pattern of development. Thus the professional made war on the disconnected nature of amateur scholarship.

A cooperative ethic had, however, the disadvantage of putting more emphasis on attainment of a general level of competence than on the creation of unique achievements. The cultivation of talent discouraged to some degree a quest for genius. One of the founders of the American Historical Association, J. Franklin Jameson, grasped very early the nature of the choice that was being made, and accepted it. "Now it is the spread of thoroughly good second-class work," he wrote in 1891, ". . . that our science most needs at present; for it sorely needs that improvement in technical process, that superior finish of workmanship, which a large number of works of talent can do more to foster than a few works of literary genius."[2]

The standards of craftsmanship for which Jameson spoke took on

[1] Quoted in David D. Van Tassel, "The American Historical Association and the South, 1884-1913," *Journal of Southern History,* XXIII (1957), 466.
[2] J. F. Jameson, *The History of Historical Writing in America* (1891), pp. 132-33.

such importance in professional eyes that content could easily suffer at the expense of technique. Moreover, the guild-enclosed historian could not escape the standardization of goals and activities that is inherent in organizational life. In spite of a self-critical spirit built into professional history, the insular and fraternal habits of professional association tended to perpetuate the high level of mediocrity that Jameson regarded as a necessary but temporary stage in preparing the way for truly great and profound work. Perhaps the teaching function of the professional historian also sustained a good-natured tolerance of routine performance. In the protected atmosphere of the classroom a man continually responsible to others younger and less mature than himself does not easily hold to an extravagant and selfish ideal of achievement.

The amateur historian, on the other hand, cherished his independence. John Bach McMaster, a self-made historian who secured a professorship at Pennsylvania because he wrote an outstanding book, a scholar who was notably absent at the founding of the American Historical Association, illustrated the amateur spirit in opposing the Carnegie plan for pensioning retired professors. "I believe that in this and in all professions, as in business, each man should stand on his own basis, and on that alone," McMaster announced in his highly unprofessional way.[3] Similarly, the amateur historian expected his work to survive or perish on its individual merits; he was little concerned about its status as a "contribution" to some continuing collective inquiry. Having no feeling of corporate identity (except in a local or ethnic sense), the amateur historian did not write primarily for other historians. He chose his subject for its intrinsic interest and wrote either for his own satisfaction or for a public that would accept him on his own terms. He might have too little knowledge and appreciation of technique, but he never had too much.

So, in time, many amateur historians grew contemptuous of their professional brethren. "After a while," Theodore Roosevelt recalled, "it dawned on me that all of the conscientious, industrious, painstaking little pedants, who would have been useful in a rather small way if they had understood their own limitations, had become because of their conceit distinctly noxious. They solemnly believed that if there were only enough of them, and that if they only collected

---

[3] Eric Goldman, *John Bach McMaster, American Historian* (1943), pp. 70-71.

enough facts of all kinds and sorts, there would cease to be any need hereafter for great writers, great thinkers." [4]

One might suppose, in view of this sharp divergence, that the professional summarily thrust the amateur aside, that lines of battle were drawn from the outset, and that the victory of one meant the defeat of the other. Things were not that simple. Neither a professional ethic nor a mature professional organization came into being overnight in 1884. These developed gradually and did not become distinct until the twentieth century. The new school of Ph.D.'s, although quite self-conscious in the eighties, had not yet found its place in American culture. It needed the help and sought the aid of everyone seriously interested in history. Aid was readily extended, for the better amateur historians fully shared the professionals' interest in raising the standards of cultural activity in America. Much of the character of modern American historiography will remain obscure unless we appreciate that it sprang from the combined efforts of independent gentlemen and professional scholars, who comprised initially a homogeneous class with a common mission.

The rise of a professional outlook in the field of history was an integral part of a broad movement for the establishment of authority in American intellectual life. In almost all fields of cultural endeavor, associations that defined standards and goals appeared in the late nineteenth century. The American Historical Association was one among a great number of such bodies. The American Philological Association made its debut in 1869. At least 79 learned societies were organized in the next decade, and 121 in the Eighties. The new universities not only introduced graduate schools of arts and sciences but also multiplied and immensely invigorated the nation's professional schools. Beginning in the 1870's, physicians underwent increasing regulation by state examining boards. The spread of state and local bar associations and the organization of the American Bar Association in 1878 strengthened the professional consciousness of lawyers.[5] The National Education Association (1870) tried to do the same with teachers.

[4] Quoted in Howard K. Beale, "The Professional Historian: His Theory and His Practice," *Pacific Historical Review,* XXII (1953), 228.
[5] Merle Curti, *The Growth of American Thought,* 2nd ed. (1951), pp. 586-88; James Bryce, *The American Commonwealth,* 2nd ed., vol. II (London, 1891), p. 502; Richard Harrison Shryock, *The Development of Modern Medicine* (London, 1948), p. 284.

Other agencies stepped forward to exercise custodial jurisdiction over literature and the arts. The great metropolitan art museums, most of which were established in the 1870's, served as weighty arbiters of taste. New nonpartisan, nondenominational magazines— the *Atlantic Monthly,* the *Century, Scribner's*—labored to elevate and guide a national middle-class audience in the pursuit of culture and respectability. The *Nation,* edited by E. L. Godkin, was the most distinguished and influential of these journals. Throughout the last third of the nineteenth century it was the authoritative voice of the patrician and academic intelligentsia. In 1868 Godkin had complained that all groups in America were organized except "the chaotic mass of persons scattered from Maine to California to whom mental culture is one of the great objects of this mortal life." [6] By the end of the century the chaotic mass had undergone an organizational revolution comparable to the trust movement in American business. There was even, after 1898, a National Institute of Arts and Letters, an honorific, self-appointed body modeled on the great European academies.

Scholars inevitably participated prominently in this movement of consolidation, since it blended with a long-term trend toward specialization and technical refinement in intellectual life. It also enlisted the cultivated patrician class, for the movement represented a profound reaction against the democratic openness and rawness of the pre-Civil War era. America in the midnineteenth century had had a paucity of effective intellectual institutions. Its strikingly undisciplined culture had thrown off institutional restraints on the individual. It valued the omnicompetence of the common man above the tutelage of any elite. In the late nineteenth century, urbanization, conservatism, and a general weakening of democratic values contributed to a reassertion of leadership by established authorities.

Thus patricians readily joined professional scholars in enterprises calculated to uplift and codify American culture; they could not anticipate how far the codification would go, or how much their own intellectual pre-eminence would ultimately suffer. The academic men, for their part, felt at home in patrician circles. James Bryce noticed in the late Eighties that American professors, in spite of modest salaries, seemed always to be among the local social aristocracy. They were dignified, frock-coated gentlemen, and at Columbia Uni-

6 E. L. Godkin, "The Organization of Culture," *Nation,* VII (1868), 486-88.

9

versity before the turn of the century professors were almost automatically listed in the New York *Social Register*. (At the best universities even the salaries of the top professors were substantial. A few exceeded $5,000 in a time when many school teachers earned $500 and maids were available for $3.50 per week.) [7] As if to symbolize the alliance of academic authority with aristocratic traditions, universities in the late nineteenth century adopted ceremonial robes for formal occasions, and enclosed their new laboratories in ivy-covered Gothic.

Moreover, most academic scholars shared the social ideals of their patrician associates. Both groups conceived of themselves as guides for a democratic society that overestimated material success and undervalued "the higher ideals of life." Both felt a common mission to civilize the masses on the one hand and subdue the upstart nouveaux riches on the other. Both echoed the *Nation* and the *Atlantic* in calling for "an educated class amongst us, to be the guardians of the traditions and feelings and aspirations of high culture, and the diffuser of an atmosphere of thought and study—a kind of barrier, too, against the gross materialism of the time, the growing tendency to estimate the value of everything in dollars and cents, and to despise or shirk all discipline of mind or body which does not promise a speedy return in hard cash." This class would constitute, said William T. Harris, U.S. Commissioner of Education, an "aristocracy of culture," disputing alike the claims of mere wealth and the prerogatives of birth.[8]

Accordingly, the early professional historians regarded their

[7] Bryce, *op. cit.*, p. 549; John D. Davies, "The 'Old' Faculty," *Princeton Alumni Weekly*, LXI (November 25, 1960), 6-9; W. R. Harper, "The Pay of American College Professors," *Forum*, XVI (1893), 96-109; Hugh Hawkins, *Pioneer: A History of the Johns Hopkins University, 1874-1889* (1960), pp. 42, 129. M. Halsey Thomas, to whose knowledge of New York social history I am much indebted, has checked his recollections of faculty conversation by looking up the Columbia faculty of 1900 in the *Social Register* of that year. He found nearly all of the full professors listed, leaving aside three Jews and the notoriously unconventional Harry Thurston Peck.

[8] *Nation*, IV (February 21, 1867), 151-52; Thomas Wentworth Higginson, "A Plea for Culture," *Atlantic Monthly*, XIX (1867), 29-37; William T. Harris, "The Use of Higher Education," *Educational Review*, XVI (1898), 160. See also G. Stanley Hall, *Aspects of German Culture* (1881), p. 307; James Russell Lowell, *Representative Selections*, ed. Harry Hayden Clark and Norman Foerster (1947), pp. 436-51; Henry Dwight Sedgwick, "The Mob Spirit in Literature," *Atlantic Monthly*, XCVI (1905), 14-15.

scholarly activity as an essential component of the whole movement for consolidating American culture. In Germany, where many of them in the 1870's and 1880's went for training, they acquired an austere conception of specialized research that would before long separate them from amateur connections; but they also found in Germany the example of a professoriat active in civic enterprise. The German idea of the professor as the conscience of the state corresponded roughly to the American ideal of an aristocracy of culture. John W. Burgess, German-trained historian who inaugurated graduate work at Columbia in history and political science, hoped to produce statesmen and public officials as well as scholars. The first American guidebook to historical scholarship, Charles Kendall Adams' pioneering *Manual of Historical Literature* (1882), contained a long digression on current national problems that would require historically informed leaders. Early meetings of the American Historical Association reverberated with pleas to historians to serve society, raise the level of political debate, and restore integrity in public life.[9]

The chief architect of the American Historical Association exemplified and fostered the union of professors and patricians. Herbert Baxter Adams, director of historical studies at Johns Hopkins during the Eighties and Nineties, though not a noteworthy scholar in his own right, was the first indefatigable promoter of professional history. Through his outstanding students, through the *Johns Hopkins University Studies in Historical and Political Science* (1882-    ), which he founded and edited, and through his secretaryship of the American Historical Association during its first sixteen years, Adams probably did more than anyone else to Germanize American historical scholarship. Yet he took special care to involve amateur historians in the Association and thereby make it a broadly national institution.

A New Englander "of sound Puritan stock" though unrelated to the more famous Adamses, Herbert Baxter was a product of Phillips Exeter Academy, Amherst College, and the University of Heidel-

[9] Charles Kendall Adams, *A Manual of Historical Literature*, 3rd ed. (1889), pp. 19-23; Herman Ausubel, *Historians and Their Craft: A Study of the Presidential Addresses of the American Historical Association, 1884-1945* (1950), pp. 38-39; Andrew D. White, "European Schools of History and Politics," *Johns Hopkins University Studies in Historical and Political Science*, V (1887), 471-546.

berg. He worshiped his Heidelberg master, Johann Bluntschli, who (Adams thought) had arrived at a truly historical jurisprudence by participating in the politics and legislation of his time. Adams' own enthusiasm for public service expressed itself through his connection with the U.S. Bureau of Education, for which he wrote and edited a long series of pamphlets on the history and current state of American education. His favorite project for a time was a scheme for a national academy at Washington to train professional civil servants as West Point and Annapolis trained officers. Adams all the while enjoyed the pleasures of Baltimore and Washington society, particularly the Cosmos Club and the Saturday Evening Literary Club that met at the home of a wealthy and cultivated lawyer, Horatio King. In 1891, when Adams was offered a lucrative post at the new University of Chicago, he drew up a balance sheet, comparing the two situations, which presents a revealing profile of patrician values. Among other, more personal considerations, he listed: [10]

| East | West |
|------|------|
| Quiet | Rush |
| Continuity | Broken |
| Society | New People |
| Conservatism | Boom |
| Duty | Advantage |
| Settled | Moving |
| Identification | Lost |

Not surprisingly, Adams decided to stay at Johns Hopkins.

Privately, Adams had a rather superior attitude toward the many local historical societies and the amateur historians of the country. But he realized keenly, as he told a friend, "the importance of corporate influences, of associations of men and money." [11] So he launched his plan for a national historical society with the aid of the American Social Science Association, a kind of clearing house for knowledge about social and educational issues that concerned the aristocracy of culture. The President of the Social Science Association, John Eaton, who was also Commissioner of Education at the time, joined

[10] W. Stull Holt, ed., *Historical Scholarship in the United States, 1876-1901* (1938), p. 157. See also *Herbert B. Adams: Tributes of Friends* (1902).
[11] Holt, *op. cit.*, p. 469.

Adams and two other professional historians in summoning an organizational meeting of historians, to be held in conjunction with the annual meeting of the social science group. Of the forty-one people who answered the call and constituted themselves the American Historical Association (AHA) only a minority had any professional historical training. The charter members included patrician historians, like William B. Weeden and Charles Deane, and men of affairs, like Carroll Wright, Rutherford B. Hayes, and William T. Harris. Nevertheless the professionals controlled the organization from the outset; and at the second annual meeting they declared their fundamental allegiance by electing Leopold von Ranke, then approaching his ninetieth birthday, as their first and only honorary member.[12]

Determined to bring all the historical resources of the nation within the purview of his Association, Adams continued to direct its energies outward. For two decades he and his cohorts on the Executive Council rarely selected a professional historian as their annual president. (The only clear exceptions were Andrew Dickson White and Charles Kendall Adams, both university presidents.) Sometimes the AHA recognized a great patrician scholar like the revered George Bancroft, heavy with years and honors. Sometimes it honored a distinguished clergyman with historical tastes, like Richard Salter Storrs. Sometimes it chose a conservative and cultivated man of affairs, like Simeon Baldwin, chief justice of the Connecticut Supreme Court and one-time president of the American Bar Association. Meanwhile, Adams took pains to gather the state and local historical societies under the Association's paternal wing. When in 1889 some of them seemed on the verge of creating their own federation, Adams headed them off with a special invitation to participate in the Association's work. He also initiated an elaborate bibliography of their publications.[13]

Just as Adams associated himself with the U.S. Bureau of Education, so he strove to attach the American Historical Association to the federal government. American governments, in contrast to European, had shockingly little interest in subsidizing research, publishing historical documents, or maintaining usable archives. Adams was de-

[12] American Historical Association *Papers*, I (1886), 22-23, 483; J. F. Jameson, "Early Days of the American Historical Association, 1884-1895," *American Historical Review*, XL (1934), 1-5.
[13] Holt, *op. cit.*, pp. 126-28; A. P. C. Griffin, ed., "Bibliography of American Historical Societies," AHA *Annual Report* (1905), vol. II.

termined to rouse Congress to a consciousness of its historical responsibilities. Reciprocally, he wished to clothe the AHA with the dignity of the national state. After the first two annual meetings at the headquarters of the Social Science Association in Saratoga, New York, Adams shifted the base of operations to Washington. For a decade the AHA met there regularly, except one year when it went to Boston to honor Justin Winsor and another when it met at the World's Fair in Chicago. Adams delighted in the attendance of a few Congressmen and governmental officials at these meetings. Furthermore, he prevailed upon their good will to secure from Congress in 1889 a federal charter for the American Historical Association. This unusual act of incorporation fixed the principal office of the Association permanently in Washington, and authorized it to report annually to the Smithsonian Institution. The latter was directed to transmit to Congress the AHA's proceedings and its reports on the condition of historical study in America. Adams thereby secured at government expense both office space and the printing of his annual reports.[14] More important, he opened a channel through which the aristocracy of culture might, in historical matters, exert a vigorous, uplifting influence on national policies.

These expectations proved false. The governmental connection never matured. In America, unlike Adams' beloved Germany, professors and other guardians of culture did not succeed in establishing a solid partnership with the state. During the Jacksonian period the intellectual class in America had lost its political eminence, and all efforts to recover that eminence in the late nineteenth century were unavailing. In the early 1890's committees of the American Historical Association began memorializing Congress to take heed of the nation's scattered and neglected historical records. The scholars wanted a unified management of the national archives; they also pleaded for a Historical Manuscripts Commission that would—like the British agency of that name—inventory important papers in private hands. Congress did nothing. Any prospect that it would seriously notice the annual reports it still receives from the Association soon vanished. The arrangement continues today as a useful economy in scholarly printing expenses and as a memorial of the forgotten hopes of Herbert Baxter Adams.

14 The story may be followed in the annual *Papers* and *Reports* of the AHA and in the articles by Jameson cited above.

Another, greater Adams also tried vainly in the 1880's to close the gap between government and culture. While Herbert Baxter used the new device of a professional organization, Henry Adams relied on his own brilliant salon. He established himself at Lafayette Square in Washington in 1877, partly to pursue historical research and partly to be where he expected political, scientific, and historical talent to converge in a new concentration of national energy. Washington failed to live up to these expectations. It never became a genuine capital in the sense in which almost every European country had a national center of wealth, knowledge, intellect, fashion, and political power. Nor did Henry's personal circle become a society. Instead, it contracted as his life darkened. Even the presence of a fellow historian in the White House after 1901 did not unite the world of learning and the world of politics.[15]

In the absence of a political system capable of binding the patrician intellectual and the academic teacher to a common center of authority, the two groups eventually drifted apart. Each was thrown too exclusively on its own intellectual resources. The drive toward a stricter professionalism gradually pulled the academic men away from patrician associations and from the wide culture that patrician life at its best embraced. To this trend the patrician offered little effective counterpressure. After the 1890's the number of amateurs producing important historical books diminished drastically. There is no reason to suppose that professionals crowded them out; they quit of their own accord. James Ford Rhodes, speaking to the Harvard undergraduate History Club in 1908, advised young men of ample means to devote their lives to independent historical scholarship; [16] but very few took such advice, and Rhodes himself had in the early twentieth century no real successor. A similar disengagement evidently occurred in other fields of cultural endeavor. One thinks of Edith Wharton's literary isolation in upper-class New York, her descriptions of delicate American dilettantes in Europe, and her own nostalgia. The aristocratic revival in American culture during the post-Civil War decades had spent much of its force by the turn of the century. In the increasingly democratic atmosphere of the Progressive Era the aristocracy of culture very largely went to pieces; and

[15] A. Hunter Dupree, *Science in the Federal Government* (1957), pp. 296-300. On Henry Adams see Ernest Samuels' *Henry Adams: The Middle Years* (1957).
[16] James Ford Rhodes, *Historical Essays* (1909), pp. 77-78.

many of its patrician elements became—like Henry Adams himself in his later years—peevish, precious, and aloof.

We can observe the other side of this separation beginning in the American Historical Association in the 1890's, as the professors moved to take full charge. After a decade of Herbert Baxter Adams' leadership, dissatisfaction broke out in 1895. On the surface the issue was simply one of where to meet. A group of professors, led by George Burton Adams of Yale, William A. Dunning of Columbia, and Albert Bushnell Hart of Harvard, complained that the annual meetings were dull and poorly attended because Washington was not an adequate center of literary and academic life. The protesters demanded and won a new policy of rotation that would bring the Association each year to one of the major university communities.

Behind this specific change it is not hard to see a broader professorial rebellion against Herbert Baxter Adams' careful balancing of academic and nonacademic interests. The programs to date had included a large number of papers by nonprofessional historians, mostly light and trivial performances. The Association had largely avoided discussion of pedagogical problems and had maintained on its Executive Council an even balance between professionals and amateurs. In all these respects the emphasis now shifted decisively in a professional direction. More professional historians were elected to the Executive Council. Their papers henceforth dominated the annual meetings. And in 1896 the AHA appointed its famous Committee of Seven (all professors) to improve historical instruction in the secondary schools. The new policies quickly produced a gratifying expansion. Between 1895 and 1899 membership doubled (reaching 1,400), and attendance at meetings increased from 50 to more than 200.[17]

The same group that broke the Washington axis of the AHA simultaneously launched a strictly professional historical journal. Several Ivy League professors, headed by George Burton Adams and Hart, met in New York in April 1895 and founded the *American Historical Review* (*AHR*) independently of the American Historical Association. Since they wished to have an American publication with the highest technical standards, they created an entirely professional editorial board. J. Franklin Jameson, a young professor at Brown

17 AHA, *Annual Reports* (1895-99); Jameson, *op. cit.*, *AHR*, XV (1909), 15-19.

University, was installed as managing editor. Three years later the Association began to subsidize the *Review* and elect new members of its editorial board. In 1915 an amateur member of the AHA, Frederic Bancroft, backed by some disgruntled southerners, made ugly charges of fraud and favoritism against the editors; whereupon the Association formalized its control of the *Review* by acquiring legal ownership.[18] The independence of the *Review* during its early years, however, insured its uncompromising professionalism at a time when the Association was still in transition.

Finally, the new leadership that emerged in 1895 recognized that history could not depend on the federal government for any considerable support or initiative. In the absence of congressional action, the AHA appointed its own Historical Manuscripts Commission "to edit, index, or collect information in regard to unprinted documents relating to American history." Over the succeeding years the Commission swelled the annual reports of the AHA with a variety of useful documentary and bibliographical publications. Then, to prompt some improvement in the disorderly archives of American governments, a Public Archives Commission, formed in 1899, turned its attention to the states. Methodically, it surveyed the records of one state after another and published its findings each year. Within ten years the Commission's reports had stimulated twenty-four states to make formal provisions for the preservation and custody of their unpublished records. Here was a major achievement to be credited to the organized, systematic outlook of the professional historian.

For all of their increasing self-confidence, the professional historians were not so foolhardy as to ignore their amateur brethren. The myriad of state, local, and ethnic historical societies commanded immensely valuable resources. The AHA continued, therefore, to welcome into membership everyone seriously interested in history and to strengthen ties with the other historical societies. In 1896 the recently established American Society of Church History was absorbed into the American Historical Association as its Church History Section. In 1904 the Association organized, in conjunction with its annual meeting, a regular Conference of State and Local Historical Societies to

---

[18] The formal account in Jameson, *op. cit., AHR,* XXVI, (1920), 1-17, should be supplemented by "The Reminiscences of Frank Maloy Anderson" (Oral History Research Office, Columbia University, 1957) and the Frederic Bancroft Papers (Columbia University).

stimulate greater cooperation among them and with the national Association.

The degree of cooperation actually attained depended on the responsiveness of the amateur bodies to a professional spirit. By and large, the eastern societies, which were privately endowed, socially prestigious, and genealogically inclined, held to a prosy, traditional course. They continued to putter with muster rolls, the military records of colonial wars, and the obituaries of their own members; they took little interest in anything outside their particular local jurisdictions. Their leaders were likely to be club men with nothing to do, interested in small antiquarian objects. On the other hand, the western state historical societies, having less tradition behind them, were more vigorous, adaptable, and cooperative.[19] The major societies in the Midwest relied heavily on state support, as did the major universities. Their leaders were active men, close to public affairs, like J. Sterling Morton, Nebraska railroad promoter and Secretary of Agriculture in the second Cleveland administration, or Reuben G. Thwaites of Wisconsin, a former newspaperman with the mind of an entrepreneur. Eager to learn and to improve, the principal western societies participated willingly in the AHA's Conference of State and Local Historical Societies. Moreover, they associated themselves with the history faculties in their respective state universities. Thwaites, who ran the best subsidized of all of the societies, persuaded the state of Wisconsin in 1901 to locate the state historical society on the campus of the University in a single building together with the University library and the graduate seminars in American history. In other states, notably Alabama and Mississippi, the strongest historical work was done by the newly created official departments of archives and history, which the AHA's Public Archives Commission had inspired; and there too professional attitudes took hold.[20]

The formation of the Mississippi Valley Historical Association in 1907 was another evidence of the vigorous midwestern entente between professional historians and state-supported historical agencies.

19 Elizabeth Donnan and Leo F. Stock, eds., *An Historian's World: Selections from the Correspondence of John Franklin Jameson* (Memoirs of the American Philosophical Society, vol. 42, 1956), p. 284.
20 H. Hale Bellot, *American History and American Historians* (1952), pp. 26-34.

The initial impulse for a unifying organization to advance research and conserve historical materials throughout the Mississippi Valley came from the secretaries of several state societies. Instead of holding themselves aloof from academic men, however, the secretaries proposed at the outset to link their regional association with the AHA by meeting conjointly each December. On the urging of Clarence W. Alvord, a German-trained professor at the University of Illinois who organized the first program of the new association, it decided against any effort to popularize history and turned its attention to scholarly publication.[21]

By the time the Mississippi Valley Historical Association appeared, the formative era in the creation of the American historical profession was over. The patrician historians, with very few exceptions, had either retired from the scene or subsided into ineffectual antiquarianism; and all amateur scholars of any note were following the lead of the professionals. By now, the American graduate school had come fully of age. Some sixteen American universities were training doctoral candidates in history. Altogether, they had produced about 250 Ph.D.'s since 1882.[22] Young men no longer went to Europe in large numbers for a professional degree. The attraction of Germany had declined perceptibly in the 1890's and more sharply after the turn of the century, though some Americans still went to Paris and Oxford.[23]

By now, too, the American professoriat had imposed its authority on historical instruction below the collegiate level. The AHA's Committee of Seven, disturbed by the haphazard, routine character of history in the secondary schools, proposed a sweeping revision in 1899. It called for a four-year history requirement in the college preparatory program, encompassing ancient history, medieval and modern Europe, English history, and American history. The Committee also insisted on supplementing rote-learning in textbooks with collateral reading and other projects. Within eight years these recommenda-

[21] James L. Sellers, "Before We Were Members—The MVHA," *Mississippi Valley Historical Review*, XL (1953), 3-24.
[22] William B. Hesseltine and Louis Kaplan, "Doctors of Philosophy in History: A Statistical Study," *AHR*, XLVII (1942), 766, 771.
[23] Richard S. Barnes, "German Influence on American Historical Studies, 1884-1914" (Ph.D. dissertation, Yale University, 1953), p. 68; Jameson, *An Historian's World*, p. 254.

tions became the accepted standard, greatly improving the position of history in the secondary schools.[24]

We may consider the year 1907 as the end of an epoch in respect also to the actual accumulation of research. The twenty-six-volume "American Nation Series," published between 1904 and 1907 and edited by Albert Bushnell Hart, constituted the first great professional synthesis of American history. Planning for it had begun at meetings of the American Historical Association in the late 1890's as a consequence of dissatisfaction with an earlier cooperative work edited by Justin Winsor, *A Narrative and Critical History of America* (8 vols., 1884-89).[25] The latter was only quasi-professional. The contributors, with a few exceptions, were amateur scholars. Although each provided a careful, unadorned summary of existing knowledge, their chapters had no integrative principle, no analytical pattern. All but two of the authors of the "American Nation Series," on the other hand, had had graduate training in history. Each volume in the series undertook to explain a sequence of development. The work represented a triumphant appropriation of the whole span of American history by professional historians.

Finally, the spearhead of professional activity, the American Historical Association, had acquired by 1907 approximately the form in which it survives to this day. Meeting that year at Madison, Wisconsin, the Association installed for the first time a president who was purely and exclusively a professional historian. The custom of choosing influential patrons of history was decisively put aside. Occasionally during the next two decades the AHA might still honor an outstanding patrician historian like Theodore Roosevelt or Henry Osborn Taylor; otherwise the presidency was henceforth exclusively in the hands of university professors. Appropriately, the first of this largely unbroken line was John Franklin Jameson. He was then only forty-eight years old; three decades of single-minded dedication to scholarship lay ahead. His elevation to the presidency in 1907 was a tacit acknowledgment that the American historical profession had developed its own unique leader.

Jameson was the first notable professional historian who did not

24 William MacDonald, "The Situation of History in Secondary Schools," *Nation,* LXXXV (1907), 225-26; AHA, *The Study of History in Secondary Schools: Report . . . by a Committee of Five* (1911).
25 W. A. Dunning, "A Generation of American Historiography," AHA *Annual Report* (1917), pp. 350-54.

study in Europe. Son of an unsuccessful New England school teacher and postmaster, he attended Amherst College while living at home with his parents. Having no money to go abroad, he went to Johns Hopkins for graduate study. There, in 1882, he received the first Ph.D. it awarded in history; and there he was fired by a vision of the coming transformation of American scholarship by "the professorial class." Jameson absorbed Herbert Baxter Adams' zeal for the new Germanic methods, but he scorned his teacher's indiscriminate promotional activities, particularly his truckling to the "elderly swells who dabble in history." [26] Austere in manner and conscientious to a fault, Jameson resented deeply anything that smacked of pretentiousness, bias, or careless and hasty workmanship. In himself he cultivated a breadth of knowledge so wide and an accuracy so impeccable that—in the words of one of his oldest friends—"it was always an act of audacity to question the reliability of his statements." [27]

Jameson had many of the qualities of a great historical writer: massive learning, precision of expression, a penetrating understanding of motives, and a subtle sense of relationships. Why he abandoned historical writing when he was scarcely forty remains something of a mystery. Part of the explanation lies in the cautiousness and severity of his critical standards, which quarreled and contended with the constructive power of his ideas. He was, in this sense, our American Lord Acton. As a young man, Jameson wrote a great deal, including an impressive study of William Usselinx, for which he learned Dutch, some illuminating essays on historiography, and a brilliant series of lectures on the American Revolution, which with characteristic diffidence he left unpublished for thirty years. None of this satisfied him, and his confidence in his ability to do the big books he really valued failed before he could put it to a test.[28]

Whatever feelings of personal inadequacy prompted this surrender, his decision had the support of a historical rationale. Jameson believed that he lived in a period uncongenial to great individual

[26] Jameson, *An Historian's World*, p. 47. The best biographical sketches are in the introduction to this volume and in the *Dictionary of American Biography*, vol. XXII.

[27] Memo by Charles M. Andrews in AHA Files 1936-40, Box 23, Archives of American Historical Association (Library of Congress).

[28] Note the confessions of inadequacy in Jameson, *An Historian's World*, pp. 86, 125, and compare with the bibliography of his early publications in *Herbert B. Adams: Tributes of Friends*, pp. 80-82.

achievements in history. He compared his own era to the seventeenth century. Then as now, historical scholarship was advancing "more by extensive accumulation and critical sifting of the evidences than by new endeavors toward their interpretation." The time-spirit required historians to work within modest limits. Against the dryness of such an atmosphere, they might take comfort in recalling that when the earlier "Age of Erudition had done its work of accumulating and sifting evidence, there emerged upon the Europe of 1750 the coordinating and philosophical ideas of the *Aufklärung.*" [29] So Jameson felt sustained by history as he turned away from creative effort and sought opportunities to guide and organize the work of Erudition.

In 1895, while teaching at Brown University, Jameson undertook both the editorship of the *American Historical Review* and the chairmanship of the Historical Manuscripts Commission. Thus he assumed central responsibility for mobilizing sources and for setting standards of publication. But how much could be accomplished in the vast documentary and bibliographical field without strong institutional support? Clearly, the voluntary efforts of men who stole a little time from their own teaching and writing would hardly suffice. Jameson was soon dreaming of a national center for historical research. The establishment of the Carnegie Institution of Washington in 1902 opened such a possibility; for the Institution was designed to promote research in the liberal arts and sciences, especially such fundamental projects as might lie beyond the scope of governmental support and beyond the strength of a particular university. Jameson headed the advisory committee that recommended a program for history.

Jameson's committee formulated a precise and extensive plan for coordinating professional scholarship in American history. The principal service of an endowed institution, Jameson always believed, should be to make unprinted sources accessible to others. The proposed center should therefore prepare reports and indexes of the manuscript materials in the federal archives in Washington. It should hire scholars to do the same for materials on American history in European archives. It should undertake a continuing program of editing and publishing important national documents, as the *Monumenta Germaniae Historica* had long done in Germany. Furthermore, the full-time director of the center should run a kind of

29 Quoted in Barnes, *op. cit.,* p. 87.

clearinghouse for scholars throughout the country, advising them on research opportunities and keeping them informed of one another's work. The center should also include, on a rotating basis, professors on leave of absence from their universities, who would guide graduate students coming to Washington to work on theses.[30]

This last function never materialized. The trustees of the Carnegie Institution, intent on a purely research operation, vetoed any arrangement for the instruction of students. Otherwise, the committee's proposals were fully adopted. The trustees even permitted the director of their Department of Historical Research to edit the *American Historical Review* as one of his official duties; and in 1905, after Andrew McLaughlin had served for two years, Jameson came to Washington to assume both posts. From the outset he had about him a small group of young assistants, the chief of whom was Waldo G. Leland, one of his former students at Brown.

For twenty-five years the Carnegie Institution's Department of Historical Research pursued undeviatingly the goals set forth in the original plan. When funds permitted, the Department occasionally subsidized a professor's independent research; but the energies of the permanent staff and of most of its temporary appointees went exclusively into elaborating the apparatus for research. Before Jameson took over, the Department had already published a preliminary guide to the Washington archives of the federal government, had begun collecting the letters of the members of the Continental Congresses, and had sent Charles M. Andrews to England to survey the manuscript materials for early American history in the British Museum. The Department had also inaugurated in 1903 an indispensable annual bibliography of *Writings on American History*. Jameson carried these projects forward, adding others of a similar nature from time to time. Meanwhile, he gave time and advice freely to the many scholars who called at his office while visiting Washington, and maintained a prodigious correspondence with all who asked for counsel. In spite of his frosty exterior, Jameson incarnated the professional ethic of cooperation; and this, together with his meticulousness in detail, made him tireless in helping others less talented than himself.

Jameson's energies reached well beyond the official circle of his duties. As a service to graduate students and their advisers, he insti-

[30] Carnegie Institution of Washington, *Year Book* (1902).

23

tuted and maintained an annual list of historical dissertations in progress in American universities. Since the Carnegie Institution refused to continue the *Writings on American History,* Jameson each year scraped together private donations sufficient to pay for it.[31] In 1908 his right-hand man, Leland, became secretary of the American Historical Association, and thereafter the two offices functioned almost as one. As the chairman of successive AHA committees, Jameson kept a drum-fire of criticism on Congress for neglecting its historical responsibilities; and each incoming administration was confronted with his patient, courteous insistence on centralized management of the nation's archives.

No other foundation has ever given history the sustained support that the Carnegie Institution provided between 1903 and 1928; that it did so was largely due to Jameson's determination and prestige. The real interest of the president and trustees of the Institution lay in the natural sciences. The only humanistic disciplines that secured a regular place in its structure were history and economics, and the Department of Economics was virtually deprived of support within a decade. The president and trustees had doubts about Jameson's program too; yet they let it go ahead, with modest but regular increases in appropriations. This enabled Jameson to play a more central role in organizing historical research than anyone before or since. Libraries then lacked professional bibliographers, and governments lacked professional archivists. Encouraged by Jameson and others, the historical profession undertook the work of both. Soon professional historians were infiltrating state historical societies and spreading higher standards of documentary publication; as early as 1904 C. W. Alvord became editor of the *Illinois Historical Collections* published by the State Historical Library. Jameson's example and initiative must have counted for more than anyone now can measure.

Yet there were serious limitations in a program so largely devoted to the tools and materials of scholarship rather than its results. Jameson's Department never became, in the full sense, an institute of historical research. Its activities acquired, therefore, too routine a character. Jameson perceived some of the new problems and needs of scholarship that were developing in the years after 1907. But he was a modest man of settled habits and convictions, and so maintained the unchanging tenor of his ways. "I struggle on," he told

31 Jameson, *An Historian's World,* p. 314.

Henry Adams in 1910, "making bricks without much idea of how the architects will use them, but believing that the best architect that ever was cannot get along without bricks, and therefore trying to make good ones." [32] Many of the bricks produced in his kiln came forth with painful slowness. Leland, who began work in 1907 on a guide to materials for American history located in Paris, published the first volume in 1932. Completion of a historical atlas of the United States took even longer. One member of Jameson's staff, Edmund C. Burnett, spent almost thirty years editing the letters of the members of the Continental Congress. Another, Elizabeth Donnan, worked fifteen years before publishing the first volume of her *Documents Illustrative of the History of the Slave Trade.*[33] These were valuable, painstaking aids to American historiography. But long before they were completed other agencies, including the federal government, were doing work of similar kind and calibre; Jameson's Department of Historical Research no longer played an innovating role.

At last, in 1928, this sedate and dignified operation was brusquely terminated. Jameson retired at the request of the president of the Carnegie Institution. Projects still outstanding were put on a terminal basis, and the appropriation for history was transferred to the support of archaeology.[34] Jameson, now approaching seventy, moved to the Manuscripts Division of the Library of Congress, where he remained the wise and honored elder statesman of the historical profession. But the world of the American historian had now grown too various, complex, and disjoined to allow any one person to exercise the institutional leadership that Jameson provided in the early years of the century.

---

[32] *Ibid.,* p. 136.
[33] Waldo G. Leland and J. J. Meng, eds., *Guide to Materials for American History in the Libraries and Archives of Paris* (2 vols., 1932 and 1943); C. O. Paullin, *Atlas of the Historical Geography of the United States* (1932); Edmund C. Burnett, ed., *Letters of Members of the Continental Congress* (8 vols., 1921-38); Elizabeth Donnan, ed., *Documents Illustrative of the History of the Slave Trade to America* (4 vols., 1930-35).
[34] For much further detail see the annual *Year Books* of the Carnegie Institution.

# GROWTH SINCE 1907

In the first decade of the twentieth century, when Jameson emerged as the administrative genius of the historical profession, it was relatively small and uncomplicated. Total membership in the American Historical Association came to something more than 2,000, of whom about 300 attended the annual meetings. No participant could miss the Association's still heavy involvement in the organization of historical work. The program regularly featured a conference of state and local historical societies, a session on the teaching of history, and reports of the Public Archives Commission and the Historical Manuscripts Commission. The sessions devoted to scholarly papers were neither numerous nor very diverse. A typical program might have one session on European history, two sessions on American history, and perhaps a session of a general topical nature cosponsored by another scholarly society meeting at the same place.[1]

A comparison with the present situation gives a measure of the altered scale of professional activity. Between 1907 and 1962 membership in the American Historical Association increased fivefold; and since distances have shrunk, the annual meeting attracted ten times as many registrants in 1962 as it had in 1907. Instead of one joint session, in 1962 nineteen cooperating societies participated. Instead of two sessions on American history, there were thirteen. Instead of one session on European history, about seventeen took place. Some fourteen additional sessions were given to ancient, Russian, Latin American, African, and Asian history. In this vast concourse of subject-matter specialists, some attention still went to curricular problems (two sessions) and to the reproduction of research materials (one session).[2] But these obviously occupied a minor place in the total program. While the range and variety of historical research had grown enormously, much of the responsibility for surveying and indexing historical documents had devolved into other hands. Profes-

[1] See, for example, AHA *Annual Reports* (1906-1908).
[2] "The Chicago Meeting, 1962," *AHR*, LXVIII (1963), 880-83.

sional librarians, archivists, and curators, through their own societies and journals, were now doing a large part of the job.

The growth of historical activity, except for interludes during the two world wars, had been steady. It had also, for a long while, been slow. The very rapid expansion of the historical profession that occurred at the turn of the century did not resume until after World War II. For many years membership in the American Historical Association, for example, remained relatively static. Having reached 2,700 in 1909, it never climbed above 3,000 until 1926, or above 3,500 until 1939. During a span of three decades, in other words, AHA membership increased only 30 per cent, although the total number of college teachers in the United States rose almost 500 per cent in the same period.[3] The big boom came in the late 1940's and 1950's. AHA membership spurted from 3,800 in 1945 to 9,400 in 1960. The Mississippi Valley Historical Association grew at a comparable rate. The number of students receiving doctoral degrees in history reached a prewar high of 162 in 1938; in 1960 it climbed to 375.[4] Scholarly books and articles poured from the presses in greater volume and in more fields than ever before.

The major shifts in the growth rate—its decline in the early twentieth century and its spectacular upswing in recent years—correlate with important changes in the historians' milieu. Subsequent chapters will take up those cultural changes, which may account for a loss of momentum in some sectors of the profession after 1907 and for a new vitality after 1945. Before entering into such hazardous questions, however, it is necessary to notice an underlying, cumulative improvement in the capabilities of the American historical profession. Beneath all fluctuations of talent, status, and outlook, the total research effort has steadily expanded throughout the twentieth century. This expansion has resulted from a continuous proliferation of the institutional support for professional historical work.

To that support many agencies contribute: universities, libraries, private historical societies, governments, and foundations. In fact,

[3] Bureau of the Census, *Historical Statistics of the United States: Colonial Times to 1957* (1960), p. 75. All membership figures come from AHA *Annual Reports*.
[4] Figures compiled from various volumes of *Doctoral Dissertations Accepted by American Universities* and from *Index to American Doctoral Dissertations, 1959-1960*.

variety of sponsorship and diversity of output have strikingly characterized historical research in the United States. The sprawling, multitudinous nature of the whole institutional complex is evident in both of its major components. One of these is an intricate communications network, which has widened access to sources and multiplied channels for scholarly publication. The other is the system of higher education, which has given more and more people livelihoods as teachers of history and incentives for research in the area of their teaching. Although the two spheres of activity have developed simultaneously and in close relation to one another, each deserves separate consideration.

Since the past cannot be invented, all historical inquiry depends on the sources that a scholar is willing and able to consult. These may be physical remains, oral testimony, or written records. Relatively few historians in America have paid serious attention to nonverbal sources—to pictures, monuments, and other physical marks of the past. Perhaps because ours has been so largely a culture of the word, our historians have generally been librarybound, and their first concern in research has been access to adequate libraries.

In the nineteenth century most historians in the United States necessarily studied local history, since only local collections were within reach. An occasional wealthy gentleman like Francis Parkman and Henry C. Lea might employ copyists in foreign capitals to supply him with material. Others like George Bancroft might make effective use of diplomatic appointments. One pioneering scholar, Jared Sparks, America's first full-time professor of history, secured from the U.S. Department of State the financial backing that enabled him in 1818 to visit archives in London, Brussels, and Paris.[5] But these were men with very special advantages. The transformation of American scholarship began in the late nineteenth century with the creation of great research libraries of wide scope, which admitted any properly qualified student.

The pacemaker was the Library of Congress under the leadership of Herbert Putnam. The son of a distinguished New York publisher,

[5] Herbert Baxter Adams, *The Life and Writings of Jared Sparks,* vol. II (1893), pp. 5-8, 42-51. On the further significance of this trip see C. K. Webster, "Some Early Applications from American Historians to Use the British Archives," *Journal of Modern History,* I (1929), 416 ff., and Galen Broeker, "Jared Sparks, Robert Peel, and the State Paper Office," *American Quarterly,* XIII (1961), 140-152.

Putnam illustrates again the fruitful impulse that an aristocracy of culture gave to the institutionalization of scholarship. Partly through chance and partly through a love of books, he became a director of public libraries, first in Minneapolis and then in Boston. In 1899, yielding to a sense of duty, he accepted a call to the Library of Congress. Putnam found it a cluttered, dingy, understaffed institution, concerned principally with serving Congress. He made it the national library, undergirding research everywhere in the country and standing—in his own words—"foremost as a model and example in assisting forward the work of scholarship in the United States." [6]

Two years after Putnam took charge, the Library of Congress inaugurated three path-breaking policies. It started distributing its printed catalog cards to other libraries, thereby creating a uniform system of cataloging. It built up, adjacent to its own card catalog, a national union catalog of books located in other major American libraries. And, most remarkably, Putnam announced the willingness of the Library of Congress to lend books to other libraries for the use of scholars at a distance from Washington. In all these ways the Library of Congress prompted the consolidation of scholarly activity on a national scale.

Simultaneously Putnam was helping the Library of Congress to become the great American repository of historical manuscripts. In 1902 he brought from Boston another distinguished patrician scholar, Worthington C. Ford, to head the recently created Division of Manuscripts. Ford soon launched a historical publications program with the first volume of the *Journals of the Continental Congress* (34 vols., 1904-37). With the aid of Jameson's Bureau of the Carnegie Institution, Putnam also amassed vast quantities of transcripts of manuscripts in foreign archives pertaining to early American history.

Elsewhere research libraries grew prodigiously under the auspices of the leading universities, some of the states, and many wealthy individuals. If independent gentlemen ceased to write the most important historical books, they compensated generously by providing the materials for others to use. The Harvard University Library, which

[6] David C. Mearns, *The Story Up to Now* (Librarian of Congress *Annual Report, 1945-46*), pp. 184-94. See also *National Cyclopedia of American Biography,* vol. IX, p. 249, and Herbert Putnam, "Relation of the National Library to Historical Research in the United States," *Educational Review,* XXIII (1902), 217-32.

had 577,000 books in 1900, contained 882,000 in 1910 and continued to receive outstanding collections. The New York Public Library, whose vast research holdings were acquired and sustained by private endowment, was organized in 1895. The Newberry Library, launched in Chicago in 1887, amassed great resources for British and American history and literature. The John Carter Brown Library of early American history opened as a semiautonomous institution at Brown University in 1904. The old private historical societies gradually extended a warmer welcome to outsiders who wished to use their specialized holdings.[7]

During the 1920's many special libraries were founded: the Pierpont Morgan Library in New York, strong in medieval manuscripts and incunabula; the William L. Clements Library in Ann Arbor, concentrating on early American history; the Folger Shakespeare Library in Washington, D.C.; the Henry E. Huntington Library in southern California, emphasizing Tudor and Stuart England; and the Hoover Library at Palo Alto, California, specializing in modern international relations. A more recent creation, the Dumbarton Oaks Research Library in Washington, D.C., which Mr. and Mrs. Robert Woods Bliss gave to Harvard University in 1940, has made possible a tremendous upswing in Byzantine studies. All of these institutions take pains to serve visiting researchers. Some of them even attract foreign scholars who gladly come to the New World to study the Old.

Increasingly, the research libraries were staffed by professional librarians trained in library schools that excelled those in any other country. The new librarians, following in the footsteps of bookmen and amateur bibliophiles like Richard Rogers Bowker, developed the elaborate bibliographical guides and indexes that have become so indispensable to recent scholarly work. Before the 1920's, for example, there were virtually no general lists of the location of newspapers, periodicals, and manuscripts. Today, at any considerable library, a scholar can learn a great deal about the special resources of any other. In the last decade, as a consequence of foundation support

[7] Arthur E. Bestor Jr., "The Transformation of American Scholarship, 1875-1917," *Library Quarterly*, XXIII (1953), 164-79; Walter Muir Whitehill, *Independent Historical Societies* (1962), especially pp. 20-22. The Harvard statistics are taken from the Harvard University *Reports of the Librarian*, 1900, p. 217, and 1910, p. 7.

and increased cooperation among research libraries, progress toward national bibliographical control has been more rapid than ever before.[8] The Council on Library Resources, a subsidiary of the Ford Foundation created in 1956, has made possible such splendid projects as the *National Union Catalog of Manuscript Collections* (1962-      ). The American Historical Association, under the energetic secretaryship (1953-63) of Boyd Shafer, has recovered an active role in such projects. Shafer secured over a million dollars in grants for special aids to research and teaching.[9]

Together with these improvements in bibliographical armament, historians have acquired in recent years the means to conquer distance. The movement of the historian to his sources, and of the sources to the historian, proceeds on a scale and with an ease scarcely imaginable forty years ago. Although a handful of universities provided sabbatical leaves in the 1890's, before World War I very few academic scholars had both the time and the money to travel to distant archives; most of their research rested entirely on printed sources.[10]

In the prosperous 1920's, sabbaticals became widely available and research grants also materialized in more than exceptional cases. The John Simon Guggenheim Foundation, uniquely and exclusively devoted to the support of talented individuals, began its distinguished career in 1925, and over the next decade made more grants in history than in any other field.[11] The new Social Science Research Council, financed with Rockefeller money, inaugurated a program of research fellowships in the same year. It too subsidized at least as many historians as scholars in other disciplines. In 1930 the American Council of Learned Societies, a federation of national societies representing many disciplines, acquired sufficient foundation funds to

---

[8] Robert B. Downs, *American Library Resources, A Bibliographical Guide: Supplement, 1950-1961* (1962), p. vii.

[9] Boyd C. Shafer, "Partial List of Expanded, Renewed or New Activities Since 1953" (mimeographed report).

[10] C. W. Alvord, "The New History," *Nation*, XCIV (1912), 458; T. F. Tout, "History and Historians in America," *Transactions of the Royal Historical Society*, fourth series, XII (1929), 1-17.

[11] Lewis B. Cooper, *Sabbatical Leave for College Teachers* ("University of Florida Education Series," vol. I, 1932), p. 9; Bernard Peach, "John Simon Guggenheim Memorial Foundation: Investment in Free Individuals," *South Atlantic Quarterly*, LX (1961), 151, 202.

award its first postdoctoral fellowships, usually for travel abroad.[12] After World War II these and other opportunities, notably the Fulbright awards that sent American students and scholars to many foreign lands, increased prodigiously. Sixty Americans attended the International Congress of Historical Sciences at Paris in 1950; ten years later 170 Americans went to the Congress at Stockholm,[13] and it is doubtful that any large number of these paid their own way across the Atlantic. The American historian had become a global traveller.

Thanks to technology, historical records acquired a still more remarkable mobility. New machines enabled the historian to bring exact copies of many of his sources to his own study instead of going to them. The photocopying of historical records originated sometime before World War I, but it remained too costly to have any considerable application in individual research. The most ambitious of the early undertakings was carried out between 1927 and 1932, when John D. Rockefeller Jr. gave the Library of Congress $450,000 to acquire from various European archives nearly two million photostats of documents bearing on early American history.[14] Then, in the late 1930's, far cheaper techniques of photoreproduction—microfilm and microcard—became available. With the generous support of foundations, vast programs of microfilming materials in foreign archives began during World War II and continued with the aid of Fulbright scholars in subsequent years.[15] American libraries, learned societies, and commercial enterprises such as University Microfilms, published and sold photocopied editions of large categories of sources. By 1960 a revolution in the distribution of research materials had occurred, though its end was not yet in sight.

The more sources historians had at their command, the more out-

---

[12] Roy F. Nichols, "History and the Social Science Research Council," *AHR,* L (1945), 493; Waldo G. Leland, "The American Council of Learned Societies and Its Relation to Humanistic Studies," *Proceedings of the American Philosophical Society,* LXXI (1932), 179-89.

[13] *AHR,* LVI (1951), 746; LXVI (1961), 891.

[14] Elizabeth Donnan and Leo F. Stock, eds., *An Historian's World: Selections from the Correspondence of John Franklin Jameson* (Memoirs of the American Philosophical Society, vol. 42, 1956), pp. 335, 351-52.

[15] George L. Anderson, "Mechanical Aids in Historical Research," in *In Support of Clio: Essays in Memory of Herbert A. Kellar,* ed. William B. Hesseltine and Donald R. McNeil (1958), pp. 80-91; Homer C. Hockett, *The Critical Method in Historical Research and Writing* (1955), pp. 261-63.

lets they needed for publishing their researches. In the early years of the historical profession, such facilities were meager. Commercial publishers printed the best scholarly books, and one of them, G. P. Putnam, rendered a signal service between 1885 and 1910 by publishing reasonably accurate editions of the writings of the Founding Fathers. Four or five universities instituted presses in the 1890's for the benefit of their own faculty and graduate students.[16] Otherwise, professional historians had virtually no vehicle, except the annual reports of the American Historical Association and its *Review*, capable of reaching a nationwide scholarly audience.

The effective development of university presses as agencies of the whole academic community dates from the founding of the Yale University Press in 1908 by a New York broker, George Parmly Day. He welcomed manuscripts from all scholars, regardless of their institutional connections; and he published serious books of general intellectual interest in addition to research studies. In the 1920's a dozen universities organized presses; the output of university presses more than doubled; and the best of them, following Yale's example, advertised widely and served not merely as organs but as ornaments of their respective institutions. By 1960 there were about fifty university presses, and they accounted for about 10 per cent of the new titles published annually in the United States.[17]

Meanwhile, a phenomenal multiplication of the number of periodicals publishing professional historical research was under way. For professors of American history the long-established organs of the state and private historical societies furnished outlets once their editors became receptive to professional work. Before World War I the amateur societies confined themselves almost entirely to printing documents and the writings and addresses of their own members. The rising influence and insatiable needs of professional scholars have since turned these journals to an ever-growing diet of scholarly articles. In 1925 one-sixth of the contributors to five leading state historical journals were academic people. Thirty years later two-thirds of the contributors to the same journals had academic connections.[18]

[16] George H. Putnam, *Memories of a Publisher, 1865-1915* (1915), pp. 67-71; Chester Kerr, *A Report on American University Presses* (1949), pp. 17-19.
[17] Nelson A. Crawford, "American University Presses," *American Mercury*, XVIII (1929), 210-14; Helen L. Sears, *American University Presses Come of Age* (1959), p. 12.
[18] Based on a tabulation of the contributors to the following journals at ten-year

Meanwhile the professionals were also creating their own specialized organs. Some of these spoke for new scholarly societies; others came from the initiative and dedication of a single man. All of them arose from a desire to foster some previously neglected domain of historical knowledge. Among the earlier additions, the *Catholic Historical Review* (1916) reflected the incipient professionalization of Catholic historiography under the auspices of The Catholic University of America. The *Hispanic-American Historical Review* (1918) was founded by Professor Charles E. Chapman with funds supplied by a wealthy San Franciscan of Mexican descent. *Isis* (transplanted to the United States in 1922) was part of George Sarton's heroic labors in behalf of a professional history of science. The Twenties saw the launching of *Speculum* by the new Mediaeval Academy of America, *Agricultural History* by the Agricultural History Society, the *Journal of Economic and Business History* by the Business History Society, the *New England Quarterly* by a group of Harvard professors with aid from the Colonial Society of Massachusetts, and the *Journal of Modern History* by the University of Chicago Press. The Institute of the History of Medicine, created at Johns Hopkins University in 1929 with funds from the Rockefeller Foundation, established the *Bulletin of the History of Medicine*. The list of scholarly journals has since lengthened steadily, particularly under the influence of the interdisciplinary activities represented by such publications as the *Journal of the History of Ideas* (1940), the *Far Eastern Quarterly* (1941), the *American Quarterly* (1949), *Comparative Studies in Society and History* (1958), and *History and Theory* (1960). Today, instead of lacking outlets, a historian writing on almost any subject can choose among several.

What stands out in this extraordinary proliferation of the institutions of scholarship is the diversity of initiative and the relative weakness of centralized direction. Virtually every new development has democratized the opportunities for research achievement. In recent years, it is true, the American Historical Association and other agencies have striven to improve coordination of scholarly activity. But

intervals from 1925 to 1955: *Ohio Archaeological and Historical Quarterly, North Carolina Historical Review, Pennsylvania Magazine of History and Biography, Wisconsin Magazine of History,* and *Proceedings of the Massachusetts Historical Society.*

34

nowhere, since Jameson's heyday, has a single focus of authority and leadership materialized. Instead of a national center of historical research, Americans have created their own peculiar welter of voluntary associations, special projects, and particular agencies. Characteristically, the federal government has been exceedingly slow and hesitant in sponsoring historical inquiry. When Congress in 1958 finally provided some "National Defense" fellowships for graduate students in the social sciences, it acted on the quixotically democratic assumption that too few universities were producing the scientists and scholars of the future.[19] The National Defense fellowships have served therefore to decentralize still more the pattern of scholarly activity.

The reluctance of the federal government to assume historical responsibilities dogged Jameson at every step in his lifelong campaign for federal expenditures in behalf of history. As early as 1891 he pointed out that the United States gave less official care to the publication of historical documents, and to the preservation of unpublished records, than did even the smaller countries of western Europe. Yet his repeated insistence on centralized management of the nation's archives did not bear fruit until 1934, three years before his death, when the great National Archives Building on Pennsylvania Avenue was at last completed, and the principal records of all branches of the federal government became available to scholars in one efficient establishment.[20]

Jameson's desire for a systematic, governmental program of publishing historical documents proved even more difficult to realize. A few specialized projects, notably the long-established series "Foreign Relations of the United States" (1861-    ), did enjoy official sponsorship, though even "Foreign Relations" was not edited by a trained historian until 1921. Four years later, on Jameson's recommendation, Congress authorized publication of the *Territorial Papers of the United States* (25 vols., 1934-60), a task to which Clarence E. Carter devoted a lifetime of meticulous care. Another

[19] U.S. Office of Education, *Guide to the National Defense Education Act of 1958* (1959), pp. 11-12.
[20] J. F. Jameson, "Expenditures of Foreign Governments in Behalf of History," AHA *Annual Report* (1891), pp. 33-61; J. F. Jameson and Edward Channing, *The Present State of Historical Writing in America* (1910), pp. 5-10; G. Philip Bauer, "Public Archives in the United States," in *In Support of Clio*, pp. 65-67.

suggestion from Jameson prompted publication by Congress of *The Writings of George Washington,* edited by John C. Fitzpatrick (39 vols., 1931-44).[21]

Beyond these piecemeal ventures, Jameson strove to interest the United States in maintaining a permanent commission on national historical publications. His plan fell on deaf ears when a committee of leading historians recommended it in 1908, and made little headway when the American Historical Association urged it again in the 1920's.[22] The idea finally came alive in the 1950's—not because the federal government was prepared to assume real responsibility but because a number of private sponsors for grand documentary publications were appearing.

The precipitating factor was issuance in 1950 of the first volume of Julian Boyd's masterly *Writings of Thomas Jefferson,* underwritten by the *New York Times* in conjunction with the Princeton University Press. On this occasion, Wayne C. Grover, head of the National Archives, interested President Truman in making a call for a broad national program of works such as Boyd's. As a result, a National Historical Publications Commission, which had been quietly authorized in the National Archives Act of 1934, was reorganized and brought to life. The Commission, composed of public dignitaries as well as historians, was charged with laying plans for important documentary publications. After a general survey of needs and opportunities, it has initiated and sought sponsors for a large number of projects, chiefly critical editions of the papers of American statesmen.[23] Universities, foundations, and business enterprises are providing most of the funds. Not until 1964 did Congress make federal money available to the Commission for grants in aid of these important works. The success of the whole campaign is another indication of the dependence of American historical scholarship on dispersed and disparate auspices.

---

[21] Jameson, *An Historian's World,* pp. 308, 364-65; Richard W. Leopold, "A Centennial Estimate," summarized in *AHR,* LXVII (1962), 860.

[22] Clarence E. Carter, "The United States and Documentary Historical Publication," *Mississippi Valley Historical Review,* XXV (1938), 3-24.

[23] "Historical Activities," *Mississippi Valley Historical Review,* XLVIII (1961), 176-77; John Tebbel, "Safeguarding U.S. History," *Saturday Review,* XLV (June 23, 1962), 24-25, 52; "The Reminiscences of Guy Stanton Ford" (Oral History Research Office, Columbia University, 1956), pp. 892-94; "The Reminiscences of Solon J. Buck" (Oral History Research Office, Columbia University, 1957), pp. 16-19.

Since the 1930's the federal government has employed substantial numbers of historians, particularly in the Defense Department and the National Park Service. Nevertheless, seven out of eight Ph.D.'s in history make their careers in colleges and universities.[24] So the fundamental economic basis for the growth of the historical profession has been a massive spread of college education. Without the jobs and the research incentives thereby provided, the demand for sources and publication outlets would have been far weaker. Consequently it is useful, in following the expanding content of historical scholarship in the twentieth century, to keep always in mind the flexible and expanding character of the educational setting.

By the beginning of the twentieth century American universities conventionally taught ancient, European, and American history; and the first task of research was to establish a sound basis of scholarship within those fields. The earliest efforts of professional scholars were concentrated overwhelmingly in American history, for which original sources were most accessible and patriotic motives strong. Almost nine-tenths of the historical dissertations written in American universities in the Eighties and Nineties dealt with native subjects. Herbert Baxter Adams insisted on the title Professor of Institutional History rather than Professor of American History, but he assigned American thesis topics even to students like Charles Homer Haskins and Charles D. Hazen, who became distinguished European historians.[25] Jameson deliberately limited the work of his Department of Historical Research at the Carnegie Institution to American history, although his own knowledge and interests ranged far beyond. In the early years most of the contributors to the *American Historical Review* wrote about American history, which still received as late as the 1920's slightly more space than European history. The period from 1900 to World War I, however, marked the emergence of outstanding professional scholars in the principal non-American fields.

At first ancient history was taught chiefly in classics departments,

24 *Report and Recommendations of the Committee of the American Historical Association on the Historian and the Federal Government* (mimeographed report, n.d. [1952?]); Dexter Perkins and John L. Snell, *The Education of Historians in the United States* (1961), p. 21.
25 *Ibid.*, p. 30; W. Stull Holt, ed., *Historical Scholarship in the United States, 1876-1901* (1938), pp. 145-46. Other men who became prominent European historians after writing dissertations on American subjects included James Harvey Robinson, Robert L. Schuyler, William Shepherd, E. R. Turner, and E. P. Cheyney.

for it grew out of philological and archaeological studies already transplanted from Germany during the nineteenth century. The gentleman-classicist Charles Eliot Norton inspired the American School of Classical Studies at Athens (1881), which supplied graduate fellowships and a base for excavations.[26] Another American School of Classical Studies followed in Rome in 1895. Of America's pioneer ancient historians, both Tenney Frank and William Lynn Westermann got their training in Latin literature in the late Nineties and later shifted to history. In a series of magnificent books, Frank combined literature, history, and archaeology to interpret Roman civilization as a whole. On the other hand, America's first outstanding authority on Greek history, William Scott Ferguson, was from the outset a political historian. In three major books published between 1899 and 1913, he added significantly to the history of Athens and Greek imperialism.

The greatest of America's ancient historians, James Henry Breasted, developed from a background in biblical rather than classical philology. As a student in a midwestern theological seminary, he became fascinated with Hebrew and doubtful of Christianity. He transferred to Yale, whence his Hebrew professor sent him to Berlin for training in Egyptology; this resulted in a Ph.D. thesis (1894) on the solar hymns of Ikhnaton. Like Tenney Frank, Breasted mastered archaeological, literary, and official documentary sources. His *History of Egypt* (1905), the first scholarly, well-balanced history of the ancient Nile, was still the standard work at the time of his death thirty years later. His *Development of Religion and Thought in Ancient Egypt* (1912) expounded an exciting interpretation of the evolution of moral ideas. After World War I he developed the great Oriental Institute at the University of Chicago and gave most of his attention to its archaeological excavations in the Near East.[27]

Important professional scholarship in medieval history also began around the turn of the century. Although the American medievalists did not write on the scale that Breasted, Frank, and later Michael Rostovtzeff achieved in ancient history, they did distinguished work

<hr/>

[26] Louis E. Lord, *A History of the American School of Classical Studies at Athens, 1882-1942* (1947), pp. 1-48.
[27] W. F. Albright, "James Henry Breasted, Humanist," *American Scholar,* V (1936), 287-99. On Frank see *Dictionary of American Biography,* vol. XXII, pp. 203-205; on Westermann, American Philosophical Society *Year Book* (1955), pp. 509-12.

at an equally early date. Perhaps the first significant monographs were Charles Gross's dissertation on *The Gild Merchant* (1890), done at Göttingen, and Charles M. Andrews' *Old English Manors* (1892). Gross, the first Harvard historian to contribute to the literature of European history, inaugurated a great bibliographical enterprise with the publication in 1900 of *The Sources and Literature of English History to About 1485*. (Cooperation between the Royal Historical Society and the American Historical Association has carried this forward to the nineteenth century, but the series is only today approaching completion.) Other American medieval historians, notably L. J. Paetow, have also helped to confirm the prophetic remark that Jameson made back in 1891: "No nation in the world is so addicted to bibliography and indexing." [28]

Like Gross and Andrews, most of the early American medievalists concentrated on English history. England was the most accessible country with a medieval past, and its history before 1600 seemed peculiarly our own. As the principal source of American liberty and the incarnation of tradition, stability, and conservative social evolution, English institutions made a powerful appeal to the American aristocracy of culture. In 1900, George Burton Adams, who built Yale's Department of History practically from scratch, announced in the *American Historical Review* an impressive interpretation of the evolution of limited monarchy from the feudal principles preserved in Magna Carta. To Adams, the survival of feudal restraints upon power saved England from absolutism. Ultimately Adams synthesized this and many other contributions in his *Constitutional History of England* (1921), the first full-scale treatment after Maitland. Charles H. McIlwain's Harvard dissertation, *The High Court of Parliament* (1910), was perhaps an even more seminal book. Meanwhile, Charles Homer Haskins, surely the most learned and energetic of American medievalists, a full professor at Wisconsin at the age of twenty-two, was also studying Norman institutions; but Haskins ransacked archives across Europe and pursued the Normans wherever they had gone. His *Norman Institutions* (1918) remains the standard treatise on the subject.[29]

---

[28] J. F. Jameson, *The History of Historical Writing in America* (1891), p. 151. A good summary of Gross's career is in *Proceedings of the Massachusetts Historical Society*, XLIX (1916), 161-66.

[29] Reginald E. Rabb, "George Burton Adams," in *Some Modern Historians of*

Haskins' work illustrates another striking characteristic of American medieval scholarship. In contrast to the insularity of English historians leading Americans had, even in the Anglophile atmosphere of the early twentieth century, an unusual freedom from national or local parochialism. American scholars studied trans-European movements, and sought to grasp medieval civilization as a whole. Institutionalists moved in an increasingly comparative direction, which led to McIlwain's brilliant analysis of the medieval estates in the *Cambridge Medieval History* (vol. VII, 1932). Dana C. Munro awakened—first at Wisconsin where he taught from 1902 to 1915, then at Princeton—a strong American interest in the Crusades. Munro thought of the Crusading movement as a frontier of European expansion and in that sense analogous to American experience. Until very recently his students and disciples have maintained Crusading history as a feature of American medieval scholarship. After World War I the rise of intellectual history turned attention to another kind of contact between Eastern and Western civilizations. Haskins, deserting the Normans, became the principal authority on the transmission of Greek and Arabic learning to western Europe, while Columbia's Lynn Thorndike launched a massive *History of Magic and Experimental Science* (8 vols., 1923-58).[30]

Modern European studies have their own place later in this book. It is sufficient here to say that they too were established on a professional basis around the beginning of the century, but progress was slower than in the medieval field. Modern European history, especially since the Reformation, did not attract much interest and ability until after World War I. Of nearly four hundred articles printed in the *American Historical Review* before 1915, only eight related to nineteenth century Europe. As late as the 1920's Harvard turned out more Ph.D.'s in medieval history than in modern European.[31]

Beyond the standard subjects, the only history that took hold at a

*Britain,* ed. Herman Ausubel (1951), pp. 177-91; F. M. Powicke, *Modern Historians and the Study of History* (London, 1955), pp. 109-17.
30 This discussion owes much to an illuminating conversation with Professor J. R. Strayer on medieval historiography.
31 W. Stull Holt, "Historical Scholarship," in *American Scholarship in the Twentieth Century,* ed. Merle Curti (1953), p. 102; Samuel Eliot Morison, ed., *The Development of Harvard University Since the Inauguration of President Eliot, 1869-1929* (1930), p. 164; Charles H. Haskins, "European History and American Scholarship," *AHR,* XXVIII (1923), 215-27.

number of universities in the early twentieth century was Latin American. This was partly because of the contemporary interest in empire and the rapid extension of U.S. power. Moreover, Latin American history abutted directly on European as well as American history; it lay in a sense between them. Just as medievalists worked into continental Europe from a background in English history, so the early Latin Americanists worked into their field from a starting point either in American or in European history. Like the Europeanists, the first generation of Latin American scholars was preoccupied with the early (or colonial) period at the expense of the modern (or national) period. Their attention centered on the origin of institutions and on the theme of expansion into frontier areas. The first important book was Edward G. Bourne's contribution to the American Nation series, *Spain in America, 1450-1580* (1904), a book that reflected the American historians' interest in the transmission and modification of European institutions.[32]

At the University of California, whose three specialists in Latin American history made it the leading center of study, Herbert E. Bolton developed after 1911 the dominant school in the United States. He attracted many students into research on Spanish soldiers and missionaries in the borderlands, where Spanish settlement impinged on that of other empires. These studies gave Bolton the idea that all of the Americas had a unitary history shaped by common experiences. Every year he preached this pan-American doctrine to a thousand students in his course on the History of the Americas, and his numerous disciples took up the refrain.[33] Bolton lacked the analytical ability to make his concept fruitful; he gave a specious appearance of significance to a program of fragmentary research. Latin American historiography attained less intellectual maturity than European. The only truly outstanding book was Roger B. Merriman's *The Rise of the Spanish Empire* (3 vols., 1918-27), and this derived from an interest in Europe. As a student of early modern Europe, Merriman saw the Spanish Empire as a natural continuation of medieval institutions, not as a product of New World conditions.

While original scholarship was developing in ancient, European,

[32] Charles Gibson and Benjamin Keen, "Trends of United States Studies in Latin American History," *AHR*, LXII (1957), 856-59.
[33] Philip C. Brooks, "Do the Americas Share a Common History?" *Revista de historia de America*, XXXIII (1952), 75-83; Arthur P. Whitaker, *The Western Hemisphere Idea: Its Rise and Decline* (1954).

and Latin American history, the content of American higher education was steadily widening in all directions, most especially toward the present. An increasingly pragmatic attention to current problems and to the experience of the contemporary world was apparent before World War I. Thereafter this trend spread through the whole educational system. The expansion of historical scholarship proceeded mainly along similar lines. The most striking increase of effort after 1917 occurred in recent history, in the penetration of areas outside of western Europe and America, and in the numerous interdisciplinary interests an exploding curriculum produced.

A new course that embodied these objectives, a course usually entitled History of Western Civilization, became the staple of historical instruction between the two world wars. At Columbia College, where it originated in 1919, the course was named Contemporary Civilization.[34] Everywhere it emphasized recent history and the spread of European influences throughout the world. Everywhere it endeavored to bring the multiplicity of modern knowledge within a unifying historical perspective. Thus "Western Civ" renewed the function of the historian as a generalist in a present-minded culture. It did much to save history from the pedagogical decline that philosophy—another generalizing discipline—was undergoing. Although it did not arrest specialization in research, the teaching of Western Civilization surely encouraged the newer areas of research into which historians were moving.

A dramatic increase of activity in modern European history after World War I was only one manifestation of the shift of historical and educational interests toward the present. The balance of effort also shifted within the better established fields. The study of American colonial history suffered while modern American history boomed. In English history, through the work of Wallace Notestein and Conyers Read, the most distinguished American scholarship now concerned the Tudor and Stuart rather than the medieval period. In Latin American history a virtually exclusive preoccupation with the colonial period gave way to a new attention to the nineteenth and twentieth centuries.

As recent times came to the fore, the spectrum of historical scholarship widened to embrace the whole non-Western and semi-Western

34 Arthur M. Schlesinger, "The History Situation in Colleges and Universities," *Historical Outlook*, XI (1920), 103-106.

world that was pressing in upon the United States. Slowly between the wars, and then with pell-mell speed since 1945, Russian history, east Asian history, and Islamic history have crowded upon the American academic scene.

The entry of professional scholarship into these areas followed the pattern we have glimpsed in the development of Latin American history. Historians gradually reached outward from established academic interests and appropriated the related or similar aspects of a new area. Thus the few American historians before World War II who wrote on Russian and Asian history stressed the Western aspects of the former and the Westernization of the latter, with special attention to diplomatic relations with the West. As in medieval and Latin American history, the theme of expansion appealed to Americans. Apparently the first American monograph on Russian history was Frank Golder's *Russian Expansion on the Pacific, 1641-1850* (1914), and possibly the most important American contribution to Chinese history before World War II was Owen Lattimore's *The Inner Asian Frontiers of China* (1940).[35]

In the 1920's and 1930's European dictatorships drove into exile many scholars trained outside the American historiographical tradition and capable therefore of widening its scope and enriching its substance. The emigré professors brought with them a more intimate understanding of cultures that American scholars had viewed from the perspective of the outsider, who can observe external forms more readily than their inner spirit. Not only Russia and the Far East, but also many other neglected fields of knowledge benefited. One of the early arrivals, Alexander Vasiliev, imported Byzantine history to America. Fleeing from Hitler, Ernst Kantorowicz brought an unprecedented grasp of medieval intellectual history. Stephan Kuttner's Institute of Canon Law at The Catholic University of America raised medieval church history to an importance it had lacked due to native preoccupation with American church history. In Spanish history a scholar uprooted by Franco, Americo Castro, revealed an endogenous pattern of development that Americans surely would not themselves have perceived. In the Russian field, Michael Karpovich at Harvard trained a new generation of American scholars, and

---

[35] John S. Curtiss, "History," in *American Research on Russia,* ed. Harold H. Fisher (1959), p. 23; Charles O. Hucker, *Chinese History: A Bibliographic Review* (1958), *passim.*

George Vernadsky at Yale wrote a monumental *History of Russia* (vols. 1-4, 1943-59) from the point of view of its internal dynamics. For the Far East, perhaps the most remarkable contribution came from Karl A. Wittfogel and Feng Chia-sheng. Their *History of Chinese Society: Liao* (1949) disproved conclusively the hoary idea that the Chinese had always assimilated their conquerors. Wittfogel went on to make a daring comparative analysis of *Oriental Despotism* (1957).

In the 1930's a second impetus quickened the expansion of historical scholarship into areas beyond America and western Europe. Foundations and scholarly organizations became concerned about the allegedly narrow scope of humanistic scholarship in the United States. The American Council of Learned Societies exercised decisive leadership. Sparked by Mortimer Graves, who later became its executive secretary, the ACLS in the early Thirties created "development committees" to promote underdeveloped fields of knowledge—Chinese, Japanese, Indic-Iranian, Byzantine, and Latin American among them.[36] The ACLS, a loose federation of learned bodies dominated by the humanities, had struggled along with scant support from the large foundations, whose humanistic interests rarely extended beyond the photogenic glamor of archaeology. Now the prospect of awakening America to an understanding of far-away peoples touched a responsive chord, particularly at the Rockefeller Foundation where international cooperation was an article of faith. Persuaded that humanistic studies were too largely snobbish and antiquarian, the Rockefeller Foundation decided to help culture become more "democratic and inclusive."[37] Its support made possible special conferences on non-Western areas, intensive language courses, traveling fellowships, and annual bibliographies (e.g., *Handbook of Latin American Studies,* 1936-   ). Initially, the dominant concern was with language training; very few of the American professors who wrote about the Far East knew any Far Eastern language. By the

---

[36] Kenneth Scott Latourette, "Far Eastern Studies in the United States," *Far Eastern Quarterly,* XV (1955), 6; American Council of Learned Societies, Committee on the Promotion of Chinese Studies, *Progress of Chinese Studies in the U.S.A.* (1931); Lewis Hanke, "The Development of Latin American Studies in the U.S., 1939-1945," *Americas,* IV (1947), 33.

[37] Raymond B. Fosdick, *The Story of the Rockefeller Foundation* (1952), pp. 239-42.

end of the Thirties the intriguing term *area programs* was beginning to circulate.

World War II dramatically forced the pace and altered the character of area studies. As in no previous war, American forces were deployed everywhere in the world. Suddenly the need for access to non-European societies became enormous. The federal government intervened in the history of scholarship on a massive scale. Army and Navy training programs and subsequent overseas experience gave a vocation to many of the young men who now—no longer young— are assuming leadership in area studies. The State Department promoted an exchange of professors with various countries and attached cultural officers to many embassies. The Library of Congress vastly augmented its resources in Asian, Russian, and Latin American fields. Many professors served in Washington agencies, where the need to answer immediate questions about a particular area convinced them of the value of pooling information controlled by several disciplines.[38] Ever since, historical scholarship in the "underdeveloped" fields has had a markedly interdisciplinary character.

In this respect the underdeveloped fields were not entirely unique. The urge to combine several disciplines for the understanding of a civilization as a whole goes back a long way. Ancient historians had always thought of themselves primarily as classical scholars or as Orientalists, as the case might be; and since the establishment of the Mediaeval Academy of America in 1925 medieval historians have increasingly identified themselves as medievalists. The distinctive feature of the area studies stimulated by World War II, however, was the utilitarian and contemporary stamp that the war put upon them. Programs initiated in the Thirties under literary, linguistic, and historical auspices passed, as a result of the war, chiefly into the hands of social scientists. This has created an educational pattern that now attracts to the study of Russian, Asian, and Latin American history students interested in analytical relationships and comparative generalizations. They try to understand the indigenous society in its own terms instead of seeing it merely in the perspective of Western expansion; but their social-science training has also given them a strong interest in testing general social theories.

[38] Philip E. Mosely, "The Growth of Russian Studies," in *American Research on Russia*, pp. 1-22; Hanke, *op. cit.*, pp. 32-35.

45

By the 1960's Persian history, African history, and comparative tropical history had found a place in the repertoire of American scholarship; its global embrace was virtually complete. Meanwhile, the range of human activities included in historiography had expanded as phenomenally as its geographical scope. At first, professional historians confined themselves in practice to certain kinds of political and economic subjects. Eventually, they learned to write about child-rearing habits, mass hysterias, and events in the laboratory. Like the movement into new geographical areas, the topical expansion of history has proceeded more or less consciously along interdisciplinary lines; and it too has reached a point at which further enlargement of the realm of history seems hardly possible.

Topically as well as geographically, historical scholarship expanded by reaching out from a familiar subject to the contiguous fringes of the unfamiliar. Thus political historians, on turning to economic history, initially concentrated on the economic operations of government; institutional historians, attracted to educational history, first studied educational organizations rather than the content of instruction; social historians drawn to the history of science could understand its social context more readily than its theoretical structure. In time, professional historians found their way closer to the center of these topics; and scholars inside the relevant disciplines assisted them, much as foreign-born historians helped Americans to penetrate unfamiliar areas.

The spread of professional history into new types of human activity is not so clearly visible a process as its chronological and geographical extension. New area-histories almost automatically crystallized into coherent divisions of historical knowledge; for each area possessed a culture and a tradition that needed to be understood in its own terms before it could be related satisfactorily to the history of other areas. But the addition of new topics to any single area-history produced in most cases a much more fluid situation. Most of the neglected strands of social and cultural activity that twentieth century historians uncovered were so interwoven with other strands of the same area-history that clear-cut specialization has been arbitrary and artificial. Certain labels, like *social history* or *intellectual history,* proved necessary, of course. Since no historian could be equally receptive to all phases of human activity, we needed convenient indicators of the wavelengths to which individual historians

46

were most attuned. But the labels seldom designated a coherent sphere of reality, and they have sometimes confined the historian instead of clarifying history. In practice, historians have widened their coverage of an area in response to changing interpretations of it; and have embraced whatever range of data their own sensitivity permitted or their interpretive pattern suggested.

Sometimes, however, a topical strand virtually requires a more distinct specialization, involving the whole career of many scholars. This is the case when professional historians become interested in the development of an organized body of skills and knowledge. Like constitutional law or the practice of medicine, an appropriate subject must, of course, affect powerfully many other strands of history and thus need the attention of the professional historian, not just the subject specialist; yet the topic must also present such technical difficulties that general historical syntheses cannot do it justice. These conditions are most apparent, and most conducive to historical specialization, when a body of skills and knowledge has had a continuous internal development, transcending the histories of individual countries and belonging therefore to no one of them. Two examples of such specialties will serve the present discussion: military history and the history of science.

The history of warfare and of science deserve to rank as important branches of professional historical scholarship. Both war and science exert a major impact on civilization; and both depend on an elaborate development of theory and technique on the part of a dedicated elite over many centuries. Although international in character, each takes a coloration from the society that contains it. Americans have written military history at least since Increase Mather's *Brief History of the War with the Indians in New England* (1676), and the history of science since Samuel Miller's *Brief Retrospect of the Eighteenth Century* (1803). In the twentieth century each has become a branch of professional history. Of the two, military history is the less recondite; yet the history of science, for all of its difficulty, has established itself more easily in the American historical profession.

Until the twentieth century the history of science suffered from polemical enthusiasm and from fragmentation. Those who treated the theme broadly celebrated the progressive triumph of science over religious superstition; specialists confined themselves to histories of the separate sciences. At one extreme stood such hagiographic works

47

as Andrew Dickson White's *History of the Warfare of Science with Theology* (1896); at the other were monumental compendia like Florian Cajori's *History of Mathematical Notations* (2 vols., 1928-29).

Twentieth century historians have had the task of working out a general history of science that would be more than a one-sided story of progress, and more too than the sum of the histories of the separate disciplines. Although the foundations of such a history were laid in Europe, since World War I some of the major advances have been made in the United States. The principal achievement—not wholly American—has been to show the continuity between modern and premodern science. Lynn Thorndike elaborately demonstrated the interlocking of magical and scientific thinking, while George Sarton, who emigrated to the United States from Belgium during World War I, produced a practically boundless encyclopedia, *Introduction to the History of Science* (5 vols., 1927-48), covering the subject to the end of the thirteenth century.[39] With Sarton's aid, Harvard University established a doctoral program in the history of science in 1935, and since World War II many other universities have competed feverishly for the few well-equipped scholars in the field. The study of medieval science continues to flourish. For the modern period the social history of science has received most attention, but Charles Gillispie's important book, *The Edge of Objectivity* (1960), offers a unifying view of modern science as a structure of knowledge.

In contrast, the study of military history has remained on a much lower level of generalization. The only American work of outstanding importance was done in the 1880's by a captain assigned to prepare a course of lectures on naval history at the new naval War College at Newport. Alfred T. Mahan's *The Influence of Sea Power Upon History, 1660-1783* (1890), followed by similar surveys of the French Revolution and the War of 1812, brilliantly demon-

39 Herbert Butterfield, "History in the Twentieth Century," *The Historical Association, 1906-1956* (London, 1957), 71; C. Doris Hellman, "George Sarton, Historian of Science and New Humanist," *Science*, CXXVIII (1958), 641-44. A helpful review essay is I. Bernard Cohen's "Some Recent Books on the History of Science," *Journal of the History of Ideas*, XV (1954), 163-92. On the present organization of the field see Richard H. Shryock's "The History of Science in American Universities,' *Proceedings of the American Philosophical Society*, CV (1961), 512.

strated how control of the seas affected the outcome of these conflicts. Subsequent Army and Navy scholars have rarely rivaled Mahan's grasp of the geographical, technological, and strategic aspects of military history. The American military establishment has hardly ever produced historians equal to Generals Sir Frederick Maurice and J. F. C. Fuller in England, and American soldiers have continued to read of their great commanders in the works of Maurice, Fuller, G. F. R. Henderson, and Liddell Hart.

World War II aroused much popular interest in America's own military history and some stirrings among professional historians also. Samuel Eliot Morison, nautical scholar par excellence, persuaded a nautical President to make him the Navy's historian. After seeing all the naval action one man could reach, Morison wrote from the vantage point of participant as well as scholar. Through fifteen volumes, which appeared on an average of one per year, his *History of United States Naval Operations in World War II* (1947-62) maintains an unflagging vigor and acumen. At the Pentagon, Kent Roberts Greenfield assembled a staff of young scholars who are telling the story of ground operations. Their individual volumes, detailed, learned, and sometimes very penetrating, will someday comprise a vast eighty-volume history of the *United States Army in World War II* (53 vols., 1947-61).

Some of this activity has spread backward into the study of earlier wars and military systems. As yet, however, scholars in the universities have studied little more than the politics of military groups and the details of particular military campaigns. The general history of war as an institution remains only a dimly perceived ideal. Academically speaking, military history is still a sideline.[40]

Why does the historical profession treat the history of science as a broader, more important domain than the history of war? The question opens an instructive view of the influences that have shaped the topical spread of research. Most obviously, the dominant intellectual interests of the profession play a part. The strong movement of inquiry in recent decades into areas of life beyond the scope of governmental affairs has aided the history of science while working against

---

[40] John Bowditch, "War and the Historian," in *Teachers of History: Essays in Honor of Laurence B. Packard,* ed. H. Stuart Hughes (1954), pp. 322-27. See also Richard Glover, "War and Civilian Historians," *Journal of the History of Ideas,* XVIII (1957), 84-100.

the grain of military studies. The quest for breadth in historical writing proceeded on the assumption that social and intellectual subjects are intrinsically "broad," whereas interest in the theory and practice of war smacked of the bad old "drum-and-trumpet" school, which, never having existed among professional historians, was all the more easily discredited. Thus the vast study of World War I sponsored in the 1920's by the Carnegie Endowment for International Peace was explicitly an economic and social history that excluded military and diplomatic policy. Even so, only half of the volumes originally projected were published; only three of these dealt with the United States; and none of the three was written by an academic historian.[41]

The antimilitarist bias inherent in the thrust of professional historical interests has received wider support from an old American predisposition to keep military and civil affairs separate. Viewing war as abnormal and episodic, American intellectuals have generally wished to leave military questions to military technicians. The new international situation after 1945, charged with persistent military danger and feverish scientific competition, greatly emphasized the continuous importance of both; but scholars have responded more readily to the scientific challenge. Doubtless the organization of academic life confirms this preference by denying to the military the prestige enjoyed by scientists. Historians venturing upon the terrain of the natural sciences enter willingly and profitably into interdisciplinary relations with fellow scholars in the disciplines most concerned; but the professors of "military science," assigned to campuses to indoctrinate students in reserve training programs, lack the scholarly attainments or intellectual prestige requisite to real participation in the academic community.[42]

Conceivably it might be possible to demonstrate how every extension of the subject matter of professional history has come from the intrinsic logic of historical study, from the general cultural milieu, and from the organization of academic life. But then we should miss much else. In general, we may conclude that the remarkable diversity of American historical scholarship today betrays the flexibility of

---

41 The genesis of this project, which Harry Elmer Barnes called "the most stupendous example of historical cooperation yet known to man," is reported in James T. Shotwell's *Autobiography* (1961), pp. 134-55.
42 Louis Morton, "The Historian and the Study of War," *Mississippi Valley Historical Review,* XLVIII (1962), 605.

these conditioning factors, the relative permissiveness of the whole setting. In spite of fashions and prejudices, no large topic has been entirely neglected. For this we may thank especially the eclecticism of the modern American university. By making a place for everything from home economics to African languages, it has encouraged academic historians to take seriously every dimension of human experience.

# 3

# DISTRIBUTION AND RECRUITMENT OF TALENT

Thus far our story has been one of almost uninterrupted expansion, diversification, and increase of capacity. In a span of three generations, America developed the biggest and most comprehensive historical profession of any country. Yet any process of growth creates new problems, and the American historical profession has had its share. Internally, these have to do with the distribution of effort among fields of specialization and with the level of ability in the profession as a whole. In the twentieth century too rapid expansion in some fields occurred at the expense of others; one may even speak of a decline in certain areas of historical scholarship. More generally, the quality of professional historiography probably did not keep pace with the impressive growth of effort and spread of coverage. Evaluation of these differentials is not easily made; yet some tentative estimate seems essential to a balanced view.

On the question of "neglected" fields, it is hard to speak impartially, since all enthusiastic historians tend to believe that their own fields, or at least the most important aspects of them, suffer sad neglect. Historians in America, perhaps because they are so numerous and so loosely organized, have a propensity to make constant appeals to their brethren in behalf of neglected subjects, hoping thereby to win recruits in the everlasting competition for talent and effort. What stands out, however, above the clamor of so many voices, is the quiet fact that a few large areas of research have experienced a marked decline of attention and support during the last generation. The most notable of these losses have resulted from the passion for contemporaneity that has so stimulated interest in modern history at the expense of the remoter past.

Before World War I, freshmen in American colleges very commonly had a choice between ancient history, medieval and modern European history, and English history. By 1919—the year in which Columbia College launched the famous course significantly entitled "Contemporary Civilization"—ancient history had lost its time-honored place as a freshman elective in the great majority of leading universities and colleges.[1] A significant decline in scholarly activity did not become evident, however, until World War II. Many of the major historians of antiquity remained active through the 1930's, when Tenney Frank was supervising a five-volume *Economic Survey of Ancient Rome* (1933-40) and Michael Rostovtzeff was writing his great three-volume *Social and Economic History of the Hellenistic World* (1941). After World War II Americans continued to make notable archaeological discoveries, such as those of William F. Albright in Palestine and B. D. Meritt in Greece, and to publish an occasional major work like John A. Wilson's *The Burden of Egypt* (1951);[2] but ancient historiography dwindled to a very small fraction of the total historical effort. An attrition in graduate enrollments reduced the number of American graduate students working on doctoral dissertations in ancient history from a high of 36 in 1938 to as few as 15 in 1961.[3] Perhaps not coincidentally, this shrinkage closely followed the reallocation of foundation support in favor of more recent times and more exotic areas. In contrast to the handsome support the Rockefeller Foundation gave James Henry Breasted in the Twenties and Tenney Frank in the Thirties, it has given nothing in recent years for classical or for medieval studies.

As one might expect, the Middle Ages have attracted more students than antiquity, though not nearly a fair share. Over the decades the number of Ph.D.'s slowly increased. In the 1950's it rose somewhat above the level reached in the late 1930's; the loss has been relative rather than absolute. In recent years many more universities than ever before have had doctoral candidates in medieval history, but none any longer has more than a handful. The seventeen doctoral dissertations on medieval history completed in 1960 were done at fifteen different universities, a fact that illustrates both the general decentralization of American scholarship and the lack of a predom-

[1] Arthur M. Schlesinger, "The History Situation in Colleges and Universities," *Historical Outlook*, XI (1920), 103-106.
[2] Mortimer Chambers, *Greek and Roman History* (1958), pp. 11-13; Miriam Lichtheim, "Ancient Egypt: A Survey of Current Historiography," *AHR*, LXIX (1963), 37-39. Albright has sketched his autobiography and credo in *History, Archaeology, and Christian Humanism* (1964), pp. 287-327, but see also G. Ernest Wright, ed., *The Bible and the Ancient Near East* (1961), and Herbert F. Hahn, *Old Testament in Modern Research* (1954).
[3] I have counted the number of dissertations listed in successive editions of the AHA's *List of Doctoral Dissertations in History Now in Progress at Universities in the United States*.

inating leader or school.[4] As in other non-American fields, the arrival in recent decades of continental European scholars has helped to widen American academic horizons. A slow emergence of interest in social and economic themes and the penetration of American scholarship into geographical areas untouched before the 1930's—notably Byzantium, medieval Islam, and medieval Russia—have brought diversity in place of the concentration of an earlier day. It is no longer possible to accuse American medieval historians, as one of their number did in 1934, of regarding the Middle Ages almost exclusively from a classical, Western Christian standpoint.[5]

While ancient and medieval history have clearly not received the attention they deserve as the matrix of our civilization, it is less certain that the quality of scholarship in those fields has suffered to a pronounced and special degree. Wherever the technical difficulties of research are unusually formidable and the interested segment of the intellectual community is small, the general dangers of academicism increase. A preoccupation with minutiae is encouraged, the larger action of the intellect clogged. Nevertheless, all the major divisions of history have continued to recruit lively, talented minds. And if, as seems true, Americans trained since World War I have produced very few major books on premodern history that break new ground in a large way, a similar judgment may also be made of the far larger company of modern historians. For all of its growth, the American historical profession in the twentieth century has not wholly lived up to the high expectations of its early leaders.

Although the discovery of new fields and techniques of investigation has never ceased to excite professional historians, many of the best of them grew disappointed with the general state of their discipline after its formative era ended. In the Eighties and Nineties enthusiasm for the new movement of historical research was unqualified. "It was a time of exhilaration and almost religious fervor among the younger scholars," Andrews remembered.[6] The humblest young

---

[4] S. H. Thomson, "A Note on American Doctoral Disertations," *Progress of Medieval Studies in the United States,* Bulletin 20 (1949); *Index to American Doctoral Dissertations, 1959-1960,* p. xvii, and preceding annual editions. See also Loren MacKinney, "Medieval History and Historians during World War II," *Medievalia et humanistica,* no. 5 (1948), pp. 24-35.

[5] Charles W. David, "American Historiography of the Middle Ages, 1884-1934," *Speculum,* X (1935), 125-37.

[6] Charles M. Andrews, "These Forty Years," *AHR,* XXX (1925), 233.

teacher, going out from one of the new seminars to a torpid southern or western college, could feel himself anointed for a pioneering role. A conviction that they were laying the intellectual foundations for great historical work gave the early professional historians a wonderful zest; they confidently expected to produce successors greater than themselves. In 1904 Woodrow Wilson, one of the early Hopkins Ph.D.'s, opened the historical sessions of the Congress of Arts and Sciences at the St. Louis Exposition with the happy announcement, "We have seen the dawn and the early morning hours of a new age in the writing of history, and the morning is now broadening about us into day." [7] After 1907, when the pioneering was over and the modest record and limited accomplishments of the second generation of professional scholars became gradually evident, disappointment set in.

"Time and the vast hordes of youths eager to acquire collegiate education have somewhat undeceived us," confessed Jameson in 1910, while Edward Channing challenged anyone to "see if he cannot count the really first class works of American historical writers within the last twenty-five years on his fingers; and yet conceive of the number of persons engaged in historical pursuits and the number of books constantly published under the guise of history!" Jameson continued to hope for better things. After World War I he predicted that it would—like the Napoleonic wars—usher in "an age of generalization, of synthesis, of history more largely governed and informed by general ideas." [8] The new era did not arrive on schedule, and leading academic historians continued to remark sadly on the amiable mediocrity that their movement, now become a settled institution, seemed to produce. In the late Twenties a committee of the American Historical Association deplored the waning of the historian's influence. One of the judges of the Guggenheim fellowships commented privately in 1946 on the surprisingly small number and poor quality of the applicants in history. On retiring from the executive secretaryship of the American Historical Association in 1953, Guy Stanton Ford made much the same observation on "the poor

[7] *Congress of Arts and Sciences, Universal Exposition, St. Louis, 1904,* vol. II (1906), p. 3.
[8] J. F. Jameson and Edward Channing, *The Present State of Historical Writing in America* (1910), pp. 12, 29; J. F. Jameson, *The American Historian's Raw Materials* (1923), p. 41.

status of history," which he attributed to overspecialization and lax standards in the schools.[9]

In 1948 the American Historical Association asked the members of its Council to rank the six greatest American historians no longer living The only trained, academic scholar who received first place on anyone's list was Frederick Jackson Turner. The other front-runners were gentlemen-historians: Henry C. Lea, Henry Adams, George Bancroft, William H. Prescott, and above all Francis Parkman. In general, the rulers of the AHA, despite the bias one might expect them to have shown in favor of professionalism, cast slightly more votes for amateur historians, whose chief work was done in the sixty-year period from 1840 to 1900, than for professional scholars who wrote in the fifty-year period from 1890 to 1940. The results might have been a bit different if Charles A. Beard had not still been alive, but it is interesting that Beard's own list of six included only two professionally trained historians, Jameson and Andrews, whom he ranked toward the bottom.[10]

All of this suggests a surprisingly persistent, long-standing dissatisfaction among the senior statesmen of the historical profession. Obviously, some of their melancholy should be discounted. Even if the complaints were otherwise entirely accurate, they would tell us nothing about the accomplishments of recent years or about the present trend of scholarship, which is in many respects encouraging. Also, as an appraisal of past performance, such retrospective judgments are open to the charge of nostalgia. Encouraged by the self-critical habits of scholarship, historians in their later years may yield as easily as anyone else to an undervaluation of the present in comparison with the remembered promise of an earlier day. There is always a special temptation to underrate the young men coming forward by magnifying the titans of the past.

[9] Jean Jules Jusserand *et al., The Writing of History* (1926), pp. v-vii; Edwin F. Gay to Arthur H. Cole, January 28, 1946, in "Economic History: Memoranda and Reports," Files of the Social Science Research Council; "The Reminiscences of Guy Stanton Ford" (Oral History Research Office, Columbia University, 1956), pp. 145-47.
[10] "Council Business 1948," Archives of the American Historical Association (Division of Manuscripts, Library of Congress). For another prestige rating made about the same time by the chairmen of about 130 history departments and confined to "the distinguished professors of American history since 1875," see Gladys A. Wiggin, "Selecting and Appraising Personnel," in *Democracy in the Administration of Higher Education,* ed. Harold Benjamin (1950), p. 133.

The very character of historical research may lend a certain objective credibility to this sense of declining greatness. After the first broad surveys of a topic or a period are worked out, historical study necessarily becomes more demanding and complex, making the execution of ambitious books progressively more difficult. Only if advances in historical thought keep pace with the growing burdens of research can scholarship avoid an appearance of narrowing scope and diminishing effectiveness.

Allowing for the difficulties of such comparisons, one may still suspect a modicum of truth behind the feeling of declension that haunted many leading scholars. Although the number of good historians has steadily increased with the growth of the profession, the generation that came of age after the formative era was perhaps not so rich in outstanding talent as the one preceding. Of the men who secured graduate training between 1880 and 1905, one may nominate at least seven who became scholars of enduring distinction. To the field of American history belonged Frederick Jackson Turner, Edward Channing, Charles Maclean Andrews, and—the youngest of the lot—Charles A. Beard. In European history their peer and contemporary was Charles Homer Haskins, in ancient history James Henry Breasted, and doubtless we should also include, as a thinker and essayist, Carl Becker.[11] Did as many Americans of equivalent stature emerge from the graduate schools during the next quarter century? In European history William Langer may be ranked with Haskins. In American history Arthur M. Schlesinger Sr. has probably in his own way had an importance comparable to that of Andrews, and either Allan Nevins or Samuel Eliot Morison may deserve a place beside Channing. But how many of the doctoral graduates of 1905 to 1930 can we put in the company of Turner, Beard, Breasted, and Becker? Judgments about individuals will differ, and such ratings easily become invidious; the likelihood remains that few present-day scholars would wish to challenge the pre-eminence of the best historians educated in the late nineteenth century over the best of the succeeding generation.

The complaints about a shrinkage of outstanding talent have generally been coupled with a broader criticism of the recruitment and motivation of professional historians generally. It has often been

[11] Becker actually received the Ph.D. degree in 1907, but his days as a graduate student ended in 1899 when he started college teaching.

said, for example, that too few graduate students have a genuine research drive, and that the average historian therefore does not produce *enough*. As early as 1909 Jameson lamented that the *American Historical Review* was not getting an increasing number of articles and that at least half of the professors of history published nothing at all. The American Historical Association in 1926 appointed a committee to investigate why graduate study was leading to so little productive research. The committee estimated that no more than 150 of the 600 men and women with Ph.D.'s in history engaged persistently in research and publication.[12]

These figures tell us little about the vitality of the profession, and less about the trend of excellence. From the outset, teaching has been the primary obligation of a Ph.D. in history, and a large proportion of our professors have devoted themselves, by choice or necessity, exclusively to that. In all likelihood there has never been a time when much more than half of the profession has done any effective postgraduate research. A careful study has shown that Jameson's estimate of the proportion of nonproducers in 1909 held true in the late nineteenth century as well. Fifty per cent of those who received Ph.D.'s in history from American universities before 1892 published nothing at all in the next decade.[13]

Productivity apparently reached a peak during the decade of the Great Depression, when competition for academic posts was at its keenest. By 1939 more than 60 per cent of the historians who received doctoral degrees in the late 1920's had publications to their credit. Since World War II the percentage of productive scholars among younger members of the profession has declined, probably because the immense demand for college teachers has enabled throngs of students to secure degrees and to settle comfortably into teaching careers. In a recent study that seems closely comparable to the earlier report on the 1930's, a social scientist has found that only 34 per cent of those who secured doctorates in history in 1947-48

---

[12] Elizabeth Donnan and Leo F. Stock, eds., *An Historian's World: Selections from the Correspondence of John Franklin Jameson* (Memoirs of the American Philosophical Society, vol. 42, 1956), p. 125; Jameson and Channing, *The Present State of Historical Writing*, p. 12; Marcus W. Jernegan, "Productivity of Doctors of Philosophy in History," *AHR*, XXXIII (1927), 1-22.

[13] William B. Hesseltine and Louis Kaplan, "Doctors of Philosophy in History, A Statistical Study," *AHR*, XLVII (1942), 795.

published anything during the next eight or nine years.[14] Historians produced more under the spur of hardship than they do with all of the affluent opportunities and soft inducements of today.

We should not conclude that either the average quality or the total quantity of scholarship has fallen off. Because of the enormous postwar expansion of the profession, American historians collectively publish far more than ever before. In some fields, notably American history, the deluge of print has become an intellectual menace, threatening the capacity of scholars to keep abreast of research while maintaining a large and coherent view. Yet this outpouring has not depressed the average quality of historical publication. Anyone who looks back at the frequently stiff and pedestrian articles in the leading historical journals during the Twenties and Thirties may feel reassured about the general level of contemporary work: it is more deft, often more perceptive, and usually more substantial. We have, then, no reason to suppose that the American historical profession has ever lost ground as a result of a slackening of the drive and skill for research. Indeed, European scholars have often been amazed by our sheer assiduity.[15]

On the other hand, the relative paucity of major historians who have come out of the graduate schools during a good part of the twentieth century does point to some limitations in the composition or training of the American professoriat.

The easiest explanation of talent shortages has always been the Ph.D. system. Allegedly, it forces graduate research into tight little subjects unsuited to significant generalization, deprives students of a ranging and reflective education, stifles creativity and rewards conformity. The criticisms have been made for decades, although always by a relatively small minority in the profession. At the 1904 meeting of the American Historical Association George Burton Adams proposed that the doctoral dissertation be abandoned, and from time to time other leading historians have recommended a relaxation of the requirement. The difficulties that such critics stress have surely existed; but there is reason to suspect that the recurrent complaints have generally served a ritualistic rather than a constructive purpose.

[14] *Ibid.;* Bernard Berelson, *Graduate Education in the United States* (1960), p. 55.
[15] For a recent instance see the *Economist,* March 17, 1962, p. 1030.

By blaming "the system," which in fact could be as flexible as individual departments and professors might desire, critics have attributed to Germanic techniques the deficiencies in American performance.

The curious thing about the American Ph.D. program is its concern over technique. As American students discovered the doctoral dissertation in Germany in the nineteenth century, it was simply an exercise demonstrating one's capacity to do original research and to defend publicly an argument based thereon. Historical theses ran to about seventy pages; they occupied only a few months of a student's time. At first, American universities simply copied these procedures. Consequently, the dissertations their students executed in the 1880's were clearly works of apprenticeship, which did not involve so heavy a commitment of time and energy as to determine a man's subsequent career. Fears that America—with all of its heterogeneity—would permit the high standards of a European degree to deteriorate encouraged a progressive raising of the formal requirements. What had originally been a two-year graduate program lengthened in the Nineties to three years, and the student was expected to devote a full year to his thesis.[16] While the concept of defending an argument became perfunctory, the object of making a substantial display of newly discovered information was more and more insisted upon. By the 1920's it was generally reckoned that getting a Ph.D. meant four or five full years of graduate study, and the average candidate, in the words of Wilbur C. Abbott, was "almost always in a state of nervous hurry from at least the beginning of his second year." [17]

Although the stultifying effects of such extended labors were apparent, academic folkways proved exceedingly inflexible. Ironically, the swollen size of theses and the inflation of printing costs after World War I gradually forced universities to suspend the traditional rule that theses must be published, thereby permitting a further sacrifice of quality. A conference on graduate study called by the American Historical Association in 1932 urged a shortening of dissertations and an improvement in literary standards. The same recommendations, sternly repeated twenty-five years later by a committee of grad-

---

[16] Association of American Universities, *The First and Second Annual Conferences* (1901), pp. 23-24, 39; Ephraim Emerton, "The Requirements for the Historical Doctorate in America," AHA *Annual Report* (1893), pp. 79-90.
[17] Jusserand, *op. cit.*, pp. 43, 134.

uate deans, remain to date largely unrealized.[18] In spite of the deans' recommendation in 1957 that dissertations ought not to exceed 250 pages, the average length of doctoral theses in history accepted in six major universities actually increased from 351 pages in 1950-52 to 357 pages in 1959-61.[19] Evidently the problem did not inhere in the formal requirements of the system but rather in the people who operated it and the students whom it recruited.

A second shortcoming that leaders in the profession have repeatedly emphasized over the last forty or fifty years takes us closer to the human factor and may have more to do with the dip in scholarly distinction that seems to have occurred after 1905. At least from the early twentieth century until fairly recently, history and the social sciences—to judge from the complaints of their elder statesmen—failed to attract at the graduate level the brightest and most enterprising of their undergraduate majors. Instead, the ablest students usually entered business or such professions as law or medicine. "What we have then," declared W. E. Dodd stonily, "is to take in the main the poorest material and make of it the thinking element of the country." Evarts B. Greene added the depressing reflection in 1933 that the low level of intellectual interest prevailing among graduate students deprived the few promising novices of valuable stimulus.[20]

Two interconnected explanations have customarily been advanced for the diversion of talent into other careers: American society is excessively materialistic, and professors' salaries are accordingly too low to attract the most vigorous people. Men such as Turner and Jameson, who remembered the more spacious life of the late nineteenth century, thought that a "steady diminution of the salaries of professors" accounted for the supposedly poorer quality of the students of 1920 as compared with those of the 1890's. Actually, college professors had always felt aggrieved by their modest remuneration; and average salaries at the better institutions, except briefly after World War I, kept pace quite well with the rising cost of living

[18] "Conference on Graduate Study," AHA Files 1933, Box 6, Archives of American Historical Association; *New York Times*, November 13, 1957, p. 28.
[19] Figures compiled largely from *Dissertation Abstracts* and based on theses presented at Columbia, Princeton, Pennsylvania, Illinois, Michigan, and North Carolina.
[20] Jernegan, *op. cit.*, p. 19; *AHR*, XXXVIII (1933), 303. See also Jameson, *An Historian's World*, pp. 190, 255; "Research," *Encyclopedia of the Social Sciences*, vol. XIII, p. 333; Thomas C. Cochran, "A Decade of American Histories," *Pennsylvania Magazine of History and Biography*, LXXIII (1949), 179.

during the long inflationary era that began in 1897. The great prizes of academic life—the chairs that paid four or five thousand dollars in the 1890's—did become relatively less rewarding as time went on. Moreover, the great multiplication of Ph.D.'s forced an increasing proportion of them into those innumerable respectable but struggling colleges where a professor's income allowed no margin at all for buying books, for travel, or for major illnesses.[21] This was not a prospect to attract a highly select student body.

Nevertheless, the problem of recruiting outstanding students after the early years of the twentieth century surely arose from less tangible difficulties, which bad pay served mainly to objectify. The basic hindrances the profession encountered were social and cultural rather than economic. The social status of the humanistic professor and the cultural status of history deteriorated in the early twentieth century. They have only recently begun to revive. Although these trends were interconnected and concurrent, it will be useful first to trace the social question, which relates more directly to recruitment. Essentially, the life of scholarship was being democratized and therefore detached in greater degree from patrician associations. As that happened, history became less attractive to young men of inherited culture, excellently qualified by background for scholarly pursuits.

This is not to say that the historical profession ever drew its talent preponderantly from any one stratum of society. The persistent, nostalgic myth that our foremost professors of history used to come predominantly from elite families needs serious qualification. Of the many Adamses who played so large a part in historical scholarship before World War I, for example, none who made history a professional career had prominent parents or notable family connections. Charles Kendall Adams was a poor farm boy; Herbert Baxter's father was a local lumber merchant; George Burton and Ephraim D. sprang from plain Congregational ministers. Academic life has always offered an avenue of social mobility to young men of modest means and unpretentious background.

By examining the social origins of professional historians suffi-

---

21 Reliable figures translated into real purchasing power are given in Beardsley Ruml and Sidney G. Tickton, *Teaching Salaries Then and Now* (Fund for the Advancement of Education, Bulletin No. 1, 1955), pp. 46, 54, 65. For further data see Claude C. Bowman, *The College Professor in America* (1938), and—for the darker parts of the picture—"The Small College and Its President," *Popular Science Monthly*, LXXXIV (1914), 450.

ciently eminent to be included in the *Dictionary of American Biography* and similar compendiums, it is possible to understand more precisely how changes in American society in the early twentieth century influenced the recruitment of talent. Attribution of family status on the basis of such sources must often be approximate. Nevertheless, a rough classification of ninety-seven prominent, native-born historians who completed their graduate training between 1882 and 1946 throws some light on their geographical and social origins.[22]

These origins have always been diverse. Leading historians hailed from almost every part of the country, although New England was somewhat overrepresented before World War I, and the states west of Kansas produced only two members of the entire group. At least half of those who took their degrees during the 1920's and earlier grew up in communities of less than 10,000 population. Over the years a consistently large proportion of the historians in my sample— 23 per cent before World War I, 26 per cent after—were sons of unpretentious men engaged in quasi-intellectual pursuits: school teachers, clergymen, and journalists. This suggests that intellectual incentives in the family have always counted for academic success more heavily than any particular social rank.

Still, it is noteworthy that the proportion of distinguished historians recruited from wealthy or otherwise prominent families declined substantially after the early years of the twentieth century. Of the leading historians trained before 1918, 26 per cent originated in this high status category. Only 13 per cent of the notable historians trained in the 1930's and early 1940's sprang from families of comparable standing. Moreover, the dwindling elite group no longer included, as it did at the beginning of the century, a good many sons of highly successful businessmen. The offspring of bankers and man-

[22] In order to avoid any criteria other than reputation, I included in this analysis every professional historian for whom I could find a fairly adequate biographical sketch. Since my interest was specifically in the most eminent historians, I did not undertake to determine the composition of the rank and file of the profession, and some of my results may not be representative of the whole group. (For data on the whole body of history graduate students in 1958, see Dexter Perkins and John L. Snell's *The Education of Historians in the United States*, 1961, pp. 42-46.) A limitation of my method is the inevitable decline in the number of usable biographies as one approaches the present. I felt able to tabulate both the geographical and social origins of 47 historians who completed their training before 1907, 19 who did so from 1907 to 1918, 16 from 1919 to 1930, and 15 from 1931 to 1946. I included only historians born in the United States or Canada or of American parentage.

ufacturers now fled from the Groves of Academe. "Men of means," Frederick Jackson Turner noted in 1922, "like the type of Coolidge and Merriman in their younger period, seem to prefer to carry on in their own environment." [23] As the representation of elite groups fell, my statistics show a corresponding increase in the proportion of leading historians recruited from the children of shopkeepers, salesmen, and urban immigrants.

This shift was undoubtedly not in itself unfavorable to first-class historical work, for we know such work can be done by men of many sorts and conditions. The diminished appeal of academic pursuits to sons of illustrious families was symptomatic, however, of a more general status problem. Here we must return to a very large subject already touched upon in another connection: the breakup of the aristocracy of culture.

Although the old-time college professor of the mid-nineteenth century was a man of uncertain repute, commonly considered an ineffectual refugee from active life, the enrichment of the leading colleges and universities after the Civil War lifted their faculties to a position of some eminence. Men of dignity and sober rectitude, these professors enjoyed an intimate connection with the local social elite while participating increasingly in the culture of a wider world. They had, therefore, a status not inappropriate to sons of the "best families"—young men like Archibald Coolidge, Edwin F. Gay, Roger Merriman, William A. Dunning, Allen Johnson, James Harvey Robinson, and Conyers Read—whose fathers were distinguished merchants and manufacturers and whose mothers might read Greek as well as charm a drawingroom.

In the twentieth century matters changed. The absorption of scholarship within a nationwide professional system separated the life of the professor from that of the cultivated layman. Typically, a professor now derived prestige from a display of expert knowledge within his academic discipline or in practical affairs, not from his social standing in the community. We have already observed a separation of professional from patrician at the turn of the century in the transformation of the American Historical Association. Another

[23] Turner to Jameson, November 14, 1922, J. F. Jameson Papers, Box 85 (Division of Manuscripts, Library of Congress). In the group I studied, 12 per cent of those trained before World War I were sons of very substantial businessmen. Only one such historian appeared after World War I, and he became a college president.

gulf opened between college trustees and college faculties: they ceased to move in the same sphere.

To many, the change signified a loss of status. Some observers spoke hopefully of the public approval that a new type of professor was winning, "practical, hustling fellows, live wires," who knew all about public utilities and industrial efficiency and tainted meat. The humanistic scholar more often felt elbowed aside. When thoroughly professionalized, he counted for less in local society, received less respect as a model of character and culture, and accepted perforce the plain title of Mr.[24] By World War I, a new literary genre, the academic novel, was dramatizing his self-denigration. As an absentminded fellow, he was a prime butt of popular jokes.

Thus, an academic career separated from patrician association lost attractiveness to the social class possessed of the fullest cultural advantages. This seems plain enough. More important is the likelihood that the lower status of the professorial office put it at a disadvantage in the competition for the ablest young men of middle- as well as upper-class origins.

Few today will wish to return to the social distinctions of the late nineteenth century. Nor need we, in the interest of the historical profession, want to do so. The depressing sense of a loss of status, which was so widespread in the first quarter of the twentieth century, has been dramatically reversed since World War II. Instead of looking backward to the esteem attached to "character" and "culture" among the genteel classes of the late nineteenth century, college professors have become conscious of their rising importance as a relatively autonomous group on the national scene. The jibes that cultural critics of the 1920's leveled at the ineffectuality of academic men have all but vanished; and the stock figure of the absentminded professor is gone from our folk humor. Fears of his dangerously growing influence, so pronounced in the 1930's and 1940's, have also subsided into acceptance and respect. "Intellect," declared Lionel Trilling in 1952,

[24] Robert Morss Lovett, *All Our Years* (1948), p. 62; George Trumbull Ladd, "The Degradation of the Professorial Office," *Forum*, XXXIII (1902), 270-77; John James Stevenson, "The Status of American College Professors," *Popular Science Monthly*, LXVI (1904), 122-30; Carl Becker, "On Being a Professor," in *Detachment and the Writing of History: Essays and Letters of Carl L. Becker*, ed. Phil L. Snyder (1958), pp. 91-113. A different and I think too simple picture is presented in Richard Hofstadter's *Anti-intellectualism in American Life* (1963), pp. 204-206.

"has associated itself with power, perhaps as never before in history, and is now conceded to be in itself a kind of power." More recently, the 1960 Republican candidate for president wrote a book about himself partly—he tells us—because his successful opponent had advised him that authorship "tends to elevate [the politician] in popular esteem to the respected status of an 'intellectual.' " [25]

Certainly the university has never before played so large a part in American intellectual activity as it does today, nor has it ever before so completely controlled access to social and economic opportunity. The increasing services of university men to governments, businesses, and civic organizations have dramatized for all to see the power of specialized knowledge in contemporary life. The enormous expansion of college enrollments, and now the frantic clamor for admission, reveal a general acceptance of higher education as essential to nearly every position of responsibility. The professor has emerged, therefore, not only as the visible possessor of intellectual authority but also as the gatekeeper at the citadel of all of the elites, whom every aspirant for honor must pass. In place of the reputation once derived from association with a social class, the professor has acquired a new, occupational prestige from his entrenchment in a mighty institution.

Salaries too have risen substantially. After a painful decline in the 1940's, the purchasing power of faculty salaries moved upward in the 1950's, aided by increasing national concern over education. By 1953 professors in large state universities had almost regained the purchasing power they had fifty years before. In the next decade, salaries soared, to say nothing of unprecedented fringe benefits.[26] The change was swift enough to loose talk about "the affluent professors," and an influential columnist in the *New York Times* expressed some concern that too many, rather than too few, of the ablest young people might be choosing academic careers.

[25] Lionel Trilling, *A Gathering of Fugitives* (1956), p. 66; Richard Nixon, *Six Crises* (1962), p. xi. See also *Detroit Free Press,* March 14, 1963, p. A-11. An early and still useful discussion of status trends is in Richard H. Shryock's "The Academic Profession in the United States," American Association of University Professors *Bulletin,* XXXVIII (1952), 50-54.

[26] Ruml and Tickton, *op. cit.,* pp. 54, 65. By applying to 1962-63 statistics on average salaries of professors the same arithmetical procedures Ruml and Tickton used, one reaches the conclusion that the average professor's purchasing power (not including fringe benefits) was 40 per cent greater in that year than it had been in 1904. Based on AAUP *Bulletin,* XLIX (1963), 142.

Since historians mature slowly, it is probably too early to appraise the consequences for historical scholarship of this striking improvement in professorial status. Whether great historians are developing today, we do not yet know. Nor is it yet clear how large a share history is receiving of the new talent that is going into graduate study. We have, however, some reason to be optimistic. Historians have pretty much ceased to complain that their brightest undergraduate majors are spurning the graduate schools. An extensive survey of college seniors in 1957-58 showed that 55 per cent of the history majors with A averages were planning to undertake graduate study.[27] If, as seems likely, the proportion is higher today, the trend in academic recruitment augurs well for historical scholarship in the years ahead.

It would be wrong to suppose that social incentives fully explain the trend of recruitment or that those incentives are really separable from other considerations. Genuine distinction in historical work depends at least as much on how Americans value history. We turn, therefore, from changes in the status of the professor to concurrent changes in the status of history in American culture.

[27] Perkins and Snell, *op. cit.*, p. 38. By contrast, in the late 1920's only 20 per cent of the undergraduates in "selected institutions" who took honors in the social sciences (including history) became graduate students in those subjects. "Conference on Graduate Study," *loc. cit.*

# 4

## THE HISTORIAN AND HIS AUDIENCE

Looking back to the dazzling success of the great literary historians of the mid-nineteenth century, the professionals and their critics have often deplored the existence of a wide gulf between modern academic historians and the general public. Usually responsibility is laid at the door of the ivory tower in which professional historians supposedly dwell. "They have abdicated their whole position in our culture," said a disgruntled Alfred Knopf recently.[1] The complaint is an old and chronic one, going back at least to the early years of the twentieth century. Always, it charges the professional historian with failing a waiting public by making history dull, jejune, and overly specialized.

That there is constant tension between the built-in objectives of a profession and the changing demands that society makes upon it cannot be denied. But the nature of the demand is a critical factor in this relationship. We shall examine the objectives of the professional historian at length in the next chapter. Meanwhile, it is reasonable to assume that a country gets, for the most part, the sort of history that it wants. A survey of the demand for history since the late nineteenth century should help to correct an oversimplified, unhistorical view of relations between historians and the general culture.

These relations involve other kinds of historians as well as professionals. In spite of the relative decline of the gentlemen-historians after the turn of the century, America has never lacked good amateur scholars. Ordinarily we expect that the best of them will reach a wider public than will their professional peers, who for their part will have more interest in basic problems of methodology and interpretation. The difference is never absolute, and the best amateur history has never been mere popularization. History, because of its fluidity and openness, is not an arcane discipline. Although its critical operations are exacting, its fundamental tasks of organizing data into a design and thereby recreating the life of the past does not depend on

[1] Interview with author, March 1961.

68

any systematic methodology. Nor has history a special language of its own. Consequently, professional historians are unable to immure themselves completely within a specialized sphere, and writers unblessed with special training are often capable of doing important historical work. Then the professional faces stiff competition. To understand the situation of the professional historian requires, therefore, an understanding of the changing nature and appeal of the amateur.

All historians in America were amateurs when the famous historical spirit of the nineteenth century was at its height. In the 1830's —forty or fifty years before the era of the professional began—history became the most remunerative of all literary genres. Its popularity and prestige diverted Washington Irving from light belleslettres and for several decades supplied an immense market for cheap reprint editions of the historical works of Jared Sparks, Joel T. Headley, Irving, and others. A taste for solid historical instruction, aided in America by the moral and intellectual earnestness of the Puritan tradition, extended far beyond the limits of any single class. Prescott's weighty and expensive *Conquest of Mexico* (1843) appealed so widely that seventy or more American newspapers reviewed it within a month of publication. When the first half of Macaulay's *History of England* appeared in 1849, four American publishers seized upon it instantly, and the first year's sale in the United States was estimated at no less than two hundred thousand copies. This would amount to one copy for every fifteen white families. The publishers could not recall another work of any kind that had ever so completely taken the whole country by storm.[2]

By the end of the nineteenth century, when professional historians were appearing on the scene, serious historical interests were still considerable but apparently less widespread. Prestigious, dignified monthly magazines such as the *Atlantic* and the *Century* teemed with historical essays in the Eighties and Nineties. The *Century* serialized Nicolay and Hay's monumental biography of Abraham Lincoln month by month for two and a half years. The bustling popular journals, on the other hand, paid virtually no heed to the past. In the

[2] William Charvat, *Literary Publishing in America, 1790-1850* (1959), pp. 74-77; Harry Hayden Clark, "The Vogue of Macaulay in America," *Transactions of the Wisconsin Academy of Sciences, Arts, and Letters*, XXXIV (1942), 238.

casual view of *Harper's Weekly,* the disappearance of "links that still connect us with the past . . . is one of the inevitable consequences of progress and improvement." [3]

The works of leading historians accumulated on the shelves of gentlemen's libraries. John Fiske, the best-selling American historian of the period, wrote as vividly as most of his more popular predecessors; yet few of his books sold as many as fifteen thousand copies in their year of issue. Perhaps the most brilliant of all American historical works, Henry Adams' profound and scintillating *History of the United States during the Administrations of Jefferson and Madison* (1889-91), sold a mere three thousand sets during the entire decade of the Nineties.[4] Expecting no better, Adams took a compensatory pride in the class character of the whole historical enterprise. In dismissing the possibility of a businesslike return on his literary property, Adams told his publisher:

> In truth the historian gives his work to the public and publisher; he means to give it; and he wishes to give it. History has always been, for this reason, the most aristocratic of all literary pursuits, because it obliges the historian to be rich as well as educated. I should be very sorry to think that you could give me eight thousand a year for my investment, because I should feel sure that whenever such a rate of profit could be realised on history, history would soon become as popular a pursuit as magazine-writing, and the luxury of its social distinction would vanish.[5]

The luxury of its social distinction! This, much more than sales, sustained the chief nonacademic historians who carried on after the turn of the century. A number of men of independent means who had taken up historical pursuits in the late nineteenth century continued active in the early twentieth, and all of them addressed a still smaller audience than Fiske in the 1890's. The most renowned was James Ford Rhodes, a retired Cleveland industrialist who moved to Boston to write his muscular *History of the United States from the Compromise of 1850* (1892-1906). Each volume sold about two or three thousand copies in its first year in print. Henry Osborn Taylor,

[3] *Harper's Weekly,* XV (1871), 1022.
[4] Milton Berman, *John Fiske, the Evolution of a Popularizer* (1961), pp. 258-59; Harvey Wish, *The American Historian* (1960), p. 172.
[5] Quoted in Roger Burlingame, *Of Making Many Books: A Hundred Years of Reading, Writing, and Publishing* (1946), pp. 157-58.

author of *The Classical Heritage of the Middle Ages* (1901), *The Medieval Mind* (1914), and many other books designed to show what men throughout the past had deemed best and highest, made nothing from his distinguished books.[6] Of lesser note were William Roscoe Thayer, member of the Harvard Board of Overseers and biographer of Cavour; the Virginia gentleman Philip Alexander Bruce, who made himself the leading authority on the early history of his state; Ellis P. Oberholtzer, a proper Philadelphian who devoted his life to continuing the work of his teacher, John Bach McMaster; Frederic Bancroft, witty and sometimes venomous Washington bachelor and student of the slavery controversy; and Hiram Martin Chittenden, who spent his leisure as an Army officer in the Missouri River Valley writing *The American Fur Trade of the Far West* (1902).[7] The occasional journalist, like Ida Tarbell, who found time and incentive for historical biography was distinctly rare.

None of these authors appeared on any best-seller list during the first two decades of the century; nor did any other historical book except a biography of Mark Twain.[8] After the turn of the century even the upper-class interest in history declined. The excitement of reform in the Progressive Era caught up many of the "best people," and the elite magazines held their readers to the extent that they dropped a leisurely retrospective view in favor of a critical examination of the contemporary scene. Ida Tarbell shifted from the grandeur of Lincoln to the reality of Rockefeller; Brooks Adams turned from the laws of history to the principles of business administration; Winston Churchill abandoned historical romance for political fiction. During the Eighties and Nineties Theodore Roosevelt, Woodrow Wilson, and Henry Cabot Lodge had written much history; neither they nor any

[6] Robert Cruden, *James Ford Rhodes* (1961), pp. 90-91; H. O. Taylor to James Truslow Adams, April 30, 1929, James Truslow Adams Papers (Columbia University).

[7] Thayer, *The Life and Times of Cavour* (1911), and *Life and Letters of John Hay* (2 vols., 1915); Bruce, *Institutional History of Virginia in the Seventeenth Century* (2 vols., 1910), and *History of the University of Virginia* (5 vols., 1920-22); Oberholtzer, *History of the United States Since the Civil War* (5 vols., 1917-37); Bancroft, *Life of William H. Seward* (2 vols., 1900); Jacob E. Cooke, *Frederic Bancroft, Historian* (1957); Gordon B. Dodds, "Hiram Martin Chittenden, Historian," *Pacific Historical Review*, XXX (1961), 257-69.

[8] Alice Payne Hackett's *Sixty Years of Best Sellers, 1895-1955* (1956), p. 29, summarizes data from *Publisher's Weekly*. The *Bookman* published monthly lists throughout the period; these too are barren of history.

other politically active patrician continued historical work amid the whirlwind of reform after the turn of the century.

Beneath the obvious ferment of progressivism, a deeper change in the intellectual temper—less specific, less easy to define—worked in the same antihistorical direction. The genteel and conservative cultural standards with which history had long associated itself were breaking down. A passion for intense life, for the vitality of immediate experience, was challenging the dignified, elevated attitudes that history had always suggested. The impetuous modern temper did not become fully evident until the 1920's, whereupon a reaction against it appeared; but the historical spirit was already reaching a low point as early as 1905, when even the costume novel went clearly out of fashion.[9]

In view of this unreceptive atmosphere, criticism of the professional historians for failing to speak to a general audience misses the mark. There was no general audience. It dissolved in the excitements of contemporaneity and scattered in the winds of democracy. Even a scholarly work so controversial and contemporary in interest as Charles A. Beard's *An Economic Interpretation of the Constitution* (1913) sold fewer than eight thousand copies over a span of four decades, and then only with the aid of a second edition published during the Constitutional crisis of the 1930's. Academic historians had good reason to feel thrown upon their own resources: the decline of their status as professors coincided with a vast indifference to their work as authors. One can sympathize with the complaint made by the secretary of the American Historical Association in 1917 about the public image of his guild. It is customary, he said, to regard historical scholarship as "a harmless, though amiable pursuit, but one of little if any 'practical' use, and to look upon the student of history as a person who, having too few red corpuscles in his blood, is content to bury his head in the dust of the past, oblivious to the interests and exigencies of the present."[10]

As if to confirm the diminished status of their craft, historians found their control over secondary school curriculums waning. The four-year pattern of history courses the AHA persuaded the schools

[9] Ernest E. Leisy, *The American Historical Novel* (1950), pp. 16-17.
[10] Waldo G. Leland, "Concerning Catholic Historical Societies," *Catholic Historical Review*, II (1917), 387. Beard's sales are given in *Charles A. Beard: An Appraisal*, ed. Howard K. Beale (1954), p. 310.

to adopt at the beginning of the century began to break down before World War I. First civics, then other contemporary "social studies," demanded recognition for contributing directly to "social efficiency." [11] History had patriotic uses; otherwise it was something of a bore.

Under such circumstances the professional historian who desired to be heard beyond the circle of his colleagues addressed himself to the one audience that was growing visibly before his very eyes: his students. Historians of the highest caliber lent their talents to the writing of textbooks, both for college and for high school. These had been dull and lifeless compendiums, the products of second-rate minds. Scholars like Becker, Breasted, Beard, and James Harvey Robinson made history textbooks in the United States outstanding. But the profession paid a price for this achievement. Habituated to writing blandly for their students, as the natural and profitable alternative to writing technically for their colleagues, historians fell captive to an artificial and immature audience. The requirements of such an audience may have lessened their desire to find, and their ability to satisfy, a genuine historical public.

After World War I a new audience for the serious writer emerged in America, and it has been gaining maturity ever since. It has neither the homogeneity nor the assurance of position and tradition that belonged to the aristocracy of culture. That older audience was unified by its consciousness of itself as a social class with certain well-defined responsibilities, and it also shared common intellectual interests shaped by the standard educational curriculum that prevailed through most of the nineteenth century. The new audience, much more fluid and diversified, rests on a broader basis. It has grown from the extraordinary expansion of higher education in recent decades, from the multiplication of specialized white-collar occupations, and from a concomitant increase in leisure time. Its intellectual interests reflect the multifarious content of modern higher education and the immense variety of opinion-making agencies. It seeks knowledge, not out of a moral imperative but out of a need to integrate and understand its discordant experience. The current "cultural explosion" is only the most recent manifestation of the rising level of taste and activity on the part of this hungry and restless audience.

[11] E. Dawson, "For Recognition of the Social Studies" and "History and the Social Studies," *Educational Review*, LXVIII (1924), 22-25 and 67-70.

Early manifestations of the new American "middlebrow" appeared in the 1920's, when nonfiction books and major novels sprang into prominence on the best-seller lists. For decades the best sellers had consisted almost exclusively of sentimental fiction. Now Sinclair Lewis, F. Scott Fitzgerald, Thornton Wilder, and Theodore Dreiser ranked among the top novelists. More surprisingly, sales of books on history, popularizations of science, and analyses of current events often equaled or surpassed the sales of novels. For one example, H. G. Wells's *Outline of History,* issued by a hesitant publisher at an exorbitant price in 1920, sold one and a half million copies—one copy for every twenty homes in the country—within twelve years. Circulation data from public libraries show a tremendous rate of increase in book reading under way in the 1920's and continuing since that time. Moreover the underlying trend toward nonfiction, strongest among college graduates, has steadily advanced with the spread of higher education.[12]

The surprisingly avid interest of this new public in history was twofold. First, it wanted a framework to provide some sense of order and stability behind a world in tumult; it wanted some ground on which to stand. The very emancipation and turbulence of the modern temper bred a compensatory demand for large-scale, panoramic history. This accounts for the spectacular success of such universal history as Wells's *Outline,* Hendrik Van Loon's *The Story of Mankind* (1921), James Harvey Robinson's *The Mind in the Making* (1921), and, after World War II, the abridgment of Arnold Toynbee's *A Study of History* (1947). The same need, expressed in nationalistic terms, explains the huge popularity of the sagas of American experience written between the wars by James Truslow Adams, Mark Sullivan, Claude G. Bowers, and Van Wyck Brooks.[13]

Second, the new audience wanted biography—not formal, discreet, the life heavily overlaid with the objective circumstances of the

12 William S. Gray and Ruth Munroe, *The Reading Interests and Habits of Adults: A Preliminary Report* (1929), p. 48; Henry C. Link and Harry Arthur Hopf, *People and Books: A Study of Reading and Book-Buying Habits* (1946), pp. 71, 158, 163; *Wilson Library Bulletin,* XXXVI (1962), 402-404. On Wells see his *Experiment in Autobiography* (London, 1934), p. 719, and W. Warren Wagar's *H. G. Wells and the World State* (1961), p. 40.
13 Adams' *The Epic of America* (1931) was the top nonfiction bestseller in 1932. Sullivan's *Our Times* (6 vols., 1926-35), Bowers' *Jefferson and Hamilton* (1925), and Brooks's *The Flowering of New England* (1936) were also among the most popular books of their day.

times, but rather vividly personal biography in which portraiture and the interpretation of subjective experience play a large part. The boom in biography doubtless catered to a desire for familiar contact with dominant personalities, thereby offsetting the anonymity and impersonal standardization of modern urban life. The rise of humanized biography coincided with the emergence of the newspaper columnist and radio commentator and with an extreme exploitation of personality in the entertainment world. All served the same function. The biographies might be as shallow and romanticized as Emil Ludwig's *Napoleon* (1927) or as flippant and precious as Lytton Strachey's *Queen Victoria* (1921); they might also rise to the commanding historical stature of Douglas Southall Freeman's *Robert E. Lee* (1935).

The cultural revolution that called forth the popular demand for history and biography also produced its suppliers. The new historical writers of the Twenties and Thirties came chiefly from the world of journalism and literature. Never before had so many journalists and free-lance writers possessed the ability and incentive to undertake serious historical research. Their movement into this kind of nonfiction reflected the same broadening of intellectual interests, and the same desire for a stable background, that was creating their audience. Occasionally these amateur scholars had connections with the old aristocracy of culture. Such was the case, for example, with James Truslow Adams and Van Wyck Brooks. But Brooks had rebelled partially against his patrician background; and Adams, who deserted a career in Wall Street to pursue historical studies, became partially dependent on selling his literary wares. Literary ambitions, sometimes linked with political interests, inspired the postwar amateur historians. Unlike their late nineteenth century predecessors, they felt toward history little sense of the luxury of its social distinction.

Two great Lincoln biographers in the 1920's gave an example and impetus to amateur scholarship. Albert J. Beveridge, a former United States senator and an accomplished writer on current events, had done an astonishingly successful four-volume biography of John Marshall (1919) before he retired completely from politics and surpassed all previous biographers of Lincoln in breadth of research and in critical acumen. During the first six months of publication, Beveridge's *Lincoln* (2 vols., 1928) earned $51,000 in royalties. Carl Sandburg was no less successful. The first two volumes of his

Whitmanesque biography (*The Prairie Years,* 1926), written while he was a Chicago newspaperman, enabled him to quit his job. He spent the next decade as a wandering troubador, reading folk songs and collecting material for a four-volume continuation of the work (*The War Years,* 1939).[14]

A few others, by inheriting or marrying money or by frugal living, managed to dispense with a steady job and put their energy primarily into history. Van Wyck Brooks, forsaking a distinguished career as literary critic and editor, spent all of his time for nineteen years on a finely wrought, deeply informed, and highly personal history of American literary culture (5 vols., 1936-52). Matthew Josephson, who was schooled in the 1920's to the insecurity of the literary life, developed in the 1930's—partly under the influence of his Connecticut neighbor Charles A. Beard—into a vivid portraitist of the leaders of the Gilded Age. George Dangerfield, an English immigrant, left the literary editorship of *Vanity Fair* in 1935 and devoted himself to an increasingly disciplined fusion of art and scholarship.[15] At the age of sixty Irving Brant forsook a newspaper career and by frugal living devoted himself intensively to the life and times of James Madison (6 vols., 1941-61).

Such men were relatively uncommon. Most journalist-historians pursued research in time bought by much routine work. Bernard De-Voto edited magazines while lavishing on a three-volume history of the American West (1943-52) "an effort whose intensity and cost no one but me will ever appreciate." [16] *Harper's* editor, Frederick Lewis Allen, wrote deft and often perceptive history on the side. Douglas Southall Freeman, editor of the *Richmond News Leader,* gave half of his very long working day between 1915 and 1934 to *Robert E. Lee.* George Fort Milton produced major books on the politics of the Civil War era while editing the *Chattanooga News.*

14 James Truslow Adams to Mark Howe, March 18, 1929, Adams Papers; Alfred Harcourt, "Forty Years of Friendship," *Illinois State Historical Journal,* XLV (1952), 396.
15 Brooks describes the writing of his *Makers and Finders* in *From the Shadow of the Mountain* (1961); Josephson's memoir, *Life Among the Surrealists* (1962), stops in 1930. His principal books on American history are *The Robber Barons* (1935), *The Politicos, 1865-1896* (1938), and *Edison: A Biography* (1959). Dangerfield's main contributions are *The Era of Good Feelings* (1952) and *Chancellor Robert R. Livingston of New York, 1746-1813* (1960).
16 Bernard DeVoto, "On the Writing of History," *Chicago History,* II (1951), 314.

Henry F. Pringle was associate editor of *The Outlook* during the writing of his impressive and scholarly *Theodore Roosevelt* (1931); thereafter he taught journalism at Columbia. Wilbur J. Cash composed a solitary masterpiece, *The Mind of the South* (1941), at his desk as associate editor of the *Charlotte News*. Walter Millis found time, amid editorial duties at the *New York Herald-Tribune,* to write influential books on military and diplomatic history.

Although the rewards of historical writing could be substantial, the struggle to attain financial independence was grueling and usually unsuccessful. Marquis James, who did a vivid biography of Sam Houston (1929) while supporting himself as a staff writer for the *American Legion Monthly,* lost that job in the Depression. He holed up in an attic to complete the first volume of an excellent life of Andrew Jackson (2 vols., 1933-37). The second volume was written with money paid by Bernard Baruch for ghostwriting his memoirs. After that James became entangled in a succession of subsidized undertakings and never got free until it was too late. Allan Nevins, on the other hand, found time and security to do his best work in an academic chair. During the 1920's he produced six substantial historical books at night after spending a full day on a New York newspaper. Like his friend Claude G. Bowers, a more popular but more partisan historian who also worked for the *New York World,* Nevins often left his downtown office at four in the afternoon, raced to 42nd Street, and squeezed in a half hour of research in the Reserve Room of the New York Public Library before it closed at five.[17] At the end of that herculean decade he settled into a professorship at Columbia University.

These writers, all scholars addressing a general audience, answered a demand that professionally trained historians were not filling. The only professionals who reached a large, adult public in the Twenties and Thirties were two who had cut loose from an academic environment: Charles A. Beard and James Harvey Robinson. Both wrote runaway best sellers in the 1920's after resigning from Columbia University in disgust with its policies; and if Robinson's *The Mind in the Making* (1921) was no more than a polemic, Beard's *The Rise of American Civilization* (1927) was an intellectual as well as a popular triumph. Many other professional historians would have liked to have the public's ear. Some of the younger ones, overcoming

[17] Bessie R. James to author, May 18, 1964; Nevins to author, June 1, 1961.

the profession's earlier disinterest, responded in the 1930's to the vogue of biography. None equaled the popular success of amateurs in this genre, and most professional scholars either ignored or positively distrusted the new public.

Their aloofness was partly a function of their social and institutional situation. It has already been suggested that the academic environment subjected the relatively few gifted writers in the profession to the tempting and devitalizing burden of textbook writing. Other scholars found their environment inhibitive to any communication with unspecialized readers. The security the professional historian enjoyed in a university sheltered him from the daily necessity that disciplined the free-lance writer to the utmost clarity and pungency of expression. The increasing number of seminars and professorships in each of the major universities encouraged more and more division of labor and specialization, the reverse of what the layman wanted. Then too, every form of resistance to a general audience was perhaps stiffened by the academic man's general feeling of being unwanted and unappreciated outside his own realm. The wound to his self-esteem inflicted in the early twentieth century remained unhealed. To the academic scholar in the Twenties, Thirties and Forties, no improvement of status was apparent. Rather the public success of the amateur historians suggested the reverse. The failure of the public to appreciate the professional historical expert—as it appreciated both the popular historian and the scientific expert—rankled deeply.[18] This aggravated the professionals' defensiveness.

At the same time, professional historians had strong reasons of principle to shrink from catering to popular taste. The reigning theory of history in the universities, which will concern us more extensively at a later point, distinguished sharply and invidiously between science and art. It is perhaps equally important that general readers of history in the interwar period rarely cared for any complex formulation of man's experience. The pursuit of an audience therefore en-

---

[18] Charles M. Andrews, "These Forty Years," *AHR*, XXX (1925), 226-27; Raymond J. Sontag, "On the Study of Diplomatic History," *Pacific Historical Review*, XV (1946), 212-13. Some of the professionals felt outclassed: "One day up at Columbia [Dixon Ryan] Fox and some others were talking on that very point and the general opinion was that at present more and better historical writing was being done by men with no academic connection than by those who had such." James Truslow Adams to Allan Nevins, September 20, 1925, Adams Papers.

tailed grave intellectual risks from which professional historians wished to guard their discipline. The public's hunger for "human interest" fed upon an episodic display of personality rather than an integrated analysis of process, which was history's more fundamental concern. In 1935 Henry Steele Commager, one of the most vivid and popular of professional scholars and an excellent biographer withal, complained that the rage for biography had become "so extreme that history as such has all but disappeared." [19]

In overpersonalizing history, the popular writer was tempted to strain for effect. The desire for excitement and color easily degraded history into melodrama, a tendency that subtly corrupts both the detachment of the historian and the integrity of his art. No one put the case against melodrama better than the great Dutch historian Johan Huizinga. In the late 1920's, he said of the kind of historical writing then fashionable:

> Overestimating the emotional content of everything it touches upon, it interprets the taut figures of history according to an unkempt generation's need for edification. It gluts itself on poorly understood and poorly understandable -isms. It knows the riddles of the soul of every saint, every wise man, every hero. It concocts tragic psychological conflicts for artists who created their greatest work while whistling a tune. . . . Soberness, restraint, a certain skeptical reserve in investigating the deepest emotions of the heart—all of which are the duty of true historical writing—do not please the contemporary reader.[20]

As an accurate description of the history that sold well in the Twenties and Thirties, Huizinga's statement went too far, doing less than justice to Beveridge, Beard, and Freeman and their countless readers. But as a general characterization of popular taste, the judgment struck home; and as a warning of the vulgarity that a would-be popular historian courts, it made a valid point.

In addition to the risks of simplified causation and cheap histrionics, popularization raised another hazard, which many professional historians felt keenly. Preoccupation with dissemination might undermine the cherished value of discovery. The scholar's great com-

---

[19] Henry Steele Commager, "The Literature of American History, 1935," *Social Studies,* XXVII (1936), 252.
[20] Johan Huizinga, *Men and Ideas: History, the Middle Ages, the Renaissance* (1959), pp. 45-47.

mitment to the acquisition of new knowledge might suffer from too eager a quest for an audience, as the experience of some historical museums and societies indicated. In contrast to the universities, most of the historical societies and museums welcomed the boom in American history. Timidly in the Twenties, then with mounting gusto in the Thirties and since, societies that had given all of their attention to scholarly endeavors criticized themselves for having been too pedantic and aloof. They inaugurated radio programs, traveling exhibits, lavish historical reconstructions, and many other forms of salesmanship. Although some societies gained new resources for scholarship from their public activity, others allowed scholarly functions to wither.[21] Might that not happen in the universities and professional organizations too?

The issue was posed acutely at the end of the 1930's by an incident in the American Historical Association that revealed how wide the gulf between professor and public remained. By then a number of members of the AHA had become restive. Critical of the stodginess of the organization and respectful of the achievements of some of the amateur scholars, they wished to cooperate with the latter in promoting public interest in history. One such man was Conyers Read, executive secretary of the Association, who had managed a textile firm during a long interval (1920-33) between professorships at Chicago and at Pennsylvania. Another was Allan Nevins. Although many professionals adopted a clubby, disparaging attitude toward Nevins's phenomenal productivity, he tried more than anyone else to unite the values of the free-lance historian with those of the academic scholar. In 1938 he published *The Gateway to History,* a book at once learned and inspirational, which sought to communicate to the general reader Nevins's own vivid and eclectic sense of the meaning and excitement of history.

In the preface to the book, Nevins urged the establishment of a popular magazine of history. Conyers Read fell in with the idea enthusiastically, as did William L. Langer of Harvard, who saw an op-

21 David D. Van Tassel, "Historical Organizations," in *In Support of Clio: Essays in Memory of Herbert A. Kellar,* ed. William B. Hesseltine and Donald R. McNeil (1958), pp. 145-46. See also *Proceedings of the Conference of State and Local Historical Societies* (1937, 1938). The trend is severely criticized in Walter Muir Whitehill's *Independent Historical Societies* (1962) and Wilcomb E. Washburn's "Scholarship and the Museum," *Museum News,* XL (October 1961), 16-19.

portunity to "revitalize" the profession. Nevins, who had hitherto avoided historical conventions, joined the American Historical Association, and his allies quickly arranged his election to the Council of the Association. At the annual meeting that December, Read and Nevins put forward a plan for a popular historical magazine to be sponsored by the AHA and published by Condé Nast. The Council approved the scheme by a narrow margin, but the Association itself, after an impassioned debate, rejected it. The opponents detected a commercial taint to the enterprise. They wanted the AHA to stick to pure scholarship.[22]

The rebuff so enraged Nevins that he lost his customary urbanity. A few weeks later he published in the *Saturday Review of Literature* a blistering attack on academic pedantry, entitled "What's the Matter with History?"

> The pedant . . . has found means in our university system and our learned societies to fasten himself with an Old Man of the Sea grip upon history. . . . Though the touch of this school benumbs and paralyzes all interest in history, it is supported by university chairs, special foundations and funds, research fellowships, and learned bodies. It is against this entrenched pedantry that the war of true history will have to be most determined and implacable.

Most of our best historical writers, Nevins concluded, are still outside academic life, and a body uniting them with the best of the university writers should be formed to promote history as literature.[23]

This blast, with its dire implications of dual unionism, created an uproar. One leading department of history was reportedly shaken to its foundations. Nevins and Read went ahead with the organization of a new society to back the proposed magazine; but they failed for many years to raise adequate funds. Meanwhile the dominant forces in the profession turned coldly against them. Read, whose imperious ways had offended in other matters also, was eased out of the executive secretaryship of the AHA. His successor, Guy Stanton Ford, followed an extremely conservative policy throughout a twelve-year

[22] AHA *Annual Report* (1938), pp. 6, 10-11, 32, 58; Robert L. Schuyler to Charles A. Beard, February 14, 1939, AHA Files 1936-40, Box 24, Archives of American Historical Association (Division of Manuscripts, Library of Congress). See also Professor Langer's review of *The Gateway to History* in *New York Herald-Tribune, Books*, XV (September 18, 1938), 4.

[23] "What's the Matter with History?" *Saturday Review of Literature*, XIX (February 4, 1939), 4, 16.

Twenty years passed before the Association called Nevins to
ɪor of its presidential office; whereupon he returned to its
gs and, in his presidential address, renewed with gentleness
gnity his old plea for union of academic and lay historians:
ɯ ᷅ ɪre all amateurs, we are all professionals." [24]

It seems clear in retrospect that no amount of tact and goodwill
could have bridged the distance between the two groups in the
1930's. Too few individuals had, like Nevins, a foot planted in both
camps, and each side had too much cause for distrust and resentment
of the other. On the whole, the historical profession *was* stuffy, defensive, pedantic. The lay public on the other hand, was inchoate, undisciplined, unselective. Gratifying its emotional demands, writers
dependent on the public—in spite of often admirable scholarship—
cared too much about dramatic effects and too little about intellectual problems. Only a few of the widely read, free-lance historians
dealt seriously and critically with relations between past and present;
very few raised speculative or interpretive questions of any substance. The great middle-class audience for history was too new and
unformed to relish genuine intellectual encounters.

Since World War II the relations between professional historians
and the reading public have moved gradually into a new and more
hopeful phase. The sharp intellectual cleavage of the Twenties and
Thirties has diminished, just as the social grievances of the academic
man have lessened. Considerable public interest in the past persists.
What is more important, much of that interest operates now on a
higher plane. The spectacular and florid types of historical literature
that flourished in the 1930's, the historical novel and the romantic biography, have greatly declined. Nor do sweeping surveys, like *The
Outline of History* or *The Epic of America,* any longer answer our
cultural needs. Instead, a better educated public is, with more self-
assurance, buying substantial histories of a war, an age, or a single
episode.

This advance in sophistication has brought part of the reading
public within reach of professional historians. Many of them, in turn,
are welcoming the chance to be heard without demeaning themselves. For the first time since the days of Motley and Macaulay, an
intensive study in European history, such as Garrett Mattingly's *The
Armada* (1959), can win a great company of readers. For the first

24 Allan Nevins, "Not Capulets, Not Montagus," *AHR,* LXV (1960), 253-70.

time since the days of George Bancroft, a scholarly, multivolume narrative of a whole period in American history, notably Arthur M. Schlesinger Jr.'s *The Age of Roosevelt* (3 vols., 1956-60), has received immense acclaim.

In the study of history, as in other disciplines, communication between the academic and the extra-academic world has become more continuous and diversified than ever before. Father Walter J. Ong has remarked upon the interaction that is occurring as the academic study of literature and the writing of literature grow together.[25] A like trend seems to be under way in the historical field. We do not have today so many highly talented amateur historians as flourished between the wars. The emergence of Bruce Catton and George Kennan hardly balances the passing or retirement of Freeman, Beveridge, Sandburg, Brooks, Cash, and others. Today, more completely than ever before, serious historical writing is done under the auspices of academic institutions. This near monopoly creates public responsibilities that academic life as presently organized does not adequately fulfill. Still, the public standing of the professional scholar has surely benefited from his clear possession of the field. It is no longer possible to say that most of our best historical writers are outside academic life.

Nor is it now possible to say, as Jameson gloomily did forty years ago, that no American magazine of the first class ever prints a historical article. Late in 1962 the *Nation* devoted an entire issue to historical thought and activity in America today, while the *New Yorker* simultaneously made an unprecedented foray into similar territory, printing a book-length report on the intellectual doings of professional historians in Britain.[26] The *New Yorker* has not yet found American historians so interesting, doubtless with good reason. America has a less developed historical consciousness, and our historians do not belong to so well defined an intellectual community. We seem to be moving, however, in that direction.

One milestone was passed in 1954. The fruition of Nevins's long-held dream of a popular magazine of history marked both the substantial progress and the peculiar problems of connecting profes-

25 W. J. Ong, "Synchronic Present: The Academic Future of Modern Literature in America," *American Quarterly*, XIV (1962), 256-57.
26 "The Uses of History," *Nation*, CXCV (November 24, 1962); Ved Mehta, "The Flight of Crook-Taloned Birds," *New Yorker*, XXXVIII (December 8 and 15, 1962), 59-147 and 47-129.

sors with an American lay public. A skillful promoter, James Parton, a former editor of *Time,* organized an impressive coalition of sponsors for a magazine designed to meet the standards and enlist the talents of academic scholars as well as journalists. Parton combined the group that Nevins had organized in 1939, the Society of American Historians, with an association of state and local historians that was publishing a magazine for teachers on how to use local history in the schools. This magazine, *American Heritage,* was transformed under the sponsorship of both groups into a slick, elegant monthly for the general, upper middle-class reader. The distinguished free-lance historian Bruce Catton became editor. Within a couple of years circulation reached two hundred thousand.[27]

The realization of Nevins's dream has revealed its limitations. *American Heritage* proved to have great appeal, high technical finish, and no intellectual challenge at all. The sharpness, freshness, and variety of its historical vignettes could not conceal its studied avoidance of controversial issues. Evading analysis, desiring always to please and never to dare or to disturb, *American Heritage* has maintained a nice compromise between nostalgia and realism.

Its blandness was the inevitable result of a successful penetration of the adult historical audience as an undifferentiated whole. The basic defect lay in the terms in which the problem had always been conceived: professor *versus* public, technical specialization *versus* a democratic culture. The search for a "mass" audience necessarily homogenizes it, reducing the actual diversity of tastes and interests to the most common denominator of "human interest." The historian, encouraged to write for everyone who will take some instruction along with entertainment, addresses no one in particular. The readers, encouraged to accept a passive role, discover what they have in common with one another (i.e., their "heritage"), instead of exercising their capacity to discriminate.

As a reflection of the old ideal of one unified democratic culture, *American Heritage* may not be representative of current trends. Today the pursuit of excellence and the intense concern over the quality of American life are working against intellectual homogeneity. As the upper strata of the reading public come into greater prominence and significance, we are becoming conscious of many publics, at

27 "The Reminiscences of James Parton" (Oral History Research Office, Columbia University, 1959), *passim.*

varying levels of sophistication. The fading of a simple antithesis between professor and public has also made these differentiations within the supposedly amorphous, unspecialized popular audience more visible. Consequently, a professional historian can feel the possibility of communicating with a special, though not an exclusively technical, audience that is eager for the kind of history that makes an argument, offers a new idea, or reveals a fresh dimension of experience. Today's professor, if he has something to say and knows how to say it, need not choose between writing for his professional colleagues on the one hand or "popularization" on the other, with the radical change of pace and method that implies. He may speak to a selective public, confident at least of its growing size and importance.

The selective publics—there must be many of them—do not put books at the top of the best-seller lists. They take their pick of the quality paperbacks and the special-interest book clubs that have appeared within the last fifteen years. History enjoys no special status with the elite audiences, as it once did with the aristocracy of culture. It competes and blends with other intellectual interests. To do so successfully, it must meet critical standards that are neither exclusively literary nor exclusively professional; it must engage the modern mind.

Bemused by the seductive clamor of textbook publishers on one side and intimidated on the other by the production schedule of his dean or department, the academic historian may not easily discern the waiting presence of an intellectual audience. If only because of such obstacles, he needs that audience almost as much as it needs him. Most historical work, of course, will—and should—continue to have more special aims. The vast majority of research studies necessarily treat subjects of purely professional concern; and a legitimate place remains for popularization. But great history speaks to cultivated, unspecialized minds, and surely it will speak most strongly and clearly in a culture that listens. Whatever advances the present trend in listening strengthens the capacity of the historian to speak.

Thus the sanctions of the cultural milieu, along with the distribution of institutional support and social prestige, have played a part in the ebb and flow of excellence. All of these conditions, as they impinge on the professional historian, interact with his own conception of his task. This too has altered over the years. Having appraised the external conditions of historical work in America, we shall now look inward, to understand the idea of history as it has developed in the American historical profession, and to gauge the direction in which it is moving.

# ❧ II ❧

# THEORY

American historians in recent years have shown a special predilection for writing about historical writing. Although still uncomfortable in the rarefied regions of philosophy of history, they have become addicted to the more tangible sort of commentary we call historiography. The sheer quantity is astonishing: historians ordinarily know that their own history is too small and provincial a part of their whole jurisdiction to deserve a large share of their attention.

A practical problem of communication accounts in part for the change. In an age of multitudinous specialization, few specialists can keep their bearings unaided. The historiographer has stepped in as a middleman in scholarly discourse, taking over where the book reviewer leaves off. He conserves the scholarship of the past that seems currently relevant. He directs attention to convergent aspects of current scholarship, helping individual historians discover the relation of their own interests to larger currents of thought.

Historiography has also a less routine but more dangerous appeal: it is a critical weapon. Since it blends historical explanation with critical appraisal, it provides a vehicle of emancipation from ideas and interpretations one wishes to supersede. Accordingly, it flourishes in response to conflict and revision in historical thought. In its polemical function historiography has ratified many a rebellion. Unfortunately, it usually loses thereby some of its historical integrity. Historiography is ordinarily written by the winning side, which tends to present the losers' intentions and presuppositions in a partisan light. Over the course of time the criticisms that successive generations make of their predecessors may accumulate in the historiographical record.

This is so much the case in American scholarship that the course of historical theory in this country appears on the surface quite desultory and confusing. One gets the general impression of a seemingly circular debate over objectivity. We call the early professional historians the Scientific School; for they disparaged preceding historians like Bancroft and Parkman as men of letters lacking in the scientific spirit essential to a proper objectivity. The Scientific School, in turn, came under attack in the twentieth century from a group of scholars who ultimately called themselves Objective Relativists. They charged the Scientific School with failing to understand the limits of objectivity and with stultifying history in the pursuit of an impossible goal. Since World War II most historians have tended to accept all of these criticisms, while adding that the relativists went too far in denying objectivity and thereby made history too "present-minded."

A dimension very much lacking from this composite picture is that of agreement and continuity. Throughout the long and sometimes bitter argument, differences of principle were actually less sharp than they seemed. No one, including the "literary" historians, rejected the ideal of objectivity in the ordinary sense of unbiased truth; no one gave up the effort to attain it; and no one thought it wholly unapproachable. Consequently, we must go behind the distorted picture that each generation has left of its predecessor in order to tell what all the shouting was about. A more coherent pattern begins to emerge once we ask each group—the early professionals, their critics, and their critics' critics—about itself instead of taking the word of its successor. How did historians in each group perceive their own situation and their own tasks?

In asking this question, the social history of the profession sketched in the preceding chapters offers a point of departure. The views that scholars have had of themselves as participants in American life evolved hand in hand with their ideas about history. Academic historians in the 1880's and 1890's, we have seen, marked out a role for themselves in American culture with splendid confidence. At the same time, they put a high estimate on their capacity to grasp objectively the patterns of history. In the twentieth century they lost much of this confidence, becoming simultaneously doubtful of their status, dissatisfied with their achievement, and skeptical about the character of historical knowledge. In recent years their self-esteem has significantly revived; and as it has gone up, their faith in history as a form of knowledge has also risen. Historians have taken the self-sufficiency of their principles and of themselves for granted at one time, and have fallen into doubt and self-criticism on both scores at another. Their theoretical premises have changed as they have altered their image of themselves.

Accordingly, historical theory in America has moved within a circle of confidence and doubt. What the early professional historians overestimated was not the ideal of objectivity, but rather their own ability to take charge of history independently of its former connections with literature and philosophy. What the relativists discovered was not the limits of scientific objectivity (which their predecessors had recognized), but rather the limits of a discipline that was failing to live up to expectations. What the contemporary critics are reacting against is the deflation of historical consciousness that occurred when twentieth century scholars fell into an excessive skepticism about the possibilities of historical knowledge. At each of these stages Americans took from the ample storehouse of European precept and example what served their own purposes and mood.

# 1

# SCIENTIFIC HISTORY:
# THE AMERICAN ORTHODOXY

Scientific history—if we may so designate the formative orthodoxy of the early professional historians—came to America in the third quarter of the nineteenth century. It arose from no single source, and it materialized without programmatic announcement. By the beginning of the twentieth century the academic historians were convinced that they alone had established a "scientific" approach to history in America, and that they had transplanted it directly from the German universities where about half of them had studied.[1] Actually, what they called scientific history had already taken root in America outside of academic circles. It did not become fully self-conscious and systematic until sustained by a professional apparatus and professional training. But some of the principal attributes of scientific history first appeared in the work of a good many amateur historians, beginning perhaps with Richard Hildreth, whose six-volume *History of the United States* was published between 1849 and 1852. No one represented the ideals of scientific history more fully or more ably than the Philadelphia publisher, Henry C. Lea, whose first books on medieval history came out in 1866 and 1867. Neither Hildreth nor Lea nor many other amateur pioneers of scientific history studied abroad.[2]

In a large sense, the new historical movement was part of the turn in American culture from romanticism to realism. The contemporaneous novels of John W. De Forest and William Dean Howells, and the paintings of Winslow Homer and Thomas Eakins, came out of the same world view that shaped the writing of scientific history. In

[1] J. F. Jameson's "The American Historical Review, 1895-1920," *AHR*, XXVI (1920), 2, estimates that half of the academic historians of 1895 were trained in Germany.

[2] Donald E. Emerson, *Richard Hildreth* (1946); Edward Sculley Bradley, *Henry Charles Lea: A Biography* (1931); William M. Armstrong, "Henry C. Lea, Scientific Historian," *Pennsylvania Magazine of History and Biography*, LXXX (1956), 465-77. For a valuable account of other "critical historians" who emerged in the 1850's see David D. Van Tassel's *Recording America's Past, 1607-1884* (1960), pp. 121-34.

fact, one of the early literary realists, Edward Eggleston, was also a leading scientific historian. In every genre, realists distrusted imagination. The realistic artist, novelist, or scholar did not necessarily achieve a more truthful representation of human experience than the romanticist did, but he adopted a more impersonal tone. The realistic historian did not necessarily surpass the romanticist in factual accuracy, but he felt a special zeal to correct errors of subjective judgment. Unlike the romantic thinker, the realist avoided identifying himself with his subject. He stood apart from it, observing from the outside. He did not submerge himself in the mood and feelings that a situation suggested.

In all fields, realists were reacting against the romantic disposition to idealize and spiritualize life. Consequently, they shrank from exploring the mysterious depths of human character. They looked away from the uniqueness of personality in order to emphasize concrete, external relationships. Similarly—but less successfully—they refrained from elucidating timeless moral verities. In contrast to the intensive inwardness of romantic thought, realists cultivated an extensive view of the tangible and the multifarious. In these respects realism resembled photography, which was also coming into vogue during the third quarter of the nineteenth century. Justin Winsor in 1890 touched a major aspect of the whole cultural change in comparing the historian's task with that of the camera, which "catches everything, however trivial," and in assuming that "everything" registers on a photographic plate.[3]

Since the attention of the realist ranged across an extended surface, his transcription of life was open-ended rather than self-contained. Romantic artists and historians, endeavoring to concretize universal values, cast their work into a symbolic design; but realists presented theirs as a fragment of experience, which continued indefinitely beyond the somewhat arbitrary limits of the canvas or the narrative. For the romantic Francis Parkman, *The Discovery of the Great West* (1869) had a representative unity in the career of La Salle. But realists considered this sort of thing episodic; and for Frederick Jackson Turner *The Rise of the New West* (1906) was a segment cut from a seamless web.

All forms of realistic expression reflected, of course, the growing

[3] Justin Winsor, "The Perils of Historical Narrative," *Atlantic Monthly,* LXVI (1890), 296.

influence of the natural sciences in the latter half of the nineteenth century. This immense, diffuse influence spread through many channels: through the systematic organization of knowledge, through the replacement of traditional superstitions by matter-of-fact habits of mind, through the transforming impact of technology on practical life. Far from beginning in 1850, scientific influences had been gathering strength for a long time, and in American historical writing had made themselves felt since the early eighteenth century. In fact, romantic historians could never have achieved the effects they desired without already possessing the critical outlook associated with scientific inquiry. The change that occurred in the age of realism was not the introduction of scientific methods into humanistic studies but rather a sweeping displacement of the countervailing elements of romantic thought and feeling. What we call scientific history involved much more than a critical approach to evidence; it also subordinated romantic values to a scientific spirit. That spirit was impersonal, collaborative, secular, impatient of mystery, and relentlessly concerned with the relation of things to one another instead of their relation to a realm of ultimate meaning. Scientific history incorporated these attitudes.

It also incorporated, and put a new emphasis upon, evolutionary theories. The concept of cumulative, on-going change, operating through an endless chain of tangible causes and effects, became for scientific historians the very essence of historical wisdom. The meaning of every event, every form of experience, inheres in its location in the chain; and the historian's task is to make each link intelligible by discovering its genetic connection with what preceded and what followed. So applied to human affairs, the evolutionary hypothesis sealed the partnership between history and science; and history became Darwinian while biology became historical.

Actually, the idea of evolution—broadly defined as a continually unfolding process of development—entered historical thought long before Darwin. It was, as John B. Bury said, "the great transforming conception" that enabled history in the nineteenth century to take front rank among humanistic studies. Romantic historians, in spite of an emphasis on representative men and moments, had a deep feeling for the organic interconnectedness of human experience through time. A romantic historian like George Bancroft was more of an evolutionist than some of the early realists, such as Hildreth and

Winsor, who treated historical changes one by one with no concern for underlying continuity. Winsor confessed with positive pride that he made history "a thing of shreds and patches." [4]

From a realistic point of view, the weakness of the romantic idea of development was its idealistic character: it signified chiefly an emanation of spirit. By the 1870's, however, evolutionary ideas under the impact of Darwin and Spencer were losing their transcendental associations; evolution was becoming naturalized. A mechanistic and materialistic version of evolution thereupon completed the transition in America from romantic to scientific history.

As a doctrine of biophysical change, evolution strengthened the realistic approach to history immensely. It showed that history was not a thing of shreds and patches, and this made the revolt against romantic history coherent and intellectually exciting. The evolutionary sequence seemed self-explanatory, containing its dynamism wholly within itself. Consequently, it discredited the romantic emphasis on ideal, transcendental principles. Evolutionary science also justified abandonment of the romantic concentration on great, representative moments of human experience, for evolution reduced every moment to a link in the chain and imputed significance to the chain rather than the individual microcosm. Similarly, the unbroken continuity of evolution justified an open-ended narrative in place of the artistically contrived design of romantic history. To historians who saw the possibility of approximating in their work an all-embracing, objective pattern, the personal shape and flavor of romantic history became illusion.

In addition to its sheer intellectual appeal, scientific history suited the practical interests of a good part of the American aristocracy of culture in the late nineteenth century. To appreciate fully the dominion that "objectivity" won, and the enthusiasm it awakened, one must take its social relevance into account. As we have already observed, the patrician intelligentsia of the post-Civil War era was bent on establishing standards—on bringing discipline, stability, and solidity into what had been a chaotic, excessively individualistic intellectual life. The impersonality of scientific history met this demand exactly. Both in method and in content scientific history subordi-

[4] *Ibid.*, p. 297; John B. Bury, "The Science of History," in *The Varieties of History*, ed. Fritz Stern (1956), p. 214. On the romantic historians see David Levin's *History as Romantic Art* (1959).

nated individuals to institutions. It replaced the waywardness and subjectivity of romanticism with a sense of regular, uniform processes. It stressed cumulative scholarship and revealed a cumulative development in the organization of society. The scientific historian resembled, in his concern with impersonal standards, the civil service reformer of the same period. Both were subjecting passion and caprice to objective law.

While advancing the work of consolidation, scientific history was also congenial to the high-minded, cosmopolitan conservatism that the aristocracy of culture upheld. The lesson of continuous, unbroken development taught a sober respect for the dependence of the present on the past. From history so conceived, a nation prone to precipitate impulses might learn due caution; a people falsely convinced of its youthful exemption from the problems of older societies might learn responsibility. Charles Kendall Adams's *Manual of Historical Literature* pointed out:

> We see that the strongest and most lasting work is not that which is set up complete by act of independent creation, but that which has been framed little by little into the affairs of life as it has been needed. Perhaps, most important of all, we in America come to see that we are not under that exceptional protection which Von Holst has sneeringly said was long supposed to be vouchsafed by the kindness of a partial Providence to Americans as well as to women and children. On the contrary, we find that we are under the same rigorous laws that have shaped the destinies of nations on the other side of the Atlantic. We are awakened to the fact that our tendencies are essentially the same that have shown themselves in other republics.[5]

As a group the early professional historians not only shared the conservative evolutionism of their patrician associates; they had further reason of their own for zealous allegiance to the principles of scientific history. Scientific history was in fact their explicit raison d'être, and they embraced it with a special fervor because it constituted a declaration of independence for their academic discipline. For professional historians the scientific approach cut the fetters that had en-

[5] Charles Kendall Adams, *A Manual of Historical Literature*, 3rd ed. (1889), pp. 17-18. In this as in most respects Frederick Jackson Turner's youthful essay of 1891, "The Significance of History," was simply representative of current historical thought. See *Frontier and Section: Selected Essays of Frederick Jackson Turner*, ed. Ray Allen Billington (1961), pp. 11-27.

tangled history with older academic subjects and had subordinated it to literature and philosophy.

History had been a minor aspect of the classical education offered in American colleges. The new professional historians, therefore, were taking over functions formerly performed—or more often neglected—by teachers of languages and literature. Similarly, the professionals were pushing toward the leadership in historical writing that had formerly belonged to literary gentlemen. The criticism that scientific history made of the romantic school served the professional historians' need to dissociate themselves from literature.

Accordingly, the professional historian staked out a special claim to the ideal of objectivity and denied that the literary artist could faithfully serve so jealous a master. Distrusting the dramatic and the rhetorical, professionals insisted that "the appetite for literary effects requires constant curbing lest it betray the writer into distortion of the truth." History should not be regarded as an art. "The false assumption that history is a branch of literature, that an historical narrative must be a work of art, has seriously hampered the progress of scientific historical work," a methodologist sternly counseled. "It leaves the field open to a horde of amateurs." [6] An emphatic differentiation between history and literature fortified the professionals' sense of superiority toward a "horde of amateurs."

In making this differentiation, the professionals also registered their scorn for "mere narrative." [7] In practice, they arranged their facts according to patterns of narration inherited from their predecessors, but they considered themselves engaged in a very different kind of enterprise. Whereas literary amateurs dealt extensively in personalities, the professionals prided themselves on tracing the evolution of institutions. Institutional history exemplified their cult of objectivity by providing an impersonal, external framework for historical events. Moreover, institutional history expressed their own sense of organizational solidarity: it shaped history to the pattern of their own group consciousness, their own corporate spirit.

[6] Homer C. Hockett, "The Literary Motive in the Writing of History," *Mississippi Valley Historical Review*, XII (1926), 476; Fred Morrow Fling, *The Writing of History: An Introduction to Historical Method* (1920), p. 157. See also Frederic A. Ogg, "Literary Decline of History," *Dial*, XXXII (1902), 233-235.

[7] R. H. Dabney, "Is History a Science?" *The University Magazine*, X (January 1894), 3-9.

Next to literature, the early professional historians dreaded most an entangling alliance with philosophy. The connection of history with philosophy was almost as old as its connection with literature; history had long been defined as philosophy teaching by example. The rebellion against this tie had begun in Europe in the early nineteenth century, much before the professionalization of history in the United States. In a large sense, the whole historical movement of the nineteenth century was antiphilosophical. History was struggling to free itself from teleological assumptions, and historians who followed in the footsteps of Leopold von Ranke saw that philosophy imposed an arbitrary pattern on history, alien to reality. They tried to replace formal truths with particular, inductive relationships, and thus to make philosophy itself historical. Among American professional historians, however, the distrust of philosophy went to an almost paralyzing extreme.

The special bête noire of American academic historians was philosophy of history. They commonly equated it with "preconceived opinions" and with the introduction of moral judgments in historical writing. In recommending standard requirements for the Ph.D., Ephraim Emerton of Harvard conceded hesitantly that students might "venture upon a brief excursion" in philosophy of history; but he quickly added that it was a "dangerously speculative subject better reserved for later years in any deep way." [8]

A particular objection to philosophy of history was that it had usurped the name of science. Before the professional historians arrived on the scene, philosophy of history in the Anglo-American world had become positivistic. Following Auguste Comte, the positivists believed they could reduce history to a natural science by hypothesizing a system of unvarying evolutionary laws. The historical positivist most influential in America was the Englishman Henry T. Buckle, whose *History of Civilization in England* appeared in 1857. Throughout the rest of the century, certain amateur scholars in the United States, chiefly John W. Draper, Brooks Adams, and Henry Adams, carried on the effort to create a fullfledged science of history.[9]

---

[8] AHA *Annual Report* (1893), p. 87. See also Henry E. Bourne, *The Teaching of History* (1905), p. 15, and John Martin Vincent, *Historical Research: An Outline of Theory and Practice* (1911), pp. 8-9.

[9] Buckle's impact, although not yet adequately appraised, is attested in almost

Modestly construed as a search for specific, piecemeal laws of development, the science of history had a real fascination for the early professional historians. But even this became increasingly suspect; and systematic attempts to work out general laws of history they considered decidedly premature. They shrank from the apriorism of such undertakings, which seemed "dangerously speculative" rather than truly scientific. A systematic science of history threatened to subordinate history again to philosophy just when it was winning independence. In the face of this jurisdictional conflict, a fixation on the criticism of documents and the patient accumulation of facts hardened. The empirical outlook of the professional historian was, on one side, a reaction against positivistic theories, as it was at the other extreme a reaction against romantic subjectivity.

Scientific history tended toward a rigid factualism everywhere in the late nineteenth century, but perhaps nowhere more strongly than among American professionals. Unlike their contemporary colleagues in England, France, and Germany, the Americans made not a single, sustained effort to discuss the nature of historical knowledge. Even in the handbooks they wrote on historical method, American scholars dispensed with the theoretical sections of the European treatises—chiefly Ernst Bernheim's *Lehrbuch der historischen Methode* (1889)—on which they otherwise relied.

Americans consistently attributed to Ranke the happy severance of history from philosophy, and acclaimed the German historian as the founder of their own severely factual, realistic approach. Yet only a couple of Americans studied under Ranke, who retired in 1871; few read his work extensively; and no American translated any part of it. Ranke himself, as most German historians recognized by the end of the nineteenth century, was a romantic idealist, who always sought an intuitive apprehension of the universal within the particular. For Germans in the idealist tradition, history embraced and fulfilled the task of philosophy; for American empiricists the two were worlds apart.[10]

It is easy enough to say, in accounting for this curious difference be-

---

all the early manuals on history. See Winsor, *op. cit.*; *Autobiography of Andrew Dickson White,* vol. I (1905), p. 42; Charles Francis Adams Jr., *Massachusetts, Its Historians and Its History* (1893).

[10] Georg G. Iggers, "The Image of Ranke in American and German Historical Thought," *History and Theory,* II (1962), 17-33.

tween American scholars and the German academic world in which many of them were trained, that Americans are a practical people who do not respond congenially to speculative discourse. Consequently, science and scientific history had a down-to-earth, nontheoretical meaning for Americans. In German culture, on the other hand, the realm of spirit was never so sharply distinguished from the concrete realities of science; the German word for "science" (*Wissenschaft*) refers broadly to every kind of organized knowledge. Americans welcomed the practical techniques of German scholarship, but were more impervious to the German philosophical tradition, which in fact was at a low point in the 1880's when American professional history crystallized.[11]

Undoubtedly an American ethos did encourage hardheaded preoccupation with tangible facts, but not so decisively as to account for the tone of early American professional history. On the hypothesis of national character, one might have expected American academic philosophy in the late nineteenth century to exhibit the same practical-scientific bent that history displayed. Among American professors of philosophy, however, a highly abstract idealism reigned triumphant, and it was German idealism at that.[12]

The difference lay primarily in the contrasting situation of historian and philosopher. The academic historian confronted an essentially practical problem of establishing his own separate, autonomous status. He had to show what history was not: not literature, not philosophy. The academic philosopher, on the other hand, already belonged. His problem was to defend what philosophy was: the spokesman in American education for the "higher" truths of religion. Now the rising natural sciences threatened philosophy's traditional role. Meeting this intellectual challenge called for the profoundly theoretical resistance that German idealism supplied.

Unlike the philosopher, the historian faced no difficulty on the

11 Richard S. Barnes, "German Influence on American Historical Studies, 1884-1914" (Ph.D. dissertation, Yale University, 1953), p. 112, points out that the peak influx of American students to Germany coincided with the brief flowering of positivism there. It should, however, be said that J. G. Droysen had a certain influence on some American historians. See especially John W. Burgess, "Political Science and History," AHA *Annual Report* (1896), vol. I, pp. 203-219.

12 Herbert W. Schneider, *A History of American Philosophy* (1946), pp. 441-490.

level of basic principles. He already had, all unwittingly, a philosophy of history. He believed, serenely and implicitly, in progress; and his confidence in the general advance of wisdom and virtue enabled him to ignore theoretical problems in going about his practical business. If the historian took care of the facts, the values would take care of themselves. We may conclude, then, that the narrow conception of scientific history among American professional historians reflected their struggle against older rivals and their intellectual security in waging it.

This self-confidence becomes still more impressive when we consider closely the attitude of the early academic historians toward their vaunted objectivity. They did not, as modern critics would have us believe, think themselves capable of complete objectivity. The early professional historians freely acknowledged the contingent, fragmentary nature of historical evidence. Modestly, they denied that historians could attain the certainty possible in the "exact" sciences; for they appreciated the difficulties that chance and the unpredictable actions of individuals introduce into the problem of historical causation. Moreover, they recognized that no historian can eliminate his own predilections from his work. Indeed, they conceded that the shift of attitudes and interests in each generation requires a constant rewriting of history. "New conditions give rise to new problems, and these to new conceptions; and when we turn again to examine the past, we put to it questions never before asked." [13]

But such admissions did not vex or dispirit the men who made them. Against skepticism, their faith in progress stood them in good stead. They taught the inexactness of history with the intention and expectation of attaining an ever-increasing precision. They welcomed changes in historical perspective as cumulative, expecting that each partial truth would enrich the whole corpus of historical knowledge. When Henry E. Bourne noted in *The Teaching of History* (1905) that every generation looks back on the past from a changed point of view, he added that it therefore discovers "fresh significance in many a fact that hitherto appeared commonplace.

[13] Quoted in Ogg, *op. cit.,* p. 235. See also Charles Kendall Adams, *op. cit.,* pp. 4-7; Vincent, *op. cit.,* pp. 300-302; Allen Johnson, *The Historian and Historical Evidence* (1926), pp. 160, 172; and the influential work of the prominent English historian Edward A. Freeman, *The Methods of Historical Study* (London, 1886), pp. 122, 148-51.

The scope of history itself has by this means been several times enlarged." [14]

In sum, the founding fathers of professional history proudly capitalized on many a negation. In the name of history, they denied literature, philosophy, and even the certainties associated with the natural sciences. Yet they did not restrict themselves solely to the determination of facts, nor did they stand apart from the general intellectual advances of their age. They were, after all, enthusiastic evolutionists, eager to explore genetic relationships, to discover developmental patterns. The same kind of inquiry was flourishing in other fields of study, particularly in jurisprudence—where Oliver Wendell Holmes Jr.'s *The Common Law* (1881) left a powerful impress—in biblical scholarship, in philosophy, in political economy, and in anthropology. The historians felt themselves part of a great movement, in which the historical method was invigorating many disciplines simultaneously. They welcomed these allies gladly, doubtless thinking themselves at the head and front of the whole advance. To such collaborators the historians readily recognized their own indebtedness. They appreciated, sometimes in strikingly modern terms, the value of the comparative analysis that philologists and others were employing for an understanding of continuity and change. Jameson, for example, regarded the comparative study of religions and comparative jurisprudence as two of "the most potent causes of the recent expansion of historical work." The comparative method, in the eyes of Jameson, Charles M. Andrews, and many of their contemporaries, was broadening history, as the historical method was refining comparative study.[15] Here was no narrow academic isolationism, but rather large sympathies grounded in common objectives. Whatever the limitations of scientific history in American universities, it enjoyed the great advantage of growing up during what may be called the Historical Era in humanistic scholarship.

Little wonder, then, that the early professional historians, though

[14] Pp. 85-86.

[15] J. F. Jameson, "Development of Modern European Historiography," *Atlantic Monthly*, LXVI (1890), 332; Charles M. Andrews, "Some Recent Aspects of Institutional Study," *Yale Review*, I (1893), 381-410; Freeman, *op. cit.*, p. 66. On the impressive American contribution to historical jurisprudence during this period see W. S. Holdsworth's *The Historians of Anglo-American Law* (1928), pp. 99-117; on the "golden age" of biblical scholarship, George Ernest Wright's "The Study of the Old Testament," in *Protestant Thought in the Twentieth Century*, ed. Arnold S. Nash (1951), pp. 17-31.

they lacked the faith that writes epics, possessed the faith that moves mountains. Their cautiousness, austerity, and unimaginativeness have not been an entirely happy heritage. But their confidence in the progressive nature of historical knowledge must command a wistful respect. Unlike earlier historians from Thucydides to Parkman, they did not address posterity; they wrote for their immediate successors, fully expecting to be superseded. Without hope of achieving permanence, the best of them put an inexhaustible, harmonious energy into the creation of great multivolume works. Edward Channing labored ceaselessly on a single scholarly project for thirty years, and is supposed to have said that he would be satisfied if it were of some use for twenty-five. Men of this kind had the perseverance and zest to carry out grand designs with infinite patience in detail. It is characteristic that William A. Dunning, who wrote a dull, magisterial, three-volume history of political theories since antiquity, should have enjoyed one of the happiest days of his life when he discovered, by a comparison of handwritings, that Andrew Johnson's first message to Congress was actually drafted by George Bancroft. "I don't believe," he told his wife, "you can form any idea of the pleasure it gives me to have discovered this little historical fact." [16]

[16] Letter to Mrs. Dunning, April 23, 1905, William A. Dunning Papers (Columbia University). Channing's remark is mentioned in Crane Brinton's "The 'New History' and 'Past Everything,'" *American Scholar*, VIII (1939), 147.

# 2

## THE NEW HISTORY

By 1910 a number of younger historians had launched a spirited attack on their elders. Gradually the assault gathered momentum, becoming more radical and enlisting increasing support, until it seemed finally in the 1930's to overthrow the reign of scientific history. Looking back on the quarrel today, we can see that the sharpness of the attack obscured its somewhat superficial character. The dissenters were so largely a product of the orthodoxy they wanted to change that they did not realize how much they accepted its basic principles. Only after a quarter of a century of dissatisfaction did a broad and basic challenge to scientific history take shape, and even then it was ambiguous. The hold that scientific history took on the mind of the American professional historian was extraordinarily tenacious. Nothing reveals this more than the confused struggle, from 1910 to 1945, for reform.

A running criticism of orthodox scientific history became apparent during the first decade of the twentieth century. One indictment came from laymen. A second and quite different arraignment came from social scientists. Together, these criticisms reflected—and brought home—the difficulties professional historians were beginning to face: the decline of historical consciousness in American culture, the isolation of the professional historian from a larger sphere of influence and activity. Most historians reacted defensively; a significant few accepted the challenge.

From laymen arose the accusation that the scientific school was making history unreadable. Assailing "German pedantry," leading amateur historians such as William Roscoe Thayer and Charles Francis Adams Jr. deplored the loss of literary quality that had accompanied a gain in scientific method. Between 1905 and 1909 the *Nation,* the *Independent,* the *Atlantic,* and *Putnam's Monthly* aired a number of such complaints, which Theodore Roosevelt summed up in a Presidential address, "History as Literature," to the American Historical Association in 1912. These critics argued that history must make "its final appeal not as a monument of erudition, but as a masterpiece of art." The same view was repeatedly expressed in the 1920's and 1930's in the pages of the *Saturday Review of Literature*.[1]

Ignored for the most part, the charge awoke an echo among historians whose scientific training had not obliterated a lingering attachment to the literary tradition. Contact with the English academic world, where a certain gentlemanly flourish survived, helped to keep that tradition alive. It persisted more than elsewhere at Harvard, nourished by the literary heritage that still flavored Cambridge and Boston society. At Harvard College a "field of concentration" in history and literature, established in 1906, kept open channels of communication that had elsewhere closed. Among the Harvard faculty before World War I both Edward Channing and Albert Bushnell Hart at least paid lip service to the art of history, and in the period between the wars its most accomplished and vigorous spokesman was their distinguished student, Samuel Eliot Morison.[2] In the profession at large, one gesture of concern came in 1920 from the Council of the American Historical Association. Taking cognizance of a "general public protest" against the stylistic faults of professional history, the Council appointed a committee that eventually published a small book, *The Writing of History* (1926), containing the standard laments and some ineffectual suggestions for improvement.

The terms in which these critics scolded their colleagues suggest why they accomplished so little. Invariably, they conceived of good writing as a technical embellishment, a matter of "style" and of knowing how to tell a story clearly and straightforwardly. They distinguished sharply between science as a method of investigation and art as a method of presentation. The content of historical scholarship, they assumed, is supplied by scientific method, while the form of historical scholarship should come from literary method. The content of existing scholarship they accepted as praiseworthy; the deficiency lay only in its form. This naïve distinction preserved the critics' respectability as scientific historians in good standing. It also permitted

[1] E.g., William Roscoe Thayer, "The Outlook in History," *Atlantic Monthly*, XCVI (1905), 65-78; William Garrott Brown, "Mr. Rhodes as a Historian," *Independent*, LXII (1907), 552-54; "Naturalistic History," *Nation*, LXXXIV (1907), 427-28; James Truslow Adams, "Is History Science?" *Saturday Review of Literature*, IV (1928), 497-99.

[2] A. B. Hart, "Imagination in History," *AHR*, XV (1910), 246-51; J. F. Jameson and Edward Channing, *The Present State of Historical Writing in America* (1910), p. 25; Samuel Eliot Morison, "History as a Literary Art," in *By Land and By Sea, Essays and Addresses* (1953), pp. 289-98.

them to simplify a basic problem into a practical question of technique. Since the critics asked merely that professional history wear a sprightlier dress, their colleagues naturally received the complaint as a matter of no great intellectual significance. No one in the historical profession suggested that art arises from an organic fusion of manner and matter, and that great history does also in a special way of its own.

The fundamental implications of the concept of history as art had been available since 1909, when Benedetto Croce's *Aesthetic* was translated into English. Occasional editorials in the *Nation* and the *New Republic* commented appreciatively on Croce's views,[3] but no professional historian who discussed this question before 1940 showed the slightest awareness of them. The professional historians who regretted the loss of literary qualities were very largely conservatives who looked back nostalgically to the condition of history in Macaulay's day, not forward to what history might become.

A far more influential line of criticism originated among the social scientists. Literary objections to academic history, having started among laymen, bore the taint of amateurism and could be regarded lightly. But the complaints of fellow scholars in allied disciplines carried the imprimatur of scientific authority. This criticism touched the very source of pride: it challenged the scientific status of scientific history. The ensuing controversy had all the intensity of a family quarrel. The lines between history and other social disciplines in nineteenth century universities had been very indefinite, partly because of the broad appeal of the historical and evolutionary approach, and partly because of the smallness of faculties. History did not possess separate departmental status, but rather belonged in a common department with political science and often with economics and sociology. Of these, only economics acquired its own professional organization before the twentieth century. The historically inclined American Economic Association had been formed in 1885 at the second meeting of the American Historical Association, and for many years the two societies frequently held their annual meetings together. The secession of these erstwhile allies after the turn of the century was symbolic of a deeper cultural schism.

On the surface, the trouble arose from the impatience of many so-

3 "History as an Art," *Nation*, LXXXIX (1909), 643; "The Return of Clio," *New Republic*, XXXVI (1923), 117-18.

cial scientists with the orthodox historians' reluctance to specify regularities or laws in history. In 1902 Professor Edwin R. A. Seligman, a distinguished historical economist, commended a qualified, nonsocialistic version of the Marxian economic interpretation of history to a joint meeting of the American Economic and Historical Associations. The next year, at another joint meeting, a sociologist, Franklin H. Giddings, set forth a "Theory of Social Causation." About the same time geographers, notably Ellen C. Semple, were expounding the geographical determinants of history. These arguments carried the not unreasonable suggestion that history had better establish some general principles if it was going to fulfill the program of any bona fide science. Most historians recoiled from the suggestion, which seemed to them both officious and—in the present state of knowledge—unsound. To historians, the demand for systematic interpretation looked like a dangerous reversion to the discredited theories of positivism, in opposition to which their own notion of historical science had crystallized. Replying to Gidding's proposal in 1903, Emerton exclaimed, "Under the seductive name of sociology we are here meeting once more the ghost of our ancient enemy, the philosophy of history." [4]

The scornful attitude of social scientists, appearing at the same time that laymen were turning critical of professional history, threw many historians into a defensive posture. This was the first indication of the wider loss of confidence and vigor that overtook the historical profession in the early twentieth century. A new insularity of outlook became apparent. The earlier receptiveness of scientific historians to comparative analysis and to the larger vistas of the evolutionary process diminished. Many now retreated to a virtually exclusive concern with discrete facts and the conditions immediately surrounding them.

George Burton Adams' outraged rebuttal to the social scientists in 1908 revealed the stultifying effect of their criticism on the orthodox mind. Replying to the "attack upon our position, systematic and concerted," Adams in his presidential address to the American Historical Association defined history strictly as "a science of investigation," wholly independent of the theoretical activity of the rebellious disciplines that had invaded its domain. Adams, though he knew bet-

[4] AHA *Annual Report* (1903), pp. 34-37. Cf. the sharp controversy over Ellen Semple's paper, AHA *Annual Report* (1907), vol. I, pp. 21, 47-48.

ter, spoke as if history had no object except getting its facts straight. Thereafter, orthodox historians fell into the habit of distinguishing invidiously between interpretation and synthesis. The secretary of the American Historical Association explained to a group of amateurs in 1917 that some historians "coordinate the work of others and produce histories of more general range, and there are also those who interpret, but these are called philosophers." [5]

For their revulsion against large generalizations, American professional historians in the first years of the twentieth century found intellectual support and guidance in Germany. A revitalized discussion of historical theory sprang up there in the 1890's. Echoes of it soon reached America, partly through the revisions that Bernheim made after 1900 in his influential *Lehrbuch*. Heinrich Rickert and Wilhelm Windelband brought forward a sharp distinction between history on the one hand and the natural and social sciences on the other. The systematic sciences, they asserted, make generalizations by abstracting from experience its typical, its repetitive, its deterministic aspects; but history grasps every phenomenon as unique, individual, and concrete. The implication was that history, by adhering to its own individualizing logic, gets closer to the real thing. As in their understanding of Ranke, however, the Americans once again bit only half of the Teutonic apple. The German neo-Kantians were rehabilitating the subjective and qualitative insight by which the historian apprehends values. American historians seized upon the distinction between history and social science with the opposite intention of keeping subjective thought out of their ken. They wanted to vindicate their own scientific respectability. [6]

The real problem in early twentieth century America was not one of emancipating history from science, but rather the reverse: preventing science from repudiating history. The danger that history faced was the intellectual isolation into which orthodox professors were backing. In large measure, the quarrel between history and the

[5] G. B. Adams, "History and the Philosophy of History," *AHR*, XIV (1909), 223-29; Waldo G. Leland, "Concerning Catholic Historical Societies," *Catholic Historical Review*, II (1917), 388.
[6] The first considerable report of the new German wisdom was Fred M. Fling's "Historical Synthesis," *AHR*, IX (1903), 1-22. Note Fling's defensiveness about history and his delight that Rickert has supplied "a scientific basis for the methods of history."

social sciences broke out in the United States because social scientists were deserting history. The argument over the scientific status of scientific history is best understood as an overt expression of this deeper rift.

During the first two decades of the twentieth century, historical and evolutionary interests lost the commanding position they had formerly held in the academic social sciences. The Historical School of economists retreated before the doctrine of marginal productivity, leaving Thorstein Veblen an outcast and economic history a modest special field. It was symptomatic that Seligman, who began his career as a historical economist and who urged an economic interpretation of history in 1902, thereafter published almost exclusively on public finance. In political science empirical studies of contemporary problems and policies came to the fore.[7] Sociologists and anthropologists also put aside the broad evolutionary approach of the nineteenth century. The sociological study of change shrank to an examination of specific processes evident in the existing social order. American sociologists so cavalierly neglected historical sociology that many of them after a time confused it with the history of sociology. Only in the study of primitive cultures did a historical method flourish, and there it was used against history in a larger sense. Among anthropologists, as among orthodox historians, the historical method became a means of particularizing individual phenomena and thereby criticizing general developmental patterns.[8]

Across the entire range of social sciences, the fascination of the present tended to overshadow the long record of historical experience. In its own way, the academy was behaving much like the patrician intelligentsia and the reading public. The past was becoming

[7] Joseph Dorfman, *The Economic Mind in American Civilization*, vol. III (1959), pp. 243, 256-57, 349-51; Bernard Crick, *The American Science of Politics* (1959), pp. 92-93. There are striking indications of disdain for history in *Recent Developments in the Social Sciences*, ed. Edward C. Hayes (1927), pp. 248, 315-22, and Robert Hoxie, *Trade Unionism in the United States* (1917), pp. xxviii-xxix. A less common attitude of upholding the potential value of history while denouncing all historians informs the work of Frederick J. Teggart.

[8] Harry Elmer Barnes, *The New History and the Social Studies* (1925), pp. 315-16; L. L. Bernard, ed., *The Fields and Methods of Sociology* (1934), pp. 18-32; Frederica De Laguna, ed., *Selected Papers from the American Anthropologist, 1888-1920* (1960), pp. 871-74, 877-83; Murray Wax, "The Limitations of Boas' Anthropology," *American Anthropologist*, LVIII (1956), 63-74.

unfashionable. John Dewey, although one of the most historically minded intellectuals of the period, pronounced its characteristic judgment:

> It is a familiar saying that the great intellectual work of the nine-teenth century was the discovery of history. . . . As we notice the shift of emphasis and interest which is now going on . . . would it not be nearer the truth to say that the nineteenth century discov-ered *past* history? Since what is characteristic of the present time is speculation about the future, perhaps it will be the task of the twentieth century to discover *future* history.[9]

Accordingly, the most urgent disadvantage of scientific history in the new climate of opinion was probably not that it failed to produce broad generalizations about the long ago, but rather that it paid little heed to the here and now. The social scientists, ironically enough, were plunging into a piecemeal empiricism of their own at the very time they were criticizing historians for neglecting general theories. But the social scientists' empiricism—their surveys of urban slums, their bureaus of municipal research, their statistics on commodities, transportation, and prices—was excitingly contemporary. *Their* facts concerned the practical problems that most of the American people after 1900 wanted solved. Such studies satisfied the mind, and often aided the reforms, of the Progressive Era.

The more vigorous, younger historians followed suit. Under the influence of progressivism, and particularly under the spur of criti-cism from social scientists, a liberal minority in the historical profes-sion refused to accept the isolation of history from contemporary life and from the disciplines concerned with it. Instead of reacting defen-sively to the threat to history's status, they embarked on a campaign to reform history, to bring it into line with current interests, and to keep in step with the social sciences. Surely history too must become progressive. So, in the election year of 1912, when Theodore Roose-velt campaigned for the New Nationalism and Woodrow Wilson championed the New Freedom, Professor James Harvey Robinson

---

9 John Dewey, "Instrument or Frankenstein," *Saturday Review of Literature,* VIII (1932), 581. For Dewey, as Hans Meyerhoff has observed (*History and Theory,* I [1960], 91), it was the analysis of science, not history, that was the key to philosophy. It is therefore hardly surprising that he gave so little atten-tion to philosophy of history.

of Columbia University published the major manifesto of historical reform under the title *The New History*.

Others had already said, and practiced, most of the principles that Robinson asserted. His titular phrase and much of his argument had appeared in the *American Historical Review* in 1898 in a favorable appraisal of the unorthodox German historian Karl Lamprecht written by Earle Dow of the University of Michigan. Edward Eggleston touched on aspects of "the New History," as he too called it, in addressing the American Historical Association in 1900. Frederick Jackson Turner, replying in 1910 to George Burton Adams, had stated the essential case with temperateness and discrimination. Robinson's crusading fervor was newer than his doctrine, and a sympathetic reviewer in the *Nation,* disappointed in finding so little novelty, complained that the author had set up "whole armies of strawmen . . . for the purpose of exhibiting his delightful method of putting them to rout."[10] Nevertheless, Robinson baptized a movement and speeded its attainment of intellectual ascendancy in the historical profession.

Robinson might well have attacked the conservative historians of his day for retreating into a shell, since he sought in effect to reopen the congenial relations that had obtained between historians and other social scientists in the late nineteenth century. But Robinson, intensely progressive in outlook, saw himself in a more fully pioneering role. He presented the New History as the culmination of a hitherto slow struggle against antiquated traditions. Writing with a belligerence that raised the hackles of orthodox scholars, the Columbia professor united certain fresh perspectives with conventional ideas, which he advanced with the same air of *épatant les bourgeois*.

First among the innovations the New History proposed was a deliberate subordination of the past to the present by selecting and emphasizing the aspects of the past that are most relevant to present needs. History would thereby become, as never before, pragmatically useful. Scientific historians had, of course, always considered history

[10] C. W. Alvord, "The New History," *Nation*, XCIV (1912), 457-59; Earle Dow, "Features of the New History," *AHR*, III (1898), 431-48; Frederick Jackson Turner, *The Frontier in American History* (1920), pp. 311-34. As Arthur M. Schlesinger has pointed out in a graceful appreciation, Eggleston was merely reiterating the convictions that had long guided his historical work. See Schlesinger's introduction to Eggleston's *The Transit of Civilization* (1959), p. xix.

utilitarian; their belief in it as the essential medium of civic education and political responsibility had imposed a complete four-year
sequence from ancient to American history on the nation's high
schools. But traditional scientific historians had thought their subject
so naturally useful that they felt no urge to make it so. Now that its
utility was called into question, the New Historians wanted history to prove itself.

It could do that chiefly, they thought, by stressing the recent past,
thereby explaining the origin and character of present conditions.
Excursions into remoter times should reveal "the technique of progress" by showing how outworn ideas and institutions had been overthrown. This was Robinson's particular plea for intellectual history,
of which he was the pioneer among American professional historians. In keeping with Veblen's theory of cultural lag and with Dewey's attack on absolute truth, Robinson acclaimed intellectual history as the best means of exposing the transient, relative nature of
hallowed beliefs and so enabling us to keep our thinking abreast of
changes in our environment.[11] The utility of history depended, therefore, on foreshortening it and emancipating men from it. Like the
Enlightenment, the early twentieth century was an unhistorical age,
and the New Historians were, in a sense its *philosophes*. Robinson's
scintillating course at Columbia—the History of the Intellectual
Classes of Europe—was appropriately known among the students
as "The Downfall of Christianity." [12]

Second, while foreshortening the past, the New History proposed
to widen immensely its scope. All aspects of human affairs belonged
within its generous embrace. History, according to the New Historian, had too long scanted common, mundane experience. It had
too long concentrated on political events apart from their social and
economic environment. A more inclusive outlook would strengthen
the alliance of history with progressivism. Attention to everyday life
would, presumably, make history democratic. "The older History
was essentially snobbish and exclusive," Arthur M. Schlesinger com-

[11] James Harvey Robinson, *The New History* (1912), pp. 101-31. On Robinson's relation to the earlier study of intellectual history and on some limitations
of his approach see John Higham's "The Rise of American Intellectual History,"
*AHR,* LVI (1951), 454-59, and "American Intellectual History: A Critical
Appraisal," *American Quarterly,* XIII (1961), 221-25.
[12] Arthur M. Schlesinger, *In Retrospect: The History of a Historian* (1963),
pp. 34-35.

plained. Actually, the literary historians of the mid-nineteenth century—Carlyle, Macaulay, and J. R. Green—had already broadened the subject matter of history to take in the life of the common people; but they had also celebrated heroic leaders, whereas the New Historians (to quote Professor Schlesinger again) considered "the Great Man as merely the mechanism through which the Great Many have spoken." [13]

The particular restriction of scope against which the New History contended was the formal, institutional framework that ordinarily enclosed the more traditional kind of scientific history. Scientific historians had concentrated on the evolution of towns, states, and economic organizations, emphasizing in each case the internal development of policy and structure. The New History looked outward from institution to context, from structure to environment. It sought explanation of historical change in the "social forces" (to use one of Turner's favorite phrases) surging behind and beyond the visible form of the body politic. In their determination to break down supposedly artificial compartments, the New Historians were joining the general effort of progressive intellectuals to democratize American culture. A common "revolt against formalism," designed to put the intellectual in touch with everyday life, united the New History with muckraking journalism, the pragmatism of Mead and Dewey, and the shift in social science from doctrines and systems to immediate facts.

These sympathies also help to account for the third salient feature of the New History: its enthusiastic alliance with the social sciences. To turn toward the social sciences was, by 1910, to turn toward the present. To look to another discipline for aid in understanding history was to cross conventional boundaries and so to participate in the revolt against formalism. Robinson urged history to "surrender all individualistic aspirations," recognizing that the progress of knowledge depends on cooperation between overlapping disciplines. Moreover, if historians were going to be useful in the sense of discovering "the technique of progress," they would need to participate in the search for laws or regularities having some predictive value. The special contribution of history lay not so much in its distinctive interest in the past, but rather in its ability to synthesize the results of

[13] Arthur M. Schlesinger, "History," in *Research in the Social Sciences*, ed. Wilson Gee (1929), pp. 218-19.

more specialized sciences.[14] Thus the New History revived and perpetuated the nineteenth century quest for specific laws applicable to history. But it did so in a new milieu in which the historian was becoming quite modest about his own conceptual resources and was primarily bent on assimilating and somehow integrating the wisdom of other disciplines.

The great value that Robinson, Turner, and other progressive historians put on cooperation with the social sciences sounded novel in 1910 or 1912 because those sciences were no longer historically oriented. History could no longer take its primacy among them for granted. In order to cooperate, it would have to stretch. Nevertheless, the situation had changed much more than historical theory had. The *Nation's* reviewer caught more than half the truth in calling *The New History* "this restatement of the scientific position." We might better describe the outlook of the younger scholars as scientific history reformed; but their progressive version adhered devoutly to the basic premises laid down by the first American professional historians.

Once we discount the New Historians' view of their predecessors as old fogies, their own methodological orthodoxy becomes overwhelmingly evident. They too were evolutionists, equally hostile to an "episodic" treatment of the past and equally convinced that an appreciation of cumulative change had raised history to the dignity of a science. As evolutionists, the New Historians simply attached more importance to environment and less to heredity. Similarly, in substituting a fascination with "social forces" for the older historians' interest in institutions, the New Historians practiced an impersonal kind of history characteristic of professional scholarship from the beginning. American historiography remained unresponsive to individuals or subjective states of mind, betraying at times a touch of determinism.

A related hallmark of scientific history appears in the New Historians' distrust of literature and philosophy. Turner sometimes advised graduate students against taking a minor in literature, on the score that "the old union between history and literature is now broken." Before World War I Charles A. Beard professed a sovereign disdain for theory as unreal and mythical. As late as 1921, he dis-

[14] Robinson, *op. cit.*, pp. 67-74. On the general intellectual climate see Morton White's *Social Thought in America: The Revolt Against Formalism* (1949).

missed political philosophy as merely "a great deal of talk." Robinson rejoiced at the emancipation of history from "its long servitude" to literature and philosophy; and he took pains to distinguish social scientists also from "the now nearly extinct tribe of philosophers of history, who flattered themselves that their penetrating intellects had been able to discover the wherefore of man's past without the trouble of learning much about it." [15]

Finally, the New Historians accepted essentially the same concept of objectivity that scientific historians had upheld in the nineteenth century. They cherished it without expecting fully to attain it. History, Robinson thought, must always remain a highly inexact and fragmentary science because of the nature of its evidence. Moreover, its conclusions will change as each age exercises the right to select from the annals of the past those facts that bear on present problems. The older scientific historians had reluctantly admitted as much.

Neither they nor their present-minded successors supposed that the incompleteness and relativity of historical knowledge need compromise the pursuit of objective truth. Beard as well as Robinson explicitly disapproved the introduction of moral judgments into historical writing. The interests of the present should determine the aspects of the past that deserve attention; but the objective facts that the historian then discovers will, as science progresses, more and more determine his conclusions. An underlying faith in the progress of reason in human affairs enabled both New and old historians to assume that each generation's revision of the past would be an improvement. "We have learned to recognize," Robinson concluded, "that . . . relativity is conditioned by our constant increase in knowledge." [16]

The New History was not an exercise of contemplation, not a theory finely drawn in the interest of system or logical coherence. It was a diffuse stimulus to action, a kind of yeast that worked for thirty years or more in an otherwise sluggish profession. During this long fermentation, a question that Robinson and Turner had answered ambiguously forced its way gradually to the surface. How can history

[15] Robinson, op. cit., p. 99, and "The Conception and Methods of History," Congress of Arts and Sciences, Universal Exposition, St. Louis, 1904, vol. II (1906), p. 50; Bernard C. Borning, The Political and Social Thought of Charles A. Beard (1962), p. 121. On Turner see Charlotte Watkins Smith's Carl Becker (1956), p. 15.

[16] Robinson, The New History, p. 130. See also Turner, op. cit., p. 323; Edward P. Cheyney, Law in History and Other Essays (1927), pp. 142 ff.

best reveal the "technique of progress"? By joining the social sciences in the positivist program of constructing general laws? Or by deriving criteria of progress in history from the values that are uppermost in the changing present? In effect, the formulators of the New History had recommended both without distinguishing between them; for they considered present-mindedness and science-mindedness as complementary. In time, the two policies seemed less so. As the quest for reliable generalizations grew increasingly urgent, the struggle to absorb scientific uniformities into history became incompatible with the tendency to rely on relative and changing values. In trying to hold the two halves of their faith together, progressive historians stumbled into deepening perplexities and confusions. A movement that began before World War I with the intention of making history more objective ended, in the 1930's and 1940's, in making it more relativistic.

# 3

## RELATIVISM

Throughout the 1920's and even into the 1930's the scientistic side of the New History remained in the forefront of professional attention. Getting in a right relation with the social sciences was the principal subject of theoretical discussion, and the New Historians continued to quarrel with their conservative, isolationist colleagues chiefly on this point. A student of Robinson's, Harry Elmer Barnes, emerged in the 1920's as the most rabid prophet of the coming victory of historical science over the "appalling inadequacy and narrowness" of traditional scholarship, which he identified with "pietism, obscurantism, and the political fetish." In more sober terms several presidents of the American Historical Association summoned the profession to search for laws of history, and one, Edward P. Cheyney, announced in 1923 the discovery of several tentative laws. These—including the necessity of elasticity and adaptiveness, the interdependence of the human race, the growth of democracy, and the march of progress—turned out to be the presuppositions of the New History writ large.[1]

Why did rapport with the social sciences loom so large in the interwar years? Primarily because of the importance those disciplines were acquiring in American academic life. During the 1920's the general public became for the first time conscious of at least some of the social sciences, especially economics and psychology. The secession of political scientists, economists, and others from departments dominated by historians had begun at the turn of the century and was now completed at all of the major universities. These new departments were expanding at a prodigious rate. They were also getting princely support from the great foundations. In 1921 one hundred foundations disbursed $181,471 for research and advanced education in the social sciences, including history; their outlay, rising

[1] Edward P. Cheyney, *Law in History and Other Essays* (1927), pp. 7-25; Edward C. Hayes, ed., *Recent Developments in the Social Sciences* (1927), pp. 340-41. Dana C. Munro's presidential address to the AHA in 1926 followed Cheyney in urging a search for historical laws in partnership with the social sciences.

steadily, reached $7,843,846 in 1927. But history captured a modest share of this bonanza only by associating itself with social science; the humanities were receiving relatively little.[2]

The rapid development of specialization within the social sciences and the prevailing antipathy to general theories let loose a flood of empirical research. Taking alarm, social scientists rallied around slogans of "cooperation" and "interdisciplinary research," the very gospel that the New History was preaching. In response to the cry for coordination, special research agencies sprang up. Beardsley Ruml, the dynamic young director of the Laura Spelman Rockefeller Memorial (later incorporated into the Rockefeller Foundation), supplied much of the initiative. Ruml's chief creation was the Social Science Research Council (SSRC), which from its founding in 1923 incarnated the idea of group work and "cross-fertilization." At first the American Historical Association backed off from an invitation to join the Council; but in 1925 all objections gave way to the desire to share in the Council's fellowship program.[3] The Association thereupon took care to choose as its representatives on the Council members who were in sympathy with SSRC objectives. Over the years these representatives, notably Arthur M. Schlesinger and Roy F. Nichols, played an always conciliatory and constructive role.

Yet historians had no part—until the late 1930's, and only in a small way then—in the interdisciplinary projects that the SSRC ambitiously launched. The New History was, to tell the truth, exceedingly vague in specifying how history could effectively cooperate with the social sciences and participate in their search for general laws. Robinson had suggested that the historian is better equipped than anyone else to deal with the interrelation between the various aspects of human affairs and that he performs therefore the special task of synthesis. But historians, New or old, studied the past; and toward historical synthesis most social scientists were indifferent. Moreover, the New Historians' concept of synthesis was unmanageably diffuse. They wanted so much to embrace everything, to in-

[2] Eduard C. Lindeman, *Wealth and Culture: A Study of One Hundred Foundations* (1936), pp. 70-82.
[3] Waldo G. Leland to J. S. Bassett, January 29, 1925, and February 6, 1925, Correspondence of W. G. Leland 1924-1926, Archives of American Historical Association (Library of Congress). On the origin of the SSRC see Herbert Heaton's *A Scholar in Action: Edwin F. Gay* (1952), pp. 206-209.

tegrate the whole of reality in their writing, that they could rarely analyze a single causal relationship intensively. In search of breadth and completeness, they widened the scope of history instead of isolating regularities within it.

By the mid-1930's the term *New History* had become discredited through association with an indiscriminate electicism.[4] The urge to remodel history along the lines of the social sciences was stronger than ever. Amid the national and international crises of the Thirties, the sluggishness of history in "catching up" with the supposedly more advanced sciences that treated current issues seemed intolerable.

Perhaps a more selective and intensive application to history of the concepts of particular social sciences would help. Some historians, inspired by the Lynds and their successors in sociology, thought that individual communities might provide a coherent matrix for research, and the Social Science Research Council gave its first historical committee, appointed in 1938, the job of preparing a guide for the study of local history. The anthropological concept of culture, which Ruth Benedict popularized in the early Thirties, exercised a special fascination. Culture, as the anthropologist conceived it, was an all-embracing pattern, which would satisfy the New Historians' desire to comprehend society as a whole; yet it might also reveal a unifying structure and provide a basis for selection.

With ideas such as these, some bold spirits set about shaking up the historical profession. Beard became president of the American Historical Association in 1933, just when it acquired a full-time executive secretary in the person of Conyers Read. Read's own work as a Tudor biographer was traditional; but he joined enthusiastically in Beard's determination to make history directly relevant to contemporary social thought and issues. Beginning that year, the annual meetings of the Association took on an increasingly experimental and contemporary air. In 1939 "The Cultural Approach to History" was the theme of the whole program. Scholars imported from other disciplines, to teach historians how to do it, dominated most of the sessions. "Not only the past but the historians themselves sometimes struggled for a place in the proceedings," a conservative professor

---

[4] Crane Brinton, "The New History: Twenty-five Years After," *Journal of Social Philosophy*, I (1936), 134-47; Esmond Wright, "History: The 'New' and the Newer," *Sewanee Review*, XLIX (1941), 479-91.

wryly commented.[5] Some of the best of the younger historians went seriously to work along the proposed lines. In the most striking instance Thomas C. Cochran embarked in the 1940's on a pioneering quantification of cultural trends and came to think of himself as an anthropological historian.[6] A good part of the profession, on the other hand, was antagonized by the obeisant attitude that most of the reformers evinced toward their sister disciplines.

Meanwhile, in the 1930's, the other side of the New History—its pragmatic concern with values—emerged belatedly as a more exciting issue. Robinson had invited historians to choose their facts according to canons of present relevance. So long as historians unquestioningly trusted in science to supply the canons, they did not closely examine the nature of the invitation. Only when faith in empiricism was shaken did some begin to consider their philosophical position.

Long before the relativistic implications of the New History touched other historians, they were troubling the agile mind of Carl Becker. This gentle man of irony and laconic wit—strangely sprung from rock-ribbed Iowa Methodist farmers—had gone to Wisconsin to study under Turner and then to Robinson at Columbia, and had absorbed everything that was progressive and challenging in their teaching. Yet he was a rara avis among the New Historians. No one else in the historical profession in 1910 could have written, as Becker did to Turner, "To me nothing can be duller than historical facts, and nothing more interesting than the service they can be made to render in the effort to solve the everlasting riddle of human existence."[7] Becker's suspicion of facts, in contrast to the usual desire of New Historians for the greatest possible variety of them, was one starting point of his particular heterodoxy. Closely connected was his preoccupation with "the everlasting riddle of human existence."

[5] AHA Files 1933, Box 6, Archives of American Historical Association; William C. Binkley, "Two World Wars and American Historical Scholarship," *Mississippi Valley Historical Review*, XXXIII (1946), 15; "Educating Clio," *AHR*, XLV (1940), 505; Caroline Ware, ed., *The Cultural Approach to History* (1940).

[6] Thomas C. Cochran, *Railroad Leaders, 1845-1890: The Business Mind in Action* (1953); *The Inner Revolution: Essays on the Social Sciences in American History* (1964). See also Oscar Handlin, *Boston's Immigrants, 1790-1865: A Study in Acculturation* (1941); Sylvia Thrupp, *The Merchant Class of Medieval London, 1300-1500* (1948).

[7] Burleigh Taylor Wilkins, *Carl Becker* (1961), p. 32. I am much indebted to this admirable book.

Other New Historians before World War I took the intelligibility of the universe for granted; they concentrated on the problems of society. Becker's mind delighted rather in philosophy and in literature, and was in that crucial way alien to the antiphilosophic empiricism of the New History. Yet he had little in common with the lingering literary tradition that Samuel Eliot Morison and later Allan Nevins represented. Skeptical rather than traditional, Becker was clearly on the side of the present against the past.

Virtually alone among professional historians in the early twentieth century, he was neither anchored in the security of a conservative culture nor swept confidently forward by the promise of reform. The loss in the 1890's of the trustful piety of his youth marked him permanently: he wore always a somewhat deracinated air. This ingrained sense of spiritual loss accounts for most of the attitudes that set the early Becker apart from his professional contemporaries: the distaste for hard, heavy facts, the ambivalent feelings about science, the metaphysical pathos, and the doubts of progress. All of these qualities, still bathed in personal experience, came together ultimately in his haunting view of the modern intellect:

> as the time and space world is expanded . . . the gods, withdrawing from the immediate affairs of men to the place where absolute being dwells, fade away into pale replicas of their former selves— into the Law of Nature, the Transcendent Idea, the dynamic principle of Dialectic, or whatever it may be. Philosophy in turn becomes Natural Philosophy, then Natural Science, then Science; and science, dispensing altogether with the assistance of the gods and their numerous philosophic progeny, presents for contemplation the bare record of how as a matter of fact the outer world behaves, of what as a matter of fact has occurred in past times, leaving man alone in an indifferent universe. . . .[8]

Becker began speculating about history at the point where Robinson left off. Robinson had learned from John Dewey to associate a pragmatic conception of truth with the forward march of science, and so to discredit conservative absolutes as rationalizations of transitory conditions. Becker read the pragmatists too; and like Robinson he was contemptuous of the dogmatic factualism in which conservative scientific historians were taking refuge. But Becker, as early as 1910, carried the pragmatic argument a long step beyond Robinson.

[8] Carl Becker, "What Is Historiography?" *AHR*, XLIV (1938), 28.

If history gets its point and force by selecting facts that are useful to the present, Becker asked, do not the interests of the present enter also into the very constitution of the facts? Are they not themselves merely mental images? Other New Historians distinguished between selection (or synthesis), which is the function of the present, and the facts as such, discrete and immutable. This distinction supported their expectation that each successive present could achieve a more comprehensive, better integrated selection. Becker indicated that historical facts are as much a product of the present as are historical interpretations or syntheses. His thoroughgoing subordination of past to present left no basis for the other side of the New History—its faith in becoming more and more of a social science. He even suggested, at the end of the 1910 essay, that the very ideal of objectivity, to which he was personally attached, was itself a part of a transitory present, unlikely to survive in the evolutionary process for very long.[9] While cherishing progress and reason, he lacked confidence in them, and so in historical knowledge as well.

Thus the intellectual origins of Becker's early skepticism about objective history are sufficiently clear. A combination of philosophy and temperament, his relativism resulted from the impact of a pragmatic conception of truth on a homeless spirit. He was also responding, evidently, to concrete circumstances. It is undoubtedly more than coincidence that his earliest disenchanted reflections on history appeared just at the time when the historical profession was losing momentum, when criticism of its labors was becoming widespread, and when the importance of history in American intellectual life was declining. George Burton Adams' outburst in 1908, the complaints of Jameson and Channing about the state of historiography two years later, Robinson's strident tone, and Becker's disturbing questions came out of a common milieu. Becker began that first speculative essay in 1910 by remarking on the disparaging attitude of contemporary scientists toward history, and his argument was on one level a diffident apologia for history's limitations, though on another it was a criticism of his fellow historians. In Becker the crisis in American historiography first reached full theoretical expression. Until much later, the discontent of the rest of the New Historians remained at a more superficial level. Doubly shielded from heresy—

[9] Phil L. Snyder, ed., *Detachment and the Writing of History: Essays and Letters of Carl L. Becker* (1958), pp. 3-28.

first by their profession's deafness to philosophical discussion, second by their own progressive faith—they too easily blamed history's difficulties on the pettifogging conservatives in their midst.

Becker sounded again in the 1920's essentially the same disenchanted, relativistic note he struck in 1910. It chimed now with the general, postwar disillusion so fashionable in many intellectual circles and with the pessimistic view of history so poignantly phrased in Henry Adams' posthumous autobiography. All of this awoke only an occasional echo among Becker's colleagues. One old scholar, Clarence W. Alvord, confessed that the science of history as he had practiced it now appeared "mere bunk," but for all his pessimism, he said, "I find it impossible to make myself over into a pragmatic historian." Another, convinced that the historian's purpose is to create credible myths and thus make a certain view of the world prevail, felt a sore need for a new philosophy of history. Finding none available, he concluded that historians could do no more than continue with business as usual.[10] Among the rank and file of the profession, the dogmas of scientific history, either in the orthodox or the reformed version, held fast.

Beneath the surface a subtle corrosion was occurring, and in the depths of the Great Depression it became visible at last. Becker's presidential address to the American Historical Association in 1931 received an ovation; now the profession was ready to listen. Now, restating his case, Becker put a recklessly unqualified emphasis on the necessity and value of conforming history to popular need, of satisfying Mr. Everyman, of keeping up to date his "useful myths."[11] A demand for participation, for shaping a disordered world in a more active and willful way than the pallid social-science movement promised, released a fullfledged relativist movement. The stage was set for Charles A. Beard.

---

[10] C. W. Alvord, "Musings of an Inebriated Historian" and "Changing Fashions in History," *American Mercury*, V (1925), 434-41, and IX (1926), 74; Joseph Ward Swain, "What is History?" *Journal of Philosophy*, XX (1923), 281-89, 312-27, 337-49, and "History and the Science of Society," in *Essays in Intellectual History Dedicated to James Harvey Robinson* (1929), pp. 324-25. Raymond J. Sontag remembers a long informal discussion of the causes of World War I at a meeting of the American Historical Association in the 1920's, when "the break between those whose minds were formed before 1914, and those, whatever their age, who began to think only in the years after 1918, became clear" (*AHR*, LXVII [1961], 91).
[11] *Everyman His Own Historian* (1935), pp. 233-55.

Whereas speculation about history was Becker's natural medium, Beard was driven to it by the course of history. Almost sixty years old in 1933 when he loosed the first of his relativist cannonades, Beard had taken a serious interest in historical theory only during the preceding two years. He turned to it not in a brooding mood of *Weltschmerz* but rather in a mighty effort to foresee and guide the future. Having grown up in a family of former Quakers, strongly tinged with eighteenth century rationalism, Beard had had no religious orthodoxy to lose; he had troubled himself little about the riddle of human existence. Instead, his warm, passionate nature had fulfilled itself in social issues and conflicts.

Always in the thick of things, as a college student he had visited the Chicago stockyards and had worked in Jane Addams' Hull House. While still a graduate student, he and another American had established a workingman's college at Oxford, England. During the years at Columbia (1902-1917), where Beard developed from a protégé to a partner of James Harvey Robinson, most of his teaching was on contemporary politics. He was active in the New York Bureau of Municipal Research and the National Municipal League, campaigned for a Socialist Congressman on the Lower East Side, and carried on an epic feud with the president of the university. In the 1920's he advised statesmen in the Balkans and in Japan. One of his favorite words was *dynamic,* and he once declared that the greatest passage in English literature was the conclusion to Shelley's *Prometheus Unbound.*[12]

While fighting the good fight, Beard nevertheless strained in his scholarly activity to maintain an unrelenting objectivity. Like Robinson, he associated progress with a steady extension of scientific control over human life and thought. Assuming that increasing knowledge furnishes an ever more adequate basis for political and economic policies, he rigidly excluded overt moral judgments from his own scholarly works. His early monographs were as austere as a surgical table.

In the 1920's, however, drawing on the hitherto buried resources of the English literary culture he had absorbed at Oxford, Beard's writ-

[12] Mary R. Beard, *The Making of Charles A. Beard: An Interpretation* (1955), pp. 12, 90-94; Harlan B. Phillips, "Charles Beard, Walter Vrooman, and the Founding of Ruskin Hall," *South Atlantic Quarterly,* L (1951), 186-91; Moses Rischin, *The Promised City: New York's Jews, 1870-1914* (1962), p. 233.

ing assumed a more humanistic cast. He began to defend, instead of merely putting to work, his basic values. He was worried by a widespread loss of nerve. Roused by pessimistic critics like Spengler, he turned to a defense of the cultural and moral underpinnings of modern and particularly American civilization. Beard became sharply aware that progress was not just evolutionary process but also a historical faith—"the guiding principle" of American civilization—and that belief in progress was essential to the kind of future he had before taken more easily for granted. Thus, when the Depression struck, Beard was already making articulate the philosophy of history that progressive historians had not quite known they had. The confusion and deterioration of the early Depression years thrust him deeper into a concern with values. Departing from his earlier hardboiled empiricism, he was calling by the beginning of 1932 for a scheme of ethics, "a recurrence to first principles, the hoisting of a moral standard to which all mankind may repair." [13]

Could science provide such a standard? Beard, along with Robinson and Dewey, had always thought so. Now he was not so sure. A "crisis in thought," he believed, had developed from "the discovery that science, facts, and the scientific method do not, and in the nature of things, cannot provide inescapable and irrefutable policies." [14] Like other historians who adopted a relativist position in the 1930's, he was learning that many scientists thought of themselves no longer as explaining an ultimate reality but rather as operating within sharp observational limits. [15] Perhaps more important for Beard was the criticism of natural science he encountered among European philosophers of history. Beard's plunge into philosophy apparently began with a reading of Benedetto Croce's *History: Its Theory and Practice* (trans. 1921), which taught him that the various

[13] Charles A. Beard, "A Search for the Centre," *Scribner's Magazine*, XCI (1932), 2. The best account of the gradual changes in Beard's outlook during the 1920's is in Bernard C. Borning's *The Political and Social Thought of Charles A. Beard* (1962), pp. 64-135.
[14] Quoted in Borning, *op. cit.*, p. 170.
[15] Charles A. Beard, *The Nature of the Social Sciences* (1934), p. 32, and *America in Midpassage* (1939), pp. 852-59; Carl Becker, *The Heavenly City of the Eighteenth-Century Philosophers* (1932), pp. 22-27; Charles W. Cole, "The Relativity of History," *Political Science Quarterly*, XLVIII (1933), 163, 167; Crane Brinton, "The 'New History' and 'Past Everything,'" *American Scholar*, VIII (1939), 154-55; Harry Elmer Barnes, *History of Historical Writing* (1937), pp. 266-68.

sciences are pragmatic abstractions from the more inclusive realm of history.[16]

Beard's son-in-law, Alfred Vagts, arrived on a visit from Germany in the summer of 1932 with a copy of a new book in the idealist tradition, Karl Heussi's *Die Krisis des Historismus*. Heussi described and analyzed the triumph of a subjective conception of historical knowledge in Germany in the early twentieth century. American historians were almost entirely ignorant of this development, having lost touch with German thought after the turn of the century; and Beard was amazed to learn of these "disclosures of contemporary thought." Now he saw Croce's ideas as part of a great movement. Under Vagts's tutelage, Beard went on to study other German historical theorists.[17]

As a consequence, Beard underwent a semiconversion that carried him beyond the point that Becker, in the native pragmatist tradition, had reached. Becker had humbled history, emphasizing its limitations as a science. Beard, following Croce, wanted to exalt history by restoring it to its rightful place as "the crown of philosophy." Becker argued history's inevitable bondage to the present. Beard turned the argument into a claim for freedom by announcing the emancipation of history from bondage to natural science. In contrast to Becker's somewhat fatalistic outlook, Beard centered his attack on determinism, which he associated with science and with the mechanistic causality of scientific history. He was rejecting, without openly saying so, the deterministic implications of his own earlier scholarship. He demanded that historians recognize the subjectivity of history in order to restore the primacy of values in the study of man, and thereby help to guide the history that was in the making.[18]

This first serious encounter between the American New History and German neo-idealism did considerable violence to both. It undermined, without really supplanting, the scientific theory; and left his-

[16] Charles A. Beard, "A Historian's Quest for Light," *Proceedings of the Association of History Teachers of the Middle States and Maryland*, XXIX (1931), 12-21. Beard thought so highly of Croce that he tried as president of the AHA in 1933 to bring the Italian philosopher to its annual meeting. A letter from Croce on the current state of historiography was read to the meeting following Beard's presidential address (*AHR*, XXXIX [1934], 229-31).

[17] Interview with Alfred Vagts, May 3, 1961.

[18] Beard, *The Nature of Social Sciences*, pp. 61-62, 161-63, and "Written History as an Act of Faith," *AHR*, XXXIX (1934), 219-29. See also Minutes of the Program Committee, April 2, 1933, AHA Files 1933, Box 6.

torical thought in great confusion. While using German ideas to de-limit the claims of science, Beard clung to a positivistic conception of knowledge as a structure external to the observer. He continued to hanker for an objective grasp of the totality of things while denying the possibility of attaining it; he persisted in thinking of science as the only authoritative mode of inquiry while emphasizing the unscien-tific character of history. In spite of his desire to enhance history's status as an intellectual discipline, his argument had the effect, there-fore, of discrediting it.

Beard's pragmatism added to his difficulty in assimilating the ideas he borrowed from Europe. The subjectivity that Croce and Heussi upheld was a mode of understanding, an identification of the observer with the observed. It was not an obstacle to, but rather the essential condition of historical knowledge. For Beard, on the other hand, subjectivity referred more narrowly to the historian's social goals and values.[19] It had to do with molding the future rather than un-derstanding the past. As a pragmatist, he regarded the mind of the historian as an instrument that, in serving its owner's needs, re-shapes and necessarily violates the external reality of history. He could not conceive of the subjective action of the historian as much more than arbitrary and coercive: it related always to will or to faith in the kind of future that the historian desired.

By endorsing deliberate moral judgment in historical writing, Beard made a bold, refreshing departure from the colorless neutral-ity and impersonality that American scholarship had prized since the rise of realism. He upset the easy assumption of scientific history that values would take care of themselves if historians took care of the facts. But he was left in the end without much basis for taking care of either. He could only trust—pragmatically—that the future course of history would vindicate his present values, which in turn would justify his selection of past facts.

This insistence on writing history in accordance with a vision of the future should be understood against a background of hot and ur-gent activity. The Depression had roused Beard's Promethean spirit to unprecedented exertions, as if he would now grasp destiny by the

[19] Lloyd R. Sorenson, "Charles A. Beard and German Historiographical Thought," *Mississippi Valley Historical Review*, XLII (1955), 274-87; Cushing Strout, *The Pragmatic Revolt in American History: Carl Becker and Charles Beard* (1958).

forelock and twist her once and for all in the right direction. While spelling out a philosophy of history in 1932-33, Beard was simultaneously engaged in sketching an ambitious blueprint for a planned economy to meet the domestic crisis. He was formulating a general conception of the national interest in foreign policy. He was goading an educational commission into an affirmation of collectivistic values as the foundation of all instruction in the social studies. He was even drafting a new state milk law for the angry Connecticut farmers who gathered for leadership on his lawn. In all of these respects Beard was engaged in a gigantic rescue operation, an attempt to reanimate by creative thought and purpose the progress that had lost its own momentum.

Beard's relativism, with its call to action and its renewed affirmation of progress, had a sledgehammer effect, far exceeding the impact of Becker's wistful disenchantment. Younger historians, by now thoroughly impatient with the stodginess of their profession, the stagnation of the American Historical Association, and the indifference of the public to professional history, responded eagerly to Beard's summons to controversy and interpretation. Unlike Becker, who seemed not to care much what other people did, Beard urged his colleagues to join him in reconsidering the nature of historiography; and the year after he delivered his thunderous address, "Written History as an Act of Faith" (1933), all three general sessions at the annual meeting of the American Historical Association dealt with philosophical issues.[20] Nothing like this had ever occurred before.

The indignation of conservative scholars added to the stir. In their eyes the ancient standard of objectivity was being trampled in the dust. The traditionalists guarded an essential truth, best expressed by Charles H. McIlwain, Arthur O. Lovejoy, and Robert L. Schuyler: that historical understanding requires us to transcend the biases of the present, and that history liberates us from parochialism to the extent that we succeed in doing so.[21] It was hard to listen to such voices in the midst of a world in tumult, particularly when the kind of scholarship they defended was so largely formalistic and old-fashioned. Deeply concerned about the state of their discipline but

[20] *AHR*, XL (1935), 425-28.
[21] C. H. McIlwain, "The Historian's Part in a Changing World," *AHR*, XLII (1937), 209-15; Arthur O. Lovejoy, "Present Standpoints and Past History, *Journal of Philosophy,* XXXVI (1939), 477-89; Robert L. Schuyler, "The Usefulness of Useless History," *Political Science Quarterly,* LVI (1941), 23-37.

unaccustomed to theoretical argument, historians quarreled in an atmosphere of growing confusion. Today we may look back ruefully at the partisanship that suffused this conflict between two versions of scientific history. Upholders of the orthodox version denounced the "relativists" as defeatists and sometimes associated their doctrine with fascism. They, in turn, implied that their opponents, puttering over harmless and distant facts, were practicing vicarious leisure and conspicuous waste.[22]

On the crucial matter of objectivity, the two arguments simply failed to meet. Orthodox scientific historians accused the relativists of abandoning the ideal of objectivity, when in fact they argued that the historian can become more objective by recognizing his limitations. The relativists, for their part, accused the orthodox of believing that bias can be eliminated from historical knowledge, when the latter insisted only that bias should be reduced to a minimum. One group, wishing to change the world, belabored the historian's shortcomings. The other, wishing to preserve the world, stressed his traditional ideal.

As an outgrowth of the New History, the relativist movement antagonized historians who were already hostile to a "social science approach" and appealed to historians who were sympathetic to the social sciences. Among these latter, a pragmatic desire to make history useful still united an emphasis on values with a search for scientific laws. Partly because of the ambiguities in Beard's own thinking, very few of the New Historians in the late 1930's and early 1940's realized how much the relativist argument jeopardized their own reformed version of scientific history as well as the conservative kind. The tangle did not unravel until after the New Historians made a final effort to present a coherent case.

This effort began in the interest, not of relativism, but of social science. The Social Science Research Council was looking for some concerted strategy to bring history into closer relation to the other social sciences. Roy F. Nichols in 1942 presented to the Council a report on the inadequacies of current historical research, together with suggestions for a large-scale program of fellowships that

[22] Cf. Allan Nevins's *The Gateway to History* (1938), pp. 43-44, and Eugene C. Barker's "The Changing View of the Function of History," *Social Studies,* XXIX (1938), 149-54, on one side, and on the other Walton E. Bean's "Revolt Among Historians: Interpretation in Historiography," *Sewanee Review,* XLVII (1939), 330-41.

would, he hoped, "encourage interpretive productions of value to other disciplines." At this point a major diversion occurred through the sudden entry of Beard into the deliberations. Nichols had sent a copy of his report to Beard. In reply the latter suggested that the SSRC might appoint a committee to consider not only the relation of history to the social sciences but also the basic characteristics of historical thought. The Council thereupon convened a conference of friendly historians to decide on a course of action and invited Beard to attend.[23]

Beard's recommendations, delivered in his usual grand manner, set the course that was followed. An SSRC committee chaired by Merle Curti prepared a handbook on historical methodology, which included—as Beard specified—a dictionary of terms, a treatise on historical theory, and a statement of fundamental propositions. Beard composed the propositions, wrote the introductory chapter, and exercised a predominant influence over the whole work.[24] Although the SSRC expected an analysis of the relations of history to the "other" social sciences, the book turned out instead to be a cautious, qualified elaboration of the relativist argument. Every written history, it was argued, is a product of a particular frame of reference; but we can and should become less biased by avoiding all absolutes and recognizing our preconceptions.

*Theory and Practice in Historical Study,* published in 1946 as Bulletin 54 of the Social Science Research Council, brought the controversy over relativism to a climax. For two or three years thereafter professional meetings resounded with discussions of the subject. But the debate was different now from what it had been in the Thirties. The profession was becoming more sophisticated, the concepts at issue were more familiar, and the whole atmosphere was less hectic and urgent. Historians of many persuasions now took a good part of the relativist argument for granted, and the division of opinion between progressive and conservative schools was no longer clear-cut. Perhaps the chief service of Bulletin 54 was an uninten-

23 Minutes of the Committee on Problems and Policy, July 11, 1942, SSRC Files; Nichols to author, February 19, 1963.
24 Beard's impact is clearly evident from a comparison of the final, published report with his recommendations as set forth in Beard to Nichols, July 15, 1942, and in transcript of conference on November 8, 1942, SSRC Files. The committee did balk at Beard's draft of Proposition X and accepted instead a version composed by Louis Gottschalk.

tional one. True to its divided origins, the SSRC committee had united a constant preoccupation with the relativistic limits of history and a basic allegiance to scientific objectivity. The most important chapter spoke obscurely of objective as opposed to subjective relativism. The attempt to codify the position made its internal inconsistency, and its failure to provide positive guidance in writing history, embarrassingly transparent. The pragmatic New History had reached a dead end.

# 4

# THE RENEWAL OF HISTORY

It was suggested in the first part of this book that changes in American society and culture since World War II have somewhat revived the prestige and influence of the humanistic scholar and diminished the alienation between the professional historian and the American public. A new basis has been forming for a richer historical culture. We are now in a position to observe a parallel development on the level of theory: a revival of confidence in historical knowledge. The restoration of intellectual self-respect that has taken place since 1945 has not in any simple way resulted from improvements in social status. The intellectual transformation began before a new social adjustment became apparent, and contributed to it. But emancipation from skeptical and derivative theories of history might not have gone very far if the historian's morale and his position in American culture had not hearteningly improved.

By the mid-1950's, it is worth recalling, McCarthyism was dead, and the big foundations were reacting nervously to outraged complaints that they had long neglected the humanities. A rising concern about the quality of American culture and its criteria of excellence was in the air. A reinvigorated American Historical Association was growing prodigiously in membership and activities. These and other signs of quickening vitality must be remembered as we follow the movement of historical theory.

The first indication of a new temper appeared during the late 1940's in the animated discussion of Bulletin 54.[1] Many who participated in the discussion were clearly floundering for solid ground, but the fixed point that everyone grasped was the simple axiom that history is basically an effort to tell the truth about the past. Unless the whole business is a bad joke, the historian must be able in some meaningful degree to understand the events of the past in their own terms. The label *present-minded* now loomed up as an epithet. Even

[1] Summarized in *The Social Sciences in Historical Study* (Bulletin 64, Social Science Research Council, 1954), pp. 4-16.

the relativists, who stressed the constructive role of present values in historical thought, recognized that the great problem was not to delimit but rather to realize more fully the possibilities of historical knowledge.

A clear indication of the change in atmosphere came from young scholars with obvious liberal, and even progressive, sympathies, who now drew back from the skepticism to which the relativist argument led. "I felt somewhat isolated," J. H. Hexter remembers, "from both the new-fangled and the old-fashioned historians of the thirties and early forties. . . . While wandering in the outer darkness, I felt that it might be useful—and would certainly be pleasant—to pelt the children of light, the historians *à la mode,* with whatever missiles came my way in the course of my groping about." Hexter and other disengaged spirits now argued that the relativists wrongly equated knowledge with certainty and truth with completeness: knowledge is always open to doubt, and all truths are partial. The historian's "frame of reference" includes present values, to be sure; but it also includes a large and growing mass of data about the past. The past is just as real, and just as capable of making itself felt in the formulation of historical generalizations, as is the present.[2]

At first critics hit Beard and Becker without repudiating the larger climate of opinion in which their ideas had formed. Morton White's influential book on the great liberal thinkers of the early twentieth century, *Social Thought in America* (1949), included a penultimate chapter sharply distinguishing "the later, non-synoptic gospel according to Beard" from the pragmatic and progressive ideas of the first three decades of the century. White rejected Beard's relativism as alien to the ideas of Dewey, Robinson, and Beard himself at an earlier date. Other postwar liberals, however, broke away from the whole pragmatic, evolutionist frame of mind. These historians observed that the weaknesses of historical relativism derived at least in part from its pragmatic origins. Chester M. Destler in 1950, and Burleigh T. Wilkins with more sophistication in 1959, pointed out that John Dewey stated a theory of history much like that of the rela-

---

[2] J. H. Hexter, *Reappraisals in History* (1961), pp. 1-13, 187-91. See also Harry J. Marks, "Ground Under Our Feet: Beard's Relativism," *Journal of the History of Ideas,* XIV (1953), 628-33; Perez Zagorin, "Professor Becker's Two Histories: A Skeptical Fallacy," *AHR,* LXII (1956), 1-11.

tivist historians; and that all of them slurred a necessary distinction between judgments of fact and judgments of value.[3]

A general reaction against pragmatic and progressive ways of thinking had much to do with the retreat of postwar historians from present-mindedness. Even philosophers like White, who felt a strong affinity with pragmatism, knew in the late 1940's that the movement had lost its momentum. It could not, in truth, survive the multiple catastrophes of the midcentury. It rested on a faith in progress; and the decline of the idea of progress left pragmatic philosophy and present-minded history invertebrate. Pragmatists had cheerfully trusted in the outcome of things to establish their truth or falsity. Similarly, the New Historians had subordinated past to present because they looked to the present and future direction of history for criteria of what is important and desirable. The relativism of Becker and Beard—precipitated as it was by a crisis in the progressive faith —arose from their unwillingness to surrender that faith. In disputing the historian's claim to objectivity, both of them were defending his participation in the forward thrust of life.

All of these tendencies received a decisive check when the course of history failed to vindicate progressive values. In some intellectual circles the dream of progress had faded after World War I. Among academic historians it persisted through the Twenties and into the Thirties, then dissolved during and after World War II. The breakdown of progressive assumptions freed historians, not from dependence on the present, but from an overdeveloped commitment to it. Past history escaped from deliberate subordination to future history; and a hardheaded unwillingness to rely upon the future restored a fuller integrity to the past.

An early sign of this change of heart appeared in an article entitled "Postwar Reorientation of Historical Thinking," which Roy Nichols published in the *American Historical Review* in 1948. Nichols had felt keenly the shortcomings of history vis-à-vis the social sciences; and as a great admirer of Beard, he was originally responsible for bringing the latter into the SSRC deliberations on historiography. Now, looking back over historical theory in the interwar period, Nichols concluded that historians had pushed a "doc-

---

[3] Chester M. Destler, "Some Observations on Contemporary Historical Theory," *AHR*, LV (1950), 517-20; Burleigh T. Wilkins, "Pragmatism as a Theory of Historical Knowledge," *AHR*, LXIV (1959), 878-90.

trine of uncertainty" too far. A "heedless optimism" about the future had entrapped them in the "slavery of present-mindedness." Now, he thought, less bemused by progress, historians could throw off the enslavement and become more positive and self-confident about their own intellectual functions.

In renouncing present-mindedness, Nichols also shifted ground on the question of history's relation to the social sciences. His call for a new self-confidence among historians was, in fact, a gentle "declaration of intellectual independence." In place of the widespread sense that New Historians had had of the backwardness of their discipline in comparison with supposedly more advanced social sciences, Nichols now affirmed that history will not bear such invidious comparison; for history is not science any more than it is art or literature. It is *sui generis*.[4]

This reaction against subordination of history to the social sciences was closely connected with the parallel reaction against subordinating the past to the present. Both strategies had arisen in the early twentieth century from an idolization of progress. Both reflected an urge to catch up with the exciting growth of the social sciences and to share in their influence. After World War II, the grim, intractable dilemmas of the contemporary scene, and the narrow range of alternatives it seemed to offer, sobered the claims of the social sciences. The progressive habit of grading intellectual activity according to its degree of contemporaneity diminished. In one sense the outlook of the professional historian had come full circle: the entrenchment of scientific history in the 1870's and 1880's had required a declaration of independence from literature and philosophy; the reform of scientific history in the early twentieth century brought it under the sway of the social sciences; and a declaration of partial independence from them after World War II reconstituted the historian's autonomous identity.

During the 1950's the attitudes vaguely prefigured in Nichols' essay of 1948 became the dominant outlook in the American historical profession. But the view—it can hardly be called a program, and it had no party label—spread undramatically, without the bitter de-

---

[4] Roy F. Nichols, "Postwar Reorientation of Historical Thinking," *AHR*, LIV (1948), 78-89. See also Max Savelle's autobiographical "Historian's Progress, or The Quest for Sancta Sophia," *Pacific Historical Review*, XXVII (1958), 1-26.

bate that raged in the Thirties and Forties. The absence of pyrotechnics suggests the constructive and temperate nature of the change. Neither the critique of relativism nor the affirmation of independence was dogmatic. Both trends made headway through an enlargement of intellectual sympathies and a reduction of the sharp ideological cleavage of the preceding decades.

On the score of relativism, historians did not swing back to the simple faith in a hard, external reality, and the accompanying distrust of their own shaping imagination, that characterized scientific history. The age of realism and naturalism in American culture had passed. Historians no longer considered their own subjectivity as exclusively a problem or a barrier to struggle against. It was that, of course. The task of historiography would always require the utmost divestment of bias and the penetration of a realm beyond the immediate self and its immediate society. But historians now knew that this achievement is not simply an act of self-effacement, not an effort to register passively the harmonies of an evolutionary pattern. It calls for a creative outreach of imagination and draws upon all the resources of the historian's human condition.

Accordingly, the historian can and should make use of his present in the very act of transcending it. Hexter wrote in 1954: "History thrives in measure as the experience of each historian differs from that of his fellows. It is indeed the wide and varied range of experience covered by all the days of all historians that makes the rewriting of history—not in each generation but for each historian—at once necessary and inevitable." [5] Thus the relativity of history can be accepted without apology as a challenge to intellectual adventure. Standing at the intersection between past and present, the historian can reject the pragmatic doctrine of his subservience to present purposes while welcoming the incentives and general awareness of the present in discovering new vistas of the past.

The relativity of history in this sense did not put it at a disadvantage in relation to science. The relativism of the Thirties, imprisoning the historian in his contemporary world, reflected a sense of the inferiority of history as a science. The relativity of the Fifties, emphasizing the positive opportunities of the historian's observational position, took the invidious sting out of the comparison. Physicists had learned to live as happily with their principles of relativity and un-

[5] Hexter, *op. cit.*, p. 13.

certainty as historians had learned to live with theirs. Both appreciated the importance of imaginative insight in the strategy of inquiry, and neither now drew extravagant conclusions from the downfall of the nineteenth century concept of science as a statement of absolute causal laws governing and explaining all things.

Similarly, the revival of the historians' self-respect relaxed the tensions between history and the social sciences. Less interested now in spurning others than in becoming themselves, historians seemed in some ways more receptive than they had been earlier to the teachings of their sister disciplines. Far from rejecting social science, Nichols coupled his call for independence with a continuing appeal for receptiveness to the methods of the social sciences. The principal statements of historical theory in the following years repeatedly attested the interest of leading historians in utilizing the thinking of their fellow workers in other fields. But many insisted now on utilizing such thinking in their own way and for their own distinctive ends. Instead of considering the social sciences as upstart rivals, in the manner of prewar conservative historians, or history as the handmaiden of the social sciences, after the usual fashion of the New Historians, postwar historians consider these disciplines as contributory to history. Once rid of the inferiority complex that provoked both antagonism and servility before World War II, historians look outward for intellectual stimulation and assistance without quarreling so much about the desirability of doing so. The new mood is enabling them to draw more fruitfully on the behavioral disciplines than they could under the influence of the indiscriminate enthusiasm and the reactive hostility of the 1930's.

Important differences of outlook in the profession certainly remain, and they still tend to be expressed in terms of relations with the social sciences. The debate is more temperate and constructive now. It usually presupposes a pluralistic appreciation of the many varieties of history and of social science; and hardly anyone denies that part of the contemporary culture with which historians interrogate the past resides in the social sciences. The issue goes rather to the nature of historical and scientific argument.

Some historians, in the positivist tradition, still regard scientific explanation—the testing of general laws by application to specific events—as the sole model of historical explanation. They expect by this means to achieve increasing agreement on problems of causation. They consider their colleagues regrettably vague, superficial, and short in analytical rigor. Against this view others contend that the historian is essentially a dramatist, whose narrative logic can never be simplified by any general theories and whose real task is to grasp the unanalyzable complexity of things.[6] Most historians occupy a position somewhere between these extremes: undaunted by the openness and imprecision of historical discourse, yet glad to have the help of any systematic concepts that can offer partial clarification of a particular historical problem. Most would probably agree with H. Stuart Hughes that "the historian's supreme technical virtuosity lies in fusing the new method of social and psychological analysis with his traditional storytelling function." [7]

The shift to an eclectic attitude on history's relations with its neighbors may even be followed in some of the postwar activities of the Social Science Research Council. At first the historians associated with the Council resumed their prewar campaign to teach their colleagues to be social scientists. Since Bulletin 54 had not done this, a new Committee on Historiography undertook to "sell" to the profession the "basic concepts" of the social sciences. All of the committee members earnestly espoused the "social-science approach" that had arisen in the 1930's. This they elaborated, though without the explicit present-mindedness evident before the war, in the Council's Bulletin 64, published in 1954 after many vicissitudes. Every page assumed that the social sciences provide history with its only reliable source of theory and techniques of proof; historians should therefore model themselves on their brethren.[8]

A different point of view emerged, however, from a separate conference of leading historians that the Council sponsored at Princeton in 1953. Whereas the SSRC committee concerned itself exclusively with what the historian should become, the conference discussed what he actually is. It concluded that the historian makes estimates of

[6] Lee Benson and Cushing Strout, "Causation and the American Civil War: Two Appraisals," *History and Theory*, I (1961), 163-85.
[7] H. Stuart Hughes, *History as Art and as Science* (1964), p. 77, and "The Historian and the Social Scientist," *AHR*, LXVI (1960), 35-38, 44-46. See also William B. Munro, "Clio and Her Cousins," *Pacific Historical Review*, X (1941), 403-10; René Albrecht-Carrié, "The Social Sciences and History," *Social Education*, XVI (1952), 315-18; W. Stull Holt, "History and the Social Sciences Reconsidered," *Kyklos*, IV (1955), 389-96; R. E. McGrew, "History and the Social Sciences," *Antioch Review*, XVIII (1958), 276-89.
[8] *The Social Sciences in Historical Study* (1954).

complex situations, judging which universals are present and to what extent; that he resembles in this respect an administrator rather than a scientist; and that he should not try to become a social scientist, though he should make use of abstractions drawn from social science or from any other reputable source. These sentiments did not come from old fogies, but rather from scholars like Robert R. Palmer and Oscar Handlin, whose intellectual antecedents went back to the New History and who had a healthy respect for the social sciences as well as an ability to employ their procedures.[9]

A third SSRC committee on historiography, appointed in 1956 to carry on the work of the first two, showed much less assurance about how to reform the historical profession. Composed largely of veterans of the earlier committees, the new one started with the same aim of promoting the explicit, systematic procedures associated with the social sciences. This committee was influenced, however, by the rising respect for the humanistic complexity of historical thought. It decided to find out what historians were doing for themselves in the way of arriving at sound generalizations, and accordingly solicited essays from specialists in several fields. The final report was an inconclusive confession of the difficulties of categorizing historical generalizations.[10]

Meanwhile among social scientists there were signs of a renewed appreciation for historical perspective. The predominant attitude in the decade after World War II remained—indeed became more —antihistorical under the influence of a "behavioral approach" pledged to precise quantification of the activities of the human machine. Nevertheless, in certain relatively backward fields, notably the new area studies, a genuine reciprocity between historical and systematic analysis developed. By the 1960's appreciation of the need for historical and speculative thought if the study of man was to escape triviality seemed on the rise.[11] If the vogue of behavioralism and

[9] R. D. Challener and M. Lee Jr., "History and the Social Sciences: The Problem of Communications," *AHR,* LX (1956), 331-38. See the wry comment on this and other conferences in C. Vann Woodward's "Report on Current Research: American History," *Saturday Review,* XXXVI (April 4, 1953), 16.
[10] Louis Gottschalk, ed., *Generalization in the Writing of History* (1963).
[11] It is significant that the new journal *Comparative Studies in Society and History* has attracted contributions most readily from students of non-Western areas. On the possibility of a larger historical dimension in the social sciences see Robert A. Dahl's "The Behavioral Approach in Political Science," *American Political Science Review,* LV (1961), 771.

the related vogue of cybernetics are indeed losing their sectarian exclusiveness, social scientists may be able to join historians in comparative historical studies with the mutual sympathy and advantage that have already developed in some of the area programs.

It should be evident from what has been said so far that historians, in acquiring a more confident and perhaps more sophisticated attitude toward the social sciences, have discovered more widely and deeply than ever before the humanistic implications of their own craft. As they ceased to feel inferior to, or resentful of, the social sciences, many came to regard as positive assets those human qualities of history that are neither reducible to formula nor susceptible of proof. This raised anew an old issue. Delivered from a parochial dispute over their standing as scientists, postwar historians faced the wider question of whether history is an art *or* a science. In view of the rough division of the American educational curriculum into "arts" and "sciences," it was perhaps inevitable that theoretical problems would again be posed in these classic terms. Yet the enhanced self-confidence and the eclectic outlook of most historians prohibit any simple choice. They assert the participation of history in art as well as science; they deny its possession by either.

One of the more obvious humanistic aspects of history that professional scholars have rated highly in recent years is its connection with literature and philosophy. The breach that the early scientific historians made, and most of the New Historians perpetuated, between history on the one hand and literature and philosophy on the other, began to close in the 1930's, chiefly through the influence of Becker and Beard and the search for values that they initiated. The concomitant awakening of a special interest in intellectual history among some professional scholars also pulled them toward the humanistic disciplines; and the penetration into professional circles of the popular interest in biography exerted another humanizing influence.[12] These forces were just beginning to impinge upon the still powerful currents of scientific history in the 1930's. Only since then has the academic schism between history and the humanities largely healed.

The engagement of postwar historians with literature goes beyond the question of "style" to reach the very form and texture of their

12 J. R. Strayer, ed., *The Interpretation of History* (1943), pp. 121-48.

work. Many of them, to be sure, write better than all but a few of their predecessors, and some of them use literary sources with a sensitiveness never before attained by American professional historians. In addition, there is now a widespread awareness that reality does not present a natural, perceptible pattern for the organization of historical knowledge, nor can the historian rely on any extrinsic formula for arranging his facts. His knowledge becomes meaningful only as he shapes it into a symbolic design. "The unity of past action that is seen or sensed or understood by the historian is both the starting point and the goal of his art." [13] His task is therefore akin to that of a novelist or a playwright. Whereas academic historians traditionally considered "style" as an icing on the cake of scholarship, which some liked because it would improve the taste and others distrusted because it might spoil the appetite for solid nourishment, many now realize that style as an external application is inevitably artificial; for any authentic craft blends manner and matter, form and substance, in a single creative process.

A growing sensitiveness to philosophy has accompanied the new interest in aesthetic form, and both have sprung from the same root. Both reveal a new consciousness of the human and the problematical. Both have resulted from the breakdown of the old assumptions of scientific history, chief among which was an unexamined faith in evolutionary progress. Deprived of their erstwhile assurance that human affairs fall naturally into a sequence of adaptation and growth, historians have had to probe matters they once took for granted: the overarching patterns of history, the character of historical thought, and the form of historical work. The philosophic impulse, like the aesthetic, feeds upon the need for coherent design.

Although the ability of American historians to deal with theoretical and speculative issues has matured considerably since World War II, receptiveness to such issues really began with the relativist controversy of the Thirties. Perhaps the most lasting contribution that Beard and Becker made to the profession was in awakening a philosophical consciousness. If the relativists failed to reach their own immediate goals and even lost their way in confusion, they neverthe-

[13] Loren Baritz, "The Historian as Playwright," *Nation*, CXCV (1962), 341. See also C. Vann Woodward, *The Burden of Southern History* (1961), pp. 27-39.

less ended the age of innocence in American historiography. When the American Historical Association thirty years ago published a *Guide to Historical Literature* (1931), it listed just ten works on the philosophy of history, only one of which had appeared since 1875. Presumably nothing written in the late nineteenth or twentieth century, except Spengler's *Decline of the West,* merited the attention of a professional historian. A comparable section of the new *Guide to Historical Literature* that the AHA brought out in 1961 included 59 titles, almost all published in recent decades. The best work still came from Europeans. Although American scholarly journals now welcome theoretical and speculative essays, no American historian has yet produced a major book on the nature of history. It was, however, the relativist controversy, together with the concurrent influx of refugee scholars from Europe, that reopened American access to European historical theory.

In the thirty years since Beard came seriously to grips with Croce, Heussi, and others, that access has widened immensely. Uninterrupted intellectual communication across the Atlantic has, more than any other factor, raised the level of theoretical discourse in the American historical profession. Americans have learned in the last two decades from such notable refugees as Ernst Cassirer, Karl Löwith, Carl G. Hempel, and Hajo Holborn; from such Continental philosophers and historians as Friedrich Meinecke, Raymond Aron, Henri Marrou, Ortega y Gasset, Carlo Antoni, and Pieter Geyl; and from such various Englishmen as Herbert Butterfield, Isaiah Berlin, and E. H. Carr.[14] The single greatest influence has probably been that of a formerly neglected Oxford philosopher, R. G. Collingwood, whose posthumous work, *The Idea of History* (1946), quickly attracted an important following among American historians; its imprint was

[14] Ernst Cassirer, *An Essay on Man* (1944); Karl Löwith, *Meaning in History* (1949); Carl G. Hempel, "The Function of General Laws in History," in *Readings in Philosophical Analysis,* ed. Herbert Feigl and W. S. Sellars (1949), pp. 459-71; Friedrich Meinecke, "Values and Causalities in History," in *The Varieties of History,* ed. Fritz Stern (1956), pp. 268-88; Raymond Aron, *Introduction to the Philosophy of History* (1961); Henri Marrou, *De la connaissance historique* (Paris, 1955); Ortega y Gasset, *Toward a Philosophy of History* (1941); Carlo Antoni, *From History to Sociology* (1959); Pieter Geyl, *Debates with Historians* (1958); Herbert Butterfield, *History and Human Relations* (London, 1951); Isaiah Berlin, *Historical Inevitability* (London, 1954); Edward H. Carr, *What Is History?* (1962). See also Hans Meyerhoff's influential anthology *The Philosophy of History in Our Time* (1959), and W. H. Walsh's *An Introduction to Philosophy of History* (London, 1958).

already visible upon Nichols' essay of 1948.[15] On the whole, this in-pouring of speculative thought has confirmed and strengthened the association of history with the humanities; but it has done so in-directly, by clarifying the special character of historical knowledge.

Perhaps the most fundamental methodological proposition that has come out of this latest encounter with European thought is the necessity for historians to participate subjectively in whatever past they wish to understand. No amount of scientific analysis or synthesis can take the place of that crucial act of human empathy by which the historian identifies himself with another time and place, re-enacting the thoughts and reliving the experience of people remote from himself. Thus he tries to catch the distinctive resonance of a person, a situation, and an age, as it manifests itself amid the other phenomena among which it arises and into which it passes. Scien-tific historians, both of the orthodox and of the pragmatic school, neglected this empathic function. They located themselves outside of the people they studied. Today's historians feel much more need to get inside historical situations, for they depend less on an external scheme of meaning. Here too the contemporary historian departs from the evolutionist assumption that events can be adequately ex-plained as fixed links in a continuous chain of cause and effect. Un-willing to presuppose an all-embracing framework for history— rejecting both the old framework of evolutionary progress and the cyclical framework of the newer historical metaphysics—academic historians are finding meaning in history within the specific physi-ognomy of concrete human situations.

Few Americans, however, go all the way with Collingwood's ar-gument that history is "nothing but the re-enactment of past thought," a view that allows no scope for scientific thinking, for im-personal causes, or for general propositions in historical thought. No meaning is entirely intrinsic to a single situation. An adequate his-torical explanation should include a retrospective knowledge of con-sequences and conditions that the actual participants did not have. Most historians today seem to accept the responsibility of taking their stand at no one place, either inside or outside the scene of ac-tion. Instead, they move about, viewing a situation from within and from above, blending subjective identification with objective analy-sis, uniting art with science, recognizing the complementarity of per-

[15] Nichols, *op. cit.*, *AHR*, LIV (1948), 85.

spectives and the multiplicity of relationships by which the historian —and he alone—undertakes to grasp a transition in human affairs in its full contextual significance.[16]

It is unlikely that Americans will claim for historical knowledge the radical uniqueness and preeminence that European "historicists" like Collingwood insisted upon in their dispute with the natural sciences. For the typical American historian, if my story is correct, the special character of history inheres not in a definite and superior method of its own but rather in the convergence of all sorts of techniques and insights upon the explanation of human experience, in its full existential complexity, within the limits of a definite span of time. Having regained a strong position in American academic life by foreswearing isolation on the one hand and exclusive alliances on the other, historians are not likely to revert to either stance in the foreseeable future. Instead, they can rejoice in a mediating role. They can cheerfully concede the more systematic and intensive nature of other disciplines while maintaining their own unspecialized identity. Perhaps better than any other discipline in the American university, history can resist the partition of knowledge into two cultures.

16 The following are in diverse ways illustrative: Leonard Krieger, "The Horizons of History," *AHR*, LXIII (1957), 62-74; Trygve Tholfsen, "What Is Living in Croce's Theory of History?" *The Historian*, XXIII (1961), 283-302; W. B. Willcox, "An Historian Looks at Social Change," *Journal of Social Issues*, XVII (1961), 50-65; John T. Marcus, "The Changing Consciousness of History," *South Atlantic Quarterly*, LX (1961), 217-25; "The Nature of History," AHA *Newsletter*, II (April 1964), 5-7.

# AMERICAN HISTORY

In turning from the theories that historians have professed to the actual history they have written, we should not expect to find a simple, one-to-one correlation. Connections between theory and practice in historical work are usually circuitous and indistinct. The fluid, unsystematic character of the historian's enterprise rarely permits him to go directly from a general theory to a particular proof. He is even likely to be a bit unclear about what his historiographical assumptions are. Trying to discern the shape and order of a concrete situation, he may feel his way into it quite successfully without clearly formulating the preferences that guide him.

In fact, a taste for theoretical niceties, a strong urge for clarity and precision in basic assumptions, can actually prove a handicap in dealing effectively with historical data. To move freely through the complex web of human experience, historians need to employ simultaneously a multitude of causal hypotheses. Accordingly, a good historian is not likely to operate consistently within a single theoretical framework: any one perspective restricts his range of vision. Like literature, history can gain richness from the interpenetration of conflicting ideas, from the tensions of a divided allegiance.

On the other hand, a scholar does not readily change his basic cast of mind. Although his theoretical premises may be various and ambiguous, they are relatively stable influences on the history he writes. The general view of history a man acquires at an early age may not be fully displayed for many years; for the patient, aggregative nature of historical research often postpones the publication of major books until relatively late in life. A recent analysis of the most highly regarded books on American history published between 1920 and 1950 shows that the median age of their authors at date of publication was forty-nine. Some of these books had been in preparation for only four or five years, others for twenty or thirty.[1]

During this slow gestation, the prevailing intellectual milieu is constantly changing. New theories of history gain currency. As a result, the most substantial studies may appear after the principal as-

[1] John W. Caughey, "Historians' Choice: Results of a Poll on Recently Published American History and Biography," *Mississippi Valley Historical Review,* XXXIX (1952), 295.

sumptions on which they rest have gone out of fashion. No strictly professional historian in America published a major book prior to the twentieth century. Thus the orthodox scientific historians—from whom we might offhand expect stately institutional histories in the Eighties and Nineties—produced their best work after a reaction against their philosophy had arisen in the historical profession and elsewhere. The New Historians published their master works between the two world wars, although Frederick Jackson Turner had sketched out much of their program of inquiry in the 1890's. The reaction against the New History that began twenty years ago has not yet come fully to fruition. A coherent story of historical practice must take account of this cultural lag.

It must also take account of the more specific intellectual influences that are always impinging upon and reshaping historical interests and interpretations. Even when our general conception of history remains relatively fixed, our grasp of a concrete past is continually in flux. Scholarship steadily heaps up new knowledge, testing and revising our understanding of events. Also, the unfolding of new history keeps altering the appearance of events further back. In many subtle ways the focus of attention shifts. These adjustments may go on for a long time before the theoretical framework itself gives way.

Thus the course of scholarship on American history is intricate indeed. Nevertheless, the general trends in historical theory do provide a rough guide to practice. Each of the major schools of professional historians has emphasized certain features of the American past at the expense of others. Each has also held a characteristic view of the meaning of America.

The orthodox scientific historians inherited an over-all view of American history from the leading amateurs who dominated writing in the late nineteenth century. Both the amateurs and the founders of the profession were chiefly concerned with the evolution of national unity. For them American history culminated in the achievement of a more perfect union. We may call these scholars conservative evolutionists. In contrast, it will be useful to call the New Historians progressives; for their notion of the American heritage stemmed from social protest. Rather than unity, they emphasized diversity. To the progressives the Civil War was not a culmination but an episode in a still unfinished conflict between sections and economic groups. Finally, the postprogressive historians who have emerged since World War II are taking neither unity nor diversity for granted. The old assumptions have dissolved and reformed. The central question has come to be the nature and extent of stability in American history.

# 1

# THE CONSERVATIVE EVOLUTIONIST
## AS AMATEUR

During the last quarter of the nineteenth century five American scholars published major works on American history. Moses Coit Tyler mapped out the history of American writing in the colonial period and later in the Revolutionary period. Theodore Roosevelt brought back to life the early American frontier. John Bach McMaster traversed the whole span of history between the revolution and the Civil War. Henry Adams concentrated on the years from 1800 to 1817. James Ford Rhodes, working on an equally large scale, studied the era of the Civil War.[1]

None of these men was basically a professional historian. None of them had any formal training beyond a regular college education. Roosevelt, Adams, and Rhodes did not need to engage in remunerative employment. They wrote history in the leisure afforded by their own ample financial resources. The other two, Tyler and McMaster, held academic posts during most of their adult life. Tyler, the product of a large family with modest means, and McMaster, who was left penniless as a young man by the collapse of his father's oil speculations, had to work for a living; but neither of them secured an appointment to teach history until after he had made a public reputation writing it. Tyler, escaping first from the pulpit and then from the press, launched his historical studies while teaching English literature at the University of Michigan. McMaster published his first volume while holding an instructorship in engineering at Princeton. A third member of the group, Henry Adams, taught history at Harvard during a seven-year interlude (1870-77) in his life as a literary gentleman; but his principal historical works were written later, and he left

---

[1] Tyler, *A History of American Literature, 1607-1765* (2 vols., 1878), and *The Literary History of the American Revolution, 1763-1783* (2 vols., 1897); Roosevelt, *The Winning of the West* (4 vols., 1889-96); McMaster, *A History of the People of the United States from the Revolution to the Civil War* (8 vols., 1883-1913); Adams, *The History of the United States during the Administrations of Jefferson and Madison* (9 vols., 1889-91); Rhodes, *History of the United States from the Compromise of 1850* (7 vols., 1893-1906).

more of an impression on Harvard than it left on him. In sum, the leading authorities on American history in the late nineteenth century were self-made scholars. They belonged, by background or by enlistment, to the patrician tradition of historical writing.

All five of these scholars derived from New England or New York, the areas with the oldest historical societies and the most vigorous historical culture. New England especially had dominated historical writing in America since the seventeenth century. This was largely due to the intellectual and moral earnestness of the Puritan heritage—a heritage that drove men to keep diaries, to remember the example of their ancestors and hold themselves accountable to posterity, to prefer fact over fiction, and to welcome solid instruction in the record of human responsibility. Of the five leading American historians in the late nineteenth century, only McMaster was neither by family nor by education a product of New England. The most accomplished historian of the lot, Henry Adams, had the strongest roots in that region, and the influence of New England also told on the others. Roosevelt began writing his first historical work while an undergraduate at Harvard; Rhodes yearned toward and eventually moved to Boston from the Western Reserve, in itself an extension of New England; and Tyler, who spent most of his adult life elsewhere, never mentioned the region without mentally genuflecting.

All five wrote, nonetheless, as national historians, making a conscious effort to overcome the limitations of sectional prejudice. During the late 1870's and 1880's, when they embarked upon the works that made them famous, a mood of sectional reconciliation was softening the acerbities of the mid-nineteenth century. In literature the nostalgic "local color school" transformed the vanishing peculiarities of individual regions into national possessions. In philosophy an Hegelian taste for reconciling antitheses prevailed: it expressed a similar impulse to unite conflicting values into a national synthesis.

Accordingly, the leading patrician historians in the late nineteenth century took as a dominant theme the forging of national unity and power in a crucible of sectional diversities. These historians remembered the Civil War as the great public experience of their early, formative years. Indeed, it contributed largely to their interest in history: it inspired Henry Adams' first excursion into historical scholarship, it turned McMaster's interests from science to American history, it helped to divert Tyler from the ministry to journalism and literature, and it furnished Rhodes with the subject of his master work.[2] Looking back in the aftermath of the war at earlier American history, these scholars read it throughout as a story of nationalizing principles overcoming the selfish, parochial interests of individual groups or areas.

Moses Coit Tyler explored the intellectual history of the colonial period in *A History of American Literature, 1607-1765* (1878), and in doing so he focused attention on the transition from isolated, disparate settlements to a growing "colonial fellowship." "Henceforward," he concluded, "American literature flows in one, great common stream, and not in petty rills of geographical discrimination. Our future studies will deal with the literature of one multitudinous people, variegated, indeed, in personal traits, but single in its commanding ideas and in its national destinies." Henry Adams also qualified a special fondness for New England with an embracing sense of national destiny. Like Tyler's account of colonial thought, Adams' *History of the United States during the Administrations of Jefferson and Madison* (1889-91) dwelt heavily on a contrast between the principles of New England and Virginia. Yet Adams, again like Tyler, rebuked the narrowness of both sections. He too closed his work with an apostrophe to a united people, advancing victoriously in spite of the mistakes of both the Virginia Republicans and the New England Federalists.[3]

John Bach McMaster, entirely a product of the Middle Atlantic states, carried the story of national progress forward to the eve of the Civil War. His *History of the People of the United States* (1883-1913) was distinctively the history of a whole people, observed not in prismatic patterns but in a single kaleidoscopic movement. McMaster disparaged the South for its backwardness, its sluggish response to the forces of improvement. In general, however, he sub-

[2] Adams' first historical essay, a deflation of the Pocahontas legend, was a covert attack on the southern aristocracy written in London in 1862 when his propagandist activities went awry. See Henry B. Rule, "Henry Adams' Attack on Two Heroes of the Old South," *American Quarterly*, XIV (1962), 174-84. Cf. Eric F. Goldman, *John Bach McMaster, American Historian* (1943), pp. 8-10; Howard Mumford Jones, *The Life of Moses Coit Tyler* (1933), pp. 110, 148; Robert Cruden, *James Ford Rhodes: The Man, the Historian, and His Work* (1961). Theodore Roosevelt, the youngest of the group, was less than seven when the war ended.

[3] See the fine analysis in William Jordy's *Henry Adams, Scientific Historian* (1952).

ordinated sectional differences to nationwide trends. In examining the Negro problem, the Industrial Revolution, political ideas, public schools, and a host of other topics, his eye ranged methodically from place to place across the length and breadth of the land, suggesting an infinitude of local variations upon a common theme. His work ended with Lincoln's invocation in March 1861 of "the chorus of the Union."

James Ford Rhodes plunged into the maelstrom of sectional conflict, writing like McMaster from a decidedly northern point of view. Yet his was a northernism lacking in sectional bitterness and capable of understanding the Civil War not only as grand but also as tragic. Rhodes's *History of the United States from the Compromise of 1850* (1893-1906) tempered the northern tradition with an inclusive nationalism, a widespread distribution of responsibility for slavery, and a relatively generous view of southern motives. His *History* sealed the late nineteenth century compromise between the sections; for it upheld the North on the wartime issues of disunion and slavery while upholding the South on the postwar issues of military rule and Negro suffrage.

Although a number of amateur scholars in the late nineteenth century—notably Charles Francis Adams Jr. and William B. Weeden—studied local and regional topics in a broad critical perspective,[4] only one of the most eminent patrician historians chose a sectional setting for his principal work. Theodore Roosevelt's *The Winning of the West* (1889-96) recounted the history of the trans-Appalachian frontier from 1760 to 1807. Significantly, he approached it as an arena of national adventure. His was not a story of conflicts between East and West, nor of differences between Northwest and Southwest. It was essentially a military history of how the advance agents of American destiny wrested the possession of a continent from Indians, from Englishmen, and from nature. For Roosevelt, as much as for his peers, national solidarity was the permanent result of a disappearing sectional past.

Woven through the theme of national unity was a second motif

---

[4] Charles Francis Adams Jr., *Three Episodes of Massachusetts History* (2 vols., 1892); William B. Weeden, *Economic and Social History of New England, 1620-1789* (2 vols., 1890). See also Robert L. Beisner, "Brooks and Charles Francis Adams Jr., Historians of Massachusetts," *New England Quarterly,* XXXV (1962), 48-70, and William S. Powell, "Philip Alexander Bruce: Historian," *Tyler's Quarterly Historical and Genealogical Magazine,* XXX (1949), 165-84.

that defined the nineteenth century historians' sense of America: its dedication to freedom. In the historical thought of the 1880's freedom and union did not stand opposed to one another; they formed a single national design. If America was the testing ground and the standard bearer of freedom, every step forward in its unification strengthened the fabric of freedom. Looking back from the 1880's, historians beheld the Revolution as the confluence of American history, the Civil War as its climax; and the war recapitulated the meaning of the Revolution. Both demonstrated that freedom and unity triumphed together in American experience.

From this point of view, freedom was not a particular strand of American history, distinct from and opposed to other dominant strands and therefore requiring its own particular explanation. It was a presiding genius, a pervasive energy that needed only to be exemplified. While respecting America's indebtedness and affiliation to Europe, the leading historians assumed that liberty was distinctively the essence of American nationality. Adams sketched the national character by contrasting America's open society with the "artificial," class-ridden societies of Europe.[5] Tyler interpreted the American Revolution as the outcome of principles so deeply held that the mere anticipation of possible tyranny could rouse rebellion. Roosevelt celebrated the restless initiative of western men as the essential American spirit. McMaster described the growth of national power and wealth and the widening of political and social opportunities as aspects of a single process. Rhodes felt no inconsistency in acclaiming the emancipation of the Negro from slavery and the emancipation of the postwar South from northern oppression, because both developments extended the sphere of freedom.

While the principal amateur historians shared a somewhat similar view of the meaning of American history, in choice of subject matter they displayed an impressive breadth and range of interest. Several of them, of course, concentrated on political and military events. As successors to Parkman and Prescott and Bancroft, they inherited the special interest of patrician scholarship in wars and in the actions of heroic leaders. Adams built his masterpiece upon a

[5] See especially Volume I, Chapter 6, and Adams' comment to a friend: "I have pretty much made up my mind not to attempt giving interest to the society of America in itself, but to try for it by way of contrast with the artificial society of Europe." Worthington C. Ford, ed., *Letters of Henry Adams* (1938), vol. I, p. 328.

groundwork of international relations, which he considered "the only sure base for a chart of history." Both he and Rhodes gave their best efforts to the appraisal of statesmanship. Both were also shrewd students of military affairs, as were Roosevelt and the great historian of seapower, Alfred T. Mahan. On the other hand, most of the leading amateur scholars took a wider view of the historical process than had their midcentury predecessors. Even Rhodes, who professed a sovereign disdain for "the routine of work and the round of pleasures of the majority—those blank pages of history which, if written over, could indeed be tiresome," wrote more than a few such pages.[6] Adams, a much greater historian, tried more seriously to extend the limits of political history. Troubled by "the want of some formula" to explain the social forces underlying governmental policies, he depicted individual leaders as manifestations of national traits; and he enclosed his political narrative within an elaborate cross-sectional analysis of American society at the beginning and at the end of the period he covered.

Although Adams and Rhodes never felt really at home at a distance from the centers of power, other amateur historians with a less toplofty outlook had a positive zest for exploring the common experience of the great mass of the American people. Roosevelt, while acknowledging Parkman as his master, gained from his own intimate frontier experience an unParkman-like familiarity with ordinary folk. Roosevelt's annals of border warfare embraced all the multifarious activities of the western settlements. He described vividly not only wilderness adventures but also the creation of a civilization. Tyler, in gathering up for the first time the intellectual history of early America, did not confine himself to great ideas but instead treated literature as an expression of the life and spirit of the people. McMaster made the life of the people his grand, distinctive theme, for he wrote in the conviction that no nation had ever before advanced so wonderfully in material prosperity and moral sensibility.[7]

---

[6] Harvey Wish, *The American Historian* (1960), p. 226.

[7] McMaster, *op. cit.,* vol. I, pp. 1-2. In this brief sketch I have perhaps unjustly passed over Edward Eggleston, whose one important scholarly book, *The Transit of Civilization from England to America in the Seventeenth Century* (1901), was in some ways unique. A free-lance writer without either personal means or institutional support, Eggleston had a more genuinely democratic outlook and a correspondingly broader sense of the historical process than either Tyler or McMaster.

Thus, two of the five foremost historians of the United States in the late nineteenth century, Tyler and McMaster, fixed upon previously neglected dimensions of history as their special concern, and the others widened the scope of political narrative.

In venturing out upon a broad terrain, these men were following the example of the most celebrated English historians of the third quarter of the century: the example, above all, of Lord Macaulay, who gave a model of how social history might be written; of Henry Buckle and his disciple W. E. H. Lecky, who created a kind of intellectual history that seemed to measure the progress of society; and finally of John R. Green, whose *Short History of the English People* (1874) outsold any other historical work in America during the latter decades of the century.[8] American historians were writing then in an atmosphere charged with increasing deference toward English society and thought. Such deference was virtually a hallmark of the American aristocracy of culture. Although American historians valued the distinctive vigor and freedom of American life, they relied on English models for improving its tone and expression.

Like their English mentors, most of the leading American historians in the late nineteenth century had not broken completely with the older romantic approach to the past. Their outlook, to be sure, was realistic and evolutionary. We may call them, on balance, scientific historians; for they wrote as modern men appraising the past from the outside, observing events and individuals as loosely connected fragments of on-going experience, more interested in the literal accuracy of photographic statement than in the intuitive grasp of a unified, symbolic design. Yet their style of thought was transitional and eclectic; their approach to history was in some ways traditional.

Most of them considered themselves engaged in a literary as well as scientific task. For Rhodes, Tyler, and Roosevelt especially, history remained a branch of literature. Objectivity must temper but should not supplant the claims of art. This, in effect, was Henry Adams' position too. Although he tried, more rigorously and strenuously than any of his contemporaries, to make history a genuine science, an unyielding dedication to aesthetic objectives irradiated his history. Adams' greatness as a historian is partly due to a sustained tension between these allegiances.

[8] Frank Luther Mott, *Golden Multitudes: The Story of Best Sellers in the United States* (1947), pp. 241-42, 310.

As inheritors of a literary tradition, the gentlemen-historians still had an interest in the role of individuals. Rhodes, for example, excelled in judicious estimates of political and military leaders. Tyler—following St. Beuve—cast his narrative in the form of a succession of biographies. McMaster, to be sure, moved steadily away from personalities, eliminating biographical vignettes in his later volumes; and some of the less prominent amateur historians in the late nineteenth century eschewed this sort of thing altogether. Nevertheless, even the pedestrian McMaster, who derived his conception of history from Macaulay, retained some sense of the scenic and pictorial.

Finally, historians who conceived of themselves as men of letters relished the making of moral judgments on men and events. The office of distributing praise and blame, and pronouncing the magisterial verdict of history, was always dear to patrician hearts. The gentlemen of the late nineteenth century, convinced of their independence from partisan bias and zealous to instruct their often misguided countrymen in the lessons of national experience, agreed with Tacitus's injunction "to let no worthy action be uncommemorated, and to hold out the reprobation of posterity as a terror to evil works and deeds." Adams did this indirectly, behind an arch and mannered pose of aloofness. Roosevelt, Tyler, McMaster, and Rhodes spoke out directly and loudly. A secure faith in evolutionary progress enabled them to suppose that they, standing at the summit of history, could truly judge the actions and standards of earlier times by their own without loss of scientific objectivity. Each of them aligned himself with the successful forces in American history, with the national unity and orderly freedom that now seemed well established.

# 2

# THE CONSERVATIVE EVOLUTIONIST
## AS PROFESSOR

Much the same can be said of the first professional historians. Drawn into graduate work in the 1870's and early 1880's, when egalitarian ideas were at a discount, they entered through the gates of the modern university into the earnest and confident world of the aristocracy of culture. They acquired, if indeed they did not already possess, the high-minded conservatism of the patrician historians. They embraced the same vision of American history as a story of freedom realized and stabilized through the achievement of national solidarity. In general, this first generation of professional historians received the work of Adams, Rhodes, McMaster, Tyler, and Roosevelt with great respect. For all their desire to set the record straight, the earliest professionals avoided challenging the interpretations of the most illustrious contemporary amateur writers. The difference between the two groups lay not in their respective social values but in the form of their historical work.

Most of the early professional scholars broke more sharply with the literary tradition. Carrying further the impersonality of scientific history, they paid little attention to the role and less to the character of individuals. They scorned scenic display and dramatic incident. They tried to withhold explicit moral judgments on people and circumstances, not because they questioned history's didactic usefulness but because they supposed that objective scholarship would reveal the evolution of morality in the march of events without intrusive comment by the writer. They assumed that the reader could make his own fair and independent judgment if given an unobstructed view of the past.[1]

Finally, the professional historians gave up the effort to encompass a wide range of social and intellectual life. Instead, they concen-

[1] The classic argument for scientific neutrality was made, however, by an amateur historian, Henry C. Lea. See his presidential address, "Ethical Values in History," AHA *Annual Report* (1903), vol. I, pp. 53-69, and Charles Homer Haskins' endorsement in "Henry Charles Lea," *Studies in Medieval Culture* (Oxford, 1929), p. 262.

trated on institutions. Whether it was the town meeting, the business corporation, Negro slavery, or something else, the institution was a form of organization, a gradually evolving structure. To study institutions was to study the morphology of history, to trace through time the skeleton of a society as biologists were tracing the underlying structure of other organisms. Not all institutional studies were specifically political by any means. At Johns Hopkins Herbert Baxter Adams encouraged the study of educational systems. G. E. Howard of the University of Chicago published a three-volume *History of Matrimonial Institutions, Chiefly in England and the United States* (1904). A vigorous interest in the history of economic institutions led Harvard in 1892 to call W. J. Ashley to the first chair of economic history and inspired the newly formed Carnegie Institution in 1904 to plan a multivolume economic history of the United States.[2] Regardless of subject, however, the approach of the institutional historians was essentially constitutional. On marriage and divorce, Howard confined himself to successive legal and ceremonial prescriptions. Herbert Baxter Adams and his students dealt chiefly with legislation, and the economic historians also focused attention on the operations of government.

Part of the appeal of institutional history derived from its impersonal, presumably objective character. To fix attention on the formal constitution of group activities was to simplify and clarify historical problems, to delimit the issue of motivation, and to bypass fortuitous, individual behavior. Institutional history lent itself to coordinated effort. A number of scholars could study the same institution—each in a different setting—in the hope of deriving by comparative analysis a larger grasp of historical development. One of the chief stimuli for institutional history came from the rise in the nineteenth century of historical jurisprudence, which in the hands of Sir Henry Maine and others revealed apparent continuities and connections between widely separated eras.

Another part of the attraction of institutional history sprang from the conservative, organic nationalism of the post-Civil War decades. Believing that the national state, now evolving toward empire, constituted the highest form of organization mankind had yet achieved, scholars studied its polity and its sanctions with profound respect. In-

[2] N.S.B. Gras, "The Rise and Development of Economic History," *Economic History Review,* I (1927), 12-34.

stitutional history taught a sober regard for constitutional processes, for "a government of laws rather than men," as the phrase went. It recorded the slow upbuilding of national organization, thereby demonstrating that neither abstract theories nor selfish interests counted for much in human affairs in contrast to the structural principles gradually unfolded over a long span of time. In sum, the institutionalists had two closely related biases: in favor of homogeneity in society, and in favor of continuity in history. At a time when leaders of opinion rejoiced in the attainment of national unity and feared the outbreak of new social cleavages, there was much satisfaction in studying the unifying ligaments within a sequence of historical development.

Before this conservative evolutionism affected American academic thought it permeated the German universities, where the study of institutional history centered. Thence institutional history spread to England, through John M. Kemble, the magisterial Bishop Stubbs, and Stubbs's successor at Oxford, Edward A. Freeman.[3] It reached America partly through the students who flocked to Germany after 1870 and partly through the influence of the English Teutonists.

One of the special fascinations of institutional history lay in a search for origins. Tracing continuities and unearthing antecedents, the institutionalists were drawn backward especially to the colonial period. There they left their strongest mark. Moreover, they characteristically sought the origins of colonial institutions in earlier European experience. The first professional historians were more consistent than some of their amateur associates in rejecting the popular patriotism that imputed a radical uniqueness to American history. In writing institutional history, conservative professors felt the solid ground of the European past beneath their feet.

At first, by an easy combination of Anglophile and Germanophile sentiment, the Americans simply followed the lead of the English Teutonists. Pursuing an hypothesis of Sir Henry Maine, the early professional historians at Harvard and Johns Hopkins tried to prove that American local institutions originated in the forests of Germany. Primitive Teutonic forms of local government—so the theory went —had been transplanted to England by the Anglo-Saxons and then carried by their descendants to New England, where they re-emerged

[3] G. P. Gooch, *History and Historians in the Nineteenth Century* (1959), pp. 271-72, 317-29.

in the shape of the town meeting. Herbert Baxter Adams made the study of Germanic origins the mainstay of his seminar in the 1880's.[4] Similarly, at Harvard in 1883 Albert Bushnell Hart included the Teutonic hypothesis in a set of "fundamental principles of American history" that defined the initial program of the conservative evolutionists:

1. No nation has a history disconnected from that of the rest of the world. . . .

2. Institutions are a growth, not a creation: the Constitution of the United States itself is constantly changing with the changes in public opinion.

3. Our institutions are Teutonic in origin: they have come to us through English institutions.

4. The growth of our institutions has been from local to central. . . .

5. The principle of union is of slow growth in America: the Constitution was formed from necessity, and not from preference.[5]

The program soon had to be amended: the shallowness of the Teutonic thesis was already being demonstrated in England. In 1883 Frederic Seebohm's *The English Village Community* argued forcefully that this institution derived from the Roman villa rather than the German mark. Several years later a skeptical young student of Herbert Baxter Adams, Charles McLean Andrews, challenged the whole theory. Having made in his doctoral dissertation a careful study of the early settlements on the Connecticut River, Andrews read a paper before the American Historical Association in 1890 pointing out that the Teutonists relied at every point on superficial similarities rather than demonstrable genetic connections. The New England town differed significantly from its supposed ancestors. Moreover, the very existence of self-governing communities of free men in Anglo-Saxon times rested on no reliable evidence. Another young colonial historian, Edward Channing, supplemented Andrews'

---

[4] Herbert Baxter Adams, *The Study of History in American Colleges and Universities* (U.S. Bureau of Education Circular No. 2, 1887), p. 173; Edward N. Saveth, *American Historians and European Immigrants, 1875-1925* (1948), pp. 16-26.

[5] G. Stanley Hall, ed., *Methods of Teaching and Studying History* (1886), p. 3.

argument two years later by explaining the genesis of Massachusetts towns in terms of immediate political experience.[6]

Thereafter the investigation of European origins turned from the remote to the immediate English background of American colonial history. Interest in local institutions correspondingly diminished. The Teutonists had postulated that the towns were the original units from which larger political organizations evolved. Andrews showed, on the contrary, that the general government created the towns. Central institutions came first. One must therefore look to the framework of British policy to understand the American colonies. From the ruins of the Teutonic school rose in the 1890's the much more impressive and lasting Imperial school. English historians had largely neglected the study of imperial organization: the Americans now told the Old World something new about itself.

The pioneer was another young man, a student of John Burgess at Columbia named Herbert Levi Osgood. In 1887 while supporting himself by teaching high school in Brooklyn, Osgood published an article identifying "the central thread" of American colonial history. It is, he said, the growth of a system of imperial administration and the problems that system engendered.[7] Osgood felt keenly the general desire of conservative intellectuals in the late nineteenth century to understand American history in a wider transatlantic context. He wished above all to show that early America had not made a sudden, radical break from the European past. The patriotic insularity of mid-nineteenth century historians like George Bancroft and Richard Hildreth had outlived its usefulness. By looking at the colonies from the vantage point of the central government in London, one could learn that all of the truth and justice did not lie on either side of the eventual quarrel. Such a point of view strengthened Anglo-American sympathies much more concretely and directly than any fanciful Teutonic thesis. Moreover, the imperial framework gave coherence to the data of early American history and permitted a realistic comparison of institutions.

On receiving his Ph.D. in 1889, Osgood quit his high school job and used his little savings to live in London. For fifteen months he

[6] A. S. Eisenstadt, *Charles McLean Andrews* (1956), pp. 14-20; Saveth, *op. cit.*, pp. 26-31.
[7] "England and the Colonies," *Political Science Quarterly*, II (1887), pp. 440-469. See also Dixon Ryan Fox, *Herbert Levi Osgood, An American Scholar* (1924).

burrowed into the vast stores of documents in the Public Record Office. It came as a great liberation to learn how the colonies looked from the unifying perspective of London. Colonial history ceased to be a mere prelude to later American history and acquired a new interest and amplitude of its own. Establishing himself at Columbia University on his return from London, Osgood embarked on a life-long task from which he never swerved. He wrote the institutional history of the colonial period as a whole.

An address to the American Historical Association in 1898 announced his program. Here Osgood stated his most important single contribution: a classification of the colonies according to constitutional structure. Historians had conventionally grouped the colonies by region—New England, middle, and southern. Osgood divided them into chartered colonies (corporate and proprietary) and royal colonies. This grouping offered a sounder basis for comparative political analysis than either a loose geographical division or remote Teutonic analogies. A comparison of colonial constitutions revealed the gradual improvement in imperial organization that accompanied the emergence of the royal colony, which provided a better balance between local and central power than either the corporate or the proprietary form.[8] The early stages of this transition Osgood expounded in great detail in *The American Colonies in the Seventeenth Century* (3 vols., 1904-1907). Before his death in 1918, he had largely completed four volumes on the colonies in the eighteenth century, which analyzed the further development of the royal colonies and the growing opposition between British executives and colonial assemblies.

In his first years of teaching at Columbia, Osgood was fortunate to have an extremely talented student, George Louis Beer. Beer concentrated on the economic aspects of British imperial policy. Like the other conservative evolutionists who investigated economic history, he concerned himself not with economic motives but rather with the political organization of economic progress. His four volumes on British colonial policy from 1578 to 1765 treated mercantilism as an honest and progressive effort to balance and harmonize the interests of all parts of the empire.[9]

8 "The Study of American Colonial History," AHA *Annual Report* (1898), pp. 63-73.
9 *British Colonial Policy, 1754-1765* (1907), *The Origins of the British Colonial*

Meanwhile, Charles M. Andrews was working independently along lines very similar to those Osgood followed. A strong interest in European history delayed Andrews' full commitment to early American history until the turn of the century; but a trip to England in 1893 to explore medieval sources disclosed to Andrews the wealth of colonial records that Osgood had discovered four years earlier. In 1898, addressing the American Historical Association, Andrews expounded an approach to American colonial history that was largely identical with the one Osgood outlined at the same session.[10]

Andrews went a step beyond his confrere in taking the imperial point of view. A genuinely comprehensive and unprovincial history, he argued, can not confine itself to the thirteen colonies that later became the United States. It should embrace the whole Anglo-American Empire before 1776. Ultimately Andrews' far-flung research extended to the Canadian and West Indian as well as the mainland colonies. Significantly, his design did not call for similar attention to the non-English empires and peoples that contributed to the formation of the United States. After discarding explicit theories of racial continuity, the conservative evolutionists remained Anglophiles, and their American history was wholly a continuation of English history.

In the long run Andrews surpassed Osgood in mastery of British administrative history, in command of the English sources, and in finesse of craftsmanship. He advanced with careful, unhurried steps. Much of his time in the early twentieth century went into producing for the Carnegie Institution two superlative guides to unpublished English sources for early American history. He contributed a volume to the "American Nation Series," sketched out his view of the whole span of colonial history in a short book of 1912,[11] but withheld his major books until very late in life.

Although the Imperial historians disregarded both the remote

---

*System, 1578-1660* (1908), *The Old Colonial System, 1660-1754* (2 vols., 1912).
[10] "American Colonial History, 1690-1750," AHA *Annual Report* (1898), pp. 49-60.
[11] *Guide to the Manuscript Materials for the History of the United States to 1783 in the British Museum* . . . (1908); *Guide to the Materials for American History to 1783 in the Public Record Office* (2 vols., 1912-14); *Colonial Self-Government, 1652-1689* (1904); *The Colonial Period* (1912).

Teutonic "germs" of colonial history and its connection with subsequent American national history, they never questioned the prevailing bias of amateur and Teutonist scholars in favor of political unity and historical continuity. In respect to unity, they found in the imperial framework an integrating principle similar to that which national organization supplied for later American history. In respect to continuity, the colonial period became in itself the matrix of a slow evolutionary process. In effect, the Imperial historians greatly lengthened American colonial history. Both Andrews and Osgood pointed out in 1898 that the middle decades between colonization and revolution, the years from 1690 to 1760, had never been studied carefully. Colonial history would lack continuity until this neglected period was brought to light. Moreover, the origins of the American Revolution should be sought in the gradual alteration of British and colonial institutions during that long span of time.

When Andrews at length published his interpretation of the causes of the American Revolution, he framed it in these terms, as did Claude H. Van Tyne and other conservative evolutionists. Imperceptibly, over many decades, said Andrews in *The Colonial Background of the American Revolution* (1924), the mother country and the colonies drifted apart. The development of new British policies of imperial control eventually precipitated a constitutional crisis, in which a rigid, aristocratic society confronted a growing individualistic one. Irresponsible agitators with an impractical philosophy of natural rights made matters worse, but no individual or group was crucially responsible. The Americans were "obeying a law of general evolution of human society toward higher and broader forms of government and social relations." [12]

Insofar as it was a genuinely revolutionary struggle, the American Revolution did not make a congenial subject for writers of the Imperial school, and most of their work lay further back in studies of the Board of Trade, British land policy, vice-admiralty courts, rights of Parliament, and the like. Meanwhile other conservative evolutionists looked past the Revolution to American national history with much the same tendency to play down dramatic ruptures in historical continuity. In studying American national history as well as

---

[12] P. 208. See also Claude H. Van Tyne, *Causes of the War of Independence* (1922); Charles H. McIlwain, *The American Revolution: A Constitutional Interpretation* (1923).

American colonial history, orthodox scientific historians interpreted change in terms of a unifying structure of institutions and principles.

Inevitably, for the period after 1776, the history of the federal constitution provided a focus comparable to that which imperial organization gave to colonial history. Andrew C. McLaughlin, one of the best of the constitutional historians, pointed out this continuity forcefully. He saw that the great problem of the early republic was the old colonial problem of reconciling liberty with central authority, and that the framers of the Constitution in 1787 in effect reestablished the old division of powers between local and central government. McLaughlin's contribution to the "American Nation Series," *The Confederation and the Constitution, 1783-1789* (1905), hailed the reorganization of these years as a conservative triumph of experience over impractical theories of pure democracy. Indeed, all of McLaughlin's writings breathed a deep respect for the continuity of the Anglo-American legal tradition.[13]

The same may be said of Edward S. Corwin, perhaps the finest of the historians of the American constitution. Corwin taught politics at Princeton from 1905 until his retirement more than forty years later. Many of his writings were historical commentaries on contemporary problems, and much of his best work appeared in the form of long articles in law reviews; so he did not leave an easily accessible corpus of historical scholarship. No one, however, matched the subtlety and precision with which he laid out the history of constitutional ideas. He looked upon constitutional law as designed primarily to set limits to legislative power. In tracing the evolution of such related concepts as judicial review, due process, and "vested right," Corwin emphasized the widespread desire of great American lawyers to give national protection to private rights threatened by legislative majorities. He depicted constitutional history as a stately interplay of doctrines that, at their best, vindicated not equality or state rights, but freedom and national power.[14]

[13] Pp. 35-42, 275; *The Foundations of American Constitutionalism* (1932).
[14] "The Doctrine of Due Process of Law Before the Civil War," *Harvard Law Review,* XXIV (1911), 366-85; "The Basic Doctrine of American Constitutional Law," *Michigan Law Review,* XII (1914), 247-76; *The Doctrine of Judicial Review* (1914); *John Marshall and the Constitution* (1919); "The 'Higher Law' Background of American Constitutional Law," *Harvard Law Review,* XLII (1928-29), 149-85, 365-409.

Constitutional issues also bulked large in the professional historians' treatment of the Civil War. Here was a time when unity and continuity had obviously and drastically broken down. Nevertheless, the main strategy of conservative evolutionists was to examine that fierce struggle as a stage in the consolidation of a united nation. In doing so, they strove to transcend sectional bias just as the Imperial school was striving to transcend a provincial bias. Most of the professional scholars went a step beyond James Ford Rhodes in withholding blame for the war and in taking a broadly national point of view. A constitutional approach was most useful in this regard; for one could argue that the South fought at least in part to defend an old-fashioned doctrine of state sovereignty that was being outmoded by the march of progress. By linking the slavery issue to a dispute over constitutional principles, historians dignified the position of both sections. The South clung to the original conception of the Union as a compact of states, whereas the North fought for the integral nation that the Union had become.[15]

On the subject of Reconstruction, the most recent period with which scholars dealt at all carefully, the acknowledged master was William A. Dunning. His doctoral dissertation, submitted at Columbia in 1885, concerned the history of the Constitution from 1860 to 1867. Although he taught a notable seminar in political philosophy and spent much of his scholarly energy on a history of European political theories, his influence on the study of the Reconstruction period proved much more enduring. Dunning published two outstanding books on that era, one a collection of essays on constitutional problems, the other a general volume in the "American Nation Series."[16] In these he maintained such Olympian aloofness from the northern bias of previous scholars that southerners flocked to Columbia to study under him. Their monographs on the reconstruction process in individual states gave substance to the "Dunning school."

---

[15] This was the view of Woodrow Wilson in *Division and Reunion, 1829-1889* (1893), p. 211. A residue of antisouthern feeling survives in John W. Burgess, *The Civil War and the Constitution* (2 vols., 1901). See Thomas J. Pressly, *Americans Interpret Their Civil War,* 2nd ed. (1962), pp. 162-63, 202-206.
[16] *Essays on the Civil War and Reconstruction* (1897); *Reconstruction, Political and Economic, 1865-1877* (1907). On the Dunning school see Wendell H. Stephenson's *The South Lives in History: Southern Historians and Their Legacy* (1955).

Essentially, Dunning agreed with the view that Rhodes was simultaneously expounding. Turbulent and unlovely as the post-Civil War years were, they could be shaped to the evolutionary pattern of national progress if one endorsed their final outcome: the reunion of North and South through the overthrow of military despotism and the restoration of white supremacy. Thus Dunning, like Rhodes and the vast majority of American historians, ratified the results both of the Civil War and of its aftermath. In the first, national unity triumphed over slavery in the South; in the second it triumphed over radical democracy in the North. This approach required, of course, a disapproval of the Radical policies of Congress in the late 1860's— a disapproval that paralleled Corwin's distrust of legislative majorities, Andrews' disdain for irresponsible agitators, and McLaughlin's criticism of the excessively democratic spirit unleashed by the Revolution.

In the case of Reconstruction, the conservative interpretation inevitably disparaged Negro claims to equality and Negro participation in government. Dunning shared the almost universal anti-Negro bias of white Americans of his day; and it is now common to assume that racial stereotypes determined his treatment of the period. Yet the distinctive feature of Dunning's book, *Reconstruction, Political and Economic, 1865-1877* (1907) was not his distaste for "barbarous freedmen" but rather the careful balance he held in discussing conditions in the South and in the North. His primary theme was the temporary breakdown and eventual recovery of probity and constitutional order in all parts of the country. Believing in reason as a restraint upon popular passions, in the educated man as a saving remnant, and above all in the majesty of the law, Dunning held no brief for the lawless tactics of the southern whites in regaining power. To him it was not only the rule of ignorance, force and fraud in the South that was deplorable but the misgovernment and commercial chicane of the whole period. The Negro was not simply an inferior race; he was a symbol of the political and economic corruption that pervaded the postwar era.

While these intensive studies of particular periods and topics were coming out, a crusty, determined little man at Harvard, Edward Channing, was methodically working his way through the whole sweep of American history on the basis of original sources. A proper

Bostonian descended from illustrious families, Channing was converted as an undergraduate from law to history by the teaching of Henry Adams. Only after establishing himself as a full professor, however, did Channing at the turn of the century take up the single task of the rest of his life. Thereafter he renounced church attendance, scholarly meetings, social engagements, and general faculty business in order to concentrate completely on *A History of the United States* (6 vols., 1905-25).

This was the most ambitious, and in some ways the crowning result of the conservative evolutionist approach to American history. The preface to the first volume declared Channing's grand theme: "the victory of the forces of union over those of particularism." "The guiding idea in the present work," he continued, "is to view the subject as the record of an evolution, and to trace . . . the story of living forces, always struggling onward and upward toward that which is better and higher in human conception." On the colonial period Channing adopted by and large the imperial point of view, arguing that the colonies and the mother country "drifted apart" in the century before 1760 through a gradual divergence of institutions. On the national period he applauded the growth of large-scale organization, praised Jefferson's loyalty to national interests, treated Jackson as a narrowly sectional man, and allowed the Old South a generous measure of sympathy.

Yet Channing's *History* does not fit neatly within a consistent style of historical thought. It was in one respect more old-fashioned than orthodox scientific history, and in another respect more modern. Educated entirely in Boston by men unblessed with German seminar training, Channing had about him something of the amateur litterateur. He gave much more attention to the role and traits of leading individuals than a true institutionalist would have done; his pages twinkled with personal comments on men and events. On the other hand, Channing also modified the conservative, institutional approach under the influence of new ideas being advanced by the reformers in the historical profession. By 1912, when Volume III dealing with the Revolution and the Constitution came out, the author was convinced that these had resulted chiefly from economic forces. "All historical development," he observed, "is founded upon industry, upon the necessity of supporting life, and the way in which it is done. . . . The historian owes a debt of deepest gratitude to the economist." [17] The last volumes of the *History* made much of the Industrial Revolution, underscored a conflict between agrarianism and capitalism, and depicted a great gulf between the divergent civilizations of North and South. Channing failed to relate effectively his social and economic data to his political narrative. He remained always in a special sense a conservative Boston Brahmin. Yet his work illustrates the fruitful interplay of competing ideas in a sensitive historical mind.

[17] J. F. Jameson and Edward Channing, *The Present State of Historical Writing in America* (1910), p. 25. In general see Samuel Eliot Morison, "Edward Channing: A Memoir," Massachusetts Historical Society *Proceedings*, LXIV (1931), 250-84.

## ·§ 3 §·

## THE RISE OF PROGRESSIVE HISTORY

In 1907 at a session of the American Historical Association devoted to American constitutional history, Professor William MacDonald read his colleagues a warning. Danger has arisen, he said, that an overemphasis on the economic and social aspects of American history will lead to neglect of the part that law has played in shaping our development.[1] At a time when legalism was so clearly dominant in historical scholarship the warning seems absurdly premature. The Imperial school and the Dunning school had only just emerged; the major works of Andrews, Corwin, McLaughlin, and others were far in the future. Yet MacDonald knew what he was talking about. A powerful undertow was at work, pulling younger men more sharply in the direction in which Channing was turning. It was the pull of the New History, already tugging strongly in those early years before James Harvey Robinson popularized its program.

To understand the history that the New Historians actually wrote we shall have to look behind Robinson's formal creed. The desire to widen the scope of history, to relate it to the present, and to link it with the social sciences were conscious objectives at a very early date; Frederick Jackson Turner espoused them in the 1890's. But these objectives do not in themselves explain what he and his successors did. The crucial fact underlying both their theory and their practice was a broad sympathy with the spirit of reform then developing in contemporary life. This sympathy induced an attitude toward change and continuity quite different from that of their conservative colleagues.

As progressives, the New Historians had a vivid sense that a great turning point had arrived in American experience. They wanted to participate in the transformation and to explain it. Accordingly, they studied history with more interest in interpreting change than articulating continuity. Carl Becker spoke for his own generation when he commented that the eighteenth century *philosophes* had little use for the conception of continuity in history, which nineteenth century historians established: "The reason is that the eighteenth-century

[1] AHA *Annual Report* (1907), vol. I, p. 79.

171

Philosophers were not primarily interested in stabilizing society, but in changing it." [2] Moreover, the kind of change that seemed important to the *philosophes* of the twentieth century was not the slow unfolding of institutions through an inner logic of their own, but rather the kind wrought out of conflicts of interest and clashes of purpose. To be progressive was to believe that the progress of society was neither automatic nor secure, but had to be won at every step, over entrenched opposition.

For progressive historians, then, the dynamics of change constituted the great issue of historical inquiry. Their rebellion against the dominant kind of institutional history did not arise from indifference to politics or constitutions; much of their research concerned political organizations, particularly political parties. But they wanted above all to know how and why these agencies responded to and effected transformations in a wider field of action. Whereas conservative evolutionists concentrated on the character of institutions, understood in terms of their origins, progressives focused on changes in institutions, explained in terms of a surrounding environment.[3] Their insistence on broadening the scope of history was, therefore, in large measure a search for the causes and conditions of change. Earlier explorations of social and economic history had proceeded from other motives, so it is little wonder that progressive historians paid only grudging compliments to such predecessors as McMaster and Macaulay. Their portrayal of historical environments seemed too static for progressive tastes, too little designed to explain the changes in human affairs.

In turning outward from institutional to environmental history, progressive scholars were in another respect turning inward. They were becoming in a certain sense more nationalistic than their conservative colleagues. The latter, seeking the European origins of our institutions, had inveighed against a provincial Americanism. The progressives, by diverting emphasis to environment and change, tended to lose sight of European origins and backgrounds. They took the Old World heritage for granted and asked how the American environment modified it; or they associated that heritage with reactionary elements resisting the life-giving forces of change. This, of

---

[2] *The Heavenly City of the Eighteenth-Century Philosophers* (1959), pp. 96-97.
[3] Oscar Handlin, "The Central Themes of American History," *Relazioni del X congresso internazionale di scienze storiche*, vol. I (1955), pp. 152-53.

course, was the emotional significance of Turner's celebration of the frontier as the crucible of a new nation and the matrix of a unique society. The nationalism of conservative scholars was, on the whole, not so positive and assertive. For them the growth of national unity provided a great theme because it was synonymous with stability, order, and the preservation of an ancient freedom. The progressives, on the other hand, cared less about the form of American unity and more about the content of American uniqueness.

Accordingly, quite a different vision of America shone through the pages of progressive historiography. For one thing, it was a livelier America, constantly in flux, full of real and vital conflicts between contending groups. It was less stable and more deeply divided than the America of the conservatives; it was less securely anchored in traditions reaching back across the centuries. It was a nation that had progressed, and achieved its own special identity, by breaking away from the bonds of a European past. For another thing, the essential meaning of America was differently construed. To progressive historians that meaning inhered not so much in the achievement of national unity as in a continuing struggle toward democracy. Significantly, the emergence of the progressive school coincided with an immense growth in popularity of the principal symbols of American democracy. Around the turn of the century Lincoln overtook and surpassed Washington as the most popular biographical subject. Simultaneously the reputation of Jefferson recovered from the long eclipse of the preceding forty years.[4]

The new historical attitudes that progressivism engendered spread quickly, widely, and selectively. To a remarkable extent the outstanding progressive historians sprang from two sections of the country: the Midwest and the South. Turner hailed from a Wisconsin town that still served in his youth as a trading post for nearby Indians. Robinson came from Bloomington, Illinois. Becker and Beard grew up on midwestern farms, one in Iowa, the other in Indiana. James T. Shotwell was a product of a country town in western Ontario. The list might be greatly extended. Most of the prominent conservative professors of history, on the other hand, were easterners: Herbert Baxter Adams, Andrews, Osgood, and Channing bore the

[4] Harry R. Stevens, "Contemporary American Biographical Writing: Trends and Problems," *South Atlantic Quarterly,* LV (1956), 362; Merrill Peterson, *The Jefferson Image in the American Mind* (1960), p. 229.

indelible stamp of New England; Beer and Dunning were affluent sons of New York and New Jersey respectively.

Many midwesterners and southerners felt that an eastern elite had too long monopolized the writing of American history. Resentfully, they complained that the typical eastern historian could scarcely see west of the Hudson River and that American history was being written mainly as an extension of New England.[5] Though not entirely untrue, the complaint was exaggerated. Its very extravagance proclaims the sense of cultural inferiority with which a new generation of home-trained scholars confronted the established citadels of academic authority. Their drive to democratize American history, to embrace its continental dimensions, and to read it as a struggle against privilege reflected the democratization of academic life itself.

The first and most influential of the new men was Frederick Jackson Turner. Never has an American historian had so much impact in so few pages; rarely has one acquired great influence at so young an age. Alert, strikingly handsome, enthusiastic, and quite without idiosyncrasies, Turner arrived at Johns Hopkins in 1888 to study for a Ph.D. under Herbert Baxter Adams. He brought with him the conviction that the present age surpassed all previous eras, that its glorious hallmarks were science and democracy, and that its heroes were Darwin, Spencer, and Lincoln. He had already learned at the University of Wisconsin to write institutional history. He had already discovered a special interest in the history of his Midwest. Having little to learn from Adams, Turner reacted against the latter's overemphasis on European origins. He was more impressed by the pioneer progressive economist, Richard T. Ely, who opened to him the exciting possibilities of an economic interpretation of political and social change.[6]

Nevertheless, until after his return to Wisconsin to teach, Turner

[5] C. W. Alvord to Carl Becker, April 23, 1917, Archives of Illinois Historical Survey (University of Illinois); Curtis Nettels, "Frederick Jackson Turner and the New Deal," *Wisconsin Magazine of History*, LVII (1934), 258.
[6] The best biographical account to date is Fulmer Mood's "The Development of Frederick Jackson Turner as a Historical Thinker," *Publications of the Colonial Society of Massachusetts*, XXXIV (1943), 283-352. I am also indebted to Lee Benson's *Turner and Beard* (1960), pp. 1-91; Henry Nash Smith's *Virgin Land: The American West as Symbol and Myth* (1957), pp. 291-305; "The Reminiscences of Guy Stanton Ford" (Oral History Research Office, Columbia University, 1956), pp. 77-92; and *The Early Writings of Frederick Jackson Turner*, ed. Fulmer Mood (1938).

was somewhat of a conservative evolutionist, seeing America primarily in terms of continuity and connections with Europe. Then he took his stand against the "wise men from the East," as he called his conservative, European-oriented colleagues; and in a relatively few years all of his major ideas flowered. Impressed by the deep agricultural unrest of the early 1890's and the apparent exhaustion of good cheap land, he concluded that America had reached a momentous turning point. He came upon the writings of an Italian economist, Achille Loria, who taught that access to land dominated the evolution of society. These ideas, converging perhaps with similar theories of Henry George and with a rich legacy of popular myths about the West, convinced Turner that natural conditions largely determined American history. In effect, he turned to nature for the key to history. His famous address of 1893, "The Significance of the Frontier in American History," argued with a poetic lilt that the encounter with the wilderness explained the distinctive features of America: above all, its democracy and its amalgamation of many peoples and sections into a united nation.

In 1893 Turner was still more interested in national unity than in conflict and diversity. He still thought of the frontier as if it were an institution, to be described as a single, organically unfolding process. Consequently, his frontier thesis was relatively easy to accept. It evoked an old grass-roots pride; it explained all of America—East as well as West—as a product of the same experience; it did not break with the conservative emphasis on homogeneity. Thus the frontier thesis mediated between old and newer styles of interpretation. It greatly eased the transition to more abrasive types of progressive historiography.

Turner never repudiated his frontier thesis; indeed, he invoked its imaginative appeal on many subsequent occasions. But his empirical research turned in another direction. Keenly aware of tensions between East and West as well as North and South, he put his seminar to work on a study of sections, which he defined as "natural economic groupings in American history." [7] From the mid-Nineties to the end of his life, the character and interplay of sections was his principal scholarly interest. He organized the whole program of teaching in American history at Wisconsin along sectional lines. His only com-

[7] Preface to Orin G. Libby, *The Geographical Distribution of the Vote of the Thirteen States on the Federal Constitution, 1787-8* (1894), p. vii.

pleted, integrated book, *Rise of the New West, 1819-1829* (1906), had as its main theme the transition from a predominantly nationalist to a predominantly sectionalist outlook in the United States during that decade; and Turner treated the politics of the period as expressions of unstable sectional alliances. Laboring prodigiously to define his sectional units, he made original use of maps and statistical data.

The sectional interpretation went much beyond the frontier thesis in revealing conflict and diversity while stopping short of the rigid categories of a class interpretation. Sections appealed to Turner as historical configurations partly because of their fluidity and complexity. They offset a deadening uniformity in national life without destroying its organic wholeness. Turner thought of his own beloved Old Northwest not only as a section but also a balance wheel between other sections; he thought of sectional politics as a politics of compromise. Like many early twentieth century progressives, Turner both discerned and deplored class conflict. To him the "common man" was an undifferentiated American: and the section, as a "natural economic grouping," seemed more American than "artificial" class alignments. Professor Charles G. Sellers Jr. has pointed out that "Turner and his followers muted the discordant note of class struggle by transposing it into conflict between distinct geographical sections." [8]

In fact the sectional approach was so fluid that it proved for Turner a will-o'-the-wisp. The sections refused to remain distinct. The more intensively he studied, the more they blurred, overlapped, and subdivided. For many years he struggled to write a sequel to *Rise of the New West,* a sectional interpretation of the period 1830-1850. When he died in 1932, the magnum opus was still unfinished.[9] Nevertheless, he had reached some striking insights and opened an immense domain to others. It is not too much to say that he supplied the first dynamic design for a history of American society.

Although applied to all parts of the country, Turner's method was especially influential in raising to professional importance the history of the West and the antebellum South. Around 1910 scholars working independently of one another discovered that various major

[8] Charles G. Sellers Jr., "Andrew Jackson versus the Historians," *Mississippi Valley Historical Review,* XLIV (1958), 626.
[9] *The United States, 1830-1850: The Nation and Its Sections* (1935).

issues, previously interpreted in other terms, arose from western expansion. One put forward the thesis that western land hunger produced the War of 1812, another that it brought on the Mexican War. A student of British policies toward the frontier thought he found there a new key to the American Revolution. Behind the notorious Kansas-Nebraska Act a Kansas professor detected legitimate western aspirations for a transcontinental railroad.[10]

This kind of economic "realism" tended to downgrade both the constitutional and the moral aspects of the slavery question and to encourage a new look at the Old South. Inspired by the Turnerian approach, southerners probed the "natural economic groupings" within southern history, distinguishing between the planters of the Black Belt and the farmers of the up-country, and between the Virginia of Jefferson and the South Carolina of Calhoun. Some—notably William E. Dodd and Thomas Jefferson Wertenbaker—analyzed conflict and change in southern history with a strong democratic animus against the planter aristocracy. On the other hand, Ulrich B. Phillips, who was no less indebted to Turner, dedicated one of his books "To the Dominant Class of the South," with whom he largely identified himself.[11] As a conservative Turnerian, Phillips gave his best efforts to studying slavery not as an abstract legal system but as a way of life revealed in the account books and other records of the great plantations. His genial, immensely learned *American Negro Slavery* (1918) argued that it had failed as an economic institution but succeeded as a form of social accommodation between a superior and an inferior race.

Actually, all of the important Turnerian studies bore upon na-

10 Warren H. Goodman, "The Origins of the War of 1812: A Survey of Changing Interpretations," *Mississippi Valley Historical Review*, XXVIII (1941), 173-74; William E. Dodd, "The West and the War with Mexico," *Journal of the Illinois State Historical Society*, V (1912), 159-72; C. W. Alvord, *The Mississippi Valley in British Politics* (2 vols., 1917); Roy F. Nichols, "The Kansas-Nebraska Act: A Century of Historiography," *Mississippi Valley Historical Review*, XLIII (1956), 190-94. Alvord's book was actually a hybrid offspring of the Imperial school and the Turner school.

11 Phillips, *A History of Transportation in the Eastern Cotton Belt to 1860* (1908); William E. Dodd, *Statesmen of the Old South* (1911), and "Profitable Fields of Investigation in American History, 1815-1860," *AHR*, XVIII (1913), 522-36; Thomas Jefferson Wertenbaker, *Patrician and Plebian in Virginia* (1910). Turner's influence on Dodd and Phillips is elucidated in Wendell H. Stephenson's *The South Lives in History: Southern Historians and Their Legacy* (1955), pp. 29-94.

tional issues, if only because Turner approached sections and frontiers as parts of a larger whole. His specific influence intermingled readily with other strains of progressive thought. For example, John R. Commons, another Hopkins-trained student of Richard T. Ely, cast the history of organized labor in a form similar to that Turner gave to the history of the West. Commons and Turner sat in the same seminar at Johns Hopkins, came from similar midwestern small-town backgrounds, and carried on their historical studies in the same milieu. Commons joined the Economics Department at Wisconsin in 1904, and when Turner went to Harvard six years later he tried to persuade the Wisconsin History Department to appoint Commons as his successor.[12] Commons shared Turner's conception of history as a conflict between competing interests. He shared equally an enthusiasm for the stabilizing effects of balance and compromise. In 1893, the very year of Turner's epochal address, Commons published a book on the distribution of wealth in America, which argued that a momentous turning point had arrived now that free access to land was disappearing. Later, in a four-volume *History of Labor in the United States* (1918-35), largely written by his students, Commons explained the distinctive traits of the labor movement in much the way that Turner explained the distinctive traits of America as a whole. For both men the key was opportunity in the form of free land. Commons' best student, Selig Perlman, brilliantly restated the point. The American environment produced a labor movement that was characteristically job-conscious rather than class-conscious.[13] For more than a generation most labor historians remained true to the spirit of Frederick Jackson Turner.

Turnerians were too sensitive to economic conflicts, however, to ignore class struggle; and sectionalism was simply not relevant enough to contemporary interests to contain fully the progressives' sense of social reality. Most political discussion in the early twentieth century transcended sectional lines. In all parts of the country progressives rallied against a presumably monolithic opposition. They commonly thought of America as fundamentally divided between

[12] "George Clarke Sellery Room Dedication," *Wisconsin Magazine of History,* XLI (Autumn 1957), 50; John R. Commons, *Myself* (1934), pp. 43, 128-37; George D. Blackwood, "Frederick Jackson Turner and John Rogers Commons— Complementary Thinkers," *Mississippi Valley Historical Review,* XLI (1954), 471-88.
[13] Selig Perlman, *A Theory of the Labor Movement* (1928).

two socio-economic strata: the democratic many and the privileged few. This simple dualism had been part of the ideology of democratic protest movements in America throughout the nineteenth century. Even conservatives customarily regarded American political history as an enduring contest between Jeffersonian and Hamiltonian principles.[14] Progressives simply restored a rich social content to a dualism that conservatives figured in abstract constitutional terms. In their rising desire to curb big business, progressives interpreted the polarity of American politics as a persistent struggle between the great mass of the people and an overly powerful economic class. By 1910 Turner himself was writing with a new sense of the solidarity of a "monied aristocracy" in American history. "We may trace the contest between the capitalist and the democratic pioneer," he averred, "from the earliest colonial days." [15]

Although chiefly attributable to American reformist attitudes, this hardening of the progressive view of social conflict also owed something to Marxist influence, now seeping into American scholarship for the first time. In the process of convergence, Marxism softened at least as much as progressive history stiffened. Following E. R. A. Seligman, some of the more advanced progressive intellectuals found they could separate Marxism as an analytical tool from socialism as an ideological credo. Moreover, they vastly simplified the tool. They dispensed entirely with the dialectical pattern of true Marxist analysis, and they diluted its historical materialism into a simple emphasis on the political importance of property. In effect, Marxism helped to educate American scholars to the historical significance of other sorts of property relations in addition to the ownership of land.

The conception of American history as primarily a conflict between over- and underprivileged classes emerged most clearly at Columbia University. There Seligman's influence was strong. There James Harvey Robinson declared early in the twentieth century that a "sober and chastened form" of Marxism "serves to explain far more of the phenomena of the past than any other single explanation ever offered." [16] There too Carl Becker, already a student of Turner's,

[14] John Fiske, *Essays Historical and Literary* (1907), vol. I, pp. 169-70; William A. Dunning, *Truth in History and Other Essays* (1937), p. 45.
[15] *The Frontier in American History* (1920), pp. 110-11, 325.
[16] James Harvey Robinson, *The New History* (1912), p. 51. Seligman's influence on Beard stands out in the latter's review essay, "A Socialist History of France," *Political Science Quarterly*, XXI (1906), 120.

came under Robinson's instruction; and Becker's powerful dissertation, *The History of Political Parties in the Province of New York* (1909), related the rise of a revolutionary movement to lower-class aspirations for a larger share of the political and economic power held by the great provincial magnates. In contrast to Turner, Becker identified the urban workingmen as the quintessentially revolutionary group.

It was at Columbia also that Charles A. Beard pressed the knife of class conflict to the very heart of American political institutions. In two famous monographs published in 1913 and 1915, Beard offered belligerently revisionist accounts of the writing of the Constitution and the subsequent formation of American political parties. More than other progressive historians, Beard aimed deliberately to overthrow conservative institutional history, with its emphasis on the slow unfolding of abstract principles.[17] He interpreted both the Constitution and the rise of Jeffersonian democracy as convulsive shifts of power dictated by severely materialistic considerations.

Beard's tough-minded zeal to purge history of false idealism drove him to specify the property interests of both sides—the interests of opponents of the Constitution as well as those of its makers. He was thus more consistent than many progressives, and in a sense more impartial; but his typology suffered from excessive concreteness. Adhering to the usual dualism of progressive thought, he fixed upon the small debtor farmers and the large holders of public securities as the central antagonists. Out of a desire to shock and to prove the case in a very literal way, his *An Economic Interpretation of the Constitution* attributed the Founding Fathers' statecraft to the immediate, personal gain they could realize through appreciation of their own security holdings.

This narrow attention to personal motivation gave the book much notoriety and obscured Beard's larger concern with general class interests. Actually, his stress on security holdings was functional to a broad distinction he drew between two classes of property owners.

---

17 This is especially apparent in Beard's attack on McLaughlin for exaggerating the continuity of the Anglo-Saxon legal tradition and the role of ideas in history (*AHR*, XVIII [1913], 379). See also Beard's *An Economic Interpretation of the Constitution* (1913), pp. 8-13, and *Economic Origins of Jeffersonian Democracy* (1915). On Beard's relation to his intellectual milieu see the suggestive essays by Richard Hofstadter and others in *Charles A. Beard: An Appraisal,* ed. Howard K. Beale (1954).

Beard divided American political society into "personalty" interests on one hand and "realty" interests on the other. The Constitution and the Federalist party were the instruments of merchants, manufacturers, and associated speculators and creditors; Jeffersonian democracy rested on a broad farming basis. Essentially, Beard arrayed capitalists, whom he considered for the most part creditors, against resident landowners, whom he regarded chiefly as debtors.

Behind this somewhat unreal distinction it is not hard to discern a rural midwesterner's sensitiveness to the alien world of commercial chicanery and financial manipulation. Although Beard approved of the concentration of political power the capitalists brought about, he disliked their speculative motives. Until late in life he avoided stock investments because he regarded them as gambling.[18] One may also see in Beard's interpretation how the ideas of a fellow midwesterner, Frederick Jackson Turner, were being adapted to a sharper class analysis of American history. In effect, Beard was combining Turner's stress on property in the form of land with Marx's stress on property in the form of capital.

Having written nothing on American history prior to 1912, Beard arrived on the scene of United States historiography late in the progressive era. His impact was chiefly felt after World War I. Two imposing dissertations that Beard's students at Columbia wrote before the war testify, however, to the immediate possibilities of extending his ideas backward and forward through American history. Arthur M. Schlesinger's *The Colonial Merchants and the American Revolution* (1918) and Dixon Ryan Fox's *The Decline of Aristocracy in the Politics of New York* (1919) were written under the formal supervision of Osgood, but their inspiration came primarily from Beard.[19] Studying the politics of the American merchant class in the 1760's and 1770's, Schlesinger interpreted its opposition to British policies in a manner quite similar to Beard's explanation of the role of that class in creating a national government. Both saw the merchants as defending existing business interests against hostile legislation, by Parliament in one case, by state legislatures in the other; but in the revolutionary situation the merchants confronted a cruel dilemma when popular mobs outreached their own limited in-

[18] Interview with Miriam and Alfred Vagts, May 3, 1961.
[19] Arthur M. Schlesinger, *In Retrospect: The History of a Historian* (1963), pp. 43, 53.

tentions. Fox carried the story forward from 1800, detailing the continued efforts of the New York merchant class to defend business interests while it gradually and painfully adjusted to the popularization of power. He portrayed the Whig party of the 1840's as the outcome of this adjustment. Although he could not detect a persistent division between real and personal property, he saw the Whigs like the Federalists as the party of large property interests.

# 4

# THE ASCENDANCY OF PROGRESSIVE HISTORY

Prior to World War I conservative evolutionists and progressives shared in approximately equal measure the work of a young, eagerly developing profession. The progressive view dominated Columbia and Wisconsin; conservatism ruled Yale; Harvard, after the coming of Turner, had some of both; and so did Chicago, the home base of McLaughlin and Dodd. Although the balance was clearly tipping toward progressivism after 1910, controversy and rivalry between the two schools was minimal. There seemed room enough and problems aplenty for all professional historians while they were staking out their claims. The common cause of superseding amateur scholarship united their varied undertakings.

In the 1920's and 1930's the old conservative school, although strongly entrenched in many institutions, suffered a steady and ultimately disastrous loss of intellectual vitality. Its work was far from finished; great parts of our institutional and administrative history remained still unwritten. But that kind of history no longer seemed relevant to an age in which, as Walter Lippmann said, "Whirl is king." Of the livelier young men entering academic life, very few felt the sense of national unity and historical continuity that had inspired so many of the first generation of professional historians. Change and a passion for modernity were the order of the day. At a time when all values were in flux, and government seemed either irrelevant to life or an instrument for remaking it, who could find in the formal constitution of political authority an inspiring theme?

By the early Thirties, the eclipse of constitutional history was widely recognized. "Constitutional history, with its emphasis on the permanent rather than the transitory aspects of government and politics, has been falling into neglect," one elder statesman mourned in 1934.[1] He might have added that constitutional history itself was becoming less concerned with the permanent and more with the transitory. The best of the younger men who stayed in the field turned their attention from the framework of law to a realistic appraisal of

[1] *AHR*, XL (1934), 426.

individual judges. This was the strategy that Carl B. Swisher and Alpheus T. Mason followed, a strategy that attuned them to behavioral changes rather than institutional continuities. Other young historians deserted the field, as James G. Randall did after publishing *Constitutional Problems under Lincoln* (1926).[2] Some of the established authorities carried on, of course, in a traditional vein. A scholar settled in an area of research does not ordinarily switch to another in response to new intellectual fashions. McLaughlin, for example, published his weighty *Constitutional History of the United States* in 1935. Corwin, on the other hand, shifted increasingly from history to contemporary problems; and when he retired in 1946 he remarked that he had outlived his subject.[3]

In American colonial history the constitutional or institutional approach retained for some years an appearance of continuing vigor because of the prestige of the Imperial school. Its London-centered view of early American history seemed to some scholars more valuable than ever after World War I; for the popular mind seethed with isolationist, 100 per cent American sentiments, to which a transatlantic perspective offered a salutary corrective. The Imperial school was also sustained by the massive, undeviating strength of Charles M. Andrews. Andrews survived to a ripe old age, producing good students, extending his indefatigable researches, and finally in the evening of his life releasing his long awaited magnum opus. The four great volumes of *The Colonial Period of American History* (1934-38) dealt largely with the seventeenth century. Andrews did not live to treat the eighteenth century in the same way, but he had the last and most authoritative word on what he covered.

Moreover, Andrews had one remarkable student who carried forward his lifework with the same matchless fidelity to a youthful purpose. Lawrence H. Gipson, a one-time Rhodes scholar who received his Ph.D. under Andrews in 1918, settled in the 1920's into writing a "definitive" history of the last twenty-five years of the old British Empire prior to the American Revolution. Gipson proceeded with complete fidelity to the social values of conservative evolutionism.

[2] But Randall pointed out the direction of future scholarship in "The Interrelation of Social and Constitutional History," *AHR*, XXXV (1929), 1-13. A detailed account of research trends is in Paul L. Murphy's "Time to Reclaim: The Current Challenge of American Constitutional History," *AHR*, LXIX (1963), 64-79.
[3] Reported to me by Professor A. T. Mason, May 1961.

His sympathy for the harmonious strength of old English institutions, and his distaste for the radical spirit of '76, quite exceeded that of his austere master. He lingered through nine affectionate volumes upon a description of the Empire in its last moment of tranquility and equilibrium.[4] Few now wished to read so leisurely a work; but Gipson considerably modernized the imperial approach. He reached well beyond the institutional framework, taking much account of individual motives and geographical groups and analyzing social and economic conditions. By assimilating the methods of both amateur and progressive historians, Gipson carried the Imperial school as far as it could go.

He had, however, no students and—by the 1930's—hardly any fellow workers. By then the Imperial school was breaking up in all the leading universities; the progressive approach was ascendant. Old J. Franklin Jameson, who had seemed serenely independent of any school or theory, thrilled younger scholars in 1926 by publishing an almost radical economic and social interpretation of the American Revolution.[5] Students trained in institutional history in the Twenties changed the direction of their research in the following decade. Leonard Labaree and W. F. Craven undertook studies of colonial society, Richard B. Morris investigated the control of the colonial labor force, Stanley Pargellis and Charles Barker moved into intellectual history.[6]

[4] *The British Empire Before the American Revolution* (1936-56). In the tenth volume, published in 1961 thirty-seven years after he began the work, Gipson at last moved into the story of the coming of the Revolution. The relation of his efforts to those of his predecessors is summarized in Max Savelle's "The Imperial School of American Colonial Historians," *Indiana Magazine of History,* XLV (1949), 123-34.

[5] *The American Revolution Considered as a Social Movement* (1926). In response to an enthusiastic review by Charles A. Beard, Jameson said that "nearly everything that is a matter of doctrine" was in an earlier text he had read in 1895 to a small audience at Columbia University. Nevertheless, the imprint of subsequent scholarship and of World War I on Jameson's thinking are visible. Elizabeth Donnan and Leo F. Stock, eds., *An Historian's World: Selections from the Correspondence of John Franklin Jameson* (Memoirs of the American Philosophical Society, vol. 42, 1956), p. 319.

[6] Leonard W. Labaree, *Conservatism in Early American History* (1948); Wesley Frank Craven, *The Southern Colonies in the Seventeenth Century* (1949); Richard B. Morris, *Government and Labor in Early America* (1946); Stanley Pargellis, "The Theory of Balanced Government," *The Constitution Reconsidered,* ed. Conyers Read (1938), pp. 37-49; Charles A. Barker, *Henry George* (1955). An older institutionalist, Evarts B. Greene, also devoted himself in-

Reviewers of Andrews' volumes complained that he wrote in a "legalistic" spirit, touched only incidentally on economic developments in the colonies, ignored sectional conflicts, and paid little heed to the common man. Progressive historians were rectifying these deficiencies. In the spirit of Turner, Thomas Jefferson Wertenbaker produced a panoramic account of the Americanization of a transplanted European civilization. In the spirit of Beard, Curtis Nettels published a strongly class-angled synthesis of American colonial history.[7]

The title of Nettels' book, *The Roots of American Civilization* (1938), suggests the particular interest progressive historians had in the indigenous aspects of the colonial scene. While infusing a democratic bias into the writing of early American history, these scholars were also linking it with subsequent national history. Imperial historians had reached a dead end on coming to the American Revolution. Although they cherished the principle of continuity, their special insistence on treating the colonies as part of English history blocked them from looking forward to American national history. The Progressive school studied the colonial period in the light of the national period as so integrated the two. But the progressives' nationalistic concentration on the internal dynamics of American development reversed the fault of the Imperial school: in uniting colonial history with later national history, progressive scholars separated it too much from European history.

Still, the progressive approach offered a valuable counterbalance to the extrinsic and formal emphasis of the Imperial school. If research had flourished under these new auspices, the change might have been a substantial improvement. Unfortunately, however, colonial history declined between the wars almost as much as constitutional history. In textbooks the space devoted to the period before 1776 contracted drastically; the research talent it attracted decreased markedly in comparison with more recent fields. Undoubtedly, pro-

---

creasingly to social history; see *The Revolutionary Generation, 1763-1790* (1943).
[7] Wertenbaker, *The Founding of American Civilization* (3 vols., 1938-47); Nettels, *The Roots of American Civilization* (1938). See also Thomas P. Abernethy, *Western Lands and the American Revolution* (1937); Robert A. East, *Business Enterprise in the American Revolutionary Era* (1938); Carl Bridenbaugh, *Cities in the Wilderness* (1938) and *Cities in Revolt* (1955); Merrill Jensen, *The Articles of Confederation* (1940). The reception of Andrews' work is summarized in A. S. Eisenstadt's *Charles McLean Andrews* (1956).

gressive ideas contributed to the diversion of talent both from the colonial period and from constitutional themes. If one was too formalistic, the other was too remote to engage fully the progressive mind. The so-called present-mindedness of progressive history was in effect a predominant interest in the outcome rather than the origins of a situation or period in the past. Progressive historians saw the colonial period as a time of origins, and their attention tended to move from that starting toward what followed. Most of them neglected the origins of American history in favor of the changes it subsequently underwent. Thus, the best of Osgood's later students, Schlesinger and Fox, worked largely in the nineteenth century. When Andrews on one occasion twitted Schlesinger for deserting the colonial field, Schlesinger replied that he regarded the Revolution as the beginning of the national era rather than the closing stage of the period of dependence.[8]

The drift of historical interest from colonial to national history after World War I opened a field of research in which some of the functions of the old Imperial school found a new and relevant application. This was American diplomatic history, an area of study not completely ignored before 1914 but very nearly so. On the whole, professional historians before the war had trained their sights either on the domestic scene or on the European origins of American history. The continuing relations of the United States with Europe remained largely neglected except in the work of a few amateur scholars like Henry Adams and Alfred T. Mahan. The war fostered in professional circles a somewhat clearer awareness of American involvement in European politics. Accordingly, diplomatic history emerged as a recognized subdivision of American national history.

One could, of course, study diplomatic history in various ways. Followers of Turner, such as Julius Pratt, Arthur P. Whitaker, and Frank Owsley, came at the subject from an interest in the internal social and economic pressures affecting American policies.[9] On the

---

[8] "The Reminiscences of Arthur M. Schlesinger" (Oral History Research Office, Columbia University, 1959), p. 60.

[9] Julius Pratt, *Expansionists of 1812* (1925); Arthur P. Whitaker, *The Spanish-American Frontier, 1783-1795* (1927); Frank L. Owsley, *King Cotton Diplomacy: Foreign Relations of the Confederate States of America* (1931); Frederick Merk, "Oregon Pioneers and the Boundary Settlement," *AHR*, XXIX (1924), 681-99, and subsequent publications; Thomas A. Bailey, *Theodore Roosevelt and the Japanese American Crisis* (1934).

other hand, American diplomatic history in the 1920's strongly attracted scholars in the conservative evolutionist tradition. It offered them a congenial yet up-to-date substitute for the formal, institutional scholarship that was going out of fashion. Diplomatic history, like constitutional history, called for a mastery of public documents. It required a discriminating eye for official phraseology and for the architecture of official policies. It offered scope for tracing the continuities underlying such policies as the Monroe Doctrine and the Open Door.[10] Moreover, diplomatic history carried down into the national period the conservative evolutionists' appreciation of an international framework connecting American with European history.

So it is not surprising that a good part of the research on American diplomatic history in the 1920's dealt with Anglo-American relations, much of it written with the attention the Imperial school had given to British views and strategies. The most considerable specialist who emerged at this time was Samuel Flagg Bemis, a student of Channing with a fine passion for archival research. From the outset Bemis took his stand in Europe. Largely disregarding domestic conflicts, he examined the evolution of early American foreign policy against a background of international rivalries and intrigues. Unlike most of the Imperial historians, Bemis harbored a strong patriotic animus against the "corrupt" statecraft of the European powers. His account of how Americans shrewdly reaped advantage from Europe's distress smacked of postwar disillusion with the Old World; yet his insistence on a transatlantic perspective was clearly an inheritance from the Anglophile spirit of conservative scholarship.[11]

The flush of postwar interest in American diplomatic history did not last. The ranks of conservative evolutionists thinned; and progressive historians, who regarded foreign policy as subordinate to domestic concerns, became more wholly absorbed in the latter. Probably what most discouraged scholarly activity in the diplomatic field was the increasingly isolationist atmosphere in the United States. Iso-

[10] Dexter Perkins' three-volume history of the Monroe Doctrine (1927-37), summarized in *Hands Off: A History of the Monroe Doctrine* (1941), is one of the notable works of the period. See also Tyler Dennett, *Americans in Eastern Asia* (1922).

[11] Bemis, *Jay's Treaty* (1923) and *The Diplomacy of the American Revolution* (1935); Ephraim D. Adams, *Great Britain and the American Civil War* (2 vols., 1925); Donaldson Jordan and Edwin J. Pratt, *Europe and the American Civil War* (1931); Dora Mae Clark, *British Opinion and the American Revolution* (1930).

lationist sentiment reached an apogee in the Thirties. In 1941 one scholar thought it was "fortunate" in view of the widespread disinterest that as many as three major universities gave a position of importance to the study of American foreign policy.[12]

Since historians engaged in studying other countries were relatively immune to isolationist influence, they took over a good share of the work. A disproportionate amount of the best research on American diplomacy was done by scholars primarily interested in the history of Europe, Latin America, or the British Empire. Such was the case with major books published by Charles Seymour and Alfred L. P. Dennis on America's assumption of the responsibilities of world power, by William Spence Robertson and J. Fred Rippy on relations with Latin America, and by John Bartlet Brebner and A. L. Burt on the interwoven destinies of the United States, Canada, and Great Britain.[13] Specialists in American history, if they did not neglect foreign policy, viewed it in a more parochial and carping way. In an atmosphere heavy with distrust of "power politics" and "propaganda," isolationists and their opponents agreed at least on a profound dissatisfaction with the general record of modern foreign policy. Accordingly, in the 1930's a fixation on the mistakes and shortcomings of our diplomacy conditioned much of the writing that American specialists did in this field.[14]

One may conclude, then, that diplomatic history encountered in the intellectual climate of the late Twenties and Thirties essentially the same difficulties that impeded work in constitutional and colonial history. All three fields came under the influence of progressive thought, which was critical of tradition, insensitive to institutional continuities, and preoccupied with domestic conflict. Neither diplomatic nor constitutional nor colonial history provided an entirely attractive or suitable medium for major progressive scholarship. Their

[12] Statement of Carroll S. Alden in *AHR*, XLVII (1941), 167.
[13] Seymour, *American Diplomacy During the World War* (1934) and *American Neutrality, 1914-1917* (1935); Dennis, *Adventures in American Diplomacy, 1896-1906* (1928); Robertson, *Hispanic-American Relations with the United States* (1923); Rippy, *United States and Mexico* (1926); Alfred L. Burt, *The United States, Great Britain and British North America from the Revolution to the Establishment of Peace After the War of 1812* (1940); Brebner, *North Atlantic Triangle* (1945).
[14] This is emphasized in Ernest R. May's "Emergence to World Power," in *The Reconstruction of American History*, ed. John Higham (London, 1962), pp. 186-92.

vicissitudes are one index to the dominant position the progressive school won between the wars. The other index is what that school accomplished in the realm that concerned it most: the history of conflict and change within an indigenous environment.

Between the two world wars progressive influence became so great in American historiography that it seemed for a time virtually to overwhelm all other conceptual possibilities. World War I neither interrupted nor diverted this widening stream of historical thought. Instead, the ideas of Turner, Beard, and their younger associates spread through the historical profession in the 1920's without any really sustained opposition. Certain new currents fed into the stream; and ultimately it grew vexed and turbulent. But these complications arose, for the most part, within the progressive tradition.

The outstanding achievement of progressive scholarship between the wars was a broadening of the scope of historical narrative. The New History had from the outset pledged itself to a grasp of the past as inclusive as life itself, and American historians were now redeeming the pledge. Clearly delimited research on specific institutions languished; loosely defined studies of situations and relationships abounded. It was an age of social history. Surprisingly little first-rate political history was written. The few good political histories that did appear, like John D. Hicks's *The Populist Revolt* (1931) and Howard K. Beale's *The Critical Year* (1930), stressed the social and economic context of political action. Economic history as such fared no better than political history. Most of the work in this field had been done by economists, who by the time of World War I were lured away from history by new developments in theory.[15] Historians, while busily applying economic interpretations, took the underlying economic processes largely for granted. Impatient of studying any single department of life in its own terms, they neglected economic history in pursuing the undifferentiated flux of life.

The quest for breadth received considerable impetus from a series of conferences that the American Historical Association sponsored in 1931 for planning future research. Both of the conferences on American history, one meeting in the East, the other in the Midwest, bewailed the relative neglect of local history and of sociocultural matters like education, religious folkways, and the impact of

[15] Of the forty leading colleges and universities that had offered courses on economic history in 1902, nine had dropped the course by 1920; AHA *Annual Report* (1920), pp. 153-62. See also Thomas C. Cochran, "Research in American Economic History: A Thirty Year View," *Mid-America*, XXIX (1947), 6.

technological change. Roy Nichols prepared for the eastern conference a long list of such topics. Both meetings assumed that the most
urgent task of scholarship was to reach beyond political, military, and
constitutional themes. Published in a little volume entitled *Historical
Scholarship in America* (1932), these recommendations accelerated
a movement already strongly under way.[16]

One important dimension of the movement was a steady expansion of the progressive historians' conception of "the people." Before
World War I the common man was an abstract figure in American
historiography, hardly visible except in the classic image of the pioneer. This image revealed little of the multitudinous variety that
democrats had long considered one of the glories of the American
people. In the 1920's and 1930's many of the younger scholars became fascinated with the concrete experience of particular groups in
distinctive environments. They wrote, usually with a close feeling of
identification, about such folk as dirt farmers, indentured servants,
cowboys, missionaries, Indians, and immigrants. In so doing, progressive historians were specifying the rich diversity of the American
people.

They were also reacting against the repressive, 100 per cent Americanism of the war years, which contributed especially to a new interest in the religious and ethnic divisions in American society.
Academic scholars had hitherto left the story of such groups in the
keeping of their own amateur chroniclers. Progressive historians still
give little heed to the Negro as a fullfledged participant in American history. Within the white population, however, they recognized
that the American people were in significant ways Methodists and
Catholics and Germans and Norwegians as well as frontiersmen,
workers, and planters.

The first notable efforts to integrate religious and ethnic groups
into the mainstream of American history came from midwesterners
heavily indebted to Frederick Jackson Turner. It was Turner who
inspired the leading authority on the history of American Protestantism, William Warren Sweet. A professor at DePauw and later at the
University of Chicago, Sweet revised the old denomination-centered

---

16 Committee of the American Historical Association on the Planning of Research, *Historical Scholarship in America: Needs and Opportunities* (1932).

"church history" by relating the major Protestant groups to political and social forces. All of his books, including the widely read *Story of Religions in America* (1931), emphasized especially the democratizing effects of the frontier.[17]

A similar stress on the frontier in general and the rural Midwest in particular attended the treatment of the foreign-born. After World War I several second-generation midwestern historians realized that the interaction of European emigrants with the American environment was one of the great, neglected aspects of the making of America. Arthur M. Schlesinger, himself an Ohioan of German parentage, called attention to this theme in an essay published in 1921. Other young midwesterners had recently embarked on just such studies. George M. Stephenson and Theodore C. Blegen specialized respectively in the Swedes and the Norwegians. Marcus L. Hansen, a second-generation Dane, took the whole sweep of emigration from northern and western Europe for his field. He began work on the subject in 1917 as a student of Turner's at Harvard; and like Turner he explained migration primarily in economic terms. His fundamental contribution was to internationalize the Turner tradition. He viewed America as the frontier of an expanding Europe and took as much account of the changing European environment as he did of the American. Hansen's work, almost all of it unpublished and incomplete at his untimely death in 1938, went far beyond the usual limits of progressive history.[18]

While these researchers were expanding the base of American history, other scholars were constructing a new synthesis of the whole story. The empirical knowledge for a genuinely democratic history they had only begun to amass. But the outlines of an interpretive pattern lay ready at hand, and the leading progressive historians were eager to sum up. The task of synthesizing the full sweep of demo-

[17] Sidney E. Mead, "Prof. Sweet's Religion and Culture in America," *Church History*, XXII (1953), 33-47.

[18] Arthur M. Schlesinger, "The Significance of Immigration in American History," *American Journal of Sociology*, XXVII (1921), 71-85; G. M. Stephenson, *The Religious Aspects of Swedish Immigration* (1932); Theodore C. Blegen, *Norwegian Migration to America* (2 vols. 1931-40); Carl Wittke, *We Who Built America* (1939); Marcus L. Hansen, *The Immigrant in American History* (1940) and *The Atlantic Migration, 1607-1860* (1940). See also Allan H. Spear, "Marcus Lee Hansen and the Historiography of Immigration," *Wisconsin Magazine of History*, XLIV (1961), 258-68.

cratic experience appealed irresistibly to their comprehensive spirit. Accordingly, most of the major works published in the 1920's were not strikingly original essays on particular topics. They were massive codifications of the progressive version of American history.

The most influential book of this kind came from Charles A. Beard. *The Rise of American Civilization* (2 vols., 1927) was his first serious historical work in a long time. He resigned from Columbia University in 1917 and subsisted principally thereafter on textbooks for elementary and high school students, which he and his wife turned out rapidly and successfully. Beard had long wanted to produce a general survey of a different order, one that would do for the United States what John R. Green's *Short History of the English People* had done for England. The ferment among postwar intellectuals over the quality of the American heritage quickened his resolve, and an extended visit to the Orient in 1922-23 gave him a deep sense of the differences between civilizations. He returned home determined to write a history testifying to the restless, inextinguishable vitality of the American people.[19] Cutting loose from the restrictions of the textbook, as he had already broken away from academic fetters, Beard created with his wife's assistance a work of great power and eloquence.

In line with his earlier interpretation of the Federalist period, Beard portrayed an ever renewed struggle throughout American history between a dominant minority of businessmen and their various adversaries, notably British ruling classes, American farmers and workingmen, and southern planters. In this perspective Jacksonian democracy became an uprising of farmers and workers, and the Civil War a "Second American Revolution" in which northern businessmen drove the planter aristocracy from power. Beard told the story with few regrets for the vanquished. He admired the daring enterprise and the technological innovations engendered by the acquisitive spirit, and with each upheaval he associated—as cause or effect —a forward thrust of democracy. To these political and economic forces Beard related an impressive array of educational, cultural, and social activities, venturing brashly into fields (like music) that he knew little about, dwelling on the progress of scientific and secular values, and seeking wherever possible to interweave material and

[19] Interview with Miriam Vagts, May 3, 1961.

ideal phenomena. He conveyed a strong sense of the importance of rational purpose in human affairs, but his rhetoric was profoundly naturalistic. The Civil War he described as an "Irrepressible Conflict." In other contexts he wrote of "an inexorable process beyond the will of any man or group," of the "forces of the age beating pitilessly . . . driving . . . men and women before the storm," of the "havoc [that] fate play[s] with the little schemes of men."[20]

While Beard was writing *The Rise of American Civilization,* some leading academic historians were collaborating on another synthesis, much less compelling but more scholarly and painstaking. In 1922 Arthur M. Schlesinger inaugurated at the State University of Iowa a course entitled "Social and Cultural History of the United States," the first of its kind in any college. At the same time he proposed to a publisher a scheme for a multivolume, cooperative history of "the formation and growth of civilization in the United States." The first four volumes appeared in 1927; nine more came out in succeeding years. The series, under the general editorship of Schlesinger and Dixon Ryan Fox, was called *A History of American Life.*

Whereas Beard never underrated the importance of political power, Schlesinger wanted to get away entirely from the predominantly political substance of general history. In this he followed consciously the example of another of his Columbia teachers, James Harvey Robinson. Schlesinger's original conspectus for *A History of American Life* defined as its theme the events and influences that touch the everyday life of the people. He relegated politics and government to the background, convinced that they impinge only remotely on the sphere of the average citizen. The series had much to say about health, social welfare, prosperity, depression, poverty, recreation, and agitation for reforms, but very little about the actual exercise of power. This was, in Schlesinger's view, not only the democratic but also the truly American way to write history.[21]

Through the editors' scrupulous care, the series achieved a high degree of uniformity in style and content. It did not, on the other hand, have a unified conceptual scheme. Although the authors often

[20] *The Rise of American Civilization* (1927), vol. I, p. 635; vol. II, pp. 479, 544.
[21] Schlesinger, "What American Social History Is," *Harvard Educational Review,* VII (1937), 57-65. On the genesis and execution of this project Professor Schlesinger's "Reminiscences" are much fuller than his published autobiography.

made cautious, implicit use of economic interpretations in organizing their material, their attempt to be comprehensive and eclectic without specifying the locus of power gave their work a largely descriptive cast. The editors had divided American history into chronological segments according to the prominence at one time or another of some general process like the *The Rise of the Common Man, 1830-1850, The Emergence of Modern America, 1865-1878,* and *The Rise of the City, 1878-1898.* Periodization of this sort sharpened the usual progressive emphasis on rapid social change; for no contributor could take a long-range view of the process in question.

The third of the major syntheses published in 1927 dealt with the history of ideas. It came from the pen of a teacher of English at the University of Washington, Vernon L. Parrington. Professional historians were barely beginning to write intellectual history. Although Robinson and John Dewey had assigned it a prominent place on the agenda of the New History, and Carl Becker demonstrated in *The Declaration of Independence* (1922) how beautifully a professional historian could handle it, nearly all of his colleagues clung to the tangible stuff of social and political affairs. A severe conception of scientific objectivity inhibited professional historians from venturing into a realm where subjective values, speculation, and opinion composed the very substance for investigation. Parrington, having missed the rigors of graduate training, was not afraid of ideas. He was much closer than were the professionals to the nineteenth century humanistic tradition, in which men like W. E. H. Lecky, Leslie Stephen, and Moses Coit Tyler turned to intellectual history as a historical-evolutionary substitute for metaphysical systems. Parrington followed their example in producing *Main Currents in American Thought* (3 vols., 1927, 1930), the first grand formulation of its subject.

While his sense of the sweep and range of ideas derived from a literary background, Parrington belonged essentially among the progressive historians. He started work on *Main Currents* in 1913 captivated by the economic interpretation of history and "impatient with the smug Tory culture which we were fed on as [Harvard] undergraduates." He considered himself part of a generation that had "dedicated itself to history and sociology, accepting as its immediate and particular business a reexamination of the American past in order to forecast an ampler democratic future." [22] To organize his narrative Parrington relied on a Turnerian dialectic that arrayed East, West, and South against one another; and within each section he pitted the spirit of capitalistic exploitation against that of agrarian democracy. His book richly elaborated the old antithesis between Hamiltonian and Jeffersonian principles. It traced the evolution of the latter from the chrysalis of Puritan autocracy through infusions of enlightened and romantic idealisms to an eventual encounter with industrial consolidation and scientific pessimism. The architecture of the book, though much too ambitious to withstand close examination, was imaginative, intricate, and splendorous.

Amid the hosannas that greeted Parrington's epic, few progressive readers noticed how profoundly troubled his vision of American history was. Unlike Beard, Parrington did not celebrate an advancing partnership of science, democracy, and faith in progress. Unlike the authors of *The History of American Life,* he did not at every stage emphasize the *rising* forces and the indications of progress. Many progressive historians escaped—or in the case of Beard deliberately combatted—the disillusion that invaded American intellectual life after World War I. Parrington, who in this sense resembled Becker, felt the bite of postwar disillusion keenly. He was a hopeful man, eager "to forecast an ampler democratic future," quick to praise the children of light and to scold the children of darkness; but the general movement of history since the Civil War seemed inimical to the Jeffersonian ideals he cherished. His discouragement arose only partly from nostalgia for a decentralized society, from repugnance for the consolidated power and colorless standardization of the twentieth century. As an idealist, he was also disturbed by the deterministic implications of his own intellectual weapons. The economic interpretation of history taught the subordination of ideas to material realities. The whole scientific, naturalistic outlook of his generation endangered humanistic values. Consequently, Parrington could not cast American intellectual history in the pattern of continual progress. He saw it rather as cyclical. Starting from the wasteland of Calvinistic pessimism, he traced the rise of liberal democracy to an

---

[22] *Main Currents in American Thought,* vol. III (1930), p. 403. I am indebted to the careful analysis by Robert A. Skotheim and Kermit Vanderbilt, "Vernon Louis Parrington: The Mind and Art of a Historian of Ideas," *Pacific Northwest Quarterly,* LIII (1962), 100-13.

apogee before 1860 and its descent thereafter into the realistic but disillusioning jungle of scientific pessimism. At the end of the story the best he could see were "sunset skies that gave promise of other and greater dawns." Just as Carl Becker's writings in the 1920's signaled a crisis in historical theory, Parrington's marked the onset of crisis in the progressive interpretation of American history.

# 5

## CRISIS IN PROGRESSIVE HISTORY

All of the leading historical journals ignored *Main Currents in American Thought,* presumably considering it outside their purview. The profession as a whole came to accept intellectual history only gradually in the 1930's and 1940's.[1] Nevertheless, during the inter-war years the concerns that weighed so heavily on Parrington's mind did infiltrate professional scholarship. They appeared first in the handling of certain concrete topics, then provoked wider controversies over interpretation, and led finally to new perspectives on American history.

It was becoming evident in the Twenties, and increasingly so in the Thirties, that history had somehow gone wrong. The course of America's progress was strewn with too many mistakes, failures, and illusions to have unfolded with the neat, intrinsic logic that Turner and Beard had sketched. A number of progressive-minded historians between the wars dedicated themselves to explaining the failures and puncturing the illusions. We have already observed this highly critical approach in the study of diplomatic history; it appeared just as strongly in a re-examination of America's domestic record. Tough-minded progressives, though still intent on vindicating democracy and saving a faith in progress, set out to expose the most unpleasant "realities." This naturally led to an intensified use of economic interpretations. Some historians, however, recoiled sharply from the fatalistic implications of so impersonal a view of history. By the late 1930's an emerging revolt against economic determin-ism was beginning to threaten the intellectual foundations of pro-gressive historiography.

The roots of these developments, most of which became visible in the 1930's, go back to the disillusion that followed World War I. The general influence of the postwar disillusion was to call into question the status of ideals in American culture. Many Americans in the Twenties wanted to exorcise the crusading, self-righteous ideal-

[1] John Higham, "The Rise of American Intellectual History," *AHR,* LVI (1951), 462-67.

ism of the war years. They associated much of it with New England —a land of Puritans, abolitionists, and other moral fanatics. Accordingly, the principal literary and social critics mounted a withering attack on New England culture and on traditional moral authority in general. In this assault some progressive historians joined. They were already skeptical of abstractions and appearances; they had already spied the cloven hoof of self-interest beneath the seats of the mighty; and they were already in revolt against New England. As southerners and midwesterners, progressive historians had never had any sympathy for the moneyed and patrician groups of the Northeast. They equated democracy with the common man, especially the frontiersman, not with the New England tradition. After World War I their economic and sectional animus interlaced with the popular "debunking" mood.

The explosive effects of the combination may be observed in the work of two amateur historians who became widely respected and influential in professional circles. James Truslow Adams gave the sanction of scholarship to the repudiation of Puritanism, and Albert J. Beveridge did the same to abolitionism, though neither had set out with any such intention. Both launched their historical studies in a highly conventional vein. Adams, a New York gentleman brought up to regard that city as an outpost of English culture, started in 1919 upon a history of New England with the simple purpose of presenting it from the viewpoint of the Imperial school.[2] About the same time Beveridge, a midwestern progressive who had written an adulatory biography of John Marshall, embarked on a biography of Lincoln intending to eulogize his exalted moral leadership.

The postwar disillusion hit both of them hard. The revulsion against Puritanism provoked Adams to inquire iconoclastically into the economic motives of the early settlers. He decided that they had come more largely to fish than to pray. Adams soon dropped the Imperial approach and made his history of New England a study of conflict between Puritan "theocracy" and frontier democracy. Beveridge, also looking behind appearances to realities, was appalled to discover a shifty, partisan Lincoln, entangled in vested interests. The

[2] In a book review in the *New England Quarterly*, III (1930), 742, Adams explains the original intentions with which he began work on the three-volume series, *The Founding of New England* (1921), *Revolutionary New England, 1691-1776* (1923), and *New England in the Republic, 1776-1850* (1926). The James Truslow Adams Papers at Columbia University are also illuminating.

splenetic, trouble-making abolitionists shocked him still more.[3] Beveridge managed to redeem Lincoln somewhat by contrasting his down-to-earth politics with the abolitionists' destructive fanaticism. In place of a noble idealism, both historians found jobbery and hypocrisy.

Along similar lines, a highly critical view of the whole Civil War experience was shaping up. Disillusion with World War I called into question the moral grandeur of the earlier holocaust; and progressive emphasis on the common opposition of the South and West to New England focused attention on northern misdeeds. The Civil War seemed now, in its consequences at least, a betrayal of democracy. Fred Shannon won a Pulitzer Prize for a book describing the inefficiency, corruption, and profiteering in the Union armies. The already unflattering view of Radical Reconstruction that conservative scholars of the Dunning school had sketched became positively lurid in the hands of southern and western progressives who championed the white masses against the Republican "oligarchs." [4] Perhaps the war itself was an avoidable mistake. So Charles W. Ramsdell argued, with a Turnerian faith in the natural environment, which he thought would inevitably have prevented further expansion of slavery. Thus, by the end of the Twenties the idealism of the North in the Civil War era was heavily discounted. As early as 1928 Professor Dumas Malone assured his fellow southerners, "The more important positions were long ago surrendered into our hands, and the honors of war have been granted nearly all our heroes." [5]

In the 1930's revulsion against the supposedly false idealism of the

---

[3] *Abraham Lincoln, 1809-1858* (2 vols., 1928). The fascinating story of Beveridge's intellectual struggle may be followed in Claude G. Bowers' *Beveridge and the Progressive Era* (1932), pp. 569-77, and in Elizabeth Donnan and Leo F. Stock, eds., "Senator Beveridge, J. Franklin Jameson, and Abraham Lincoln," *Mississippi Valley Historical Review*, XXXV (1948), 639-73.

[4] Shannon, *Organization and Administration of the Union Army, 1861-1865* (2 vols., 1928); Claude G. Bowers, *The Tragic Era: The Revolution After Lincoln* (1929); George Fort Milton, *The Age of Hate: Andrew Johnson and the Radicals* (1930).

[5] Dumas Malone, "A Challenge to Patriots," *Virginia Quarterly Review*, IV (1928), 486; Charles W. Ramsdell, "The Natural Limits of Slavery Expansion," *Mississippi Valley Historical Review*, XVI (1929), 151-71. There are detailed accounts of the rise of "revisionism" in Thomas J. Pressly's *Americans Interpret Their Civil War* (1962), pp. 265-306, and T. H. Bonner's "Civil War Historians and the Needless War Doctrine," *Journal of the History of Ideas*, XVII (1956), 194-97.

North blossomed into a fullfledged reinterpretation of the causes of the Civil War. A group of southern and miswestern historians with southern connections undertook to refute Beard's interpretation of the Civil War as a necessary step in the progress of the nation. It was rather, these "revisionists" argued, a horrible, needless blunder. Who then was responsible? Surely not the common man—the revisionists were too faithful to progressive values to blame the demos. Impractical extremists must have misled an innocent people. Thus George Fort Milton tried to show in a biography of Stephen A. Douglas how fanatical minorities got control of the machinery of government, flouted Douglas's "economic common sense," and brought on a war that the masses had not wanted.[6] James G. Randall's important synthesis, *The Civil War and Reconstruction* (1937), took essentially the same approach. Avery Craven of the University of Chicago set forth in *The Coming of the Civil War* (1942) the most careful analysis of how genuine economic disturbances were magnified into factitious moral abstractions. With a curl of the lip he had announced in 1935 the basic thesis of the "revisionist" school: "Each side, in the end, fought the other for principles and the glory of God, for the preservation of civilizations, for the maintenance of honor. The conflict was the work of politicians and pious cranks." [7]

While Civil War historians assailed the moral idealism traditionally associated with New England, other progressive scholars were questioning the democratic idealism traditionally ascribed to the frontier. It was, of course, more difficult for progressives to see deformities in the western spirit than to notice blemishes on eastern ideals. No one seriously criticized Turner's attribution of American democracy to the free land of the West until after World War I; no considerable dissent was heard in the historical profession until the 1930's; and even then skepticism met devout resistance from Turner's disciples. Yet the sudden outbreak of controversy revealed how serious the strains within progressive historiography were becoming.

Beard had never given much credence to the Turner thesis. From Beard's point of view, Turner was not enough of an economic realist: although starting from a materialistic basis (land), Turner had erected on it a quasi-romantic theory of Western society as free, vir-

---

[6] *The Eve of Conflict: Stephen A. Douglas and the Needless War* (1934).
[7] "Coming of the War Between the States: An Interpretation," *Journal of Southern History*, II (1936), 305.

tuous, and supremely American. Beard's reservations about the uplifting influence of the frontier, initially suggested in a book review in 1921, were much more strongly put by disillusioned cultural critics for whom the idealism of the frontier seemed as fraudulent as that of New England. In the 1930's scholars joined in the assault. Thomas P. Abernethy, one of Turner's own students, published in 1932 a path-breaking book on Tennessee politics. He described that frontier area as dominated by grasping, illiberal land speculators, among them none other than Andrew Jackson. "The first offspring of the West," Abernethy concluded, "was not democracy but arrant opportunism." Similar findings emerged from the careful studies that Paul W. Gates and Fred A. Shannon made of land disposal in the Midwest. Clearly the frontier had never offered as much egalitarian opportunity as Turner had imagined. The old notion that the frontier had provided a "safety-valve" for urban discontent and a release from urban poverty seemed a pernicious illusion in the deep economic crisis of the Thirties. Was not the escapist mythology of a western paradise somewhat responsible for America's failure to face up earlier to basic social problems? To purge our history of such beguiling fantasies, several scholars took pains to demonstrate that industrial workers had never escaped to western farms in significant numbers.[8]

In effect, economic historians were revolting against Turner while Civil War historians revolted against Beard. The coincidence of the two movements suggests their common basis in the disillusion of the interwar period. Behind the immediate target—Turner in one case, Beard in the other—the rebels were attacking older shibboleths. Each group was undermining an established piety of American culture that progressive historians had hitherto accepted: the grandeur of the Civil War and the glory of the frontier. By discrediting these cherished memories, progressive historians intended to make American history less pretty and more "realistic."

[8] Beard, "The Frontier in American History," *New Republic*, XXV (1921), 349-50; Abernethy, *From Frontier to Plantation in Tennessee: A Study in Frontier Democracy* (1932), p. 359; Shannon, "The Homestead Act and the Labor Surplus," and Gates, "The Homestead Law in an Incongruous Land System," *AHR*, XLI (1936), 637-81; Ellen von Nardroff, "The American Frontier as a Safety Valve—The Life, Death, Reincarnation, and Justification of a Theory," *Agricultural History*, XXXVI (1962), 127-34. On the background of cultural criticism see Warren I. Susman's "The Useless Past: American Intellectuals and the Frontier Thesis, 1910-1930," *Bucknell Review*, XI (1963), 1-20.

In other respects the two revolts differed. The Civil War "revisionists" honored Turner's memory. As southerners and midwesterners still teaching in America's heartland, they looked back affectionately, as Turner had, to the old rural America of farmers and planters. Craven, who was one of Turner's students and who had begun his career in agricultural history, regarded the ascendancy that the urban-industrial Northeast won during the Civil War as one of its most regrettable aspects.[9] The revolt against Turner, on the other hand, attracted many eastern historians along with a few disillusioned midwesterners like Shannon. In some measure it was a declaration of independence from midwestern domination of progressive historiography. Thus many of Turner's academic critics argued that his influence had too long delayed appreciation of the constructive importance of the city and the industrial revolution in American history. In this vein Arthur M. Schlesinger countered Turner's frontier thesis with an urban interpretation of American history, which inaugurated a sustained interest in the history of the city.[10] Another of Beard's students, Louis M. Hacker, reacted against Turner's sectionalism by insisting on the primacy of economic classes. Hacker's *The Triumph of American Capitalism* (1940) went as far in the direction of a Marxist interpretation of American history as any academic historian would ever go.

There was also another side to the anti-Turner movement, for it temporarily gave vent to very diverse discontents. While critics in the Beardian tradition assailed Turner for underrating urbanism or capitalism as against the equally impersonal processes of nature, others complained that all such approaches allowed too little autonomy or influence to ideas. Benjamin F. Wright and George W. Pierson, among others, traced American values to the cultural heritage Americans carried westward with them. From this perspective, Turner was too materialistic and even parochial in grounding ideas and behavior in the immediate physical environment. Turner, said

[9] Avery Craven, "The Turner Theories and the South," *Journal of Southern History*, V (1939), 314, and "Frederick Jackson Turner," *The Marcus W. Jernegan Essays in American Historiography*, ed. William T. Hutchinson (1937), p. 268. Craven spent his formative years in a small town in Iowa; Randall, who was a student of William E. Dodd, grew up in southern Indiana. Both married southern girls.

[10] *The Rise of the City, 1878-1898* (1933), and "The City in American History," *Mississippi Valley Historical Review*, XXVII (1940), 43-66. Cf. *The Historian and the City*, ed., Oscar Handlin and John Burchard (1963).

Pierson, derived America from real estate, not state of mind.[11] If some attacked Turner's western idealism, others criticized his economic determinism.

Actually, the latter group was striking out in the same direction in which Civil War historians were moving. Pierson's criticism of Turner chimed with the revisionists' criticism of Beard. In denying the inevitability of the Civil War they too rejected a deterministic explanation of events. Contending that agitators and propagandists precipitated a needless holocaust, these historians made much allowance for subjective and unpredictable elements in history—for passion, chance, and individual idiosyncrasies. Randall and Craven were, in fact, united with their chief northern adversary, Dwight Dumond, in believing that the Civil War resulted from folly rather than fate. Dumond, who resurrected the abolitionist indictment of slavery, was just as intent as any revisionist on discrediting economic causation.[12] It is indicative of the confused ferment of the 1930's that both the reinterpretation of the Civil War and the reconsideration of the frontier arose from a need to exorcise idealism—to be more "realistic"—yet both led in the end to a reaffirmation of ideas.

Thus, in concrete interpretive controversies, the problem of determinism, which had obsessed Parrington a decade earlier, came to a head. As a result a significant minority of progressive historians moved toward the forms of history in which Parrington had excelled: toward biography and intellectual history. There the problem of determinism was most acutely posed. Both branches of scholarship had, of course, other roots in American culture. Biography, cultivated by journalists, had already tapped a new reading public. The study of ideas was part of the unfinished business of the New History. It could be employed, as Robinson and Becker employed it, to deflate outmoded beliefs or to provide a general framework for the multifarious data history was now encompassing. But the fact that a really working interest in biography and in intellectual history emerged simul-

11 *The Turner Thesis Concerning the Role of the Frontier in American History,* ed. George R. Taylor, "Problems in American Civilization" (1956) reprints some of the major papers. Two concrete reactions against the environmentalism of the frontier thesis are H. R. Shurtleff's *The Log Cabin Myth* (1939) and Richard H. Shryock's "British versus German Traditions in Colonial Agriculture," *Mississippi Valley Historical Review,* XXVI (1939), 39-54.
12 Dumond, *Antislavery Origins of the Civil War in the United States* (1939) and *Antislavery: The Crusade for Freedom in America* (1961).

taneously in professional scholarship suggests that they also served a new and common need. Each seemed to delimit the sway of impersonal forces in history. Each opened a dimension for reasserting the capacity of men to choose their destiny.

Until the Thirties relatively few professional historians took biography seriously. Biographical dissertations were becoming popular among the increasing throngs of Ph.D. candidates for the bad reason that an individual life is relatively easy to lay out and the principal sources are often ready at hand. Mundane considerations do not account, however, for the initiative that produced the great collaborative project of the decade, *The Dictionary of American Biography* (22 vols., 1928-44). Moreover, such major scholars as Howard K. Beale, Henry Steele Commager, James G. Randall, and Allan Nevins now gave their best efforts to biography. In fact it became one of the most conspicuous and distinctive features of American humanistic studies. Through biography a remarkable number of scholars were trying to disengage themselves from the impersonal and external approach to the past that had always prevailed in American academic scholarship.

Nevins, the most indefatigible of biographers, published his first biography in 1928. He had already written three solid books of social history that reflected the strong influence of Turner and Beard. Then, partly in reaction, he became intensely interested in the role of the individual in history.[13] The long series of biographies he wrote during the next decade sought to humanize scholarly history. In each of them Nevins exhibited the character and moral force of his subject against a dense background of resistive circumstance. His career as a biographer epitomized the counterthrust of a chastened idealism arising out of the crisis in progressive historiography.

[13] Nevins to author, June 1, 1961. Among the outstanding biographies that were begun if not completed in the Thirties are Commager's *Theodore Parker* (1936), Randall's *Lincoln the President* (4 vols., 1945-55), Nevins' *Grover Cleveland, A Study in Courage* (1932) and *John D. Rockefeller: The Heroic Age of American Business* (2 vols., 1940), Charles M. Wiltse's *John C. Calhoun* (3 vols., 1944-51), Samuel Eliot Morison's *Admiral of the Ocean Sea* (2 vols., 1942), and Dumas Malone's *Jefferson and His Time* (3 vols. to date, 1948-62). Samuel F. Bemis turned to biography in the 1940's and published a notable two-volume life of John Quincy Adams (1949-55). The most imposing undertaking in this tradition today is Arthur S. Link's *Wilson* (3 vols. to date, 1947-1960). On the function and appeal of biography see Matthew Josephson's "Historians and Mythmakers," *Virginia Quarterly Review*, XVI (1940), 92-109, and John A. Garraty's *The Nature of Biography* (1957).

In considering the writings of Allan Nevins in the 1930's we leave entirely behind the pungent exhalation of postwar disillusion. Nevins evinced, along with zest for the rich human possibilities of biography, a delight in the inspirational function of history. In 1938 he wrote: "History is the sextant and compass of states which, tossed by wind and current, would be lost in confusion if they could not fix their position. . . . By giving peoples a sense of continuity in all their efforts, and by chronicling immortal worth, it confers upon them both a consciousness of their unity, and a feeling of the importance of human achievement." [14]

A sense of continuity, a consciousness of unity! These words, set down at a time when economic instability was ramifying into a fearful breakup of international stability, were more than a protest against determinism. They carried also a distinctly conservative feeling for tradition and solidarity, a feeling wholly alien to the basic progressive accent on conflict and change. They pointed to a new quest for stable values. Doubtless such a reaction against disillusion would have occurred if there had been no Depression and no threat of totalitarian power. But these disturbances raised basic questions about the general course of history and made some intellectuals more eager to find strength and sustenance in the past.

It is not commonly appreciated how far Beard himself moved in this direction. Beard's assault on scientific history during the 1930's stemmed from his desire for moral rearmament in the midst of a great crisis in human affairs. His relativism was explicitly an appeal for freedom from the coercions of fate. Consequently, his own historical writing shifted—sometimes awkwardly—toward greater stress on individuals and particularly on ideas in history. In 1939 he declared: "As in physical nature the flash of lightning always precedes the roll of thunder, so in human affairs the flame of thought has always gone before a transformation in the social arrangements of mankind." [15] The metaphor was still naturalistic, but the order of cause and effect seemed now reversed.

After giving the best years of his life to a realistic demolition of mental "fictions" and disembodied ideas, Beard was groping now for

[14] *The Gateway to History* (1938), p. 3.
[15] Charles A. and Mary R. Beard, *America in Midpassage*, vol. II (1939), p. 860; Bernard C. Borning, *The Political and Social Thought of Charles A. Beard* (1962), pp. 165-81.

the inner spirit, the unique and enduring essence, of American civilization. He never quite put his finger on it. A first attempt to identify an integral "national interest" shattered on the rock of his stubborn economic realism. Beard's *The Idea of National Interest* (1934) showed only a clash of diverse material interests, for he deliberately excluded from consideration all nonmaterial elements. A few years later, just as deliberately, Beard cut loose from materialism. He added a supplementary volume to the *Rise of American Civilization*, calling it *The American Spirit* (1942). This he considered an essential complement to the earlier volumes. It would present the "interior" rather than the "outward" aspect of civilization, describing the "intellectual and moral motivation" of Americans. Unfortunately, Beard had no method for analyzing ideas apart from material interests, so the book was a disappointingly literal summary of the documents he had read.

Beard's last historical work, written at the end of World War II, was a scathing analysis of Franklin D. Roosevelt's foreign policy. This too reflected Beard's revolt against determinism.[16] Convinced in the mid-Thirties that another war would destroy democracy in America, Beard could not regard our involvement as inevitable. He could not think that economic forces would run so contrary to the true "national interest." Nor could he, as a good progressive, hold "the people" responsible, any more than the revisionists held them responsible for the Civil War. When intervention occurred, it had to be the work of malign individuals. In a sense, Beard joined Allan Nevins in putting a new emphasis on personal responsibility in history and on the preservation of traditional values. Though Beard and Nevins disagreed completely on foreign policy, and Beard remained a critic while Nevins became a laureate of heroes, both of them reveal the approaching disruption of the progressive school.

One major historian at the height of his powers in the 1930's had never in any real sense been part of that school. This was Harvard's Samuel Eliot Morison. As Channing's student and successor, Morison inherited eclectic sympathies together with a basically conservative allegiance to the continuities in history. As a proper Bostonian living still in the house of his ancestors, he knew that those continuities be-

---

[16] *President Roosevelt and the Coming of the War, 1941* (1948). Beard's change of outlook is also shown in *A Basic History of the United States* (1944) and *The Republic* (1943).

tween the present and the remote past were still unbroken.[17] He did not find them where the older conservative evolutionists had, in the formal structure of institutions. He was enough of a twentieth century man to know that institutions are not so self-sustaining as late nineteenth century professors had believed. For Morison continuity inhered in the very stuff that progressive scholars brought to the fore, the very stuff that postwar critics held up to scorn and derision. It inhered in social relationships, in ways of life, in accustomed values, in the web of culture. Although Morison was a gifted narrative historian rather than an architect of broad interpretations, the books he wrote in the Thirties adumbrated an essentially new view of American history. Against the progressive accent on change and against the postwar revulsion from ideals, Morison wrote of the tough, enduring qualities in his cultural heritage.

Being a vigorous, explicit opponent of determinism, Morison chose biography and intellectual history as his vehicles is the 1930's. These he employed in a spirited and sustained defense of New England Puritanism. The widespread debunking of the Puritan as a gloomy moral hypocrite, especially by James Truslow Adams and Parrington, aroused Morison's regional pride. His counterattack opened with an array of biographical portraits, *Builders of the Bay Colony* (1930); it widened through an influential series of lectures, *The Puritan Pronaos* (1936); and culminated in three solid volumes on Harvard College in the seventeenth century. These books launched a revival of respect for the early religious underpinnings of American thought and society.

Morison made the Puritans relevant in several ways to the broad defense of American culture that was appearing in the Thirties. First, he humanized and somewhat modernized the Puritan image. By depicting an intellectually vigorous, broad-minded folk, comprehensible to the modern mind, he pointed up the continuity between the first Americans and their latter-day descendants. "Primitive New England is the porch to the temple," Morison concluded, "a puritan *pronaos* as it were to the American mind of the nineteenth century, and of today." Second, he repelled the economic interpretation of the Puritan emigration; they came for idealistic reasons, to preserve a

---

[17] See W. H. Hale's "Historian of the Ocean Sea," *Reporter*, XVII (July 11, 1957), 44-47, and Morison's own memoir of his childhood, *One Boy's Boston, 1887-1901* (1962).

"rugged faith." Third, Morison denied that the Puritans were Calvinistic determinists, thereby associating them with his own assault on modern determinism.[18]

In much of this program Morison had the support of a brilliant young colleague in the English Department, Perry Miller. With extraordinary subtlety, gusto, and industry, Miller elaborated the meaning of Puritan ideas on a grand scale. A Chicagoan and an atheist, he did not have Morison's conservative zeal to re-establish continuity with the fathers of New England. Miller wanted to cut through all the myths, traditional and modern alike, to decipher the authentic, unsuspected otherness of the past. Certainly the Puritans attracted him partly because of the sheer difficulty of reaching them. Yet the main point to be made here is the repugnance he shared with Morison for all social and economic determinisms. By showing that the Puritans brought with them from Europe a fully developed system of beliefs, Miller's prewar books swelled the rising assault on the Turnerian school.[19]

Miller was little read by professional historians until after the war, and it would be wrong to suppose that Morison's restoration of cultural continuity, Nevins' hero worship, or Beard's search for the American Spirit made much impression on them either. Undoubtedly most historians, in spite of multiplying schisms, remained broadly loyal to the progressive outlook. Most of them apparently held to the basic faith in progress that Parrington had come to doubt; most of them looked for "realistic" explanations of human behavior; many still viewed society as a tumultuous extension of the flux of nature. Yet the old progressive consensus was clearly under increasing strain. The notion that material forces govern history was losing ground. All of the major authorities on the Civil War, and most of those who wrote on other wars as well, had rejected the thesis of inevitability. Interest in the decision making of powerful individuals and in the impact of powerful ideas was spreading. A disillusion that had sharpened economic realism had also revealed follies and failures

[18] *The Intellectual Life of Colonial New England*, 2nd ed. (1956), pp. 11, 274; *The Founding of Harvard College* (1935) and *Harvard College in the Seventeenth Century* (2 vols., 1936).

[19] In addition to *Orthodoxy in Massachusetts: A Genetic Study* (1933) and *The New England Mind: The Seventeenth Century* (1939), see the appraisals collected in "Perry Miller and the American Mind," *Harvard Review*, II (Winter-Spring, 1964).

that realism could not explain. Current events portended a grim future for democracy. The human prospect in the future and in the past seemed less predictable than progressive historians had hitherto supposed. In compensation, some now looked for the relatively permanent features of their culture.

Two books published on essentially the same subject in the early 1940's threw these divergent views of American history into dramatic contrast. Ralph Gabriel's *The Course of American Democratic Thought* (1940) and Merle Curti's *The Growth of American Thought* (1943) were broad surveys, which brought to maturity the study of American intellectual history by professional historians. Curti's book testified to the persistent vigor of progressive scholarship. Gabriel's sketched out a new pattern that was emerging from the crisis in progressive thought.

The two men had begun their studies from similar starting points. Although Gabriel was an easterner and Curti was a midwesterner, they started from a common background of Parrington, Turner, social history, and social science. Curti was a student of Turner, and Gabriel's first book, *The Evolution of Long Island* (1921), was strongly Turnerian. Both men were primarily occupied in the 1920's with what we would today call social history. Both were drawn to intellectual history partly by an idealistic concern over the impact of war, industrialization, and modern science on American values; both wished to resist the pessimism and disillusion of the time. Curti did so in the manner of John Dewey, combining an instrumental view of ideas with an unshaken faith in science. But Gabriel, influenced by an underlying religious commitment, joined in the outcry against scientific determinism.[20] His *Course of American Democratic Thought* consisted largely of biographical portraits; Curti's *Growth* completely subordinated individuals to general social and economic patterns.

Fearful also of the danger of totalitarianism in an unstable world,

[20] On the affinity between Gabriel and Morison and the linkage between Curti and earlier New Historians see Robert A. Skotheim's "The Writing of American Histories of Ideas: Two Traditions in the XXth Century," *Journal of the History of Ideas*, XXV (1964), 269-77. The attitudes that attracted the two men to the study of intellectual history are evident in Curti's "Literature in the Synthetic Study of History," *Historical Outlook*, XIII (1922), 129, and Gabriel's reviews of the *Encyclopaedia of the Social Sciences* in *AHR*, XL (1935), 305-07, and XLI (1935), 113-16.

Gabriel adopted a conservative view of the American past. His theme was the continuity of an essentially unchanged body of ideas through the vicissitudes of the last century. He argued that the American people were basically united, even in 1861, by a faith that had survived every adversity. Curti, on the other hand, celebrated conflict, diversity, and change. His book treated democracy not as a stable faith in man but as an expanding struggle waged by and for common men with the aid of scientific knowledge. Eager to make intellectual history genuinely democratic, Curti gave special attention to popular ideas and their dissemination. He widened to the utmost the scope of the progressive synthesis, and so in a sense completed the task to which the dominant school of historians gave their best energies during the interwar years.[21] Gabriel laid the foundations of another synthesis grounded in the persistence rather than the progress of American democracy.

---

[21] Curti's impressive range—his capacity to bring into history the data of all of the social sciences—is also displayed in his collected essays, *Probing Our Past* (1954) and his pioneering quantitative study, *The Making of an American Community* (1959).

# 6

# A SEARCH FOR STABILITY

Although World War II caused a widespread lapse of scholarly activity, it did not seem for a time to change the interpretation of American history very much. In fact, as young historians came back to the universities from wartime assignments, progressive historiography entered a kind of Indian summer. Through the late 1940's and into the early 1950's most of the exciting books were written by scholars who had been trained during the Great Depression and who had responded ardently to the influence of Charles A. Beard. Their books in large measure were hearty evaluations of the tradition of democratic reform and protest. Merrill Jensen's *The New Nation* (1950) recorded the advancing struggle of democracy in the 1780's. Arthur M. Schlesinger Jr.'s *The Age of Jackson* (1945) told a similar story about the 1830's. Eric F. Goldman's *Rendezvous with Destiny* (1952) swept bravely forward from 1870 in tracing "the reform movements that culminated in the New Deal and the Fair Deal." C. Vann Woodward's *Origins of the New South, 1877-1913* (1951) focused on the upthrust of democracy under the impact of industrialism. Among somewhat older scholars, Alice Felt Tyler wrote about religious and humanitarian reform in a Turnerian vein; and Henry Steele Commager carried forward Parrington's unfinished story of modern American thought with an optimistic pragmatism the old master had lacked.[1]

A disquieting note sounded in one of the most brilliant of the postwar books. Richard Hofstadter's *The American Political Tradition and the Men Who Made it* (1948) commented mordantly on a cur-

---

[1] Tyler, *Freedom's Ferment: Phases of American Social History from the Colonial Period to the Outbreak of the Civil War* (1944); Commager, *The American Mind: An Interpretation of American Thought and Character Since the 1880's* (1950); Max Savelle, *Seeds of Liberty: The Genesis of the American Mind* (1948); Thomas C. Cochran and William Miller, *The Age of Enterprise* (1942); John C. Miller, *Triumph of Freedom, 1775-1783* (1948); John Hope Franklin, *From Slavery to Freedom* (1947); Daniel Aaron, *Men of Good Hope: A Story of American Progressives* (1951).

rent "lack of confidence in the American future" and on "the rudder-
less and demoralized state of American liberalism." This he attributed partly to the absence of really basic differences between liberal
and conservative impulses throughout the national experience. The
customary emphasis of American historians on conflict, Hofstadter
said, has obscured the underlying agreement that major parties and
movements have always shared. Ours has been "a democracy in
cupidity," which offers no coherent guidance in a new, more dangerous era.[2] Hofstadter did not press this fateful challenge to progressive historiography. He delivered it as a casual afterthought to
a narrative revealing a fascinating variety of political types. He
wrote from a position otherwise so sympathetic to Beard and so
critical of American business mores that his heresy seemed only a
step to the left.

All of these books displayed a keen interest in the role of ideas,
particularly as they bore on political action. Many of the authors still
held to a primarily economic interpretation of history; but close attention to the impact of ideas on politics inevitably pushed economic
causation into the background. From an original concentration on
external, material reality, the progressive scholar was turning more
and more to a preoccupation with values. And since the values that
many of the best books examined were those of the progressive tradition itself, historians were obviously taking stock of their own ideological heritage. While some were assuring themselves of its
strength, others probed soft spots. Hofstadter was not alone in showing a new awareness of failures and dilemmas in the liberal record.
Goldman worried about the growing relativism it displayed. Other
left-of-center historians, newly sensitive to the magnitude of American racial problems, discovered a vein of prejudice in liberal thought;
they set about rectifying the insensitivity and disinterest older progressive historians had usually shown on the subject of race.[3]

A more central and thoroughgoing reappraisal of progressive history began in monographs challenging the significance of economic
conflicts. No single monograph could make extensive claims or es-

[2] Pp. vii-x. This introduction was written, Professor Hofstadter recalls, at the
behest of the publisher; he had not written the book with any such clear design.
[3] John Higham, "Anti-Semitism in the Gilded Age," *Mississippi Valley Historical Review*, XLIII (1957), 559-78; Kenneth M. Stampp, *The Peculiar Institution* (1956); C. Vann Woodward, *The Strange Career of Jim Crow* (1955).

cape the suspicion that its findings were exceptional. By the mid-Fifties, however, the new research was having a cumulative impact on the whole shape of American history. One after another, the great crises, which progressive historians had depicted as turning points in the battle between democracy and privilege, came under fresh examination. In each case the scale of conflict seemed to shrink. Sharp divisions between periods, sections, groups, and ideologies disappeared. Over all, the new digging amounted to a massive grading operation that smoothed and flattened the convulsive dialectic of progressive history. An unsuspected degree of uniformity and agreement appeared in the welter of America's historical experience. Instead of a polarized culture—a culture eternally divided betwen over- and underprivileged groups, between a party of the past and a party of the future, between noble ideals and ignoble interests—young scholars glimpsed an essentially homogeneous culture full of small, impermanent variations. The continuity that Gabriel had observed in the American "democratic faith" and that Hofstadter criticized in the American political tradition emerged as substantial social reality.

Among the various types of cleavage that progressives dwelled upon, the sectional principle gave way most easily. An attack on sectional differences as fundamental to American history had already developed in the 1930's. It stemmed partly from the revolt against Turner: all anti-Turnerians saw the West as an extension of the East, not its antithesis. The revisionist approach to the Civil War also ran counter to an emphatic sectionalism; for revisionists assumed that North and South were not incompatible civilizations, but basically one. These views simply gained further momentum in the 1940's and 1950's. Now the defensive and aggressive sectional feelings that motivated so much scholarship in the early twentieth century were rapidly dissolving. The standardized urban milieu in which younger historians grew up deprived them of strong regional identities.

Consequently, in postwar scholarship, much that had been described as southern or western either lost significance or merged into national configurations. Following a line of research that Frank Owsley opened in the late 1930's, many southern historians called attention to the democratic features of the Old South. It was, they maintained, primarily a land of middle-class farmers, not of plantation aristocrats.[4] The notion of the antebellum South as a distinctively aristocratic society was a myth; and a northern scholar wrote a book to prove that even the myth had rested on nationwide rather than purely sectional yearnings. *The Southerner as American* (1960) was the title of a collection of essays by a group of young southern historians, and it summed up the general trend of scholarship.[5]

One might equally say of western history that it now dealt with the westerner as American. Attention shifted increasingly to the post-frontier West, to cities, economic development, and the impingement of national politics and institutions on western areas.[6] For many readers Henry Nash Smith made America's mythology about the West more interesting than the reality. Smith's powerful book, *Virgin Land* (1950), capped the assault on Turner by relegating the frontier thesis—prematurely, it should be said—to the ash heap of dead myths. Simultaneously Walter P. Webb took that thesis out of a sectional context and put it in an international context. Before World War II Webb had dwelt on the distinctive features of his own West, the Great Plains. In 1952 he published *The Great Frontier,* in which America's frontier experience is linked to European history in a general interpretation of Western civilization.

In view of the reaction against sectionalism, it is little wonder that academic interest in political conflicts between East, West, and South fell off markedly. No one could deny, of course, that the Civil War was a tremendous rupture of whatever unity and continuity America had exhibited. But few of the younger professional historians coming along in the wake of Craven and Randall found the causes of the war an attractive subject for research. While journalists served up great gobs of Civil War drama to an avid public, the number of significant contributions from professionals declined. A notable exception was

[4] Frank L. Owsley, "The Economic Basis of Society in the Late Ante-Bellum South," *Journal of Southern History,* VII (1940), 24-45, and *Plain Folk of the Old South* (1949); Charles S. Sydnor, *The Development of Southern Sectionalism, 1819-1848* (1948).
[5] Edited by Charles G. Sellers Jr.; William R. Taylor, *Cavalier and Yankee: The Old South and American National Character* (1961).
[6] Earl Pomeroy, "The Changing West," in *The Reconstruction of American History,* ed. John Higham (London, 1962), pp. 77-80; Louis B. Wright, *Culture on the Moving Frontier* (1955); Douglas F. Dowd, "A Comparative Analysis of Economic Development in the American West and South," *Journal of Economic History,* XVI (1956), 558-74.

the monumental history of the Civil War era on which Allan Nevins embarked about 1940; but Nevins, writing in the spirit of James Ford Rhodes, had an old-fashioned appreciation of the triumph of union in the midst of strife.[7]

If antagonisms between North and South failed to stimulate younger historians, conflicts between East and West proved still less inspiring. Events that had been attributed to aggressive western initiative, such as the War of 1812 and the progressive movement, were reinterpreted in national terms.[8] Most remarkably, the Turnerian doctrine that the political democracy of the early nineteenth century came out of the West received hardly any effective support in postwar research.[9] A major controversy erupted over the nature of Jacksonian democracy without any of the leading participants taking seriously the specifically western elements for which it had been famous.

Not a sectional but a class thesis was at issue in the controversy over Jacksonian democracy. Not Turner but Beard was the main target of the newer historians. Turner, having died in 1932, bore the brunt of the historiographical discontents of the Thirties; Beard's death in 1948 released a similar but fiercer onslaught. While Turner's sectionalism faded gracefully into the background, Beard's vision of an America divided between the democratic many and a privileged economic class underwent searching criticism. Throughout the late 1940's and 1950's a host of scholars mined and sapped the old economic dualism over most of the span of American history. The first sustained attack developed on Jacksonian terrain simply because a new, highly vulnerable statement of the Beardian approach materialized there.

Arthur M. Schlesinger Jr.'s *The Age of Jackson* was the work of a

[7] *Ordeal of the Union* (2 vols., 1947); *The Emergence of Lincoln* (2 vols., 1950); *The War for the Union* (2 vols., 1959).

[8] Bradford Perkins, *Prologue to War: England and the United States, 1805-1812* (1961); George E. Mowry, *The Era of Theodore Roosevelt, 1900-1912* (1958).

[9] A partial exception was the ingenious reformulation of the Turner thesis in urban terms by two easterners, Stanley Elkins and Eric McKitrick, "A Meaning for Turner's Frontier," *Political Science Quarterly*, LXIX (1954), 321-53, 565-602. Turner's stoutest postwar champion, Ray Allen Billington, gradually modified the claims of the master, muting especially the theme of sectional conflict. See "The Frontier in American Thought and Character," *The New World Looks at Its History*, ed. Archibald R. Lewis and Thomas F. McGann (1963), pp. 77-94.

brilliant, ardent, and very young man charged with the antibusiness spirit of the 1930's. Building on postulates advanced earlier by his father and by Beard, Schlesinger depicted the urban working class as the cutting edge of the Jacksonian movement. That movement involved intellectuals and other "noncapitalist groups, farmers and laboring men." It was a phase of the pragmatic, realistic, "enduring struggle between the business community and the rest of society which is the guarantee of freedom." [10] The line ran straight and true from Jackson to Franklin D. Roosevelt.

Launched in 1945 on a great wave of praise, *The Age of Jackson* soon collided with a backlash of criticism. Many historians, it will be remembered, were turning away from the urgent present-mindedness of the 1930's. They distrusted Schlesinger's heavy emphasis on the features of Jacksonian politics that resembled the New Deal. Further probing into the impressive new evidence he had assembled dissolved the polarity between "the business community and the rest of society." Jacksonian "laboring men" were often merchants and professional people; the "working class" displayed no consistent political allegiance. In fact, acquisitive, business motives entered very largely into the Jacksonian program. Evidently the common man *was* a businessman. [11]

It also began to appear that the ideological cleavage between Jeffersonianism and Hamiltonianism, which progressive historians linked with the distinction between common men and capitalists, was equally misleading. Schlesinger endorsed the usual view that the Jeffersonian spirit triumphed in the 1830's over the monopolistic schemes of the Hamiltonians. But postwar scholarship undercut this dualism too. A modest revival in the study of economic history, beginning in the 1940's, brought out startlingly close relations between government and business in the Jacksonian era.

The revival of economic history owed something to the initiative of Edwin F. Gay, Arthur H. Cole, and the Rockefeller Foundation, and something also to a new climate of opinion. The waning of eco-

[10] *The Age of Jackson* (1945), p. 307.
[11] The most effective critics were Joseph Dorfman and Bray Hammond, whose own books, *The Economic Mind in American Civilization* (5 vols., 1946-59) and *Banks and Politics in America from the Revolution to the Civil War* (1957), were among the major works of the postwar era. For a summary of the controversy see Charles G. Sellers Jr.'s "Andrew Jackson versus the Historians," *Mississippi Valley Historical Review*, XLIV (1958), 615-34.

nomic interpretations of history enabled historians to reverse their chain of cause and effect. Attention shifted from economic motives to economic processes, from the economic causes of historical development to the historical causes of economic development. Doubtless the dramatic impact that governmental policies were having on national income and wealth created a special interest in the political sources of economic growth. A Committee on Research in Economic History, appointed by the SSRC in 1941, chose as its first area for investigation the role of government in economic development. The studies it sponsored over the next decade, notably those of Carter Goodrich and his students, revealed a thoroughly mixed economy in antebellum America. An intimate, pragmatic association of state and local governments with "private enterprise" overrode all ideological scruples. One economic historian actually concluded that "it is only meretricious to contrast Hamiltonian with Jeffersonian policy." [12] Others, notably Lee Benson in *The Concept of Jacksonian Democracy* (1961), are redefining party differences with a new grasp of what was constructively liberal in Whig and Federalist programs.

Inevitably, the reaction against an ideologically divided, class-structured history reached back to the Revolutionary era. The basic dialectic of progressive historiography had been established by contrasting the Revolution and the Constitution, the one a democratic social upheaval, the other a capitalistic counterrevolution. Here was the critical test of the progressive approach; and here the sharpest clash of interpretations occurred. In 1943 a modest monograph by Philip Crowl, demonstrating an absence of class conflict in Maryland politics during and after the Revolution, went largely unnoticed.[13] In the 1950's the tide turned. It drastically reduced, though it did not wholly eliminate, the antithesis between a Jeffersonian Revolution and a Hamiltonian Constitution.

Two slashing critics went straight for Beard's *Economic Interpretation of the Constitution*. Forrest McDonald closely re-examined

---

[12] E. A. J. Johnson, "Federalism, Pluralism, and Public Policy," *Journal of Economic History*, XXII (1962), 442. On the origins of this research program see Herbert Heaton's *A Scholar in Action: Edwin F. Gay* (1952), pp. 237-48; on its impressive results, Robert A. Lively's "The American System," *Business History Review*, XXIX (1955), 81-96. Another, more recent approach to economic growth, paying less attention to government and more to markets, is in C. Douglass North's *The Economic Growth of the United States, 1790-1860* (1961).
[13] *Maryland During and After the Revolution* (1943).

the sources of income of constitutional convention delegates in order to demolish Beard's distinction between personalty and realty interests. Robert E. Brown raked Beard's logic in one book and in another assailed Becker's thesis of an internal social revolution. The widespread participation in government in colonial Massachusetts, Brown claimed, shows that Americans did not gain democracy in 1776 but rather preserved it. Instead of creating a new social order, they defended an old one.[14]

Thus a minimization of class conflict deprived early American history both of a revolutionary and of a counterrevolutionary thrust. Scholars investigating the causes of the Revolution, notably Oliver M. Dickerson, Edmund S. Morgan, and Bernard Knollenberg, discounted the impersonal economic forces and the irrepressible conflicts of Beardian history. Instead, they put forward the old patriotic view that the revolutionists were defending traditional liberties against bungling innovations of British officials. Just as historians in the 1930's rejected Beard's explanation of the Civil War for a theory of inept American leadership, so historians in the 1950's replaced Beard's explanation of the Revolution with an emphasis on inept British leadership.[15] Although the new interpretation of the Revolution was sympathetic whereas the revisionist account of the Civil War was not, the similarity of the two cases suggests again how much a repudiation of determinism contributed to the breakdown of progressive history.

As controversial breezes eddied through the staid ranks of early American historians, a new vigor seemed to enter that field. Never before had professional scholars debated so seriously the issues of the seventeenth and eighteenth centuries. The imperial and progressive schools had worked different sides of the street and had only oc-

---

[14] McDonald, *We the People: The Economic Origins of the Constitution* (1958); Brown, *Charles Beard and the Constitution* (1956) and *Middle-Class Democracy and the Revolution in Massachusetts, 1691-1780* (1955). The Beardian approach, modernized and improved, persists in Jackson T. Main, *The Antifederalists: Critics of the Constitution* (1961).

[15] Dickerson, *The Navigation Acts and the American Revolution* (1951); Edmund S. and Helen M. Morgan, *The Stamp Act Crisis: Prologue to Revolution* (1953); Knollenberg, *Origin of the American Revolution: 1759-1766* (1960); Esmond Wright, *Fabric of Freedom, 1763-1800* (1961). Other studies are summarized in Jack P. Greene's "The Flight from Determinism: A Review of Recent Literature on the Coming of the American Revolution," *South Atlantic Quarterly*, LXI (1962), 235-59.

casionally encountered one another directly. Now a frontal challenge to the progressive school made early American history, for a time at least, the liveliest area of intellectual ferment. It began to recover from the relative neglect into which it had fallen because of the progressive bias in favor of more recent history. More scholars were willing to focus on the colonial origins of American experience and to understand remote situations in their own terms. Then too, the revulsion against determinism helped to quicken colonial history. A good many postwar historians followed Morison's example of humanizing the colonial scene. Much of the best research appeared in vivid biographies of such people as Jefferson, Ezra Stiles, and Edward Livingston.[16] Fortunately, all these impulses received the timely support of a new research organization, the Institute of Early American History and Culture, which Carl Bridenbaugh started upon a productive career in 1945.

Recent American history may not be faring as well. The study of the twentieth century has shared, of course, in the general reevaluation of the American past. There too the antibusiness spirit of progressive scholarship, with its emphasis on economic conflict, has diminished. There too a revolt against determinism and a more sensitive grasp of the role of political and economic leadership characterize the latest books.[17] But major interpretive revisions, such as we have had for the history of the eighteenth and nineteenth centuries, have been less in evidence, at least for the period since 1917. No established professional historian except Eric Goldman has written seriously about the period since World War II, and some are moving their research back from the twentieth century altogether. There may be some question whether or not the vitality recent historiography had in the 1940's will persist without the explicit present-mindedness of the progressive school.

Enough has been said, perhaps, about particular periods to enable us to ask what over-all meaning the new American past is assuming.

16 Dumas Malone, *Jefferson and His Time* (3 vols. to date, 1948-62); Edmund S. Morgan, *The Gentle Puritan: A Life of Ezra Stiles* (1962); George Dangerfield, *Chancellor Robert R. Livingston of New York* (1961).

17 In addition to books by Link and Hofstadter cited elsewhere, see the numerous studies of diplomatic history by Herbert Feis; Arthur M. Schlesinger Jr., *The Age of Roosevelt* (3 vols. to date, 1957-60); William E. Leuchtenburg, *Franklin D. Roosevelt and the New Deal* (1963); Ernest R. May, *The World War and American Isolation 1914-1917* (1959); Alfred D. Chandler Jr., *Strategy and Structure: Chapters in the History of the Industrial Enterprise* (1962).

The present generation has not produced a decisive leadership such as Turner and Beard supplied in their day. No one has written a major work shaping our history into a grand design as persuasive as theirs once were. Nevertheless, alternatives to the progressive scheme have been sketched in a number of recent books, all of which depict a relatively homogeneous society with a relatively conservative history.

Historians in an age of unceasing international peril, when national security and the capacity for survival are fundamental concerns, can hardly avoid a somewhat conservative view of their country's history. They can hardly avoid an appreciation of its more cohesive and deeply rooted qualities. Nevertheless, they may trace those qualities to quite diverse sources, and they may disagree widely on the worth and durability of such homogeneity as they perceive. In rejecting a simple cleavage between two Americas, some historians may be most impressed by the wholeness of the national fabric, others by the looseness and multitude of its many strands. Their common concern is with the nature and degree of stability in American experience. Yet their answers are various and often ambivalent.

A key to the present temper of historical opinion lies in the pages of Alexis de Tocqueville's *Democracy in America* (1840), today the most respected of all interpretations of the United States. Tocqueville treated American culture as an organic whole; and his work rested heavily on the concept of national character. During the heyday of progressive scholarship this approach was somewhat suspect, and Tocqueville's influence was at a low ebb. Although progressive intellectuals sometimes indulged in generalizations about national character, they distrusted its heuristic value. Referring as it does to the pervasive, persistent features of a whole culture, "national character" neglects the environmental determination of social conflict. No edition of *Democracy in America* was published in the United States between 1904 and 1945; during most of that time it was out of print. Since World War II, however, at least six hardcover editions have appeared. With them has come a torrent of scholarship and speculation on *the* American experience, character, traits, etc.[18]

---

[18] The revival of serious discussion of national character by scholars seems to date from Margaret Mead's *And Keep Your Powder Dry* (1942) and Arthur M. Schlesinger's "What Then Is the American, This New Man?" *AHR*, XLVIII (1943), 225-44.

In addition to its integral approach, Tocqueville's classic has the special appeal today of rendering a mixed verdict on American democracy. The genial French aristocrat observed a nation at once stable and full of flux. He noticed little class cleavage. But he described a democracy that produced oppressive conformity on the one hand and kaleidoscopic variety on the other. He rejoiced in America's stability while deploring its social fragmentation. These antinomies, which Tocqueville's genius held together, jostle and contend in contemporary historical writing. Today's historians affirm on one side a need for and partial attainment of community in America. They cling on the other to values of dissent and diversity inherited from the progressive tradition. The opposing schools of interpretation that clashed so sharply in the 1930's and 1940's have partially blended, just as general historical theories have done. But the tensions that formerly divided those schools have survived their mingling.

Some of the efforts to sum up American history in recent years primarily emphasize the stability—and therefore the continuity—of American experience over the centuries. Other historians have given more attention to the reverse side of Tocqueville's model, stressing instabilities and thus allowing for a greater degree of change. To the first group belong the Harvard political theorist Louis Hartz and the University of Chicago historian Daniel Boorstin. Both of them have dwelled on the remarkable persistence of basic characteristics throughout American history. Hartz, like Gabriel before him, locates continuity in certain unifying principles or beliefs. Boorstin finds it in the pragmatic, down-to-earth way of life progressive historians often admired. Yet it is Hartz who stands closer to the progressive sympathy for friction and dissent, regretting that America has not had more.

Hartz wrote *The Liberal Tradition in America* (1955) to substitute new categories for the overworked schema of Beard and Parrington. He argued that the absence of a feudal heritage had left America with just one rather than two traditions of thought. A liberal consensus has had so unchallenged a sway, Hartz said, that most American political debate has been shadowboxing. "America must look to its contact with other nations to provide that spark of philosophy, that grain of relative insight that its own history has denied." [19]

Boorstin was equally impressed by the massive stability and un-

[19] P. 287.

philosophic harmony of America. He too explained the mediocrity of American political thought as a consequence of the absence of the deep social antagonisms that have existed in Europe. Boorstin, however, had no regrets about this. In *The Genius of American Politics* (1953) and in *The Americans: The Colonial Experience* (1958), he contended that America from the outset flourished by scrapping European blueprints, dissolving European distinctions, and moving toward a homogeneous society of undifferentiated men. A naïve practicality enabled Americans to unite in a stable way of life, undisturbed by divisive principles.

Significantly, both Hartz and Boorstin got their accent on a stable, continuous national character by looking at the United States as Tocqueville had: from the outside. They too—Hartz especially—adopted an explicitly comparative approach to American history. Hartz came to a comparative approach partly by the accident of having to teach European political theory at Harvard instead of the American theory for which he had been trained. Boorstin came to it through a European education as a Rhodes Scholar (as Lawrence Gipson had many years before) and later as a visiting professor abroad. Certainly both men were responding in a large sense to the heightened awareness of the outside world that the history of the mid-twentieth century thrust upon American historians. The domestic conflicts so apparent in an age of reform had diverted progressive scholars from the international context of American history. The neo-Tocquevilleans of the 1950's partially restored that context and so widened the horizons of scholarship. Unfortunately, their comparative interests were largely confined to contrasts between America and Europe. The insecurities of the postwar era engendered such an urge to define America—to establish its distinctive character—that the parallels and reciprocal involvements of a truly international history remained little attended.

The search for the essential and the permanent in American experience led perhaps more readily in an interdisciplinary direction, for the pursuit of national identity animated literary critics and social scientists as well as historians. One of the most persuasive general historians of the 1950's, David M. Potter, developed an integral and comparative view of American history primarily through contact with anthropology rather than contact with Europe. Like an increasing number of his colleagues, Potter found the theories of contemporary social scientists indispensable to a grasp of American society now that the progressive pattern was dissolving. He stopped writing a conventional sort of political history and made an intensive study of recent findings on culture and personality. More than most postwar historians, Potter wrote in a deterministic vein. His *People of Plenty: Economic Abundance and the American Character* (1954) is an economic interpretation, which transmuted Turner's frontier thesis into the more inclusive and systematic formulas of behavioral theory. For the transitory, sectional abundance of the frontier, Potter substituted a broadly based aptitude for productivity. Whereas the generation of Parrington and Beard had explained basic cleavages on economic grounds, Potter showed our wealth shaping a common, distinctive, and successful way of life.

On a more concrete level of scholarship one of the finest historians who has illuminated persistent features of American history is Edmund S. Morgan of Yale. Hartz, Boorstin, and Potter have explained continuity and stability largely in terms of environment and institutions. Morgan, on the other hand, has looked for and discovered a dogged adherence to fundamental principles. In writing about the Puritan founders of New England, he has emphasized the maintenance of their religious and social standards in the face of many divisive pressures. In writing about the Revolutionary generation, he has shown its undeviating pursuit of consistent principles throughout the tortuous controversy with Britain.[20]

All these historians have been aware of the other side of Tocqueville's America. All of them have noticed the diffuse instability associated in America with rapid mobility; and Boorstin's latest book, *The Image* (1962), reveals a distinct uneasiness over the formless flux he had earlier celebrated. Still, it has remained for another group of scholars, less preoccupied with contrasts between America and Europe, to deal seriously with the dimension of change. It has remained for them to formulate into new patterns the frictions within American life. Although most of the latter historians work on a relatively small scale, close to the stream of events, some of them too have tried to sketch the general course of American history. As a

20 Morgan, *The Stamp Act Crisis* (1953); *The Birth of the Republic, 1763-1789* (1956); *The Puritan Dilemma: The Story of John Winthrop* (1958); *Visible Saints: The History of a Puritan Idea* (1963).

group, they share a common fascination with the tendency of stable structures to break down in a free and fluid culture.

Movement through space and through the ranks of society forms the central theme of our latest students of conflict. Like Potter, they have taken Turner's emphasis on migration out of a sectional context. In effect, they have used the theme of mobility to explode the rigid categories of progressive scholarship while maintaining a sharp interest in conflict and change. In place of classes and sections, they have conceived of a politics of coalition between diverse interests and of a society of shifting status groups. The concept of status has seemed especially relevant because of the very fragility of the honorific and prestigeful considerations that define it. Status is something that is continually pursued and ever on the verge of being lost in a nation of mobile men. As they break free from traditional security in search of better locations, a vast process of disintegration and partial reintegration goes on.

Considering the crucial importance assigned to mobility in this version of American history, it is hardly surprising that one of the influential exponents is also the leading authority on immigration. Oscar Handlin has shaped each of his major books as a story of disintegration and mobility. Handlin's history begins, characteristically, with a stable, orderly community—a *Gemeinschaft* in the language of German sociology—which makes life meaningful and whole. Then the shock of migration disrupts the community, breeding strife and freedom; and uprooted men pursue their separate, clashing purposes. This is the story of *Boston's Immigrants* (1941), the story of antebellum Massachusetts in *Commonwealth* (1947), the story of nineteenth century immigration in *The Uprooted* (1951), and the story of us all in *The Americans* (1963). It is often an anguished story, heavy with a sense of loss and alienation. It is also highly ambivalent, for the author admires the growth of freedom while lamenting the decline of order.

A rather similar picture of American development lies behind the superficially quite different interpretations recently offered by William A. Williams and Rowland Berthoff, one of them a neo-Marxist, the other a self-proclaimed conservative. Both Williams and Berthoff look back to a time of stability and order at the beginning of American history. Both of them observe a breakdown of community in the laissez-faire world of the nineteenth century as a consequence of excessive mobility (Berthoff) or expansion (Williams).[21] The three accounts differ most sharply in their evaluation of the twentieth century. Handlin leaves the outcome confused and uncertain; Berthoff finds America gradually recovering a healthy balance; Williams sees a capitalist oligarchy restoring but perverting the ideal of community.

Through all these interpretations, through those that stress stability and those that stress change, runs a question previous generations of historians in America had never so insistently asked. Most of the major postwar scholars seem to be asking in one way or another, "What (if anything) is so deeply rooted in our past that we can rely on its survival?" This has become, perhaps, the great historical question in a time of considerable moral confusion, when the future looks both precarious and severely limited in its possibilities. The question is genuinely open-ended, because neither the partisans of stability nor the connoisseurs of change assume that history is on their side. Progressive historians, like the conservative evolutionists who preceded them, relied implicitly on a faith in progress in charting the relations between past and future. Assuming an upward gradient, they asked what each period or movement "contributed" or "added" to the march of progress. This faith, which was shaken in Parrington's day, has since 1940 been so shattered that historians must soberly ask what is permanent and what is transient in American history. Accordingly, the shedding of a progressive outlook has not left historians accoutered in the conservative evolutionism of the late nineteenth century. Conservative evolutionists were confident that unity would continue to overcome internal strife. They expected that the partnership between union and freedom, which defined their America, would continue to develop and to triumph over obstacles. Today's historians want to know how durable and meaningful are the unities and diversities that already exist. In our postprogressive culture, the relation between freedom and union seems no longer natural but tense and problematical.

Once released from the dream of progress, historians who were alert to conflict and change could face unflinchingly the tragic and

21 Rowland Berthoff, "The American Social Order: A Conservative Hypothesis," *AHR*, LXV (1960), 495-514; William A. Williams, *The Contours of American History* (1961).

ironic elements in the past. In fact, many of our best historians acquired a positive relish for the burdens, the losses, and the intractable dilemmas of history. An early indication of how profoundly this shift in sensibility could affect historical interpretation appeared in the Civil War field. The revisionist school of the Thirties had viewed the "needless" war and the "vindictive" Reconstruction as exceptional interludes in the normal progress of civilization. Like the philosophers of the Enlightenment, the revisionists believed such crimes and follies avoidable if only reason were allowed to work matters out. All of this began to look naïvely optimistic in the 1940's. Relying heavily on Reinhold Niebuhr's powerful critique of the idea of progress, Arthur M. Schlesinger Jr. in 1949 assailed the revisionists for simplifying great moral issues: "Man generally is entangled in insoluble problems; history is consequently a tragedy in which we are all involved, whose keynote is anxiety and frustration, not progress and fulfillment." Before these words were written, the leading revisionist, Avery Craven, was already modifying his position. His writings in the 1950's took more seriously the emotional realities and the moral dilemmas that led to war.[22]

Indeed, much of the best scholarship of the 1950's struck the tragic note. Instead of looking backward from the crest of a historical movement to observe its rise, as progressives usually did, the newer historians often looked forward from the crest to watch its decline. Thus Perry Miller, in resuming the Puritan studies he had commenced in the Thirties, wrote one of the finest books in our historical literature, the second great volume of *The New England Mind* (1953), as an epic of unrelieved defeat. Remorselessly, even gleefully, Miller followed the agonizing, century-long breakup of the intellectual system he had presented in Volume I in its original wholeness. In later work that reflected a growing obsession with the "meaning" of America, Miller shifted to more nationalistic themes. Meanwhile, the stable features of Puritan experience came into view again in Edmund Morgan's writings. But others carried on the analysis of dispersion and loss. Bernard Bailyn, a young historian with a keen understanding of instability in early America, traced through

---

[22] Schlesinger, "The Causes of the Civil War: A Note on Historical Sentimentalism," *Partisan Review,* XVI (1949), 891; Craven, *The Growth of Southern Nationalism, 1848-1861* (1953) and *Civil War in the Making, 1815-1860* (1959).

the seventeenth century the fragmentation of social and educational patterns as Miller had traced the fragmentation of beliefs.[23] In writing about the first half of the nineteenth century Stanley Elkins and David Donald discovered similar trends. Where earlier historians had seen a rise of democracy they found a disastrous erosion of all institutional authority.[24]

Into recent history also passed an unprecedented fascination with decline and defeat. Richard Hofstadter's very influential *Age of Reform* (1955) dwelled on the failings of the populists and the progressives. Instead of one evolutionary sequence culminating in the New Deal, he observed the degeneration of each movement into a perverse illiberalism. Henry May's *The End of American Innocence* (1959) examined the cultural ferment on the eve of World War I not as the beginning of a new era but rather as the destruction of a pre-existing scheme of things. C. Vann Woodward, who was perhaps as deeply attached to progressive values as any of our leading historians, nevertheless discovered that experiences of guilt, alienation, and defeat defined the distinctive value and pertinence of southern history.[25]

A crucial book in this mode was Henry Nash Smith's *Virgin Land* (1950), which we have already noticed for its attack on Turner's kind of western history. Although written with deceptive detachment, *Virgin Land* was essentially a study of the death of ideas. It traced three major images of the American West from the late eighteenth century to the end of the nineteenth. In each case Smith's attention fixed on a loss of imaginative richness and social relevance as the image became increasingly debased, exploited, and false to fact. An adequate account of the rise of western myths and symbols remains to be written. *Virgin Land* was the valedictory of a man alienated from the Texas in which he grew up in the 1920's.

23 Miller's *The New England Mind from Colony to Province* (1953) is complemented in social and political history by Bailyn's *The New England Merchants in the Seventeenth Century* (1955), *Education in the Forming of American Society* (1960), and "Politics and Social Structure in Virginia," in *Seventeenth-Century America*, ed. James Morton Smith (1959), pp. 90-115.

24 Donald, *Lincoln Reconsidered: Essays on the Civil War Era*, 2nd ed. (1961), pp. 209-235, and the critique by A. E. Campbell, "An Excess of Isolation: Isolation and the American Civil War," *Journal of Southern History*, XXIX (1963), 161-74; Elkins, *Slavery: A Problem in American Institutional and Intellectual Life* (1959).

25 Woodward, *The Burden of Southern History* (1960).

Smith's book also announced another theme of great significance in recent historical writing, particularly in the kind that emphasizes instability and change. He handled ideas with a psychoanalytical awareness of their emotional import. *Virgin Land* shares with Hofstadter's *American Political Tradition* (1948) the credit for introducing into professional historical scholarship a large, effective grasp of the nonrational elements in human conduct. Both authors had nourished themselves on modern literary criticism, which became penetrated by psychological interpretations in the late Thirties and Forties. Hofstadter called upon psychology primarily to explain aggression and frustration. Smith, as a professor of English, was less interested in motives than in meanings. A product of the new American Studies movement that was linking literature with history in an integrated study of art and society, he studied the dramatic symbols and pictorial images in which Americans had expressed their deeply rooted hopes and fears. He wrote the history of myths.[26]

Professional historians had been quite slow to make any real use of depth psychology. The first major study of myths in American history, *The Mind of the South* (1941), was written in the 1930's by a tormented literary and social critic, W. J. Cash; but professional historians did not follow up his brilliant insights until the 1950's.[27] Perhaps this was partly because they got little encouragement from the behaviorism that ruled academic psychology. More importantly, a reluctance to accept the nonrational as a legitimate and pervasive dimension of reality was integral to the progressive heritage of American historians. The progressive expectation of steady improvement in human affairs rested on the assumption that men are rational: they ordinarily pursue their individual or collective self-interest, and such interest is either rationally perceived or—at worst —coherently rationalized. Progressive historians treated ideas not as myths, full of extravagant fantasy, but as ideologies that interpret

[26] Smith took the first Ph.D. in American Civilization at Harvard (1940), an experience that made him a historian; but his essential intellectual experience came earlier as an editor and literary critic in the late 1920's in the Southwest, where his interest in myth was shaped by contact with the New Critics and through the influence of Hans Vaihinger and Henri Bergson. Hofstadter owed more to sociologists like Karl Mannheim and to Sigmund Freud, though his style of historical analysis was also much influenced by the approach of literary critics.

[27] E.g., Charles G. Sellers Jr., "The Travail of Slavery," *op. cit.*, pp. 40-71, and Taylor, *op. cit.*

229

life in terms functional to some interested group. Such, for example, was the method of Charles A. Beard. In the last weeks of his life in 1948 the old man still insisted, "Economics explains the mostest!" Then, after a pause, he added, "But I may have neglected the irrational." [28] The comment was an epitaph to more than one man's career.

In recent years scholarly journals have teemed with articles and university presses with books on historical myths, symbols, images, and the like. A psychological approach may, if it continues to gain momentum, reopen every question in American history. It is seductively congenial to the present climate of opinion; for it enables restless historians who are impressed by the over-all stability of their country to subjectivize the stresses within it. Psychological history turns conflict and change into an interior drama. Divisions, which the previous generation understood as basic opposition between distinct groups, become generalized tensions running through the whole culture. Acts of protest and defiance often acquire defensive, compensatory implications, so that reformers for example are seen acting out their personal and social maladjustments.[29]

Also, the study of myths and images has a special attraction in the postwar period because it focuses on kinds of thinking that unite a people rather than those that divide them. The concept of ideology refers to exclusive and rival creeds. It relates directly to social conflict. The concept of myth, on the other hand, refers to the integrating values that bind men together.[30] All in all, the psychological vogue has given an implicit sanction to harmony or adaptability. It has sustained our sense of the dynamic while expressing our need for social solidarity. It has also raised our appreciation of tragedy in history and depressed our appreciation of rational purpose.

Fortunately, American historians have not yielded wholly to the psychologizing trend. Among those who still respect the force of overt principles, a strain of rationalism persists. It is also reappearing

[28] Diary of Alfred Vagts. Evidently World War II set Beard—as it set many others—thinking more seriously about irrational motivations.
[29] See, for example, Emery Battis, *Saints and Sectaries: Anne Hutchinson and the Antinomian Controversy* (1962), David Donald, *Charles Sumner and the Coming of the Civil War* (1960), Marvin Meyers, *The Jacksonian Persuasion: Politics and Belief* (1957), and Samuel P. Hays, *The Response to Industrialism: 1885-1914* (1957).
[30] Ben Halpern, " 'Myth' and 'Ideology' in Modern Usage," *History and Theory,* I (1961), 136-37.

among a small but rising number of historians who are taking a fresh look at organizational patterns. The latter wish to know how groups and agencies—such as political parties, corporations, and communities—have molded behavior and regulated the distribution of power. Deriving partly from studies in entrepreneurial and business history and partly from contemporary American sociology, this kind of history is less concerned with motives than with structure and process. It shows men managing and being managed through rational systems of control and communication. Perhaps we may call this the new institutionalism; for it is bringing back to life a morphological study of organizations, now freed from the formalistic, evolutionary emphasis of nineteenth century scholarship.[31]

Although institutionalists thus far have not gone much beyond the monographic level, the breadth and importance of their contribution seem sure to grow. Yet it is not easy to anticipate that institutional history will in itself alter the main thrust of current scholarship. Institutions are, by their very nature, means of stabilizing the flux of society. If psychological history uncovers in the past the insecurities and pervasive anxieties that trouble many scholars and intellectuals today, institutional history projects the other side of the contemporary spirit: its rage for order. Both the psychological and the institutional approach reflect our fixation on the nature and extent of stability in our past and present. To move beyond that preoccupation historians will need more than a panoply of analytical techniques. They will need a larger and braver vision of the future than most of them now possess.

Meanwhile the profound changes in historical interpretation in the last twenty-five years have left today's scholars with plenty to do. Simply to master the new conceptual resources they have acquired is a herculean task. And the task must be well in hand before one can feel confident that the postwar generation is writing history that will live as a monument of its era, as the history of Henry Adams, of Turner, of Beard, and of Parrington lives as monuments of theirs.

[31] William Miller, ed., *Men in Business: Essays on the Historical Role of the Entrepreneur* (1952); Lee Benson, *The Concept of Jacksonian Democracy: New York as a Test Case* (1961); Morton Keller, *The Life Insurance Enterprise, 1885-1910: A Study in the Limits of Corporate Power* (1963); Chandler, *op. cit.* Far from being mutually exclusive, the institutional and psychological approaches are joined in the impressive works, already cited, by Elkins and McKitrick, and in McKitrick's *Andrew Johnson and Reconstruction* (1960).

On the concrete, empirical level, many of the newer research objectives remain substantially unfulfilled. The intricate study of social organization demanded by the collapse of the simple categories of progressive scholarship has just begun. The long stultified outward reach of American history into international and comparative dimensions, which suffered first from the environmentalism of progressive scholarship and later perhaps from the inwardness of the American Studies movement, is only now going beyond a few simplified contrasts. The sophisticated moral criticism of the past implicit in our growing psychological awareness has barely revealed its potentialities.

There is work to do also in cultivating a point of view wide enough to integrate these new interests with the unexhausted heritage from which they sprang. Much was sacrificed when the progressive historians largely ignored the constructive insights of the institutionalists. The diverse tendencies in contemporary scholarship suggest that the fault may not be so glaringly repeated. After the stirring historiographical revisions of the Thirties, Forties, and Fifties, it is a good sign that some historians are pondering "the delicate problem of developing an attitude appropriate to the process of absorbing the contributions of predecessors while trying to advance beyond them." [32] Management of this problem would seem to require all the sensitivity historians can muster—sensitivity to progress as well as decline, to the smiling as well as the tragic aspects of life, to the international background as well as the internal narrative, to social patterns as well as psychic tensions, to rational controls as well as irrational impulses, and to the great river of change as well as the bed of continuity.

[32] Lee Benson, *Turner and Beard: American Historical Writing Reconsidered* (1960), p. 96.

# ◄§ IV §►

# EUROPEAN HISTORY IN AMERICA

## LEONARD KRIEGER

PROFESSOR OF HISTORY
UNIVERSITY OF CHICAGO

❧

Americans are often accused—usually by Europeans—of lacking a genuine sense for history. The brevity and homogeneity of the American's own historical experience, the incessant challenges of growth that attract men to the present, the vaunted pragmatic attitude that orients men toward the future—these are factors in the judgment that Americans think and act as if the world were every day created anew. The relevance of this stricture is muted for American history itself, since the general feeling of consanguinity with all that has happened in one's native country and the particular continuity of the American development bestow a kind of self-evident importance upon the historical facts that, by spreading the mantle of the present over the past, obscures the problem of their relations. For the American historian of foreign lands, however, the question of a distinctive historical sense is inescapable. This sense may be defined simply as the capacity to understand the temporally distant in its own terms together with the consciousness of its relations with the familiar. It may be called into question either through the tyranny of the familiar over the understanding or through the isolation of the distant from the familiar. Since the American scholar of extra-American history finds the temporally distant extended by geographical and cultural distance, he starts by asking of his subject: "What is it to me or I to it that I should strive for it?"—and at once is imperiled by presentism or antiquarianism.

The professional features that characterize American academic life weigh with special gravity upon this brand of historian. The predominance of the undergraduate teaching function and the idea of a public educative role for history in a democratic society both call for a contemporary orientation particularly of foreign history, since for these audiences the present comprehends the familiar.[1] But over and above these special institutional influences the problem is posed by something essential in the pattern of American development. The relative isolation of American history between its Euro-

---

[1] For an early notice of the American tendency, for the sake of the market, to write European history in terms of "hot stuff on live subjects," see Charles H. Haskins' "European History and American Scholarship," *AHR*, XXVII (1923), 223.

pean origins and its post-World War II commitments—despite the running interchange from immigration, trade, and ideas[2]—created a sequence of detachment from and engagement with the rest of the world that is unique to the American experience. This sequence has had the effect of rupturing the cultural coherence of America with the rest of the world—and consequently, with the past of that world —and of unduly emphasizing the contemporary connection. The effect of this pattern was reinforced by the coincidence of the nineteenth century period of detachment from Europe with the birth of the modern European historiography that understood the past in its own terms and by the coincidence of the twentieth century period of engagement in Europe with the European historiography that laid stress upon the contemporary context of the historian.

The actual writing of non-American history in America seems to confirm the moral that such history shows a distinctive inclination toward the contemporary theme or at least toward the contemporary reference. But simply to conclude from this a categorical weakness of the American feeling for history is to commit the genetic fallacy. The conditions of American historiography set up not a conclusion but a question—not the judgment that history written from this kind of orientation must be tainted but the problem of defining the particular American approach to history that starts from this kind of orientation.

What follows will be an essay at such a definition, using the American historiography of other peoples as its touchstone. But this purpose requires certain specifications. A general review of American credits and debits in the various fields of non-American history, such has been undertaken from time to time,[3] would hardly be appropriate to the problem, however useful such an accounting might now be in itself. Of the two independent—albeit frequently related—historical impulses that have run through our civilization, the establish-

2 Daniel Boorstin maintains that until around 1914 Europe and America represented antipodes to most Americans. See his *America and the Image of Europe* (1960), pp. 19-20.

3 E.g., Haskins, *op. cit.,* pp. 217-23; Chester P. Higby, "The Present Status of Modern European History in the United States," *Journal of Modern History,* I (1929), 3-7; *Historical Scholarship in America: Needs and Opportunities,* Report by the Committee of the American Historical Association on the Planning of Research (1932), pp. 12-16; Harry Elmer Barnes, *History of Historical Writing* (1937), pp. 263-65; G. P. Gooch, *History and Historians in the Nineteenth Century,* new ed. (1959), pp. xxii-xxxix (preface of 1952 edition).

ment of the record and the elucidation of meaning from the record, Americans have, particularly since the spread of universal standards of scholarship, contributed notably to the first in the form of the monograph; but it is the second, in the form of interpretive history, that is more relevant here. Furthermore, for the purpose of defining an American historical sense the main fields of history are hardly commensurable. Ancient and medieval history are indeed not the American past, but they have a special status and raise special issues as the past of Americans. The history of the so-called exotic areas poses its own challenge in the radically alien character of its historical categories and assumptions. The history of modern Europe, as a parallel growth from a common root, spawns distinctive difficulties of recognition in its turn, since the strange is so mixed with the familiar as to appear distorted, thereby inviting either rejection, Americanization, or reportage in the American versions of European history. It is with this field and with this shape of the American historian's problem that we shall be concerned here.

## ⊷§ 1 §⊷

# THE TRADITION

It is generally agreed that the turning point in American historiography falls in the last quarter of the nineteenth century.[1] Prior to this pivotal period the writing of history in America was amateur in authorship, romantic in tone, literary in style, nationalist in mission, and multivolumed in scope. Subsequent to it the writing of history became professional, scientific, expository, and if not exclusively monographic at least limited in its canvas. There have been attempts to comprehend both halves of this history of history in a single process, but only in terms of United States history.[2] To be sure, the pioneer American historians of Europe—Motley, Prescott, Draper, Lea, White—have been duly celebrated, but, like Dante's pagan heroes, they inhabit a kind of limbo, suspended from both contemporaries and posterity. They appear to be detached from the nationalist historiography that was the hallmark of their age, and, thus bereft of a meaningful place in their own time, they appear equally irrelevant to the subsequent growth of their own genre. The fact of the matter is, however, that the historical interest of Americans in Europe did fulfill an appropriate role during the national period and that this role established an American tradition of European history that has persisted down to the present time. The conjunction of the twentieth century spread of interest in European history with the rise of "scientific" history in its various versions has converted themes into assumptions, but the essential character of the early American

---

[1] E.g., *Historical Scholarship in America*, pp. 3-8; W. Stull Holt, "The Idea of Scientific History in America," *Journal of the History of Ideas*, I (1940), 352-362; John Herman Randall Jr. and George Haines, "Controlling Assumption in the Practice of American Historians," in *Theory and Practice in Historical Study*, Report of the Committee on Historiography, Social Science Research Council (1946), pp. 25-49.

[2] Thus: Michael Kraus, *The Writing of American History* (1953); Harvey Wish, *The American Historian* (1960). Stull Holt covers the assumptions common to American historians in all fields, but only for the twentieth century, in his perceptive essay, "Historical Scholarship," in *American Scholarship in the Twentieth Century*, ed. Merle E. Curti (1953).

238

relationship to Europe passed over, with all due refinement, into the academic respectability of professional history.

If the long "amateur" era of American historiography, which stretched from the early seventeenth century to the closing decades of the nineteenth, be examined for its European history, the result is a paradox. In the seventeenth and eighteenth centuries, when American destinies were obviously tied to Europe, Americans wrote no European history; in the nineteenth century, when Americans were concentrating upon their own national development, they wrote important interpretative histories of Europe. It is true that in the colonial period men were abundantly conscious of the European context of the American experience. Puritan historians of the seventeenth century wrote Providential history that included the traditional scheme of the Four Empires, ending in Rome; the subsequent conflict of God and Satan for the souls of Christians, particularly in Europe; and the dramatic story of Reformation and persecution that furnished the setting for the narrative of New England.[3] The Revolutionary generation had a more secular point of view, but no less an authority than John Adams led it in the common belief that the history of the American revolution was part of "the history of mankind" and must be written in conjunction with the histories of the European states.[4] But in history as in other things it is a long leap between the will and the deed. A perusal of the leading histories of the colonial and Revolutionary periods shows that the Old World reference was not so much written as written about. William Bradford's introductory chapter, in his *History of Plymouth Plantation,* is rather theological than historical; his only discussion of a larger historical context is the brief denotation of the divinely sponsored spurs to the American adventure.[5] Nor does the broader framework fare any better in Bradford's successor Puritan historians. It is noteworthy only in Cotton Mather's *Magnalia Christi Americana,* where it is simply a function of his thesis that Europe was the site of the incomplete Reformation that was perfected in America,[6] and in Thomas Prince's

[3] Kenneth B. Murdock, *Literature and Theology in Colonial New England* (1949), pp. 78-79.
[4] Kraus, *op. cit.,* pp. 59-60.
[5] William Bradford, *History of Plymouth Plantation* (1912), pp. 3-60, esp. p. 44.
[6] Cotton Mather, *Magnalia Christi Americana* (London, 1702), pp. 1-4. J.

*Chronological History of New England,* where world history, in traditional chronicle style, features the introduction, simply to show "the age of the world when this part of the earth came to be known to the other." [7] The transfer of American intellectual leadership from clergymen to laymen during the eighteenth century, coupled with the technical advances, the pragmatic values, and the literary attractions of Enlightenment history in Europe, certainly stimulated the consumption of such history, but did not do much for its production. Indeed, as the exclusively colonial scope of such a typical work as Thomas Hutchinson's *History of Massachusetts Bay Colony* would seem to show, the effect of secularization upon American historiography in the eighteenth century was to weaken the common religious background that had made the European past relevant to Americans but to replace it with no other connection.

And so it was that the first noteworthy American writing of European history came paradoxically out of the "national" period of American historiography that covered most of the nineteenth century. Now this development is obviously connected with the larger problems of European influences on American thought and of American attitudes toward Europe, but it must not be identified with either of them. The impact of European study, travels, and reading upon a Bancroft, a Hildreth, a Holst, and a Burgess affected their writing of American history, but neither their experience nor their consciousness of Europe drove them to write European history. Bancroft could translate the German historian Heeren's *History of the Political System of Europe and Its Colonies* and, like Francis Parkman, he could make excursions during his New World history into cognate movements of the Old, but this kind of interest was patently derivative and in any case it was something quite different from undertaking an independent work in European history. The excursions were dominated throughout by the original extrinsic motivation, whereas an independent work of history, whatever its original motivation, neces-

---

Franklin Jameson emphasizes the similarity of European and American conditions in Mather's age and sees in Mather himself the "American analogue" of the European erudite scholarship that flourished in the decades around 1700. See J. F. Jameson, *The History of Historical Writings in America* (1891), pp. 44-45, 61-62. But note that despite the larger context Mather scarcely deals with European affairs at all.

[7] Thomas Prince, *Chronological History of New England,* new ed. (1826), pp. 23, 24-96.

sarily takes on an existence of its own and betokens another quality of historical interest. And yet these European references of the American nationalist school do offer a clue to the anomaly presented by the parallel activity of their colleagues who, similar in cultural heritage and orientation, yet turned to European history and devoted to it the same long labor and loving care for research in the sources. The clue lay in the character of the nationalism in American historiography, for this nationalism appeared, thanks to the European influence, not as an exclusive or parochial notion indifferent to outer concerns but rather as the recognition of American primacy in a universal historical destiny. From Bancroft to Turner the emphasis upon the distinctiveness of the American experience went hand in hand with the consciousness of its ultimate meaning as a part of world history. Whether a residue of Enlightenment cosmopolitanism or the synthetic habit of mind native to the nineteenth century was the cause, the result was to view the European development as the shadow-dominated section that lent integrity to the American illumination in a common work of destiny.

From this angle of vision it is not too surprising to find that the notable European histories written in the United States during the nineteenth century were addressed to the common theme that set off the American mission.[8] In one form or another this theme was the evolution of the religious, intellectual, and political freedom, which had found its chief locus in America, out of religious obscurantism and political despotism. Certainly the emphasis within this syndrome varied, from the political interests of Prescott and Motley in the first half of the century to the intellectual concerns of Draper and White in the second half, but the fundamental issue, marked by the common denominator of religion, remained the same throughout. Their subject matter and their objectives both contributed to the end of showing what America was by investigating what it was not.

The first of the American historians to receive general recognition for their work on Europe, Washington Irving for his *Columbus* (1828) and William Prescott for his *History of the Reign of Fer-*

[8] It should be noted that this interpretation differs markedly from Jameson's more casual notion that the main difference between the historians of America and of Europe during this period lay in the predominantly political interests of the former and the predominantly literary interests of the latter. For this group Europe simply furnished the more "picturesque" themes. See Jameson, *op. cit.,* pp. 113-14.

*dinand and Isabella, the Catholic* (1838), took off from the obvious point of juncture between European and American history. As Prescott wrote: "Surely no subject could be found more suitable for the pen of an American than a history of that reign, under the auspices of which the existence of his own favored quarter of the globe was first revealed. . . ." [9] This is not to deny, of course, the force of other, more objective historical drives in Prescott: the interest in Spanish culture awakened by Ticknor; the lure, tempting to so many practitioners of Clio in all ages, of a good subject that had not been done before; the awareness of newly available sources to be brought to account; the pride of the historical craftsman who writes without "national or party feeling" save for the inevitable sympathy with the actors whom he comes to know.[10] The result of these considerations was a massive and loving work of Spanish history organized by a theme common to Western culture: the development of liberal Teutonic traditions and institutions into fruitful national vitality. According to Prescott, Isabella and Ferdinand effected just this, thereby unleashing the explosion of cultural energy that founded the New World but at the same time creating the pattern of authoritarianism that led ultimately to the stifling of liberties and to imperial decline. This pattern was the function not so much of monarchy as such but of its submission to religious bigotry, and this was the organizing theme of his *Philip the Second*. The dominant principle of the age, wrote Prescott, "is to be found in the policy of Philip, the great aim of which was to uphold the supremacy of the Church, and, as a consequence, that of the crown. . . . It was this policy, almost as sure and steady in its operation as the laws of Nature herself, that may be said to have directed the march of events through the whole of his long reign. . . ." [11] Thus Prescott sought to explain both the transmission and the stagnation, in Spain, of the "seeds of liberty" whose full fruition he deemed appropriate to the "great political system" of his own age.[12]

The community of interests that was muted and transmuted in Prescott's historical passion remained open and distinct in John Lothrop Motley almost to the point of caricature. Motley was infinitely

[9] William H. Prescott, *The Reign of Ferdinand and Isabella, the Catholic*, 2nd ed., vol. I (1838), p. viii.
[10] *Ibid.*, p. x.
[11] William H. Prescott, *Philip the Second*, vol. I (1868), p. xiii.
[12] Prescott, *Ferdinand and Isabella*, vol. III, pp. 446-47, 465.

less able as a historian but infinitely more transparent in his representation of American motives in writing European history during the
first half of the nineteenth century.

> So much is each individual state but a member of the great inter-
> national commonwealth, and so close is the relationship between
> the whole human family, that it is impossible for a nation, even
> while struggling for itself, not to acquire something for all man-
> kind. The maintenance of the right of the little provinces of Hol-
> land and Zeeland in the sixteenth, by Holland and England united
> in the seventeenth, and by the United States of America in the
> eighteenth centuries, forms but a single chapter in the great volume
> of human fate; for the so-called revolutions of Holland, England,
> and America, are all links of one chain. . . .
>
> To all who speak the English language, the history of the great
> agony through which the Republic of Holland was ushered into life
> must have peculiar interest, for it is a portion of the records of the
> Anglo-Saxon race—essentially the same, whether in Friesland, Eng-
> land, or Massachusetts. . . . The lessons of history and the fate of
> free states can never be sufficiently pondered by those upon whom
> so large and heavy a responsibility for the maintenance of rational
> human freedom rests.[13]

The theme, which Motley hammered through the six volumes of the
*Revolt of the Netherlands* (1856) and its sequel (1860), was obviously "the dangers which come from superstition and despotism
and the blessings which flow from the maintenance of religious
and political freedom." [14] This theme was, for Motley, the expression
of a cosmic law, which governs "all bodies political as inexorably as
Kepler's law controls the motion of planets. The law is Progress; the
result Democracy." [15] Human history is thus a single process which
places America "on the point to which other peoples are moving." [16]
For Motley, as for Prescott, the function of European history was
dual. Primarily, it was a prenatal American history, in the period

[13] John Lothrop Motley, *The Rise of the Dutch Republic*, vol. I (London,
1896), pp. liii-lv.
[14] John Lothrop Motley, *History of the United Netherlands from the Death of
William the Silent to the Twelve Years' Truce*, vol. I (1900), p. xvi.
[15] John Lothrop Motley, *Democracy, the Climax of Political Progress and the
Destiny of Advanced Races: An Historical Essay* (London 1869), p. 6.
[16] *Ibid.*, p. 5.

when the fates of the two continents were physically joined. But a secondary function was there as well—a historical definition of America indicated by the perpetuation in Europe of the political and religious conflict that had been resolved in America. It is no accident that Motley's grasp faltered where his theme was weak. His law of history impelled him to move from the revolt of the Netherlands to the Thirty Years' War, which for him developed the same issue to a continental scale. But he never got there. As a prelude to the history of the Thirty Years' War he firmly intended to write he embarked on a history of John of Barneveldt, in which he intended to show the merging of the Dutch into the European conflict. But the parties in this arena, led by Barneveldt and Maurice, were both Protestant, both constitutional, both Dutch, and Motley could not find a handle for his treatment save for the vague speculation over whether the "great laws of the discords of the world" or "the other principle of universal harmony" would prevail.[17] He found some kind of tragic lesson for "all free states" in the internecine divisions of "the first considerable republic of modern history," [18] but this moral supplied neither substantive theme nor interpretative principle. Indeed, this phase of Motley's history showed little of either. Without the great common theme of the conflict between liberty and oppression that linked seventeenth century Europe with nineteenth century America his historical enterprise lost both its drive and its direction.

In the second half of the nineteenth century, historians registered the changes in the intellectual and institutional context of American life in their increasingly critical attitude toward the sources, in their growing veneration for science, and in the new focus upon the teaching function in the universities. And yet, for European history in America the new context produced only changes of degree. Not only did the tradition of big works on common themes persist, but in general the continuity of theme was provided by adherence to the religious motif. What did change was the concomitant of religion that made it a historical subject: where politics had historized religion during the first half of the century, science performed the same function during the second. The continuing focus upon religion was no more in the later than in the earlier era a concern for religious

[17] John Lothrop Motley, *The Life and Death of John of Barneveldt* . . . (1900), p. 35.
[18] *Ibid.*, p. xviii.

history as such. Historiographically, religion had functioned and continued to function as a constant principle of identity in terms of which the changing modes of Western culture acquired meaning and coherence for Americans. In a century of political isolation the traditional religious motif remained the main substantive theme locating America in world history. But the growing sophistication of historians in America brought with it a tendency that was to have a notable later development. Whereas in the earlier part of the century theme and material were integrally interwoven, in the second half historians began to separate them. Draper and White tackled the common religious theme directly while a growing number of historians, whose outstanding representatives were Lea and Baird, undertook particular European studies in the field and relegated the community of the theme to the status of unspoken assumption.

John William Draper and Andrew D. White addressed themselves to European history not as such but as the primary locus of the civilization that included America, and in their segregation of a common theme they founded the study of intellectual history in America. Ostensibly the theme was the struggle between science and religion that was arousing so much discussion on both sides of the Atlantic.[19] Actually they sought to demonstrate the fundamental historical necessity of the liberal, progressive, realistic piety they deemed triumphant in their own age. For both men the enemy was not religion but the wrong kind of religion; its fault was not that it was evil but that it was anachronistic; its function was not simply to be a target but to supply the unifying strand of history. That two historians of such different backgrounds, interests, and approaches should come to such a similar pattern argues much for the growth of a powerful tradition binding upon American historians of Europe.

Draper was a physiologist who desired above all to apply science to society.[20] He was also an English immigrant who saw in European history the graph of humanity and a London-trained Utilitarian who

---

[19] Thus their titles: Draper's *History of the Conflict Between Science and Religion* (1874) and White's *History of the Warfare of Science with Theology in Christendom* (1895).

[20] "This volume . . . is intended as the completion of my work on Human Physiology, in which man was treated as an individual. In this he is treated in his social relation." John William Draper, *A History of the Intellectual Development of Europe* (1863), p. iii. See also Donald Fleming, *John William Draper and the Religion of Science* (1950).

saw in the "intellectual class" the key to history.[21] His first and chief historical work, *A History of the Intellectual Development of Europe,* was designed to show that "the equilibrium and movement of humanity are altogether physiological phenomena," that "the government of this world is accomplished by immutable [natural] law," and that "man proceeds, in his social march, in obedience to it." [22] The ineluctable and universal hold of natural laws upon history is effected, for Draper, externally through conditioning by physical environment and internally through the organic cycle of life. The external role of nature determines the character of civilizations as the essential units of humanity and subjects America and Europe to a common destiny.[23] The internal role of nature produces the necessity of intellectual development within each civilization as "opinions" progress from infancy to maturity and decline to decrepitude in the society as in the individual. The theme of European history manifesting this basic natural reality is the growth of reason and science out of "the age of faith," for this development at once validates and requires the precise intellectual knowledge of the overriding "natural tendency" that is God's plan for the universe and the model for men's own organization of their institutions. Europe had evidently arrived at the stage of maturity with the triumph of rational science and the time for the intellectual planning of society was at hand.[24]

So far Draper had a historical scheme but he was not much of an American nor was he much of a historian, either by technique or by temperament.[25] It was his subsequent turn, during the Civil War, to contemporary American history that stimulated both his sense of nationality and his sense of history. He distinguished now, within his historical scheme, between the European role in destroying outmoded institutions and ideas and the American role in the intellectual construction of appropriate ones through the integration of centralized planning and individual freedom in democracy.[26]

If Draper was a cosmopolitan theorist whose scheme became historically meaningful as it grew an American dimension, Andrew

[21] Draper, *Intellectual Development,* pp. 11, 14.
[22] *Ibid.,* pp. 2, 15, 16.
[23] *Ibid.,* p. 454.
[24] *Ibid.,* pp. 616-17.
[25] Fleming, *op. cit.,* pp. 76-78, 90.
[26] *Ibid.,* pp. 98-105.

D. White showed the force of the pattern by developing it in the reverse direction. White was a professional historian who wrote on European history out of his sense of American needs. Now White, to be sure, developed an interest in European history, like so many other Americans, from his travels on the European continent and his appreciation of European culture,[27] but this kind of objective interest in European history inspired no urgency in him. In a sense the history that he did not write is as revealing as the history that he did write. He ended his career with a head full of aborted projects on subjects that had kindled his interest, like the history of Germany or of the French Revolution, but he actually came to write for publication only on those things he felt were particularly called for by American needs. Of the two motives White habitually associated with his historical studies—"labor of love" and "lessons of history"—the latter was clearly authoritative for his publications as well as for his teaching.[28] He was influenced most by the philosophical historians who wrote on themes common to the whole civilization: Ranke was a disappointment, but not Guizot, Buckle, Lecky, and Draper, through whom history became "a record of the unfolding of humanity."[29] With their themes White sought to expose Americans to the European past so that they "should understand our own time and its problems in the light of history."[30] There was, consequently, a justice in the diversion of his professional energies into teaching, university administration, and politics, since these were more direct means of encompassing his pragmatic goal.[31] What he published was similarly oriented—an article on Richelieu as an argument against slavery, an article on the *assignats* to be used in support of hard currency in America, and his *History of the Warfare of Science with Theology in Christendom*—his only important historical publication —to support the foundation of Cornell University as a nonsectarian institution.[32]

[27] *Autobiography of Andrew Dickson White*, vol. I (1905), pp. 15-16, 34-42.
[28] *Ibid.*, vol. II, pp. 489-90.
[29] *Ibid.*, vol. I, pp. 38, 42.
[30] *Ibid.*, vol. I, p. 83.
[31] For White this was a matter not only of autobiography but of formal conviction. See his *European Schools of History and Politics* (1887), in which he argues for history and historians as necessary factors in political life.
[32] Andrew Dickson White, *A History of the Warfare of Science with Theology in Christendom*, vol. I (1903), pp. viii-ix.

It is hardly surprising, then, to find the pragmatic motif built into the substance of White's *History*. Of the intellectual purpose of the work he wrote:

> I simply try to aid in letting the light of historical truth into that decaying mass of outworn thought which attaches the modern world to medieval conceptions of Christianity, and which still lingers among us—a most serious barrier to religion and morals, and a menace to the whole normal evolution of society. . . . My hope is to aid . . . in the gradual and healthful dissolving away of this mass of unreason, that the stream of "religion pure and undefiled" may flow on broad and clear, a blessing to humanity.[33]

Organizing the book in accordance with this purpose, White took up, one by one, the various fields of nature and man and showed for each field the progress in knowledge from interpretation according to divine "caprice" to understanding according to scientific law. But if White thus exemplified the persistence of the thematic emphasis inherited from the liberal Protestant tradition, he showed too the susceptibility of the thematic approach to advancing standards of historical sophistication. These found expression not only in the weakening of confessional bias that came with the more thoroughly secular orientation but even more in the historicizing of the historian's judgments. Involved here was something more than replacement of the judgment of falsity by the judgment of anachronism; it was the acceptance of past views that were scientifically false as historically true, that is, as documentary of the evolving consciousness of humanity.[34] As White himself indicated, this point of view was a product of the newer sciences like anthropology and comparative religion.[35] It was itself, then, a historical product shared by Europeans of a prior generation and many Americans of his own. White's contribution was simply to apply it to the writing of intellectual history in America.

The conjunction of a growing historical sense with the preservation of a thematic, suprahistorical American historiographical tradition was demonstrated in yet another way by White's contemporary, Henry Charles Lea. Where White started from the theme, Lea started

---

33 *Ibid.*, vol. I, pp. v-vi.
34 *Ibid.*, vol. I, pp. 17-24.
35 *Ibid.*, vol. II, pp. 393-96.

from the historical material, and if the amateur Lea turned out to be by far the more respectable and eminent historian than the professional White, the interpretive upshot of his work was not very different: like White, Lea brought the American tradition of European history to the point where it could enter into the new development toward scientific history in the late nineteenth century. A publisher by profession and a scientist by original inclination, Lea turned, as a result of an early breakdown in his health, to the less strenuous avocation of history, and particularly of medieval history, in whose chronicles he found relaxation.[36] This amateur nevertheless developed the professional standards that were to bring him international renown and domestic recognition as president of the American Historical Association. Over and above the application of critical techniques to the sources, Lea's contributions were twofold. First, he developed institutional history as the most reliable vehicle for the general study of any period. Second, he accepted no "fixed" or "universal" standard of morality and consequently denied the right of the historian to impose moral judgments that predicate an ethical continuity in history.[37] Exalting historical "objectivity" and relativizing morality, Lea insisted on the priority of "the facts" and stipulated a morality that "should educe itself from the facts" and should derive its judgments from the standards of the age under study.[38]

And yet Lea remained within the nineteenth century American tradition. If he was a historian of institutions and more particularly of legal institutions, still it was on *religious* legal institutions and practices that he did his chief work. The Inquisition and the prosecution of witchcraft engaged his primary attention, and he addressed auxiliary writings to such themes of church law as auricular confession, indulgences, sacerdotal celibacy, and the Spanish Moriscos. Second, Lea continued the American tendency to select from European history themes that represented common rather than alternate developments vis-à-vis the American. These common themes could be of two types: like Draper's and White's they could be general subjects substantively common to the European and American sectors of Western civilization, or, like Prescott's and Motley's they could be older

[36] Arthur C. Howland's preface in Henry Charles Lea's *Minor Historical Writings* (1942), pp. vii-ix.
[37] Lea, 'Ethical Values in History," in *ibid.*, pp. 56-58.
[38] *Ibid.*, pp. 59-60; Henry Charles Lea, *A History of the Inquisition of the Middle Ages,* vol. I (1888), p. iii.

subjects that functioned as a common background before the separation of European and American histories. Lea's interest in witchcraft was indeed a common theme of the first type, but he never got much beyond collecting the materials for such a study. His main concerns and his classic work were in the field of the medieval Inquisition and its sequel in the Counter Reformation, and here he can be bracketed with Prescott as an American pioneer in establishing the European background of the American experience. And even more than Prescott, the right of judgment from the point of view of subsequent American experience, which he disclaimed in principle, reentered covertly through the back door of Lea's putative historical relativism. "I have not paused to moralize," he confessed frankly, "but I have missed my aim if the events narrated are not so presented as to teach their appropriate lesson." [39] Lea's notion of historical objectivity dissuaded him from making particular moral judgments on the Inquisition as an institution, since it was produced by "a natural —one may almost say an inevitable—evolution of the forces at work in the thirteenth century," but this caution simply removed the censure from the particular institution to the whole age of men. For under the cover of summary Lea was not averse to pausing and pounding his lesson home:

> The review which we have made of the follies and crimes of our ancestors has revealed to us a scene of almost unrelieved blackness. We have seen how the wayward heart of man, groping in twilight, has under the best of impulses inflicted misery and despair on his fellow creatures while thinking to serve God, and how the ambitious and unprincipled have traded on these impulses to gratify the lust of avarice and domination. . . .
> The judgment of impartial history must be that the Inquisition was the monstrous offspring of mistaken zeal, utilized by selfish greed and lust of power to smother the higher aspirations of humanity and stimulate its baser appetites.[40]

We may well wonder what Lea's conclusion would have been if he had permitted himself to make moral judgments. Lea could argue that the judgment was not his but that of those contemporaries like St. Francis and the heretics, who represented the conscience of the age

39 *Ibid.,* vol. I, p. iv.
40 *Ibid.,* vol. III, pp. 649-50.

of the Inquisition,[41] but it is clear from the way he pointed his moral that his criteria were those of liberal Protestantism, American variety. For what his study did, according to Lea, was to set in relief the marvelous improvement that human institutions have undergone in the past two centuries, particularly in the realm of "Christian love and charity." [42]

It was, then, the comprehensiveness of the research and the historical application of institutional analysis rather than the power or originality of interpretation that raised Lea's work to classic proportions. Most of Lea's contemporaries whose historical writings on European subjects gained respect operated within the same Protestant mold and pursued the more traditional narrative approach, albeit with the more rigorous academic techniques of the later nineteenth century. Henry M. Baird's volumes on the French Huguenots, Samuel M. Jackson's biography of Zwingli, and Williston Walker's superior study of Calvin were probably the best-received exemplars of the American genre that emphasized the religious aspects of European history as most consanguine with the American experience.[43] The historiographical meaning of these works, like those of Lea, can be fully understood only if it is realized that each was imbedded in a context of general history. Baird justified his work not only by the opening of new sources but by "a lack of works upon the general theme" [44] while both Jackson and Walker surrounded their particular studies with their labors upon general church histories.[45] For American historians of this school the community of American and European history remained an explicit one.

The nineteenth century American perspective upon European history proved itself capable of absorbing technical improvements and of contributing synthetic approaches, but it can hardly be said to have provided any startling illuminations. The first intimations of the

---

[41] *Ibid.,* vol. I, p. 52.

[42] *Ibid.,* vol. III, p. 649.

[43] Baird, *History of the Rise of the Hugenots of France* (1879), *Hugenots and Henry of Navarre* (1886), *Huguenots and the Revocation of the Edict of Nantes* (1895); Jackson, *Huldreich Zwingli* (1900); Walker, *John Calvin, the Organizer of Reformed Protestantism, 1509-1564* (1906).

[44] Baird, *Rise of the Huguenots,* preface.

[45] Samuel Macaulay Jackson and others, eds., *New Schaff-Herzog Encyclopedia of Religious Knowledge* . . . (13 vols., 1908-14); Williston Walker, *Reformation* vol. 9 of *Ten Epochs of Church History,* ed. John Fulton (1900); Williston Walker, *History of the Christian Church* (1918).

creative possibilities harbored within this perspective came toward the end of the century, illuminated in a maverick representative of the American historiographical tradition, Alfred T. Mahan. That Mahan departed from the literal tradition of European history in America hardly needs elaboration. It was not only that his subject—the history of sea power—was other than the religious, moral, or ecclesiastical preoccupations of his predecessors, but that he explicitly devalued them in favor of secular interests and power as the prime moving forces of history.[46] Now certainly this position had long since become a familiar one in domestic historiography; what made Mahan important as a historian was his subscription to the figurative tradition of European history in America, for it is in terms of this tradition that Mahan's particular emphasis becomes measurable. Mahan was a loyal son of the tradition in three respects. First, although Mahan's subject in the first two volumes of his famous trilogy[47] was the history of European sea power, with America figuring only as an arena of it, his explicit context from the start was the joint "history of Europe and America," thereby perpetuating the habit of viewing European history from the angle of its community with America.[48] Second, the scope of Mahan's vision was the customary one from this angle: he wrote "general history" with reference to the bearing of his particular interest upon it.[49] Mahan's general history, moreover, was of the overt, schematic kind, akin to the Draper-White strand of the American tradition. Not only was his emphasis upon narrative synthesis and upon the reinterpretation of already published materials, but his aim was the "collection of special instances" showing the constant operation of sea power in world history and the operation upon sea power of "these constant teachings of history," these "principles which . . . belong to the unchangeable, or unchanging, order of things, remaining the same, in cause and effect, from age to

---

[46] Thus on the French wars of religion: "As the religious motive, acting in a sphere to which it did not naturally belong, and in which it had no rightful place, died away, the political necessities and interests of States began to have juster weight." . T. Mahan, *The Influence of Sea Power upon History, 1660-1783,* 12th ed. (1943), p. 92.
[47] *The Influence of Sea Power upon History, 1660-1783* (1890); *The Influence of Sea Power upon the French Revolution and Empire, 1793-1812* (1893); *Sea Power in Its Relation to the War of 1812* (1905).
[48] *The Influence of Sea Power, 1660-1783,* p. iii.
[49] *Ibid.,* pp. iii-vi.

age, . . . belong, as it were to the Order of Nature. . . ." [50] Third, for Mahan too the study of European history was essentially a pragmatic study. The "practical object of this inquiry," he wrote, "is to draw from the lessons of history inferences applicable to one's own country and service. . . ." [51] It was the persistence of principles, rooted "in the essential nature of things" and particularly in "the nature of man," which, "among all changes . . . remains much the same," that made both possible and profitable "the lessons of history," and the task of the historian was to discriminate nicely between the permanent factors that were always applicable and the false analogies evoked by evanescent conditions and tactics no longer applicable. [52]

And so it was that despite the novelty of Mahan's historical terrain his writing exhibited the familiar format of the American tradition: the description of a favored field detailed with loving care, the analytical summary of its permanent meaning, and a familiar sketch of general history, now newly illuminated by the larger meaning of the specialized events. And yet the shift of interest registered by Mahan undoubtedly meant something more than a mere change of scene, for whereas the American contribution to European history had formerly been confined to filling out a given framework with a wealth of color and detail Mahan advanced a new factor of general interpretation. Obviously, what lay behind Mahan's innovation was an expansion in the conception of the American-European community that extended the study of European history in this country from the religious and moral cohesion of Western civilization to the mutual political involvement of the expanding nations. This substantive shift was, in itself, a crucial enough breakthrough, since it adumbrated the intense professional interest in European political history that was to come, and it implied an underlying formal development that proved in the long run even more seminal. Whereas the religio-moral community that had previously impelled the American investigation of the European past was itself a community of the past, the sense of political community that was now beginning to inspire the investigation of the European past was a community of the

---

[50] *Ibid.*, pp. 7, 88.
[51] *Ibid.*, p. 83.
[52] *Ibid.*, pp. 7-13, 88-89.

present. As long as American historians assumed that the community of Europe and America lay mainly in the past they tended to assume also a disjunction in the present. Hence they limited the serious study of European history to the classical, medieval, and Reformation periods that preceded the disjunction. In intellectual history, to be sure, a general community did persist into the modern period, but, as the writings of Draper and White showed, here the specific European dimension vanished with its evolution into a set of universal principles primarily applicable to American conditions. Only with the growing sense of an American-European political community of the present did contemporary Europe recover an identity that was both concrete and pertinent, and only then did American historians seriously address themselves to the modern period of European history.

# 2

# THE TRADITION BECOMES "NEW"

The reorientation that was pioneered by Mahan began to produce results on a wide scale for European history after the turn of the century, when political events were making the rapprochement of the American and European orbits more explicit. But these results took a peculiar form, and before we can understand them we must pick up another strand in American historiography that joined the amateur tradition to produce these results. This was the so-called scientific history that rose rapidly in the last quarter of the nineteenth century to become the dominant feature of American historiography. Now a certain confusion attaches to the term *scientific history,* for it is used to cover two different historical approaches, usually—in this period —coincident but inherently separable.[1] In one sense it refers to the development of distinctive critical methods, learned in the historical seminars of Germany, propagated in graduate seminars of American universities, and appropriate to the rise of history as a separate profession administering an independent discipline. In the second sense it refers to the use of hypotheses drawn from the natural sciences as fundamental laws of reality applicable *inter alia* to history. Given the conjoint influence of Ranke on the one hand and Buckle and Darwin on the other it is not surprising to find both senses of scientific history coincident in such outstanding exemplars of the school as Henry Adams, with his Harvard seminar and his historical law of thermodynamics, and the Germanically oriented Herbert Baxter Adams and John Burgess, with their seminars at Johns Hopkins and Columbia and with their evolutionary "germ theory" of Anglo-Saxon institutional development.

By 1900 the empirical, critical tendency was clearly dominant over the lawful, systematic tendency in scientific history. This succession, which saw an initial coincidence of the two attitudes toward sci-

[1] See W. Stull Holt, "The Idea of Scientific History in America," *Journal of the History of Ideas,* I (1940), 352-57, and John Herman Randall Jr. and George Haines, "Controlling Assumption in the Practice of American Historians," in *Theory and Practice in Historical Study,* Report of the Committee on Historiography, Social Science Research Council (1946), p. 25.

ence yield to the triumph of the methodological strand, had the effect of limiting the impact of the scientific approach upon European history in America. The initial coincidence indicated that the new methods were compatible with a general framework while the ultimate decline of the *scientific* framework indicated that the framework need not be scientific. We find, consequently, that the rise of scientific history did not bring with it a dramatic alteration in the basic terms of the scholarship on European history, which, as we have seen, had predicated a general framework. Schematic interpretations were now indeed muted, on principle, but the continued relevance of the common theme appeared implicitly, as assumptions governing the choice of fields and the selection of topics. Scientific historians, like their amateur predecessors, addressed themselves primarily to fields that were common to Europeans and Americans in the sense that they formed the background to the experience of both—fields like medieval and early colonial history. Thus the great names in American scholarship outside United States history during the pre-war period worked in these general fields—Burr, Cheyney, Emerton, G. B. Adams, Haskins, McIlwain, Munro, H. O. Taylor, and Thorndike in the first and Osgood, Beer, Andrews, Shepherd, and Abbott in the second. They favored, moreover, intellectual, constitutional, and institutional subjects with a lasting impact upon the whole of Western culture. And even in those cases in which the emphasis upon particularity led to a positive denial of a substantive thematic connection between Europe and America, the logic of opposition continued to sustain the European relevance. Frederick Jackson Turner insisted on the necessity of the European context primarily to show the distinctiveness of the American experience and Henry Adams, coming to the same conclusion from his study of American history, committed himself with equal devotion to the sympathetic reconstruction of the European Middle Ages.

But for modern European history, the devaluation of explicit common themes did have a palpable effect. Writing at the beginning of the 1890's and remarking the impact of scientific history, J. Franklin Jameson associated the dull, narrow, factual solidity that it had brought to American historiography in general with a new contemporary indifference to European history.[2] We seem to have here an-

[2] J. F. Jameson, *The History of Historical Writing in America* (1891), pp. 132-36.

other round in the apparent paradox that diverts Americans from European history when American and European interests are most intertwined and sends them to it when these interests are most disjoined, but once more the paradox is illusory. It is true that the nominalist orientation of the dominant school of scientific history militated against the acceptance of larger conceptions that would relate European to American history, but if it did not encourage such ideas it did, as we have seen, tolerate them, particularly if they were traditional enough to pass unremarked. We may go even further and note that despite all appearances scientific historians also reflected the added increment of European involvement that grew toward the end of the nineteenth century and produced a Mahan. The point is simply that it did not make its appearance in great scholarly works and we should not look for it there. It does appear in the two characteristic forms that accompanied the rise of scientific history—the monograph and the textbook.

The monograph comes out of the seminar and in book form out of the doctoral dissertation. The development around the turn of the century, therefore, of monographic studies in modern European history was associated with the training of professionals for an independent historical discipline. The positive influence of these mechanics upon the study of European history stems obviously from the absorption of European subject matter along with European training methods and from a retroactive application of Parkinson's law, which required the filling out of the new history departments. But there was more to the new techniques than this. Americans had long been accustomed to borrow European methods without having to take their content, and there would have been no European history or historians in the schools had there not been an interest in it, even if the interest did come more from the supply than from the demand end of higher education. The monograph was not simply the spawn of the new professionalism. In at least one essential way it is the modern version of the old annal or chronicle—that is, it is the form of history in which the meaning behind the historical facts is presumed and omitted from the study. The monograph was an appropriate expression of an age in which Americans were still asserting their national identity vis-à-vis Europe and yet were coming to recognize their political and social involvement with Europe. It was appropriate because the monograph on European history presumed a supranational interest in the facts without having to articulate a scheme of meaning for it. On the monographic level Americans became members of an international community of scholars whose standards and whose audiences were deemed above the accident of national origins, and the inclusion of European history within the regular orbit of American scholarship pointed beyond the community of technique to the presumption of a common Western humanity in which the experience of each part was the concern of all. For a long time in the field of European history, therefore, American scholars could be content to cast their researches in the form of the monograph. The historical book and the learned journal alike became the receptacles of highly specialized studies, relieved by general essays on historiography but dispensing with general essays on history. This narrow "scientific" internationalism of American historical scholarship produced a fundamental rift within the profession of European history, for it divided what had been integral in the nineteenth century tradition: it made internally superfluous the kind of explicit general interpretations that the profession continued to need externally for its communication of the European past to the American society. It thereby created the gap between research and interpretation that has been the fundamental problem in the American history of Europe during the twentieth century.

Akin to the monograph as a product of history's independent role in American education and more revealing of its assumptions was the textbook. Accompanying the trickle of monographs, a veritable flood of textbooks on world history, European history, and the national histories of the European nations appeared before World War I. They were aimed at elementary and advanced university students and came mainly from the same school and the same generation of scientific historians that was *not* producing large-scale scholarly history in the field.[3] Superficially, the intensive monograph and the extensive textbook seemed to occupy opposite poles of the academic spectrum. Actually, however, they were associated not only by their comple-

---

3 E.g., world and European history texts by George P. Fisher (1885), G. B. Adams (1899), Ferdinand Schevill (1907), William R. Shepherd (*Historical Atlas,* 1911), Charles M. Andrews (1896-98), Charles D. Hazen (1909), Henry E. Bourne (1914)—the last three on "modern" history, i.e., since 1789. For texts on national European history, see Edward P. Cheney (1904) and Arthur L. Cross (1914) for England; G. B. Adams (1896) for France; Henry D. Sedgwick (1905) for Italy; Ernest F. Henderson (1902) for Germany.

mentary functions in higher education but also by the possibility both offered, in their different ways, for treating the European scene without constructing an interpretive framework to hang their treatment on. The textbooks tended to emphasize the political, diplomatic, military, and biographical events that could be joined by mere temporal succession without violating the empiricism of the scientific school. It is from this period and in this context that a general mode of American historiography has emerged that observers have characterized as domination by the monograph and the textbook.[4]

Yet a third indirect expression of the growing American academic interest in European history around the turn of the century was the application at long last, among historians of America, of the old abstract principle that American history should be placed in a broader context. With Osgood, Beer, and Andrews, not only was American colonial history merged into British imperial history but at least in the case of Andrews it went along with a general interest in contemporary European history.[5] In his *History of the United States of America* ( 1889-91 ) Henry Adams' focus on diplomacy drew him to pursue his theme of American-European contrast into the consideration of European as well as American political history during the Napoleonic era. William A. Dunning's emphasis upon a value-free empirical history left no place for a European-American interpretive system, but still he did combine scholarly interests in the politics of the American Civil War with the history of European political ideas not only in the ancient and medieval but in the modern eras.[6] Given the neutral and discrete mode of Dunning's analysis of political theories it would be difficult to substantiate any absorption of comprehensive assumptions from the synthetic Hegelianism of his mentor, John Burgess. In any case their example stimulated the new research in the history of political philosophy as a common West-

---

[4] Thus Charles H. Haskins, "European History and American Scholarship," *AHR,* XXVII (1923), 223-24; D. Pasquet, "Etats Unis," in *Histoire et historiens depuis cinquante ans,* vol. II (Paris, 1928), p. 502; J. F. Jameson, "Introduction," in *Historical Scholarship in America: Needs and Opportunities* (1932), p. 10; W. Stull Holt, "Historical Scholarship," in *American Scholarship in the Twentieth Century,* ed. Merle Curti (1953), pp. 93-94.
[5] Thus his *Contemporary Europe, Asia, and Africa,* vol. 20 of ed. John H. Wright, *A History of All Nations from the Earliest Times* (1902), and his *Historical Development of Modern Europe* (2 vols., 1896-98).
[6] See especially his *History of Political Theories from Luther to Montesquieu* (1905).

ern enterprise, exemplified in Merriam and Coker,[7] and the favorable environment for their younger Columbia colleagues to combine European and American themes in the expanded horizons of the "New History."

Of the philosophical meaning of the New History we have had much discussion, and intelligent discussion too, emphasizing its articulation of a "revolt" against a way of thinking represented in, among other things, scientific history.[8] And yet if the problem is considered, not philosophically but historiographically, and particularly from the angle of European historiography, a neglected dimension comes to light. For without belittling the motif of intellectual revolution and without denying the emphatically American root apparent in the adumbration of the New History by Frederick Jackson Turner and its fundamental explication by his fellow midwesterners, Becker and Beard, the fact remains that the New History represents the first constructive impulse given by European history to the American conception of history and is to be explained, at least partially, in these terms. The troubleshooter of the movement, James Harvey Robinson, was a professor of European history—the first so designated at Columbia—specializing in the modern period. During the formative phase of the movement before the war Beard not only collaborated on several of the innovating textbooks on recent European history with Robinson but he also wrote an interesting monograph on *The Office of the Justice of the Peace in England*.[9] Carl Becker had not yet begun the publications that were to make him as well known to European as to American historians, but his dual interest was already flourishing in his teaching career.[10] Among the disciples, Harry

---

[7] Thus Merriam's *History of the Theory of Sovereignty Since Rousseau* (1900) and his *History of American Political Theories* (1903); for Coker, see *Organismic Theories of State* (1910) and *Readings in Political Philosophy* (1914). It was John Burgess, the common mentor of this group, who pioneered the scholarly treatment of comparative politics to include both America and Europe with his *Political Science and Comparative Constitutional Law* (1890).

[8] See Cushing Strout, *The Pragmatic Revolt in American History: Carl Becker and Charles Beard* (1958) and Morton G. White, *Social Thought in America: The Revolt Against Formalism* (1949), esp. pp. 47-52.

[9] Published in Volume 20 of the "Columbia Studies in Economics, History, and Public Law" (1904).

[10] Becker's interest and competence in European history was one of the outstanding features of his *Beginnings of the American People*, first published in 1915. See Curtis P. Nettels' preface to the 1960 reprinting.

Elmer Barnes, Thorndike, Shotwell, and Carlton Hayes were to become prominent in the field of European history.

But what did the New History mean from the European angle? It may be said that when viewed from the European side there becomes visible in the New History the counterpoint that characterizes all revolts: it was as much a development from as a reaction against the existing constellation. The constellation created by scientific history demanded a further development, for it featured an unstable tension between the growing consciousness of American-European community and the permitted historiographical channels for its expression. The overarching conceptual framework that men like Henry Adams and Turner were calling desirable for American history was proving itself essential for European history in America. The problem did not hold for the monograph, with its built-in framework that exalted the universal value of properly disciplined knowledge, nor for fields like medieval history and the expansion of Europe, which, as backward extensions of the American past, could dispense with such a framework. But on the level of general European history the scientific approach revealed its limitations, and this held for general history in both its forms—the survey of large realms of time and space and the large interpretation of the particularized turning point.

The pressure for general history in the first of these forms was patent in the decades around the turn of the century. It appeared not only in the growing role of the historical textbook but much more revealingly in the growing market for collaborative world histories aimed primarily at the "general reader." American scholars distinguished themselves in neither category. The textbooks prior to the New History were overwhelmingly political and eschewed coherent interpretation. As for the multivolumed general histories, the discrepancy between the large American demand and the small American supply revealed the academic counterpart of the standard conditions that usually make for change in any system of production. This was the period in which European scholars initiated the publication of their classic series in the field of general history—series so advanced that they proved to be of value to the scholar as well as the interested public and indeed are in some respects usable yet.[11] Nothing

11 E.g., Wilhelm Oncken, ed., *Allgemeine Geschichte in Einzeldarstellungen* (46 vols., Berlin, 1879-93); Ernest Lavisse and Alfred Rambaud, *Histoire generale*

on this level was written in America, and since each of the European publications drew its authors overwhelmingly from the nation of its origin American scholars did not participate in them either. What did get wide publication in America was the popular general history, often of scholarly composition but political, dramatic, and ephemeral in product. Some of these were of British origin, separately published in America; [12] others were purely American publications.[13] In both cases, however, American historians played a subordinate role.

The era of scientific history was somewhat more fruitful in the sphere of that flexible second type of general history that lay between the monograph and universal history and that achieved its generality by the intrinsic importance of the chosen particular events for the larger movement of history. For we do find American historians for the first time producing works of scholarly respectability on phases of modern European history that paralleled rather than prefaced the American experience. But here again there was a discrepancy between the impulse and the execution. The impulse that sent scholars to the larger subjects in modern European history produced workmanlike jobs of politics and biography but nothing that was either a generally outstanding or a distinctively American contribution.[14] They were narratives, descriptions, or historical portraits,

---

*du 4ᵉ siecle a nos jours* (12 vols., Paris, 1893-1901); Georg von Below and Friedrich Meinecke, eds., *Handbuch der mittelalterlichen und neueren Geschichte* (23 vols., Munich, 1903-20); *Cambridge Modern History* (14 vols., Cambridge, England, and New York, 1902-12).

[12] E.g., Edward E. Morris, *et al.*, eds., *Epochs of Modern History* (1874-88), published in both London and New York.

[13] E.g., *Story of the Nations* (76 vols., 1882-1917); John H. Wright, ed., *op. cit.*

[14] E.g., for England: Roger B. Merriman, *Life and Letters of Thomas Cromwell* (2 vols., Oxford, 1902) Edward P. Cheyney, *History of England from the Defeat of the Spanish Armada to the Death of Elizabeth* (2 vols., 1914-26); Gilbert Slater, *Making of Modern England* (1913). For France: James Westfall Thompson, *Wars of Religion in France, 1559-1576* (1909); James B. Perkins, *France Under Mazarin* . . . (1886), *France Under the Regency* . . . (1892), *France Under Richelieu* (1897), *France in the American Revolution* (1911); Edward Jackson Lowell, *Eve of the French Revolution* (1892); Shailer Mathews, *French Revolution, 1789-1815* (1900); Fred M. Fling, *Youth of Mirabeau,* first and only volume of projected *Mirabeau and the French Revolution* (1908); William M. Sloane, *Life of Napoleon Bonaparte* (4 vols., 1894-96) and *French Revolution and Religious Reform* (1901). For Italy: William R. Thayer, *Dawn of Italian Independence* (2 vols., 1892) and *Life and Times of Cavour* (2 vols., 1911). For Germany: Herbert Tuttle, *History of Prussia* (4 vols., 1884-96);

important chiefly for the material they presented to the English-reading public but affording little in the way of novel approach or re-interpretation.

This was the context for the rise of the New History in the decade before World War I. Its chief spokesman, James Harvey Robinson, emphasized the European context in the various speeches and writings that were ultimately distilled into his volume *The New History: Essays Illustrating the Modern Historical Outlook* (1912), the classic formulation of the movement. The prominent European dimension of the New History makes clear its function in seeking to fill, for American historiography, the need that was most perceptible in the American history of Europe: the construction of an interpretive framework that would give meaning to historical fact.

The framework that the New Historians constructed is too familiar to require more than the refresher of a summary here. As a program for European history, it featured the following associated tenets: history is a continuous process; its chief goal should be to show how the present has become what it is as the basis for reforming it; its standards and values must change with the present; its scope must extend to all the varied interests and activities of man; it must emphasize conditions and institutions more than events; it must utilize the new and more advanced social sciences. This framework was not so much the antithesis as the modernized version of the traditional American historiography that scientific history was undermining and yet, for European history at least, could not entirely do without. It was in European history, where the empirical events did not imply their own meaning for Americans, that the conceptual framework had been traditionally strong and it was in European history that the scientific approach was leaving the most obvious vacuum.

The role of Europe in the New History was to overlay the older schemes and assumptions based on common origins with a newer one based on common contemporary connections and common destinies. The substantive relationship of the New History in its European version to the American historical tradition was analogous: it

---

Ernest F. Henderson, *Bluecher and the Uprising of Prussia Against Napoleon, 1806-1815* (1911). For military and diplomatic history, see the works by Theodore C. Dodge on Gustavus Adolphus (1895) and Napoleon (1904-07), by John C. Ropes on Waterloo (1892) and by James W. Gerard on the Peace of Utrecht (1885).

perpetuated the liberalism of the tradition but modernized it by making it more social and cultural than religious and intellectual and by assigning to the European connection not simply an original but a continuing positive function in it. The actual convergence of European and American foreign policies and of European and American social politics made it clear that the explanation of the American development lay not only in American conditions and institutions, however derived, but also in the larger process that was producing similar conditions and institutions elsewhere. The expansion of the geographical framework and of the intellectual framework beyond the local fact were parts of the same process; modern Europe could be relevant to America only as an ingredient in a common conception.

The European dimension helped to make the pragmatic impulse in the New History historiographically palatable by emphasizing the broad empirical base of its generalizing interpretations. Thus Robinson could begin his scholarly career with a study of the contemporary German Federal Council on the explicit premise that the purpose of such a study was the "broader" and "more accurate" view of American institutions[15] and he could close it with the notion that the study of European history was essential to the understanding of contemporary institutions anywhere in the world.[16] This judgment, in view of Robinson's conception of history as "making plain the world of today which can only be understood in the light of the past," [17] made the study of modern European history essential to any historical understanding whatsoever. For the New Historians the present furnished proof of the social and cultural unity behind the historical process, and the European past was its primary historical vehicle. As Robinson himself recognized, the cardinal assumption here was that of "historical continuity"—that "most fundamental and valuable truth which the past has to teach us" [18]—for it was this that made the process necessary to the fact, the present necessary to the past, and modern European history necessary to modern American history.

15 James Harvey Robinson, *The German Bundesrath: A Study in Comparative Constitutional Law* (1891), p. 5.
16 James Harvey Robinson, *The Ordeal of Civilization: A Sketch of the Development and World-wide Diffusion of Our Present-day Institutions and Ideas* (1926), pp. 4-5.
17 James Harvey Robinson and Charles A. Beard, *Outlines of European History: Part II, From the 17th Century to the War of 1914,* 3rd ed. (1918), p. iii.
18 James Harvey Robinson, "The New History," in *The New History: Essays Illustrating the Modern Historical Outlook* (1912), p. 14.

By the same token, since the unity of the present was constituted primarily by common traits of an industrial society the primary factors of history were deemed to be the social agents of this unity, to the deprecation of the political agents of differentiation.[19] The influence of the German historian Karl Lamprecht, whose stress on cultural history and on collective psychology as its central strand approached the tenets of the New Historians, was symptomatic of the connection between the emphasis on the social sciences as the source of interpretive historical concepts and the growing interest in a modern Europe whose industrial society America was coming increasingly to resemble. In the scholarly productions of Dunning, McIlwain, and Usher, as in Robinson's textbooks, the older conjunction of history and social science in America was now applied to and fertilized by the European past.[20]

But still an essential limitation operated upon this first generation of New Historians. Whatever their achievements in the older fields of American and medieval history,[21] their prime targets and accomplishments in modern European history before World War I were confined to historiography and to teaching. Their characteristic product was the essay on the former[22] and the textbook serving the latter.[23] The emphasis on historiography was natural enough, for the New Historians were developing a self-conscious philosophy of history explicitly opposed to the reigning empiricism. The concentration on the textbook is harder to explain, in view of the original approach and

---

[19] *Ibid.*, pp. 5-9. See also his "Some Reflections on Intellectual History," in *ibid.*, pp. 102-31 *passim*.

[20] For Dunning, see note 6 above. For McIlwain, who was similarly associated with political science on its theoretical side, see his brilliant *High Court of Parliament and its Supremacy* . . . (1910). Abbot P. Usher's important *History of the Grain Trade in France, 1400-1710* (1913) was published as part of the "Harvard Economic Studies." In addition, some of the important serial publications of history that date from this period include it as part of social science. E.g., the "Columbia Studies in Economics, History, and Public Law" and the Pennsylvania *Annals* of the American Academy of Political and Social Science.

[21] The works of Thorndike, Becker, and Beard mark the accomplishments of the school in these fields.

[22] In addition to the essays of Robinson and Becker in this period (see the bibliographies in L. V. Hendricks, *James Harvey Robinson* (1946) pp. 116-17 for Robinson and in Strout, *op. cit.*, pp. 168-69 for Becker), see James T. Shotwell's article on "History" in the famous 11th edition of the *Encyclopaedia Britannica* (1910).

[23] For discussion of character and influence of Robinson's textbooks, see Hendricks, *op. cit.*, pp. 64-100.

the exacting standards of critical scholarship that went into it and into its concomitant teaching methods.[24] There seem to be two main reasons—apart from Robinson's own personal equation—for this concentration.

In the first place, there is the obvious fact—but no less important for being obvious—that modern European history was a new field in America. The American tradition of European history, dwelling as we have seen it on the themes of common origins, had occupied the fields of medieval and of what Americans were later to call "early modern." The New Historians, departing from the different assumption of common destinies, included the medieval and early modern periods within the larger field extending backward from the present and were not in direct conflict with the traditional European history, with which in any case they shared the generic belief in a fundamental and continuous historical process. What they did directly oppose were the textbooks and popular histories that were filling the modern field with what they deemed aimless details of political or personal intrigue.[25] But the emphasis on the textbook was more than a matter of an address to the reigning form of historical literature in the field. For New Historians like Robinson and Beard the textbook as a form of historical writing was continuous with the general history for the public at large: [26] it was appropriate to their philosophy of history as an instrument of social reform, and—even more important for the history of history—it was appropriate to a new field that had to be surveyed before it could be sown intensively.

Second, the disproportionate weight of the textbook vis-à-vis the work of scholarship in the first generation of the European New History is also traceable to an uncrystallized quality in the conception of European-American community. The most patent facet of crystallization in history—politics—was, to be sure, not ignored, but, as Shotwell expressed it, "political events are mere externals," and since, for this view, "the universe is in motion in every part" and "the his-

[24] *Ibid.,* pp. 10-19. Note also the emphasis on publication of source collections for teaching purposes, e.g., in Volumes I-V of the University of Pennsylvania History Department's "Translations and Reprints" and Robinson and Beard's *Readings in Modern European History* (2 vols., 1908-09).
[25] James Harvey Robinson, *Outlines of European History: Part I* . . . (1914), p. iii, and Robinson, *The New History* pp. 5-13.
[26] Thus note the widespread use, by Robinson and his associates, of textbook sections in their popular works, e.g., in Robinson's *Ordeal of Civilization* (1926) and in Harry Elmer Barnes' edition of Robinson's *The Human Comedy* (1937).

torical spirit . . . has invaded every field,"[27] the New Historians seemed unable to break into the general cultural process at any particular point and tended, particularly when writing European history, rather to describe it in its totality. Disciples of the New History did, of course, like most professionals produce monographs in the form of scholarly articles and doctoral dissertations, but if they were more socially oriented than most they were still not appropriate vehicles for the characteristic tenets of the movement.

By the outbreak of World War I, then, the conditions had been prepared for a breakthrough in the American version of European history. As the beginnings of America receded into the past, the view of Europe based on its origination of America persisted but was increasingly balanced by the view of Europe based on the relevance of contemporary institutions. The scientific historians replaced the amateurs as the champions of the former connection, but they tended to assume rather than to assert it and with this attenuation the monograph replaced the large classic as its characteristic scholarly expression. The New Historians championed the latter connection, and with their emphasis on the comprehensiveness of the historical process tended to produce the textbook as its characteristic expression. The one group dwelt on the particular as implicitly meaningful to Americans; the other dwelt on the general as explicitly meaningful. It took the catalyst of war to initiate the union of the particular with the general that is a mark of creative historical writing.

[27] James T. Shotwell, "History," in *Encyclopaedia Britannica,* vol. XIII (1910), p. 527.

# 3

# THE IMPACT OF POLITICAL INVOLVEMENT
## (1914-1939)

World War I exhibited the community of American and European political interests in so fundamental a way as to make it predominant in the approach to European history for a generation and a necessary ingredient of it thereafter. The coincidence of this emphasis with the mass influx of scholars into the field had the effect of confirming the vogue of the monograph and the textbook as the characteristic forms of American scholarship, for European political history furnished especially accessible subject matter to both. At the same time, however, the political theme, coming at the stage in American historiographical development that it did, also played a most important constructive role not usually associated with political history, that favorite whipping boy of the self-styled avant garde. Past politics in its European dress broadened both the older empirical and the newer cultural streams of American historiography: for the first it introduced a dimension of meaning that was broader than the local historical fact and yet compatible with it; for the latter it introduced a historical specificity that broadened the meaning of the pass beyond its generic connection with the present. For the first group international politics produced the vogue of diplomatic history in which the historical facts themselves manifested the general tenet of an American-European community of political destiny. For the second group politics formed points of crystallization for society and culture that were noncumulative and permitted concrete and intensive historical analysis. In this way, the two wings of the American historical profession—the empirical and the synthetic—entered, on the European level at least, into a single universe of discourse and contributed to the growth of a unitary American dimension in the scholarship of European history.

The maturation of modern European history in America absorbed the two generations of scholars conditioned at either end by a world war, but each generation represented a distinct stage in this development. From World War I to the crisis of the early 1930's the emphasis was primarily, although certainly not exclusively, on the history of external relations, conformable to the prevailing judgments about the character of the forces that had brought European and American states into a common enterprise. Thereafter, the linkage of foreign policy with domestic structure in the rising dictatorships, the universal impact of the Depression, and the growing influence of the émigré scholars expanded the American-European community of interests to include the domestic as well as the foreign dimension. This succession of stages revealed in a literal way the internal relations that subsist between the specific character of American international relations at any period and the distinctive features in the American historiography of Europe. There was, to be sure, a kind of insulated, self-perpetuating mechanism built into the professional scholarship that ground out Ph.D. dissertations, but it was in the growing publication of more general and interpretive works that what was distinctive in American historical scholarship emerged.

It is obvious, of course, that World War I enormously stimulated American interest in things European. It is equally obvious that this interest included a strong historical bent. Whether through curiosity or partisanship American historians met the popular interest with occasional works of pragmatic history that ran the gamut from the diplomatic to the cultural background of the struggle.[1] What may perhaps not be so obvious is that most of these were works of journalistic or didactic rather than historical value and that the genuine historical works published during the war inhabited the main field of American involvement—the field of international politics.[2] The re-

---

[1] E.g., Arthur Bullard, *Diplomacy of the World War* (1916); William S. Davis, *et al.*, *Roots of the War: A Nontechnical History of Europe, 1870-1914* (1918); Charles D. Hazen, *Alsace-Lorraine Under German Rule* (1917); Munroe Smith, *Militarism and Statecraft* (1918); Charles H. C. Wright, *History of the Third French Republic* (1916); George M. Priest, *Germany Since 1740* (1915); Robert H. Fife, *German Empire Between the Wars* (1916); Thorstein Veblen, *Imperial Germany and the Industrial Revolution* (1915); Leo Wiener, *Interpretation of the Russian People* (1915); John Dewey, *German Philosophy and Politics* (1915); William K. Wallace, *Greater Italy* (1917). See in general the work of the National Board for Historical Service, e.g., Frank M. Anderson and Amos B. Hershey, *Handbook for the Diplomatic History of Europe, Asia, and Africa, 1870-1914* (1918).

[2] E.g., Bernadotte E. Schmitt, *England and Germany, 1740-1914* (1916); Charles Seymour, *Diplomatic Background of the War, 1870-1914* (1916); Charles D.

awakened consciousness, among historians, of an international community of political interests reached back at least to Mahan, but the impact of the war upon the young and impressionable profession of European history was to broaden the meaning of diplomatic history and integrate it into the tradition of American historiography. World War I established the precedent of enlisting historians as such in the national cause, first through the voluntary organization of the National Board for Historical Service under Shotwell and in cooperation with George Creel's Committee on Public Information, and then officially through the recruitment of such prominent historians as Shotwell and Haskins as experts in the American delegation to the Paris Peace Conference. Such activities raised, for the whole historical profession in America, the problems of "official" history that have plagued historians since the rise of the modern state, but for American historians of Europe the experience had an effect beyond this. Since their function was the provision of knowledge and analysis for American participation and policy in Europe, the war crystallized for them the political community between America and Europe and made the study of diplomacy a primary vehicle for locating the American role in human history.

The historiographical reflection of this American relationship to Europe continued through the decade that followed the war, for despite the vagaries of American foreign policy the American participation in the European peace settlement created a historical point of union that made the study of European diplomacy an abiding concern of American historians. The remarkably persistent growth of the American historical interest in Europe in the context of American isolation during the 1920's was in part undoubtedly an expression of the "antithetical" magnetism of Europe for American intellectuals in general that Boorstin has noted.[3] But even more than this, it registered the partial convergence of American and European interests that was articulated equally on the policy-making level, in the violent oscillations of American diplomacy, and on the historiographical level, in the haphazard growth of the professional concern for Eu-

Hazen, William R. Thayer, Robert H. Lord, *Three Peace Congresses of the Nineteenth Century*, together with Archibald C. Coolidge, *Claimants to Constantinople* (1917); Archibald C. Coolidge, *Origins of the Triple Alliance* (1917); Wilbur C. Abbott, *Expansion of Europe: A History of the Foundations of the Modern World* (2 vols., 1918).

[3] Daniel Boorstin, *America and the Image of Europe* (1960), pp. 23-31.

rope. The random character of historical production in this field from the end of the war to the early 1930's indicated that Americans were aware of relevant subjects in European history beyond the convergence of European and American diplomacy but that they had no controlling ideas about what constituted the relevance. A rough typology of this production may serve to ascertain the stage American historians had reached in defining their relationship to European history.

The outstanding American works were undoubtedly in the field of diplomatic history, where they dealt surely and intimately with the recent or contemporary events that led to the joint Allied war- and peace-making. In terms of the quality as well as the quantity of their performances in this field American historians attained for the first time as a group a position of parity in international scholarship. The immediate postwar mélange of memoir, report, and contemporary history of the peace-making process that Americans, as participants, had equal title with Europeans to make[4] soon gave way to the more historical, more professional, and more celebrated literature on the background and causation of the war, a literature that made the names Schmitt, Barnes, and Fay among the best known in the profession.[5] By the early 1930's Langer, Sontag, and Feis were pushing back beyond the crossroads of war with their original contributions to the general field of modern European diplomatic history.[6] Nor were these isolated achievements: they were supported by a whole battery of monographs with a similar focus.[7]

What were the qualities of this writing that moved it into the first

[4] E.g., Arthur P. Scott, *Introduction to the Peace Treaties* (1920); Ray S. Baker, *What Wilson Did at Paris* (1919) and *Woodrow Wilson and World Settlement* (3 vols., 1922); Edward M. House and Charles Seymour, eds., *What Really Happened at Paris, . . . by American Delegates* (1921); Charles H. Haskins and Robert H. Lord, *Some Problems of the Peace Conference* (1920).

[5] Harry Elmer Barnes, *Genesis of the World War . . .* (1926); Sidney B. Fay, *Origins of the World War* (2 vols., 1928); Bernadotte E. Schmitt, *The Coming of the War, 1914* (2 vols., 1930).

[6] W. L. Langer, *European Alliances and Alignments* (1931); R. J. Sontag, *European Diplomatic History, 1871-1932* (1932); Herbert Feis, *Europe: The World's Banker, 1870-1914* (1930).

[7] E.g., Edward M. Earle, *Turkey, the Great Powers, and the Bagdad Railway: A Study in Imperialism* (1923); Mason W. Tyler, *European Powers and the Near East, 1875-1908* (1925); William L. Langer, *Franco-Russian Alliance, 1890-1914* (1929); Eugene N. Anderson, *The First Moroccan Crisis, 1904-1906* (1930).

rank of the world's historical literature? What they were can be defined first by asserting what they were not. They were not qualities of originality in method or of brilliance in conception. They were the qualities of scientific history writ large—comprehensive and critical approach to the sources, isolation and control of subject matter, clarity of organization, detachment in interpretation.[8] In large measure, undoubtedly, the elevated rank attained along this well-trodden path came precisely from the appearance of comprehensiveness and detachment in this context as distinctively American attributes. The virulence of the intra-American conflict between the revisionist and anti-revisionist interpreters of the origins of the war should not be minimized, but the fact remains that in the United States this debate was carried on within the national corps of historians and that consequently Americans led the way in distilling from the debate a stimulus toward an ever more even balance of interpretation. The advantage of supranational perspective that Haskins was noting during this very period in the American historians of Europe[9] was bearing fruit. And yet the American achievement in European diplomatic history was the result of more than this. Renan once intimated that the best history is written by men who had once been personally committed to the position of their subject and had then withdrawn from it. For historians in America the sequence was either reversed or transformed into simultaneity, but both factors were present. If the quality of detachment was reinforced by the continuing American separation from Europe the quality of commitment was reinforced by the convergent policies of war- and peace-making. The diplomatic historian of this period labored under the great advantage that however specialized his subject or judicious his attitude the chain of events had themselves made his work immediately relevant to the larger stream of history that had joined America and Europe in a fateful hour. Like the religious framework for an earlier day, the political framework made the very facts of European development meaningful to Americans and thereby extended the orbit of their interests.

Diplomatic history was indeed the most prominent but it was not the only notable European history written in America during the

---

[8] See Fay's adherence to Ranke in *The Origins of the World War*, rev. 2nd ed. (1938), p. viii.
[9] Charles H. Haskins, "History and American Scholarship," *AHR*, XXVII (1923), 226.

postwar period, and the historiographical structure of the age can be appreciated only in terms of the whole body of publications it dominated. A second important type was what may be termed internationally oriented domestic history. As diplomatic history was the scientific school writ large, this second type was the "new" school writ large. The two chief expressions of this type were the enormously valuable series on the "Economic and Social History of the World War" edited by James T. Shotwell[10] and the studies around the theme of nationalism and imperalism that came out of the Columbia graduate school under the particular guidance of Carlton J. H. Hayes.[11] The American sponsorship and direction of the multinational series and the supranational standpoint for the assessment of European nationalism were equally obvious expressions of the American dimension of comprehensive detachment from the European scene. But this was not their most important aspect. What was important and what distinguished this type from diplomatic history was the way in which the urgent issues raised by the war focused and organized the treatment of domestic institutions and movements in Europe. This was obvious in the Shotwell series[12]—and it must be remembered that Shotwell was a student of Robinson—and it was true too of the studies on nationalism. Both Hayes (another Robinson student) and Moon published monographs on European social history[13] and Hayes wrote an outstanding textbook in the style of the New History[14] before the problem of aggression arising out of the war led them to synthesize domestic movements under an external theme. Thus Hayes's initial theme, in the *Essays on Nationalism*, was avowedly the "extreme militant type of contemporary national-

[10] For the Carnegie Endowment for International Peace. The series was planned during the war and the first volume was published in 1921.
[11] For syntheses on these themes, see Carlton J. H. Hayes, *Essays on Nationalism* (1926) and *Historical Evolution of Modern Nationalism* (1931); Parker T. Moon, *Imperialism and World Politics* (1926); M. E. Townsend, *Rise and Fall of Germany's Colonial Empire, 1884-1918* (1930). For monographs on these themes, see Mary E. Townsend, *Origins of Modern German Colonialism, 1871-1885* (1921); Mildred S. Wertheimer, *Pan-German League, 1890-1914* (1924).
[12] That is, in the planning of it. Most of the European volumes were written by Europeans. Two notable exceptions were Carlton J. H. Hayes, *France, a Nation of Patriots* (1930), and David J. Saposs, *The Labor Movement in Post-War France* (1931).
[13] Carlton J. H. Hayes, *British Social Politics* . . . (1913); Parker T. Moon, *The Labor Problem and the Social Catholic Movement in France* (1921).
[14] *Political and Social History of Modern Europe* (1916).

ism . . . most in evidence during and after the World War," and from this initial concern he subsequently developed his generic work on the movement as a whole.[15] By the 1930's Columbia dissertations were exploring all aspects of the theme.[16]

A third type of European history in the postwar period was one step removed in the immediate occasion of its historical interest from the second: it dealt with the general or contemporary history of areas that had been raised into prominence for Americans by the war. Its political point of reference was therefore implicit rather than explicit. This kind of interest extended far beyond Europe into the various parts of the world brought to American attention by the global nature of the war and the peace settlement. The American concern with Europe tended to concentrate, in line with this expansion of horizons, on its most exotic section—i.e., the Balkans—where the war had borne new nations, and on the vanquished nations, where the war had borne new regimes.[17] None of these works made a permanent contribution to historical understanding, either through their research or their interpretation, for they lacked both the explicit focus of the internationally oriented histories and the longer-range framework of the scholarly enterprise, but they did render aid by extending the American definition of relevance from the events of European diplomacy and warfare to the events of European history as such. Certainly general European history had been relevant to Americans before, but what had made it relevant was a process—either the process by which European events fed into American developments or the process by which European events articulated most clearly a

15 See his *Historical Evolution of Modern Nationalism* (1931), esp. p. v, and his *France, a Nation of Patriots*.
16 E.g., Jacques Barzun, *The French Race* . . . (1932); Glyndon G. Van Deusen, *Sieyès: His Life and Nationalism* (1932); H. R. Weinstein, *Jean Janres: A Study of Patriotism in the French Socialist Movement* (1936); Shepard Clough, *France: A History of National Economics* (1939).
17 On the Balkans, see Ferdinand Schevill, *History of the Balkan Peninsula from the Earliest Times to the Present Day* (1922); Eliot G. Mears, ed., *Modern Turkey: A Politico-economic Interpretation, 1908-1923 Inclusive* (1924); Charles U. Clark, *Greater Roumania* (1922); Joseph S. Roucek, *Contemporary Roumania and Her Problems: A Study in Modern Nationalism* (1932); Charles A. Beard and George Radin, *Balkan Pivot: Yugoslavia* (1929). On Germany, Ralph H. Lutz, *German Revolution, 1918-1919* (1922); John F. Coar, *The Old and the New Germany* (1924); James W. Angell, *The Recovery of Germany* (1932); Rupert Emerson, *State and Sovereignty in Modern Germany* (1928). On Austria, Oszkar Jaszi, *Dissolution of the Hapsburg Monarchy* (1929).

substantive process common to both Europe and America. What was new now—what the distinctiveness of politics contributed to American historiography—was the assumption that not simply the European historical process but the European historical event itself was meaningful, since it fed into a historical stream that not as a matter of law but as a matter of fact overflowed into the lives of Americans. Through political history the age-old assumption of the chronicler and the monographer that all events everywhere concern all men everywhere was materialized into tangible fact.

It follows, then, that the fourth type of European history in America during the postwar era was the far-flung, heterogeneous investigations into the most varied aspects of the European past for elucidation in their own terms. The growing attention that this field of research was commanding from the profession was signalized in the planning, from 1926, that eventuated in the foundation of the *Journal of Modern History* in 1929 as a periodical specializing in Europe since the Middle Ages. It was conceived as a professional periodical, it was publicly justified by little beyond the declaration of the professional need of an outlet for scholarly articles, and its founders asserted their devotion to all the substantive fields of history alike.[18] The opening of all modern European history to the specialized research of many professionals did induce a certain formlessness. It was like the occupation of any new territory, where the very breadth of opportunity scattered the settlements of the newcomers. And yet the American effort was not as undifferentiated as its statement of academic principles indicated. Not only were its most prominent achievements, as we have seen, crystallized by the recent political community of Europe and America, but even within the more insulated orbit of its miscellaneous scholarship the traditional features of American history-writing persisted, albeit in adapted forms, thereby impressing American historiography with a cumulative pattern of development.

The first of these features was the persistence of the tripartite division of historical scholarship among the textbook designed for students, the monograph addressed to the international republic of scholars, and what may be called the refinished import, beamed at

[18] See the opening declaration and Chester P. Higby's "The Present Status of Modern European History in the United States" in *Journal of Modern History*, I (1929), 1, 3-6.

the English-reading audience. The tendencies reached back into the nineteenth century: what was novel about them in the postwar period had to do mainly with the development of the third form, a hybrid historical genre that recapitulated the results of European scholarship, combined them with the intimate touch stemming from firsthand general acquaintance with the European sources, and remolded them into subjects intermediate between the monograph and the general textbook and meaningful for an American audience of advanced university students and graduates. The character of this historical form can be best sensed from its outstanding exemplars during the period: Preserved Smith's *Age of the Reformation* (1920), Guy Stanton Ford's *Stein and the Era of Reform in Prussia* (1922), Albert Guerard's *Life and Death of an Ideal* (1928), Louis Gottschalk's (1929) and Leo Gershoy's (1934) surveys of the French revolution, Harry W. Laidler's *History of Socialist Thought* (1927), Carl Becker's *Heavenly City of the Eighteenth-Century Philosophers* (1932). This orientation toward the intermediate theme or subject as the point of union between the appreciation of the particular European event and its integration into a larger framework more immediately meaningful to non-Europeans had its effect, during this period, on the extremes of the American historical spectrum as well. From the monographic side there now developed the kind of extended study that combined the specialized plumbing of primary sources with a larger scope of subject in a way only native historians of Europe had previously found meaningful. Of such a kind were Conyers Read's *Mr. Secretary Walsingham and the Policy of Queen Elizabeth* (3 vols., 1925), E. R. Turner's *Privy Council of England in the Seventeenth and Eighteenth Centuries* (2 vols., 1927-28), and the start of Gottschalk's exhaustive work on Lafayette.[19] From the other extreme, textbooks developed in the reverse direction toward a greater specialization with the separating of the different substantive fields of European history, such as the economic and the intellectual, for treatment in independent textbooks.[20] The general tendency to-

---

[19] His first volume, *Lafayette Comes to America*, was published in 1935.

[20] Thus: Frederic A. Ogg, *Economic Development of Modern Europe* (1917); Melvin Marvin Knight and Harry Elmer Barnes, *Economic History of Europe* (1928); Abbott Payson Usher, *An Introduction to the Industrial History of England* (1920); John Herman Randall, *The Making of the Modern Mind* (1926). An especially noteworthy development along these lines was the initiation of the "Berkshire Studies in European History" in 1927. Designed for use as supple-

ward the intermediate work helped to unify the scattered types of American historical writing. At the same time it created the universe of discourse within which the main issues of European history in America have been raised: the proper proportions of alien events to kindred syntheses and the criteria for syntheses that would do justice to European facts and make sense to American minds.

The role of synthesis in the American history of Europe was supported by a second traditional feature of American historiography that continued to operate in the postwar period—the subscription to the concept of Western civilization as a historical framework that included both Europe and America. The two great monuments to this concept were the American participation in the series on the "History of Civilization," in which Harry Elmer Barnes shared the editorial direction with French and English scholars,[21] and Preserved Smith's *History of Modern Culture*. Smith took explicitly as his unit the "North Atlantic peoples" in "modern times" (i.e., from the mid-sixteenth century) and saw in this unit a distinctive culture characterized by growing wealth, the spread of democracy and of popular education, the triumph of a secular attitude and the domination of science.[22] Nor was he alone in this expansive view: the Botsfords, Shotwell, Thorndike, and Randall took the history of Western "civilization" as the theme of their texts;[23] Breasted and Robinson reprinted much of their older, more orthodoxly styled texts under the rubric of *civilization*;[24] Carl Becker subtitled his "the rise of a democratic, scientific, and industrialized civilization";[25] and Carlton Hayes justified his modern European history text by denominating Europe "the seat of that continuous high civilization which we call

---

mentary textbooks, these manuals approached European history through the separate treatment of crucial intermediate subjects—e.g., *The Crusades, The Commercial Revolution, Imperial Russia*.

[21] It should be noted, however, that this series, which began publication in 1924, included several translations from two kindred French series and that its original volumes on modern Europe were written by European scholars.

[22] Preserved Smith, *A History of Modern Culture* (1930), pp. 4-6. A second volume was published in 1934.

[23] George W. Botsford and Jay B. Botsford, *Brief History of the World, with Especial Reference to Economic and Social Conditions* (1917); James T. Shotwell and Austin P. Evans, eds., *Records of Civilization* (10 vols., 1915-29); Lynn Thorndike, *Short History of Civilization* (1926); John Herman Randall, *Making of the Modern Mind* (1926).

[24] Breasted as *Conquest of Civilization*, Robinson as *Ordeal of Civilization*.

[25] Carl L. Becker, *Modern History* (1935).

'western'—which has come to be the distinctive civilization of the American continents as well as of Europe. . . ." [26] This roster confirms what was to be expected—that with few exceptions the concept of Europe as the dominant partner of a joint Western civilization defined by its *terminus ad quem* was a product chiefly of the New History and its disciples. But if this identification exhibits the continuity in American historiography it also gives a measure for assessing the development of American historiography, for the postwar work of the school shows a number of interesting changes over the prewar period of its origin. For one thing, the unit of a joint civilization that had been assumed was now the explicit unit of consideration. For another, the former investment of this framework in general texts and in historiography was now supplemented by its substantive development in such original interpretive works of joint Western history as Becker's *Heavenly City* and Preserved Smith's *History of Culture*. Finally, and most important, in this development toward the specification of the historical relevance of Europe for America an unexpected but crucial rift appeared that was not visible through the camouflage of neutral description in the general textbooks. The rift was between the contemporary joint civilization that was their framework for the history of Europe and America and the early modern period in which alone they found a genuine historical unity. Preserved Smith did not get beyond the year 1776. Carl Becker drew his famous boundary line linking the joint culture of the eighteenth century Enlightenment with the general culture of the Middle Ages and breaking it sharply off from the subsequent culture of the nineteenth century. For this later period he lost his confidence in the existence of a joint European and American culture, and if he thought in terms of a parallel development still he showed only a negative historical interest in a culture that knew "men . . . and nations, but not Man." [27] Even Carlton Hayes, despite the exercise of all due scholarly restraint, indicated clearly his disapproval of all but the earliest, "humanitarian" phase of the modern nationalism that he described.[28] Now the point here is not the approval or disapproval of a segment of history, for historians are ca-

[26] Carlton J. H. Hayes, *A Political and Cultural History of Modern Europe*, vol. I (1936), p. vii.
[27] Carl L. Becker, *The Declaration of Independence: A Study in the History of Political Ideas* (1922), pp. 224-79.
[28] Hayes, *Historical Evolution of Modern Nationalism*, pp. 289-321.

pable of writing perfectly good histories of subjects they abhor. The point is rather that, apart from the obvious connection through international politics, the one "synoptic" [29] school of historians in America was still unable to derive from its general tenet of a joint contemporary civilization the standards of relevance for specific European history, and in default of such standards had recourse to the traditional theme of the common intellectual origins of modern Europe and America. It was no mere coincidence but rather an essential relationship that associated early modern with intellectual history and recent with political history in this postwar period. But between these two sets of history and their opposite bases of relevance a crucial gap persisted.

A third aggregate within the heterogeneous growth of European history-writing in the United States during the postwar period was formed by a development that was the precise reverse of the second. Whereas the New Historians, from their assumption of a common social destiny, developed a surprising focus on early modern and intellectual subjects in their important writing, the empirical historians, from their assumption of common intellectual origins, developed an equally surprising focus on later modern and economic subjects in their important historical writing. The continued role of the traditional attitude toward Europe as an extension backward of the American past was patent in this period. Besides the further growth of medieval studies which led to the foundation of the Medieval Academy, American historians developed an unprecedented sophistication in both the intellectual history of the Reformation era and the political and constitutional history of those European nations—particularly Britain and France—whose cultural and political origins in the modern period were most akin to the American.[30] At the same time,

---

[29] The term is Preserved Smith's. See his *History of Modern Culture,* vol. II, p. iii.

[30] E.g., Preserved Smith, *The Age of the Reformation* (1920) and *Erasmus* (1923); Albert Hyma, *Christian Renaissance: A History of the "Devotio Moderna"* (1924); John J. Mangan, *Life, Character and Influence of Erasmus of Rotterdam* (1927); Wallace Notestein, *The Winning of the Initiative by the House of Commons* (London, 1934); Edward P. Cheyney, *History of England from the Defeat of the Spanish Armada to the Death of Elizabeth* (2 vols., 1914-26); Theodore C. Pease, *Leveller Movement* (1916); William T. Morgan, *English Political Parties and Leaders in the Reign of Queen Anne* (1920); Paul Van Dyke, *Catharine de Médicis* (1922); Franklin C. Palm, *Politics and Religion in Sixteenth Century France: A Study of the Career of Henry of Mont-*

however, from this core empirical history grew two new dimensions. In the first place, although European social history was more a desideratum than an achievement serious approaches were begun toward it from the side of economic history. Norman Gras set up the framework for this new emphasis with his interpretive historical surveys of the Western economy that treated it as a single process spanning both sides of the Atlantic.[31] The studies published during the postwar period remained for the most part securely within this framework: they stressed the economies of England and France, and they concentrated on the typical agrarian and mercantile institutions of the early modern period.[32] The second direction for scholarly adventure was toward the present, with the opening up of nineteenth century domestic politics to professional research and analysis. Historians before the war had worked in this field usually on the basis of the common human denominators served by biography and the spectacular event. Now, however, operating within the recognizable constitutional systems of England and France, American historians began to treat men and ideas as expressions of the characteristic institutions of nineteenth century Europe.[33] In part, of course, this chronological advance of professionalism was only natural, an ineluctable result of the passing years that keeps surrendering more and more of the recent past to the dominion of history. But this

---

morency-Damville . . . (1927); Louis R. Gottschalk, *Jean Paul Marat: A Study in Radicalism* (1927).

[31] Norman S. B. Gras, *Introduction to Economic History* (1922) and *History of Agriculture in Europe and America* (1925).

[32] E.g., Howard L. Gray, *English Field Systems* (1915); Jay B. Botsford, *English Society in the Eighteenth Century as Influenced from Overseas* (1924); Stella Kramer, *English Craft Gilds: Studies in Their Progress and Decline* (1927); Frederick L. Nussbaum, *Commercial Policy in the French Revolution: A Study of the Career of G.J.A. Ducher* (1923); Charles W. Cole, *French Mercantilist Doctrines Before Colbert* (1931). But there were scattered ventures into the economic history of the industrial era, e.g., Witt Bowden, *Industrial Society in England Toward the End of the Eighteenth Century* (1925) and Arthur Dunham, *The Anglo-French Treaty of Commerce of 1860 and the Progress of the Industrial Revolution in France* (1930).

[33] E.g., Charles Seymour, *Electoral Reform in England and Wales* . . . (1915); Herbert C. Bell, *Lord Palmerston* (London, 1936); C. Crane Brinton, *The Political Ideas of the English Romanticists* (Oxford, 1926); John M. S. Allison, *Thiers and the French Monarchy, 1797-1848* (1926) and *Monsieur Thiers* (1932); Alvin R. Calman, *Ledru-Rollin and the Second French Republic* (1922); C. T. Muret, *French Royalist Doctrines Since the Revolution* (1933); Frederick B. Artz, *France Under the Bourbon Restoration* (1931).

movement of nineteenth century Europe into historical respectability raised the problem of identifying a relevance that lay between the common origins of the eighteenth century and the tangible convergence of twentieth century international politics. In short, American historians were brought face to face with the challenge of a parallel historical experience that could be Americanized only at its initial and terminal extremes. It was this unresolved problem, perhaps, that brought European history into line with a general feature of American historiography in the 1920's: the contrast between the exalted standards of the reviewers and the limited production of the historians. The former called unremittingly for a large coherence, whether in the overt form of a conceptual unity or in the covert form of a social history that would provide a substantive unity, but what they usually got was the assemblage of material and the focus on a particular kind of activity, whether political, intellectual, or aesthetic. The discrepancy can be explained by the novelty of European history as a profession, since the higher standards of criticism, derived from the level of European historical literature, would naturally arise prior to historical creation at that level, and aside from international politics the American writing of European history in this period was in many ways the typical product of the tyro. And yet, behind these growing pains of the profession, there lurked the uncomfortable, vaguely grasped impression that the American historical dimension, like the great American novel, had not yet come to be.

It appears, then, that from the empirical as from the philosophical sides of the American tradition the gap between the reach and the grasp persisted through the postwar period. The first connections were forged in the extraordinary heat fired during the 1930's by the world depression, the development of totalitarianism into an international force, and the initial impact of the émigré scholars. These influences converged into a single massive pressure that concentrated the abstraction of a unified Western industrial civilization into a tangible reality and expanded the contact-points of international politics into a juncture all along the line of social life. The widespread economic and social crisis subjected the events of daily life to the same categories in Europe and America, while the rising threat to all countries of the omnivorous dictatorships triumphant in central and eastern Europe proved that the relevance of distant politics to America included the relevance of all human activities. The challenge of the possibility signalized in Sinclair Lewis's *It Can't Happen Here* became a beacon for a generation of politically and socially awakened intellectuals.

The historical corollary that the pasts of relevant presents are themselves relevant was driven home for Americans by the influx of refugee historians. Now certainly there was nothing new in such scholarly contacts. Not only had American historiography since the early nineteenth century received some of its most vital impulses from personal contacts with scholars in Europe but they had learned too from historians who had come to American universities for shorter or longer stays. Goldwin Smith, Edward Freeman, James Froude, Henry Morse Stephens, Karl Lamprecht, and Albert Guerard had been influential visitors or imports during the early development of the profession, and Russian historians like Michael Karpovich and George Vernadsky had initiated the tradition of refugee scholarship after the Bolshevik revolution. But where the first of these groups had had its impact upon American historiography in general and the second had extended American awareness of a still exotic historical field, the immigrant historians from central Europe during the Thirties worked a profound influence upon the general practice of European history in this country. The fact of still another immigration, the particular circumstances of the influx of the Thirties, the broad interests of historians like Hajo Holborn, Ernst Kantorowicz, Felix Gilbert, Dietrich Gerhard, Hans Baron, Hans Rosenberg, Hans Rothfels, and Gaetano Salvemini and of historically minded social scientists like Franz Neumann, Joseph Schumpeter, and Alexander Gerschenkron combined to divest academic immigration of its exceptional status and to bring the American historical scholarship of Europe soon abreast and ultimately in many respects ahead of its European counterpart. For these European scholars not only disseminated an intimate knowledge of the European heritage to American students in unprecedented numbers but they themselves represented a selection from European scholarship based on the awareness, drawn from the circumstances of their own careers, of the actual relationships that linked the various activities of man. Their feeling for historical integration was nurtured by the experience of their totalitarian homelands and developed by their intellectual naturalization in America, where, as we have seen, the conditions of cultural geography had made a general sense of historical synthesis part of the historiographical tradition. The European-born historians contributed to that tradition by connecting what had been separate in it, for the common strength of their historical teaching and writing lay in their merger of particularity and generality, in their preservation of the irreducible vitality of the one within the generic meaningfulness of the other. Hence the unforgettable impression in the American scholars who studied with these historians that historiographically as well as culturally they were recognizing their own future in the European past.

The historical writing that came out of the Thirties represented in many ways an extension of previous tendencies, as befit a growing young profession that had already evinced a lively postwar interest in Europe, but the conditions peculiar to the decade did add a dimension of large qualitative importance. This dimension involved a new appreciation of the consanguinity of the European event that permitted its research, organization, and interpretation no longer either simply as an item to be learned as such or as a subordinate component of a general tendency but as itself constituent of a common experience. The new forms of European history in America during this period, therefore, were essentially variant forms of historical integration.

First, and most obvious, was the American entry into the field of the detailed, multivolumed, general history of Europe. The "Rise of Modern Europe," better known after its editor, William L. Langer, as "the Langer series," began publication in 1934 and with all its unevenness and gaps (it is still incomplete) remains the outstanding collaborative achievement by American historians in the general field of European history. The self-conscious qualities of the series— which emphasize the synthetic as against the specialized, the social and cultural as against the political and military, the "dominant factors" as against detailed chronology, and the European as against the national—[34] are scarcely distinctive, either vis-à-vis the European counterparts of the series or the American tradition of European history, which, as we have seen, contains a whole strand whose every thread has made the same claim of innovation. What makes the series distinctive is not its opposition to its presumed antithesis—i.e., to specialized scholarship with its detailed, political, national narration or description—but its manner of negotiation with it. The series is both

[34] See William L. Langer's introduction, repeated in all the volumes of the series.

new to American historiography and different from kindred European publications in the highly analytical structure that organizes events and institutions under concepts at once immanent in and common to the whole Western civilization. The modern state, the triumph of the bourgeoisie in a commercialized and then industrialized society, the secularization of thought and culture: these familiar themes have been given periodic specification in the series through temporal categories running from Gilmore's flexible humanism to Hayes's more rigid liberalism, nationalism, and materialism. For the most part political categories predominate, but, as with Carl Friedrich's definition of the baroque in terms of power, they are categories that help to organize the other activities of the age as well. The Langer series represents a major attempt to unify the American scholarly and synthetic lines of historical tradition and thereby to create a distinctive American dimension of European history.

The welding of the particular and the general that the Langer series sought to perform *in extenso* found a second, more intensive form as well during the 1930's: the successful exploitation of social history as the nodal point of the various historical fields. This kind of history tended, in consonance with the changing international problems of the time, to complement diplomacy as a field in which basic research could elicit facts that would immediately have a general meaning for Americans. There is little doubt that American historians feel a special predilection for this kind of history. Not only has social history been for decades the single most persistent substantive desideratum raised in their critical reviews but the historical works that have been written under its aegis since the Thirties have ranked with international relations as the most original American contributions to the general field of European history.[35] The liberal tradition

---

35 Thus: Crane Brinton, *The Jacobins* (1930); Edward S. Mason, *The Paris Commune* (1930); W. K. Jordan, *Development of Religious Toleration in England* (London, 1932-40); Louis Wright, *Middle-Class Culture in Elizabethan England* (1935); Donald M. Greer, *The Incidence of Terror During the French Revolution* (1935); William Haller, *The Rise of Puritanism* (1938); Carl Brand, *British Labour's Rise to Power* (1941); Maurice J. Quinlan, *Victorian Prelude: A History of English Manners, 1700-1830* (1941); Mildred Campbell, *The English Yeoman Under Elizabeth and the Early Stuarts* (1942); Caroline Robbins, *The Eighteenth Century Commonwealthman* (1959); Charles Woolsey Cole, *French Mercantilism, 1683-1700* (1943); Henry W. Ehrmann, *The French Labor Movement from Popular Front to Liberation* (1947); Franklin L. Ford, *The Robe and the Sword* (1953); Val R. Lorwin, *The French Labor*

in American historiography favored the approach through the common man, but beyond this a clue to the special assumptions of the 1930's that sponsored it can be found in the preference for the history of the English and the French societies, whereas the social history of less kindred peoples had to wait for different assumptions to obtain.[36] The assumptions that governed the Anglo-French emphasis in social history were clearly those that were pushing historians beyond the traditional categories into more intimate perceptions of familiar societies. Thus the tendency toward social history was accompanied by American penetration into European provincial history and a more exhaustive bibliographical and biographical repertory than ever before.[37] But the social historian manifested this intimacy in a different way—not by the registration of details but by making the experience of ordinary men the common measure for the grasp of ideas and institutions, which were now viewed through their joint effects rather than as separate entities. Since formal ideas and institutions were particular to the European place concerned and since the experience of every man was conceived as common to all men everywhere, the conversion of the former into functions of the latter not only elevated social history to a central position as the point of union for the other categories of history but made every social detail *ipso facto* a constituent in the growing understanding of a common Western humanity.

Between the extensive accomplishment of the Langer series and the intensive contributions of the social historians, Americans during the 1930's developed to a new eminence that intermediate form of historical writing that was designed to reap the advantages of both. This form, particularly suited as it was to American needs in European his-

---

*Movement* (1954); Wallace Notestein, *The English People on the Eve of Colonization* (1954); Elinor G. Barber, *The Bourgeoisie in Eighteenth Century France* (1955); Warren C. Scoville, *The Persecution of the Huguenots and French Economic Development* (1960).

[36] See below. But there were notable early exceptions. E.g., G. T. Robinson, *Rural Russia Under the Old Regime* (1932); Kent Greenfield, *Economics and Liberalism in the Risorgimento* (1934); Pauline Anderson, *The Background of Anti-English Feeling in Germany, 1890-1902* (1938).

[37] Particularly in French revolutionary studies. See especially Robert R. Palmer, *Twelve Who Ruled* (1941), but note too John B. Sirich, *The Revolutionary Committees in the Departments of France* (1943) and Richard M. Brace, *Bordeaux and the Gironde, 1789-1794* (1947). Conyers Read and Stanley Pargellis compiled definitive bibliographies for sixteenth and eighteenth century England respectively.

tory, appears, as we have seen, in every stage of American historiography and furnishes an accurate barometer of its qualities. What distinguished this intermediate form during the 1930's from its previous status was the large increment of original primary research that now went into it and the large variety of limited historical subjects that, under the assumption of the seamless web of history, seemed of intrinsic general importance. Works in this genre could treat a particular historical area for several historical fields over an extended period such as Robert J. Kerner's *Bohemia in the Eighteenth Century* (1932), Ferdinand Schevill's *History of Florence . . . Through the Renaissance* (1936), and Raymond Sontag's *Germany and England . . . 1848-1895* (1938). Or they could trace a single subject or theme through many periods in the whole Western area, such as Philip C. Jessup *et al., Neutrality, Its History, Economics, and Law* (1935-36), George Sabine's *History of Political Theory* (1937), Crane Brinton's *Anatomy of Revolution* (1938), and the gifted amateur Edmund Wilson's *To the Finland Station* (1940). Or they could, finally, give exhaustive treatment to a subject large and important in itself through a limited period, like Langer's monumental *Diplomacy of Imperialism* (1935). What the works of this intermediate type had in common was a sense of totality that led their authors to prosecute their original researches beyond their wonted frameworks, a tendency most notable in Sontag's and Langer's transcendence of diplomatic history, or to ensconce their findings in a larger process, as Brinton did obviously in his *Anatomy*. It was this sense of an immanent totality that aligned this kind of history with the Langer series and social history as a generic expression of the age and that especially distinguished it from its predecessors in the American historiographical past. What distinguished it in this sense from the great thematic works of the nineteenth century was the internationalization of the general process that made the events of the European past meaningful to Americans: it was no longer the external origins of American culture or the cosmic evolution of the free spirit but a feeling for the common experience of Western man that made European events familiar and important in themselves. What distinguished it from the historiography of the earlier twentieth century was the rejuvenation of the feeling that there was a process in history. If we compare Sabine's history of political theory with Dunning's, for example, we find in Sabine an insistence upon the reciprocating relationship between the theory and the practice of politics and a developmental coherence between the analyses that are absent in his predecessor.

The momentous period between the two wars thus gave to the young profession of European history in the United States a kind of unity and purpose that could fulfill the same function as the common faith of their amateur predecessors of the nineteenth century. Continuing the latter's sense of the common origins of modern Europe and America and absorbing into it the early twentieth century sense of a common destiny, the interwar historians witnessed a contemporary community of international politics and of social crisis that helped to turn the whole of the European past from the exotic into the familiar. Within this growing circle of recognition the various activities of the profession found an unprecedented coherence: the gap between the monograph and the textbook was closed as monographs were more and more designed to contribute to larger problems and as the belief in a continuing process of history became academically respectable enough to attract a growing number of accomplished scholars to the composition of general texts. With this kind of rough consensus in the appropriation of European history by a profession of teacher-scholars the organization of the profession tended increasingly to follow European lines, specializing according to national divisions. History departments in the larger American universities began to look like microcosms of the European historical profession: the norm was to have a general European historian, who was more often than not a specialist in diplomatic history, and then a man for each of the major European countries. In part this plane of specialization was a matter of linguistic and logistical convenience in a period when the sources of modern history were multiplying to a degree calling for more intensive methods by scholars, but in part too it reflected the growth of the intimacy that Americans were feeling toward all sectors of the European past.

# 4

## THE CONTEMPORARY STATUS

It might have been expected that with the wartime community of the United Nations and the Western alliance that followed upon it the process of historical convergence would be complete and that European history would have become as immediately meaningful to American scholars as to European. In many ways this has indeed come to pass. Academic exchanges have been institutionalized to an unprecedented degree and in unprecedented forms: the whole European-American historical region has been homogenized by the development of European interest in American history and by the invitation from Europe for Americans to lecture and write on European history. Both private foundations and governmental agencies have elaborated broad programs to encourage overseas research in the interests of improved cultural and political relations, and as a result a growing proportion of young historians undergo a process that is little short of academic naturalization. American works on European history are distributed abroad by permanent arrangements among publishing houses, by European agents of presses without such arrangements, and by an increasing volume of translations that operates now as a kind of intellectual reverse lend-lease in the light of the former large surplus of English translations. A similar shift in the academic balance of trade is apparent in the new space and respect accorded American performance in the European historical reviews. There remains, to be sure, a perceptible streak of condescension vis-à-vis the converted dissertations that still comprise so much of the American publication in European history, with their Germanic earnestness and bulk footnotes magnified in book-length format. But the reception accorded the books of a Hexter, a Holborn, or a Landes shows clearly the fullfledged American membership in Clio's international peerage.

But this has not been the whole story. If Americans have grown in stature as participants in the universal republic of scholars they have not done so entirely as undifferentiated citizens of a larger political and social community. In scholarship as in politics the unexpected has come to pass since the start of World War II and in the midst of the intimate European involvement there has been a recrudescence of a distinctive American dimension.[1] American historians, in short, are now equal members of the Western historical community, not in that their historical sense has been Europeanized but rather in that, like English, French, Italian, and German historians, they represent an autonomous national dimension within the expanded historical universe. The particular shape of the contemporary American dimension is a hybrid product of the experience of the last two decades and the fundamental structure of American historiography revealed in its tradition of European history.

World War II itself witnessed both the climax of the prewar tendencies toward the growing intimacy of American historians with European history and the incubation of the newer tendencies toward a reformulation of the relationship that are prominent today. On the first count, not only did the intensive prewar patterns of exploration into European political and social history continue to produce results during and after the war,[2] but the war itself deepened the feeling for an American-European common experience that such writing predicated. The war supplied to historians as to so many other Americans a standard of relevance that conferred a kind of automatic unity upon activities previously disparate. Affecting America and Europe alike with the direct perception of its protracted span, scope, and effect, this war inspired a crisis literature that lumped the pasts of all segments of Western civilization together into a common transmission of society toward the present.[3] The deepening conviction of a general cultural crisis helped to weld the formerly discrete international and social fields of history into an integrated process that led to not only a total but a totalitarian war.[4] Such a centripetal influence

---

[1] For the counterpart of this American emphasis in the universities see W. Stull Holt, "Historical Scholarship," in *American Scholarship in the Twentieth Century,* ed. Merle Curti (1953), pp. 100-101.

[2] See pp. 284-85.

[3] Thus: Pitirim Sorokin's *Crisis of Our Age* (1941) and *Man and Society in Calamity* (1942), Sigmund Neumann's *Permanent Revolution* (1942), Hans Kohn's *World Order in Historical Perspective* (1942), Franz Alexander's *Our Age of Unreason* (1942), Karl Polanyi's *The Great Transformation* (1944).

[4] Most obviously in the theme of the 1940 convention of the American Historical Association that formed the basis for the volume edited by Jesse D. Clarkson and Thomas C. Cochran, *War as a Social Institution* (1941). Similar syntheses of domestic social and international political history under the unifying aegis of

/e even beyond the amalgamations of these fields within history
.n enforced juncture of past and present that was operated by his-
ians and nonhistorians alike.[5] These developments were confirmed
.y the prominent place now taken in the nation's historical writing
by the émigré scholars who turned to publication in response to the
urgent call of the age for the lessons of their experience.

And yet at the same time the same war produced a disruption of
these historical unities that also found its way into the consciousness
of American historians. The primary countervailing factor here was
the changed position of America in relation to Europe and the rest of
the world, a change that the conduct of the war itself made manifest.
The shift was twofold: first, the United States graduated from the
status of partnership, which characterized World War I, into the
status of leadership over all the Allies but the Soviet Union; and second, this leadership was in large part the function of the expansion of
the main military and political arena beyond Europe into the far
reaches of Asia and the Pacific. Historians are usually influenced by
their political environment, but often enough the incidence is indirect, as with the conditioning of the European cultural history written in nineteenth century America by the atmosphere of political isolation. During World War II, however, politics achieved an impact
upon the historical profession unexampled in its immediacy, not simply because of the total character of the conflict but even more directly because of the mass employment of historians, *qua* historians,
in the government. What had been, during and just after World
War I, volunteer public information service and short-term consulta-
tion affecting the comparatively few leading luminaries of the historical profession became, a generation later, years-long full-time

war can be seen in Adolf Sturmthal's *The Tragedy of European Labor* (1943)
and Franz Neumann's *Behemoth* (1942).

[5] Most obviously in such collaborative works as the United Nations series on
particular countries edited by Robert Kerner and *Makers of Modern Strategy,*
ed. Edward Mead Earle (1943), and in the unpublished reports of the Research
and Analysis Branch of the Office of Strategic Services. For examples of historians searching the past for formative factors of the present see S. Harrison Thomson, *Czechoslovakia in European History* (1943), L. S. Stavrianos, *Balkan Federation* (1944), and Hans Kohn, *The Idea of Nationalism* (1944) and its sequel,
*Prophets and Peoples: Studies in Nineteenth Century Nationalism* (1946). For
works by nonhistorians of interest or value to historians, besides Sorokin and
Neumann cited above, see Ernst Fraenkel, *The Dual State* (1941) and *Military
Occupation and the Rule of Law: Occupation Government in the Rhineland,
1918-1923* (1944), and P. Lemkin, *Axis Rule in Occupied Europe* (1944).

activity in military and political intelligence and planning for the government by all ranks of the profession, ranging from the most prominent to the novice. This group of American historians published little, either during the war or in the immediate postwar period, but the gap was compensated by the larger role that the enduring consciousness of the war has played in their current historical thinking and performance. To be sure, historians outside this group carried on both the traditions of specialized research and of general history through the war and into the postwar period and in any case the profession has by now grown beyond the wartime generation, but the fact remains that the one identifiable cohesive group among the American historians of Europe today is composed of those who applied their historical training to and nurtured it with the problems raised for the United States government by the war.[6]

Obviously this company of historians shared in the expansion of horizons that intensified the relevance of the outer world's history for the bulk of American historians, but they embody too the nationalizing features bequeathed by the war to American historiography. These features can be summarized in the observation that the war, in a kind of counterpoint to its integrating effects, reinforced the specifically American dimension in the approach toward Europe. What is important, however, is not the summary fact but the factors that fed into it, for from them the specific form of this dimension in its current phase began to take shape.

First—and probably most limited in its scope—there was the occupational factor. The critical evaluation of intelligence and the development of analyses for the consumption of American planners and policy-makers during the war made inevitable the enlargement of the specifically American point of view from which European

[6] The visible core of this grouping is composed by the veterans of the Research and Analysis Branch of the Office of Strategic Services. They have no organized existence, take no concerted action, and have even seen their war-born camaraderie and unity of purpose attenuated by more recent crosscurrents of both politics and history. And yet a complex of intellectual relations persist among them to carry on what was common in their wartime experience: their close collaboration with politically and socially conscious Europeans; their starting point from contemporary problems; the anchoring of a decidedly liberal orientation in the analysis of fascism; the resultant emphasis upon the political and social conditioning of all historical activity; the disregard for the traditional divisions of history, whether geographical, substantive, or temporal; their accessibility to the other humanistic and social disciplines, with whose representatives they actually worked to produce unified results.

events were seen. This factor was entered into the permanent historiographical record when two of the most eminent American historians of Europe were influenced by their wartime governmental functions to focus their first postwar books on the explication of American policy—William L. Langer's *Our Vichy Gamble* (1947) and Hajo Holborn's *American Military Government* (1947). But the vast majority of historians (including Langer and Holborn) departed from government service after the war, and ultimately this kind of direct address to American policy was not the war's permanent contribution to American historiography. The wartime occupational factor was important in the long run rather for the intensified awareness it brought of the new relationship between the United States and the world that developed during the war and that has persisted to the present.

Second, then, the old habit, rejuvenated by wartime government service, of using the past to explain the present developed a new dimension for European historians when they realized that the present America had become a dominant factor in Europe. The United States' authoritative role during the war brought home to the historian-analysts who were commissioned to research and plan European activities for American purposes a new sense no longer only of the convergence but now of the interpenetration of European and American destinies. This sense these historians carried over into the profession after the war. Thus both Langer and Holborn went on to turn out notable histories that, from opposite sides, traced the birth of the new political relations that comprehended America, Europe, and the world in one universe of historical discourse. Langer, in conjunction with S. Everett Gleason, took as his theme "the tortured emergence of the United States of America as leader of the forces of light in a world struggle which even today . . . is still undecided," while Holborn announced the need "to relate the history of the past to our present vital concerns" and traced the development of world politics from the angle of European history, following the progressive loss of European independence to the present point at which it could survive only as part of a larger system guaranteed by America.[7]

---

[7] William L. Langer and S. Everett Gleason, *The Challenge to Isolation, 1937-1940* (1952) and *The Undeclared War, 1940-1941* (1953), p. xvi; Hajo Holborn, *The Political Collapse of Europe* (1951), pp. vi, 189-93.

Third, the course of the war seemed to turn back the clock of history by reviving the consciousness of the American divergence from Europe. With the exception of Britain and the two small neutrals, the Europe that American analysts studied during most of the war was under totalitarian dominion, and even the resistance movements against it revealed a preponderance of social radicalism and hypernationalism that seemed, however promising for Europe, still quite different from the moderate internationalism then being permanently incorporated into the American tradition. And when Britain went socialist at the end of the war, opinion in America was divided between the view of it as an adumbration of the American future and the view of it as a confirmation of Britain's having gone European. American historians of Europe were generally sympathetic toward these movements, but with the beginning of liberation the variation between the American and the European traditions not only became a visible fact but fomented a political crisis that bit deeply into the sense of a growing American-European community. There thus recurred the old motif that pitted American against European destinies, but now under the new conditions of physical involvement that called for a new assessment of their historical relationship. The thesis of common origins was still necessary but no longer sufficient; the thesis of a common future was sufficient, but under the circumstances no longer deemed necessary. From criteria of relevancy based on the logic of kinship or opposition Americans were being forced to develop a new historical logic that could do without such rational categories and that could draw valid principles of relevancy from the multiform mixtures of the familiar and the alien in the actual history of American relations with Europe.

Fourth, one of the most definite new impulses generated among historians by the renewed consciousness of American individuality during and immediately after the war was the large-scale shift of attention to the history of the totalitarian "enemy." In practice this meant the specialization by unprecedented numbers of American historians first in German and then in Russian history. What lay behind these new specialties were fundamental factors that were given point by the war, for they have continued to produce some of the best American historical literature since the war.[8] But we are interested here precisely in the crystallizing effects of the war. The most obvious

[8] See pp. 306-308.

of these was the convergence of the histories of these countries and of America toward the successive international conflicts that have dominated American life. This tendency was reminiscent of the turn toward the new and the hostile around World War I, but the later historical concern was more intrinsic than the overt international and presentist focus of the earlier vintage. For one thing totalitarianism imputed an automatic relevance to all aspects of the past, whereas the more diffuse structure of prior political systems had called for a more partial and more selective study. Again, where the history of alien regions had been studied for the interest in the exotic or in a new bilateral relation to the United States, the history of Germany and Russia since World War II has carried with it the representative European function that historians so often have attributed to dominant powers. This function was underscored during the war by the reception in many European countries of movements taking their initiative and nature from the Nazi and Communist parent countries —a reception that has made Germany and Russia an actual ingredient in the history of other nations.

Fifth, the war broadened the horizons of American historians beyond the more exotic areas within Europe to the far reaches of the globe. The important point here is not the growth of Far Eastern, Near Eastern, and African history in the United States, however important this may be in itself. America opens out on the Pacific as well as the Atlantic, and the war found an interest in Far Eastern history, at least, that was already well established. What is pertinent and what was new with the war has been the growing consciousness of this extra-Western dimension in the minds of the American historians of Europe as the two outlooks of the nation have fused into a single network of political relations. Like so many other influences of the war upon American historiography, this awareness has had two divergent results. On the one hand, it has strengthened the sense of the Western community uniting Europe and America vis-à-vis the non-Western cultures whose history has commanded increasing attention from American historians. William McNeill's development from a European to a world historian, in his *Rise of the West* (1963), where he locates a generic Western culture in the cross-cultural history of humanity, has given a recent focus to this tendency. On the other hand, however, the conversion of what had been, to the European historians in this country, essentially a bilateral foreign relationship of the United States and Europe into a multilateral relationship of the United States to several regions of which Europe was only one has had the effect of reducing the European commitment and enlarging the American dimension. A relationship that had posited Europe as the one effective "other" vis-à-vis the United States and that had, on this basis, increasingly deemed "otherness" a category soon to be transcended had to be rethought when the new prominence of more radically alien cultures established the finality of this category, made it permanent, and thereby reduced the status of Europe to a mottled mixture of the familiar and the alien whose history would have, for Americans, neither the intimacy of the one nor the challenge of the other.

These various lessons of the war contributed to a single net historiographical effect: they rendered inadequate the former assumptions and conceptions about the relevancy of European history at the same time as they made the articulation of some assumptions and conceptions about it more necessary than ever. The older notions were rendered obsolete by the attenuation or frustration of those things that had seemed to be making Europe and America one society with one composite past. The differences in social structure manifested during the war attenuated the automatic acceptance of European social history as the central bond of unity with America, so that Louis Hartz, in his *Liberal Tradition in America* (1955), could revive with renewed relevance the nineteenth century idea of the contrasting European and American societies. Again, the simultaneous ascension of American and frustration of European power called for historical explanations rather of the divergence than of the convergence of the international politics affecting the two areas. And yet the American military and political involvement in Europe and the persistent cultural interchange with Europe seemed to point the other way: they were effective in showing a continuing connection that prevented the awareness of the divisive factors from turning into a historical indifference toward Europe. But if the resulting relationship of America and Europe was too confused to endow American historians, as it had in the past, with a stable standpoint from which to view European history, it now called upon these historians to help construct one. For whereas previous involvements had been physically sporadic and abstractly continuous they now became physically continuous. Consequently, whereas the relationship had hitherto been resolved by the alternation of the theses of divergence and convergence, these opposites were now embodied in one situation—a single Atlantic community with running differences between American and European values within it—that required their direct confrontation. This was the framework of problems which the war set for the postwar historians. In the postwar era there are, to be sure, historians who are driven by the constant motives that have ever inspired one kind of history in our civilization: the direct passion for a people, a subject, or an epoch. But for the brand of historian whose historical interests are molded by the world about him, the relationship to Europe that was once a secure assumption for his study of European history has now become a prime historical problem. What was once an answer now needs to be answered. Directly or indirectly, what is distinctive about the postwar American historiography of Europe is addressed to this issue.

Obviously, all American historians of Europe are not oriented toward this set of problems and even those who are so oriented are not exclusively so. Both the American historical profession and the distinctive qualities that mark its production of European history at present will appear distorted in a functional direction if the general professional context in which such qualities are rooted is not first noted. It cannot be emphasized too strongly that from what may be called, in its broadest sense, a quantitative point of view, the development of European history in America has continued to be the steady growth of a young profession. If the number of scholars in the field be taken as the measure, the tendency has been for the steady rise in the proportion of European historians within the American historical profession as a whole, and even the contemporary shrinkage of Europe's role in the world has not reversed the trend.[9] But it is not only a matter of warm bodies. Beyond the swelling quantity of historical publications from the increasing numbers of scholar-teachers called for by the American system of higher education, there are independent indices of growth in the increasing variety of sub-fields, the heightening level of critical sophistication, and the improving balance between specialized, intermediate, and general subjects. Despite the contemporary emphases that have as a by-product a comparative weakening in some of the traditional areas, the general picture of American his-

[9] Dexter Perkins and John L. Snell, *The Education of Historians in the United States* (1962), pp. 30-33.

torical production after an immediate postwar lull has shown a remarkable advance in the national level of solid performance across the European board, with young and recognized scholars in all fields respected both at home and abroad.[10] The recognition of this performance is necessary not only to understand that the distinctive qualities of contemporary historians represent what is new rather than what is all-pervasive in the profession but also to grasp the old-fashioned scholarly devotion to knowledge for its own sake and the undifferentiated interest in European culture that persist as the elemental bases of American historical writing in the field. The bulk of American historical literature may thus be viewed as representing America's mature subscription to the universalist traditions of scientific scholarship, a subscription that has changed in degree but not in kind since the start of the century.

But some of the shadings in this professional picture do serve as indicators of qualitative changes in the contemporary American writing of history. Even within these older fields of medieval and early

[10] Examples of such works in the "declining" fields are: For medieval history, Raymond DeRoover, *The Medici Bank* (1948) and *Money, Credit, and Banking in Medieval Bruges* (1948), Ernst Kantorowicz, *The King's Two Bodies: A Study in Medieval Political Theology* (1957); Bryce D. Lyon, *From Fief to Indenture* (1957); Brian Tierney, *Foundations of the Conciliar Theory* (Cambridge, England, 1955), and *Medieval Poor Law* (1959); Norman Cohn, *The Pursuit of the Millennium* (1957); George Vernadsky, *The Origins of Russia* (Oxford, 1959); Barnaby C. Keeney, *Judgment by Peers* (1949); Kenneth Setton, ed., *A History of the Crusades* (1955-00). For Renaissance, Hans Baron, *The Crisis of the Early Italian Renaissance* (1955); Gene A. Brucker, *Florentine Politics and Society, 1343-1378* (1962); William Bouwsma, *Concordia Mundi: Career and Thought of Guillaume Postel* (1957); Wallace K. Ferguson, *The Renaissance in Historical Thought* (1948); Myron Gilmore, *The World of Humanism* (1952); Jack Hexter, *More's Utopia: Biography of an Idea* (1952); Eugene Rice, *The Renaissance Idea of Wisdom* (1958). For Reformation, Roland Bainton, *Here I Stand: Life of Martin Luther* (1951) and *Travail of Religious Liberty* (1951); Harold Bender, *Conrad Grebel* (1950); E. Harris Harbison, *The Christian Scholar in the Age of the Reformation* (1956). For English history, Lawrence H. Gipson, *The British Empire Before the American Revolution* (1936-    ); Paul Knaplund, *Britain: Commonwealth and Empire* (London, 1956); Wallace Notestein, *The English People on the Eve of Colonization* (1954); Conyers Read, *Mr. Secretary Cecil and Queen Elizabeth* (London, 1955) and sequel, *Lord Burghley* (1960); Caroline Robbins, *The Eighteenth Century Commonwealthman* (1959); Jack Hexter, *Reappraisals in History* (London, 1961). For French history, Gordon Wright, *France in Modern Times* (1960); Leo Gershoy, *Bertrand Barere* (1962); Lynn Case, *French Opinion on War and Diplomacy During the Second Empire* (1945); Albert Guerard, *Napoleon III* (1955) and *France: A Modern History* (1959); and J. Russell Major's several studies on representative institutions in sixteenth and seventeenth century France.

modern Europe and the national histories of England and France that
represent much of the staple in American historical scholarship, innovations of approach bespeak a heightened awareness of what is
generally relevant in these traditional areas. Beyond the modernized
search of scholars like Bryce Lyons and Gaines Post for the typical
in medieval political institutions, the signal experiments are those
that broaden social history through the use of economic and sociological methods and concepts and those that broaden intellectual
into cultural history. Robert Lopez on medieval cities and commerce,
William Aydelotte's sociology of the House of Commons, and Rondo
Cameron's analysis of French economic growth illustrate the former;
Jacques Barzun's development from *Darwin, Marx and Wagner* to
*Berlioz and the Romantic Century,* John Clive's blend of history and
literature in the *Scotch Reviewers,* Carl Schorske's crossing of social
and cultural analyses in his Viennese studies, and the symbolic dimension of political ideas in the work of Ernst Kantorowicz and Michael Cherniavsky signalize the latter.

These newer dimensions of the old fields involve an extension of
historical interest into areas of human activity that are both more
universal and more inchoate than the traditional subject matter of
history. In this sense they are consistent with a second novelty of the
contemporary period that bypasses the formerly favored European
areas of American historical exploration in favor of other fields. Both
the newer dimensions and the newer fields mark a preference for the
exotic that entails a decisive shift of assumptions away from the
community of origins and the community of experience that had governed these specialties. The assumptions toward which the American
historians of Europe have shifted belong rather to the pragmatic
strain of history that has been the constant companion and benefici-
ary of the empirical scholarly tradition in Western historiography.
In America since the war the pragmatic mode has elicited a number
of approaches designed to reinterpret European history in the light of
America's new position in the world. They accept the bankruptcy of
the old unitary formulas that posited the common origins, common
destinies, or common experience of Europeans and Americans and,
appropriately to both the pluralism of our age and the prominence
of America in it, they posit only the validity of the American historiographical viewpoint as one among many possible viewpoints and interpret European history through a frank selection of what seems

relevant to it. The defining qualities of today's American history of Europe, over and above those of traditional scholarship, are made up of the new kind of questions that are being asked of this relevance. What we have is a set of issues through which the meaning of European history has become more a matter of historical discovery than of historical illustration.

The most spectacular and perhaps most revealing tendency of the current European historiography in the United States is the explicit expansion of historical fields and subjects from Europe or America to Europe and America, but now more for the purpose of exploring their internal relations than for accepting a general formula of them. The underlying assumptions here are that these relations have themselves been subject to historical change and that the special function of American historiography is to reinterpret each period and field of European history in the light of them. As happens so often in the American historical profession, the latest fashions find their way immediately into the textbooks. While there certainly has been no dearth of texts on our joint Western civilization or its main components, the period since the war has witnessed the new appearance of textbooks that take as their main theme the relations of historical Europe with the rest of the world and particularly with America—not in the old sense of the "expansion of Europe" but with a reciprocal, problematical orientation.[11] Too often the execution of this design has been through mere juxtaposition, but in a text like Solomon Bloom's *Europe and America* (1961) the history of the relations between Europe and America becomes the actual theme around which the respective histories are organized.

More enduring and more indicative of the far-reaching implications of this new horizon for American historiography have been the interpretive scholarly works that have registered it. These have been of two kinds. The broader, more analytical type deals with common themes or movements and differs from its nineteenth century prototype precisely in the care taken to differentiate the national and regional varieties within the whole. The most spectacular achievement of this kind has undoubtedly been Palmer's *Age of the Demo-*

---

[11] E.g., John B. Rae and Thomas H. D. Mahoney, *The United States in World History* (1949); R. R. Palmer, *History of the Modern World* (1950); Geoffrey Bruun and Henry Steele Commager, *Europe and America Since 1492* (1954); Louis Gottschalk and Donald Lach, *The Transformation of Modern Europe* (1954).

*cratic Revolution* (1959) with its revealing subtitle, *A Political History of Europe and America, 1760-1800,* but Alan Simpson's *Puritanism in Old and New England* (1955), Boyd Shafer's *Nationalism* (1955), and Hans Kohn's *American Nationalism* (1957) represent a similar tendency. The currency of such an approach is reflected in the theme for the regional conference of the International Society for the History of Ideas for 1962—"Ideas of Social Change Since the American and French Revolutions: The Assimilation and Transformation of European Ideas in the New World." A second, more empirical type of contribution to the history of European-American relations has been the description of the European contribution to specific American policies or movements. The two outstanding recent works along this line have been Arno Mayer's *Political Origins of the New Diplomacy* and Felix Gilbert's *To the Farewell Address.* Over and above the original elucidation of their American problems such works provide particular external—i.e., American—points of reference for European history and thereby permit selection from and synthesis of the European past on the basis of criteria that are themselves historical—i.e., that have actually been effective in the American past. This approach has already been frankly adopted on a general level as well in the still incomplete Welles-McKay series, in which each volume, usually written by a historian, is focused on the relations of a foreign country to the United States and integrates an interpretive synthesis of that country's modern history, since the American Revolution, into this framework.[12] The meaning of European history, from this point of view, is compounded of those events, institutions, and ideas that crystallized from the multiform welter of human activities sufficiently either to achieve recognition by or to enter into relations with an outside party, and American history comes to the aid of the American historian of Europe in determining what this meaning is.

A parallel development on the side of the American historians of the United States, moreover, serves to reinforce this tendency of the European historians, since the former have tended to expand their own operational horizons to include the European dimension. The most direct approach to the problem from this side has been Michael

---

[12] Sumner Welles and Donald C. McKay, eds., "The American Foreign Policy Library" (1945-    ). For one of the outstanding volumes in the series for Europe, see H. Stuart Hughes's *The United States and Italy* (1953).

Kraus's *The Atlantic Civilization: Eighteenth Century Origins* (1949). For obvious reasons the consciousness of the European connection has always been strong in the American colonial historians, who effectively incorporated it into their writing from the days of Osgood, Beer, and Andrews, and this tradition has been extended by such current practitioners in the field as Samuel Morison, Lawrence Gipson, Perry Miller, and Carl Bridenbaugh. For the national period, historians of the United States continue to lag in exploiting the European context of joint subjects, but the prewar achievements of Marcus Hansen and George Pierson still stand, for the transmission of people and of ideas respectively, and the subsequent work of Oscar Handlin and of Henry Pochmann (*German Culture in America,* 1957) keeps the field open from the American side.

More recent, more novel, and more fundamental has been the increasing postwar awareness of the larger framework as a continuing conditioner of American development and consequently as a conceptual tool for the interpretation of American history. Historically minded social scientists, with their thematic interests, have naturally been in the van here,[13] but guild historians are also turning from the blanket acceptance or rejection of the American community with Europe to the historical definition of it. Bernard Bailyn's recent interpretation of the American Revolution in the light of its problematical European associations;[14] David Potter's analyses of the mid-nineteenth century movement for American unity in the context of parallel contemporary movements in Europe; [15] and Richard Hofstadter's emphasis upon the concept of regressive classes that has proved so fruitful in the revolutionary historiography of Europe: [16] these are prominent examples of the participation by United States historians in what has become a joint enterprise to determine the development of the respective components within the American-European community.

---

[13] E.g., Hartz, *op cit;* Hans J. Morgenthau, *Politics Among Nations* (1948); Seymour M. Lipset, *Political Man* (1960); Walt W. Rostow, *The United States in the World Arena* (1960); Clinton Rossiter, *Marxism: The View from America* (1960).

[14] "Poltical Experience and Enlightenment Ideas in Eighteenth Century America," in *AHR,* LXVII (1962), 339-52.

[15] David M. Potter, "National and Sectional Forces in the U.S.," in *Cambridge Modern History,* vol. X (Cambridge, 1960), pp. 603-30; "The Historians's Use of Nationalism and Vice Versa," *AHR,* LXVII (1962), 924-50.

[16] Richard Hofstadter, *The Age of Reform* (1955).

A concomitant of the expanded framework for European history in the United States has been the devaluation of specialization in the particular European nations. This second major feature of contemporary historiography is, to be sure, restrained by the expediential requirements of American graduate training that continue to make concentration on one nation's sources the most practicable way of making and testing young scholars, but even the large universities that can afford historical specialists are calling increasingly for supranational combinations of skills, not for reasons of economy but to meet the newer standards of relevance. This feature has been especially prominent in postwar historical writing, for two of its most notable qualities may be considered as correlatives of the drift away from national specialties. The most obvious of these is what might be called multilateral European history—that is, the selection of some central movement or event in which several European nations were participant as nations and the study *seriatim* of their respective roles. Some of the above-mentioned works in which America is an overt referent—like Palmer's and Mayer's—fall into this category, but it includes also outstanding performances in which the American reference is either replaced by the Russian, as in Kennan's, or absent altogether, as in Mattingly's.[17] Whatever the variations, we have here a signal attempt to wed the "scientific" and pragmatic strains in the American historical tradition, using a phenomenological rather than a thematic mode of cohesion.

Less obviously geared to the larger canvas of contemporary European historians but scarcely explicable without it is the rising preference for substantive over national specialization, and particularly, as the most striking instance of this preference, the vogue of intellectual history. The general point can be illustrated by the development of military history and history of science from technical fields into dimensions of general history that have already produced intensive analyses of supranational problems.[18] It can also be seen in the economic historians' attention to the process of industrialization that has drawn together the various national societies of the West and requires consideration from the multinational point of view. David

---

[17] George F. Kennan, *Russia and the West Under Lenin and Stalin* (1960); Garrett Mattingly, *Renaissance Diplomacy* (1955) and *The Armada* (1959).
[18] Especially John U. Nef, *War and Human Progress* (1950) and Charles C. Gillispie, *The Edge of Objectivity* (1960).

Landes' general essay on the nineteenth century industrial revolution and Rondo Cameron's disposition of European economic growth around the problem of French capital formation show the fruitfulness of this approach for American scholarship.[19] The subject matter of intellectual history is even more integrally cosmopolitan, and the popularity of the field is explicable perhaps as much by its generic Western context as by the availability of its sources.[20] Beyond this formal function in the expanded framework of today's scholarship, intellectual history has the further attraction of dealing in general concepts that may double as historically valid principles of historical interpretation. Now, as we have seen, there is nothing especially new about European intellectual history in America, which goes well back into the nineteenth century in a continuous historiography. What is new about it at present is its employment to construct a pan-European theme rather than to illustrate a prefabricated one. It is not that contemporary historians are so much more "objective" than their predecessors but that the standards of scientific scholarship have now been fully applied to intellectual history and, more important, that historians, like so many other men of our time, have no prefabricated theme to illustrate. Intellectual historians now run the gamut from monographs to syntheses, but even within the latter category the contrast with past historiography is clear in the gulf between the tensile, questioning treatments of a Baumer, a Brinton, and a Masur on the one side and what now seems like the archaic if assured progressivism of a Draper, a White, or Robinson on the other.[21]

A third major feature of the contemporary American historiography of Europe, seemingly an antithesis of its expanded framework but actually a corollary of it, consists in the extended use of deliber-

---

[19] Landes' essay is in the new Columbia University *Chapters in Western Civilization* (1962); Cameron's book is *France and the Economic Development of Europe, 1800-1914* (1961). The expansion of military history to a dimension of general history reflects a similar development. See especially Nef, *op. cit.*

[20] Note particularly the recent emphasis on the Enlightenment as an international context for special subjects—e.g., Richard Herr, *The Eighteenth Century Revolution in Spain* (1958)—and on Russian intellectual history as the crossroads of Europe—see, for example, Martin Malia, *Alexander Herzen and the Birth of Russian Socialism, 1812-1855* (1961); Nicholas Riasanovsky, *Russia and the West in the Teaching of the Slavophiles* (1952); and Hans Kohn, *Pan-Slavism, Its History and Ideology* (1953).

[21] Franklin L. Baumer, *Religion and the Rise of Scepticism* (1960); Crane Brinton, *A History of Western Morals* (1959); Gerhard Masur, *Prophets of Yesterday* (1961).

ate focal devices to specify general history. The fact that, as we have just seen, general history tends to take form around particular international events, institutions, and ideas itself reveals the tendency toward concretion, but it is the new emphasis both on and within biography and urban history, those most particularized units of personal and social study, that exhibits the full extent of the pressure. The standards of historical vis-à-vis other brands of biography are now definitely articulate in the proposition that its subjects must register the facts and factors of their age that flowed into, through, from, and around them. This approach operates in the preferred choice of subjects from pivotal positions in mass movements as well as in their treatment primarily for the illumination of these movements.[22] City history has similarly been turned to microcosmic purposes. Franklin Ford took his stand at Strasbourg as a point to "look out from" upon Europe in his opposition to the "over-emphasis upon nationhood," while for Carl Schorske Vienna at the turn of the century was the locus for the observation of a culture in crisis.[23] The capital cities in the studies by William Jenks and David Pinkney furnished convenient frames for the depiction of national regimes and movements.[24]

The use of special, biographical, or local history as the vehicle of more general historical processes is an obvious convenience for periods in which the materials for the solution of general historical questions are too voluminous for a direct response by historians and for problems that require the use of the more intensive ancillary disciplines, whether social or humanistic. Equally obvious is the role of such methods in reconciling the demands of precise research with the larger interpretations that confer a general meaning upon the research and more particularly in perpetuating the summary distillations of European history that have always been appropriate to the

---

[22] E.g., Klaus Epstein, *Matthias Erzberger and the Dilemma of German Democracy* (1959); Rudolph Binion, *Defeated Leaders: The Political Fate of Caillaux, Jouvenel, and Tardieu* (1960); Leo Gershoy, *Bertrand Barere* (1962). It may be noted that even such a gifted amateur historian as J. Christopher Herold, with all his talent for portraiture, entitled his biography of the Madame de Staël, *Mistress to an Age.*

[23] Franklin L. Ford, *Strasbourg in Transition, 1648-1789* (1958), p. viii; Carl E. Schorske, "Politics and the Psyche in *fin de siecle* Vienna," *AHR*, LXVI (1961), 930-46.

[24] William A. Jenks, *Vienna and the Young Hitler* (1960); David Pinkney, *Napoleon III and the Rebuilding of Paris* (1958).

American angle of vision. In this quest for the representative personality or institution, these fields are similar to the intermediate genre of past American historiography.[25] But at the same time these new focal, or microcosmic, approaches—whether through crucial themes, events, individuals, or localities—have altered the status of the general meanings in European history and have thereby changed too the relationship between European history and American historiography. The unitary process—whether providential, cultural, political, or social—that historians formerly assumed to lie behind history was essentially a continuous and universal process, and consequently those categories of events that were meaningful in the process were immediately meaningful, wherever they took place, to observers everywhere. Now, however, the units that historians use to obtain coherence have become immanent and frequently discontinuous as the belief in the rational, long-range process has fallen away; consequently, the relationship between these historical units, however synthetic, and the outside historian can no longer be assumed—it must be created. For the American historian of Europe, beyond those segments of European history that have an overt external reference, the meaning of the European past emerges not from the built-in substantive relevance of certain kinds of European events but from a deliberate American approach to all kinds of European events that constructs its own meaning by investing them with a generality sufficient to make them intelligible to outsiders.[26] Thus, where the relationship between European history and the American historian used to be a function of a general interpretation of history, general interpretations of history are now a function of the relationship between European history and the American historian.

Fourth, then, American historians, conditioned by the contemporary blend of community with and separate identity from Europe, have reflected this influence in the widespread tendency to view European history from the point of view of its lost causes. This tendency

[25] See pp. 275-77, 285-87.
[26] Mattingly has testified pointedly to this evolution of the American historical point of view, indicating that whereas Mahan's generation saw the Armada as a struggle for the command of the seas and Mattingly himself in 1940 saw it as a general revolutionary war, his return to the subject after World War II was dominated by the conviction that "a fresh eye," reviewing all the evidence, could "re-create . . . a series of connected historical scenes" that would bring new vitality and new meaning to it. Mattingly, *The Armada,* pp. v-vii.

has both a professional and an intellectual facet. On the first count, American scholars in European history are impelled as much as any other scholars by the urge to "fill gaps" in previous knowledge, and national historians are wont to leave such gaps precisely in their nation's lost causes. More substantial, however, is the intellectual facet: the preoccupation with the lost cause in Europe is the present disillusioned, relativized version of that liberal faith in the progressive attainment of the international good society that has played such a large role in American historiography. The faith itself has been ruptured and as a substantive pattern is no longer meaningful for history, but it has bequeathed a point of view compounded of American reality and European potentiality that furnishes the standards of selection and interpretation for the American historians' addiction to such liberal frustrations as the revolutions of 1848,[27] French and Italian socialism,[28] German liberalism and socialism,[29] the democratic integrity of small nations,[30] and the democratic losers of the Russian revolution.[31]

The concern with such political failures is part of the general impulse to study the failure of rationality in history, and it is this same impulse that helps to mold a fifth characteristic feature of today's European historiography in America: the new emphasis on and expertise in the histories of Germany and Russia. In good measure, to be sure, the American involvement in hot and cold war with these countries has inspired this achievement, and it is undeniable that the

---

[27] E.g., Priscilla Robertson, *Revolutions of 1848* (1952); Arnold Whitridge, *Men in Crisis: The Revolutions of 1848* (1949); R. John Rath, *The Viennese Revolution of 1848* (1957); Theodore S. Hamerow, *Restoration, Revolution, Reaction* (1958).

[28] Henry W. Ehrmann, *The French Labor Movement from Popular Front to Liberation* (1947); Aaron Noland, *The Founding of the French Socialist Party* (1956); Val Lorwin, *The French Labor Movement* (1954).

[29] E.g., Walter M. Simon, *The Failure of the Prussian Reform Movement* (1955); Leonard Krieger, *The German Idea of Freedom* (1957); Carl E. Schorske, *German Social Democracy, 1905-1917: Development of the Great Schism* (1955).

[30] E.g., Charles A. Gulick, *Austria from Hapsburg to Hitler* (2 vols., 1948); Henry L. Roberts, *Rumania: Political Problems of an Agrarian State* (1951); Robert L. Wolff, *The Balkans in Our Time* (1956); John A. Lukacs, *The Great Powers and Eastern Europe* (1953).

[31] E.g., Leopold Haimson, *The Russian Marxists and the Origins of Bolshevism* (1955); Oliver Radkey, *The Agrarian Foes of Bolshevism* (1958); Robert V. Daniels, *The Conscience of the Revolution* (1960). See too George Fischer, *Russian Liberalism* (1958).

Nazism and the Bolshevism that have been the chief points of contact with America have furnished the chief points of reference for American historians. But if the explicit American connection was the starting point the performance has gone well beyond it, and we find that within the framework set by it American historians have pursued all kinds of historical problems that are internal to the national culture under study and bear only the most general of relations with the point of departure.[32]

Once again the path from pragmatic origins to genuine re-creation that American historians have traveled has both a professional and an intellectual lane. Professionally, they have come to view themselves as the utility men of European history. The nature of the Nazi and Soviet regimes has been such as to invalidate all but the monographic history written under them and to shake the nerve even of the post-Nazi historians. American historians have postulated a sufficient community of historical interests for themselves to take up the slack and a sufficient superiority in the American conditions of historical writing for their own interpretations to be more valid than those of the native scholars.[33]

The intellectual process that has led American historians of Germany and Russia to expand a pragmatic into an intrinsic historical interest starts from the usual concern to articulate the background and context of Nazism and Bolshevism[34] but is soon dominated by the problem of distinguishing between what is generic to Europe and what is distinctively national in this background and context. The predominant role of this problem stems in part from the suprana-

[32] E.g., Jerome Blum, *Lord and Peasant in Russia from the Ninth to the Nineteenth Century* (1961); Michael Cherniavsky, *Tsar and People: Studies in Russian Myth* (1961); Hajo Holborn, *A History of Germany: The Reformation* (1959).

[33] See Holborn's argument that when viewed from America German history acquires a broader perspective and a comparative dimension that makes "many events and ideas of German history . . . assume their proper proportions." *Ibid.*, p. x.

[34] This is most apparent in the several anthologies of Russian history that seek, if only by juxtaposition, to tie prerevolutionary Russia into Soviet developments. E.g., Cyril E. Black, ed., *The Transformation of Russian Society: Aspects of Social Change Since 1861* (1960); Richard Pipes, ed., *The Russian Intelligentsia* (1961); Ivo J. Lederer, ed., *Russian Foreign Policy: Essays in Historical Perspective* (1962). But it holds true too of an impressive synthesis of pre-Nazi and Nazi history like Gordon Craig's *Politics of the Prussian Army, 1660-1945* (Oxford, 1955).

tional emphasis of today's historians and in part from the actual history of these nations that made the form of receiving cultural and political influences from the West a crucial factor in their development. In this problem, then, the issues of historiography and of history meet. Not only has the totalitarian climax of these national histories helped to endow the American historiography in these fields with a more general and more analytical cast than in others but the historiographical issue of discovering appropriate categories for a partially alien culture overlaps the interpretive issue of explaining the particular national divergence from the continuity, the rationality, the humanism, and the liberalism of the West.[35] Since Western historical categories are attuned to Western values, American historians are drawn to the intrinsic categories of the more exotic European cultures not merely to understand these cultures but to increase their understanding of the departures from continuity, rationality, humanity, and freedom that now dwell in their views of history in general. Germany and Russia have thus become test cases for the renovation of the progressive conception of history, and the historian's success in merging Western and exotic categories of historical explanation for these fields becomes a prerequisite to any general interpretation of history.[36]

The tendency of German and Russian history in the United States to function as a means of reorienting the general principles of historical interpretation is but one expression of the larger tendency in the contemporary American historiography of all Europe—its sixth and final feature in this enumeration—to emphasize the counterrevolutions in European history. *Counterrevolutions* should here be taken in the broadest sense to mean those movements that arose to oppose, divert, absorb, or check the familiar "isms" that have molded the progressive conception of history. Obviously, what we have here is the obverse side of the concern for lost progressive causes. The relationship is clear in works like J. Selwin Schapiro's *Liberalism and the Challenge of Fascism* (1949) and Eugen J. Weber's *Action Française* (1962), which investigate the contrapuntal responses

---

[35] See Henry L. Roberts, "Eastern Europe and the Historian," *Slavic Review*, XX (1961), 509-16.

[36] For an extreme example of this position, see Hannah Arendt's influential *The Origins of Totalitarianism* (1951). For a more moderate position, see Carl J. Friedrich and Zbigniew K. Brzezinski's *Totalitarian Dictatorship and Autocracy* (1956).

to the progressive cause even in Britain and France, where it was apparently triumphant, but the prevalence of the tendency is confirmed, even where the connection is not articulate, in the widespread address to the history of conservative politics across the national map of Europe.[37] Some of this historical literature undoubtedly evinces a genuine conservative point of view, but since it has not yet stimulated a general conservative interpretation of European history its historiographical importance does not lie here. Where it does lie is perhaps best indicated by the analogous tendency in intellectual history, where it is not obscured by the local and divertive effects of political passion.

Certainly the latest phase of the European intellectual history of American vintage is dominated by the interest in cultural counterrevolution—that is, in the men and themes which are reactions against the standard rationalism, meliorism, secularism, and individualism of progressive intellectual history. Contemporary intellectual studies have tended to cluster around two periodic poles, the eighteenth century Enlightenment and the early twentieth century cultural crisis, but since the first is interpreted in the light of the second their historiographical meaning is conjoint. In part, obviously, these concerns reflect the effort of our generation to reinterpret the past in the light of the cultural crisis of the present, but the meaning of the effort lies not in the fact of the reinterpretation but in its content. Led by Peter Gay, Frank Manuel, and Lester Crocker, a new generation of American historians have brought to the fore the complex and tensile nature of the Enlightenment by laying stress in general on the variety and ambiguity of its points of view and in particular upon the empirical, pessimistic, mythic, and existential qualities through

---

[37] E.g., for England, see Stephen Graubard, *Burke, Disraeli, and Churchill: The Politics of Perseverance* (1961); for France, Robert F. Byrnes, *Anti-Semitism in Modern France* (1950), Albert Guerard, *Napoleon III* (1955), and Lynn M. Case, *French Opinion on War and Diplomacy in the Second Empire* (1954); for Germany, Gordon Craig, *Politics of the Prussian Army, 1660-1945* (Oxford, 1955), Klemens von Klemperer, *Germany's New Conservatism* (1957), Theodore Hamerow, *Restoration, Revolution, Reaction* (1958), Hans Rosenberg, *Bureaucracy, Aristocracy, Autocracy: The Prussian Experience, 1660-1815* (1958), Paul W. Massing, *Rehearsal for Destruction: A Study of Political Anti-Semitism in Imperial Germany* (1949); for Russia, see introduction in Richard Pipes, ed., *Nikolai Karamzin: Memoir on Ancient and Modern Russia* (1959); Nicholas Riazanovsky, *Nicholas I and Official Nationality in Russia, 1825-1855* (1959); Sidney Monas, *The Third Section: Police and Society in Russia Under Nicholas I* (1961).

which Enlightenment writers themselves limited the contrary values hypostatized in the traditional picture.[38] The tendency of this recent scholarship, illustrated in Gay's strictures upon Becker's *Heavenly City*,[39] is to make the Enlightenment more relevant to the ages that succeeded than to those that preceded it. This relevance, however, is pursued not by establishing a new substantive continuity of succession but rather by postulating the essential discontinuity of the Enlightenment at both ends and by examining, intensively and sympathetically, the status of its humane values in a complex age of rapid change analogous to our own.[40]

The recent historical analyses of European culture in the decades spanning the turn of our century are even more explicit in taking as their points of departure the developments against or beyond the rational humanism of the Western tradition. Stuart Hughes begins with the critiques of Marx, Gerhard Masur with the breakdown of nineteenth century European "rationalism," and Fritz Stern with the counterrevolution against "liberalism and secularism." [41] And yet what remains as true for these intellectual historians as for their colleagues in Enlightenment history is that their study of what we have called the cultural counterrevolution is neither a reflex of the conservative present nor even necessarily a study of conservatism. For these historians take not only as their context but as their constant points of reference the familiar liberal values that were questioned or denied by the historical agents of their inquiry.[42] Although there is

---

[38] Peter Gay, "The Enlightenment in the History of Political Theory," *Political Science Quarterly*, LXIX (1954), 374-89, and *Voltaire's Politics* (1959); Frank E. Manuel, *The Eighteenth Century Confronts the Gods* (1959) and *The Prophets of Paris* (1962); Lester G. Crocker, *An Age of Crisis* (1959). See too Henry Vyverberg, *Historical Pessimism in the French Enlightenment* (1958). For the incapsulation of the Austrian Enlightenment in a conservative cycle see Robert A. Kann, *A Study in Austrian Intellectual History: From Late Baroque to Romanticism* (1960).

[39] Peter Gay, "Carl Becker's *Heavenly City*," *Political Science Quarterly*, LXXII (1957), 182-99.

[40] The implied issue in the recent interchange between Gay and Crane Brinton on the secular religiosity of the Jacobins was precisely that of discontinuity (Gay) vs. continuity (Brinton). *AHR*, LXVI (1961), 664-82.

[41] H. Stuart Hughes, *Consciousness and Society: The Re-orientation of European Social Thought, 1890-1930* (1958); Gerhard Masur, *Prophets of Yesterday: Studies in European Culture, 1890-1914* (1961); Fritz Stern, *The Politics of Cultural Despair: A Study in the Rise of the Germanic Ideology* (1961).

[42] See Stuart Hughes' frank confession that "the base line" from which his analysis of the twentieth century proceeds is "the humane tradition" of the

a patent connection between their historical subjects and the present, these historians draw only their questions and not their interpretation from such a connection. Emphasizing the inimitable character of their period of study to lie in the running tension, conflict, and balance between the progressive forces of the Western tradition and their antitheses, they cannot explain it by assigning it a place in any continuous process of history, since the counterrevolution cuts the period off from its past and the liberal persistence isolates it from the present. The early twentieth century, then, like the Enlightenment has become one of those fertile periods in which the interruption of historical continuity entails the dependence of the general interpretation of history upon the particular interpretation. With the fragmentation of the liberal tradition that has furnished American historiography with its dominant values and interpretive criteria, American historians seek in the modern history of Europe, where the fragmentation has gone furthest, the knowledge that will permit the reconstruction of a framework of history whence assured values and interpretive criteria for historiography may once more be drawn. From present indications we may project a framework that will retain the political and social focus as the analytical measure of cultures and the liberal scale as the language of historical communication to Americans, but ensconced now in a notion of historical process that modern Europe shows to be open, plural, discontinuous, devious, volitional, and immanent in the actual events of history.

---

eighteenth century Enlightenment. Hughes, *Consciousness and Society*, p. 27. For a contemporary version of this tradition, see Shepard Clough's *Basic Values of Western Civilization* (1960).

# CONCLUSION

If we regard European history in America from the point of view of *its* history, it would appear to consist in two traditions, always somewhat involved with each other, which have grown more and more integrally together. As the conceptual framework that enclosed the European past in a process shared by America has approached the empirical scholarship that had an immediate concern with European events whatever their ultimate reference, the framework has lost much of its conceptual identity and the scholarship something of its universal "scientific" assumptions. What remains is an amalgam of analysis and research that plays a distinctive role both in American life and in the world's scholarship.

For America, European history as written by Americans has serviced the gradual ascent from the known to the unknown and has been therefore one of the channels that have led Americans from their inward preoccupations toward the understanding of the world at large. As we have seen, the development of European history in this country has been from an attitude that introduced the knowledge of the European past within the chrysalis of an already known American-European relationship to an attitude that utilized what was common to this relationship as the take-off point into the learning of what was new and alien to it. The discipline of European history, with its blend of the familiar and the exotic, has thus been a stepping stone to the confrontation of the still more exotic cultures that have challenged Americans since the war.

For the world's scholarship, the American contribution has been to make a matter of standard operating procedure what European historians do only in their more philosophical moments: to set European history in a general context without losing the vitality of the particular event. Americans do this not as a matter of historical metaphysics but as a matter of epistemological necessity: the events can be understood only when the categories linking the American subject with the European object are articulated. Just as Europe stands as an intermediary between America and world history, so does American scholarship occupy an analogous position between the European experience and the rest of the world.

Ultimately, then, the two facets of European history in America that make up its contemporary status—its position in America and its position in the world—are one. It has helped to build into the structure of knowledge meanings that are general without being abstract, and it has contributed its bit thereby to the preparation of men's minds for the admission of the hitherto unknown in ways that refine but do not violate their fundamental ideas. And this, after all, is the prime function of the historical sense.

But the American historians of Europe are paying the same price as their colleagues in American history for the evolution of their historical sense: the same process that opens their minds to the refinements of knowledge exposes to erosion the fundamental ideas and values that are being refined.[1] The skepticism toward the progressive interpretation of history and the current ambiguities of the interpretations of progressivism in history are surely signs of the common process. And yet the American historians of Europe have a counterweight that is not available to the historians of the United States. In the very nature of things the inevitable distance between an American historian and his European subject will hold his critical criteria more inviolate than will his tendency toward identification with an American subject. More important, however, the very act of historical knowledge requires, from the American historian of Europe, a set of common concepts that is closer to the level of universality—and therewith of principle—than is that of the historian of the United States. The European historian is both more impressionable and more puristic—a combination that identifies him clearly as the younger sibling of the American historical profession.

---

[1] For this development in United States history, see John Higham, "Beyond Consensus: The Historian as Moral Critic," *AHR,* LXVII (1962), 609-26. See too W. Stull Holt, "Historical Scholarship," in Merle Curti, ed., *Historical Scholarship,* pp. 97-99.

# EUROPEAN AND AMERICAN HISTORIOGRAPHY

## FELIX GILBERT

### THE INSTITUTE FOR ADVANCED STUDY

The history of modern historiography is closely bound up with national history and with the political and social developments within the nations of the Western world. A study on "French Mathematics" or "German Chemistry" would be of little or doubtful value. There might be more justification for writing a book on "English Economics" or "German Philosophy," but the reader would expect to find in such a work treatment of a period in which English economists or German philosophers made a particularly important contribution to these disciplines. But histories of historical scholarship in individual nations—of German historiography or of Italian historiography—have been written by well-known scholars, and such works are regarded as entirely legitimate undertakings.[1] Even general histories of historiography are usually divided into chapters or sections each containing rather separate accounts of the historical developments in single nations.[2] Organization according to "national principles" seems to be the most appropriate procedure in dealing with the history of history.

It is hardly necessary to give explanations for the appropriateness of this approach. Historical studies form part of the intellectual and political history of every nation. Not only have historians frequently been politicians, but history and the political ideas of any era are closely connected. Much of the historical work done in a country is concerned with that country's past, and the teaching of history serves the ends of civic education. Thus the connection of historical scholarship with political and social purposes necessarily establishes significant differences in the way in which historical scholarship is pursued in various nations.

These considerations—obvious as they are—have a direct bearing

[1] A few of the better-known "national" histories of historiography are Benedetto Croce's *Storia della storiografia italiana nel secolo decimonono,* 2nd rev. ed. (2 vols., Bari, 1930); Louis Halphen's *L'Histoire en France depuis cent ans* (Paris, 1914); and Heinrich Ritter von Srbik's *Geist und Geschichte vom deutschen Humanismus bis zur Gegenwart* (2 vols., Muenchen, 1950, 1951).

[2] See, for instance, Eduard Fueter's *Geschichte der neueren Historiographie* (1911; 3rd rev. ed., Muenchen, 1936) or George Peabody Gooch's *History and Historians in the Nineteenth Century* (London, 1913; frequently reissued). Fueter's book is very unsatisfactory, but it is still widely used because it is almost the only comprehensive history of historiography of some scholarly value.

on the subject of this essay: a comparison of European and American historical scholarship. The existing bond between historical scholarship and national history circumscribes, defines, and limits its subject.

In order to make such a comparison meaningful, it seems necessary to go back to the nineteenth century. For with the adoption of the critical method and with the professionalization of history, both European and American historical scholarship underwent the same transformation and their further historical efforts started from the same basis. Nevertheless, the developments in the various nations took their own particular forms. Because in each nation historical scholarship fulfilled somewhat different social and political needs, it would be almost impossible to make a comparison hinged on an evaluation of the relative quality of historical works. What can be attempted is a confrontation rather than a comparison, and the result should demonstrate the characteristic and distinguishing features of the European and American historical approach.

But it must also be understood that the term *European historical scholarship* does not mean much more than "the historical scholarship of the various European nations." In this essay, reference is made chiefly to historical work done in France, Germany, and Italy; this is a limitation set by the interests and knowledge—or lack of knowledge—of the author.[3] But in addition, there are certain similarities in the institutional organization of academic life in these three nations that make it possible to treat them together. If British historiography is somewhat slighted in the following essay, this is intentional. The reason is that British historical scholarship is so different from that of the Continent that it would have necessitated an almost separate treatment. Moreover, because certain similarities exist between British and American educational institutions, a confrontation of British and American historical scholarship would present less of a contrast.

---

[3] I am fully aware that I have not only neglected the historiographical developments in eastern Europe, but also the entire field of ancient history: I do not know enough about these fields to have an independent judgment.

The footnotes are not intended to present a complete bibliography: their main purpose is to orient the reader about further discussion of the problems raised in the text. Furthermore, the footnotes present in the original language the text of passages translated into English, so that somewhat free translations could be given.

In any case it is not my intention to give a full survey of the development of historiography or to deal with every important historical work or every outstanding historian. My aim is to throw light on the present status of historical scholarship in America and Europe and to explain how the present situation came about.

# THE PROFESSIONALIZATION OF HISTORY
# IN THE NINETEENTH CENTURY

The nineteenth century was the great age of history. Not only were the classics of modern historiography—the works of Ranke, Mommsen and Treitschke, Tocqueville, Fustel de Coulanges and Taine, Burckhardt, Villari, Macaulay and Maitland—produced in this century, but the study of the past was systematically organized, and history became a profession. The imperatives of modern historical scholarship—the application of a critical method to the use and evaluation of sources, the adoption of recognized techniques for editing and presenting material—as well as the existence of appropriate institutional accompaniments—prescribed courses of historical training, the establishment of historical research institutes, and the publication of specialized historical periodicals—are a legacy of the nineteenth century.

To discover the reasons for the emergence of a new approach to historical studies in the nineteenth century one must consider the general development of European thought during this period. The acquisition of knowledge about the past and the evaluation of this knowledge is a single aspect of man's reasoned effort to understand the forces that surround him and to gain insight into the meaning of his existence. The basic concepts and ideas underlying the modern development of historiography are inextricably bound up with the general intellectual trends that have shaped the modern outlook: in particular, with the secularization of thought by which religious and theological explanations of events were replaced by explanations of natural causation; with the Romantic reaction to the rationalism of the eighteenth century; and with the attempts to overcome the "revolution" by a new philosophy in which continuity was stressed. That these intellectual trends were important for the development of modern historiography is undeniable. But the development of the study of history in the nineteenth century was also directly connected with changes in the political and institutional structure of the European countries in the era of the French Revolution and Napoleon. Two of the most crucial—and lasting—achievements of this period were the centralization of administration and the active participation of the middle classes in politics. These changes in the political and social structure of the European countries, gradual though they were, were interdependent. The entrance of the middle classes into politics presupposed both the loosening of the restraints that previously had kept separate the classes of society and the abolition of the autonomous bodies that previously functioned in the interests of a particular class or group of society. Many of the duties formerly carried out by corporate organizations were taken over by the governments; their tasks were enormously increased. Education, for instance, became the "monopoly" of the state. The authority over the field of education that the governments acquired could be used for political purposes. Because of changes in the power structure, the governments were forced to give attention to views and attitudes of people whom previously they had neglected or regarded as objects to be controlled and regulated. Education could become the means by which such groups which had been oppressed and in opposition to the traditional ruling group could become integrated in the existing order. In such a program of civic education the teaching of history was a cornerstone; by demonstrating the common fate of all those living in the same political society, history served to emphasize the ties that unite people rather than the divergent interests of the various social groups.

The policy of using history to promote the political integration of society was directly expressed in a memorandum in which the Austrian Minister of Education, Count Thun, recommended to Emperor Franz Joseph the creation of the Austrian Institute for Historical Research: "It does not need lengthy explanation that the effects of a sense for national history and its awakening is of great importance and efficacy, . . . that intense study of national history promotes patriotism, loyalty, love and attachment to the inherited dynasty." [1] Likewise, Ranke explained the interest that the King of Bavaria took in

---

[1] "Von welch einflussreicher Wichtigkeit aber die Wirkung und Belebung des Sinnes fuer vaterlaendische Geschichte . . . wie foerdernd eindringliches Studium der vaterlaendischen Geschichte auf die Anregung des Patriotismus, der Loyalitaet, der Liebe und Anhaenglichkeit an das angestammte Herrscherhaus wirkt . . . scheint keiner weiteren Ausfuehrung beduerftig. . . ." Quoted in Alphons Lhotsky's "Geschichte des Instituts fuer oesterreichische Geschichtsforschung," in *Mitteilungen des oesterreichischen Instituts fuer Geschichtsforschung,* Ergaenzungsband XVII (Graz-Koeln, 1954), p. 26.

the development of historical scholarship by the particular situation in which Bavaria found itself after the Napoleonic Wars. Because "Bavaria was composed of different tribes and denominations," it was necessary "to mitigate contrasts and to merge them in a higher unit." In the opinion of the Bavarian king, historical studies were particularly suited for these purposes because "their point of departure is general history, but they give their due to particularity and individuality." [2]

From the point of view of the men in power, of the rulers or their ministers of education, the teaching of history was intended to bring about deeper understanding for the righteousness of the existing political situation and greater loyalty to the rulers of the state. Certainly Ranke regarded the legitimation of the existing political order as the principal political aim of historical instruction. [3] But in its relation to contemporary politics the nineteenth century interest in history had a Janus face. Emphasis on continuity and on the identity of the factors which determined past and present necessarily led to the idea of the nation as the primary element of historical development. In countries like Germany and Italy (or those of eastern Europe) where the national state was not yet the given form of political existence but still a revolutionary aim, historical scholarship and liberalism became allied, and historians were often protagonists of political reform. But even in established national states like England and France historians were frequently inclined to regard the political life of the middle classes to which they themselves usually belonged (and owed their influence) as a central event of history and they tended to rationalize progress rather than to defend the status quo. Whatever the original intentions of the governments in promoting historical studies, many of their practitioners became advocates of government by the people, [4] and the grandiose development of historical

2 "Wenn er besonders die historischen Wissenschaften beguenstigte, so zog er dabei in Betracht, dass das Koenigreich Bayern aus verschiedenen Staemmen und Konfessionen besteht, deren Antipathieen er zu beruhigen und in eine allgemeine Einheit aufzuloesen wuenschte. Dazu schienen ihm die historischen Studien besonders geeignet, die ihren Standpunkt in der allgemeinen Geschichte haben und dabei doch der Besonderheit ihr Recht angedeihen lassen." Leopold von Ranke to King Louis II of Bavaria, July 13, 1864; printed in Ranke's *Das Briefwerk* (Hamburg, 1949), p. 453.
3 See Ranke's introduction to the *Historisch politische Zeitschrift*, which he edited from 1832 to 1836.
4 On the relation between liberalism and history in France, see Peter Stadler's

studies in nineteenth century Europe became related to the alliance of history with the dominant and victorious forces of nationalism and liberalism.

The concepts and ideas of historical work as well as its popularity in the nineteenth century can be explained in terms of the European intellectual history of the preceding centuries and in relation to the political problems and tensions that dominated European politics since the French Revolution. But in order to understand the particular forms which the development of historical scholarship took, and which might be briefly characterized as the professionalization of history, it is necessary to describe the institutional framework—the educational organization—within which the development of historical studies was to be placed.

The prerequisite for the rise of historical studies in the nineteenth century was the reorganization of the educational system that took place all over Europe in the period of the French Revolution and of Napoleon. These reforms, particularly those in the universities, created the basis for the development of historical scholarship because through them history attained an independent position. Although history had been taught in universities and institutions of higher education all over Europe before the French Revolution, history had not been an independent subject. In the law schools legal history was offered, and in the schools of theology ecclesiastical history was studied. Universal history was taught as an adjunct to moral philosophy. Examples from history were used to illustrate the moral doctrines deduced from philosophical assumptions. Before the French Revolution, history was but an auxiliary science.[5] The recognition of history as an independent field of study and the creation of professorships

---

*Geschichtschreibung und historisches Denken in Frankreich 1789-1871* (Zuerich, 1958), then the article by Dietrich Gerhard, "Guizot, Augustin Thierry und die Rolle des tiers état in der Franzoesischen Geschichte," *Historische Zeitschrift,* CXC (1960), 290-310, and on Michelet, see the standard biography by Gabriel Monod, *La Vie et la pensée de Jules Michelet* (Paris, 1923).

[5] For the situation in Germany, see Josef Engel's "Die deutschen Universitaeten und die Geschichtswissenschaft," in *Hundert Jahre Historische Zeitschrift 1859-1959,* ed. Theodor Schieder (Muenchen, 1959), pp. 223 ff., and Emil Clemens Scherer's *Geschichte und Kirchengeschichte an den deutschen Universitaeten* (Freiburg, 1927); for France, see the following footnote. It should be mentioned that the Regius Professorships of Modern History, established in Oxford and Cambridge at the beginning of the eighteenth century, were intended to train diplomats, not historical scholars.

devoted exclusively to the teaching of history *qua* history belongs to the nineteenth century. The circumstances by which this came about varied in each country. For instance, in eighteenth century France there were frequent complaints about the lack of instruction in history. The *philosophes* criticized the abstract nature of what was being taught in the institutions of higher education and they demanded the introduction of instruction in practical knowledge. As such fields, the *philosophes* urged the teaching of history and geography, which they regarded as complementary and almost identical because both history and geography were indispensable in providing knowledge of the world in which man lived.[6] When the *ancien régime* had been overthrown there was at first the feeling that concern with the past was obsolete and that history was "a need of princes," not part of the new age.[7] However, shortly thereafter in the general overhaul of the French educational system, professorships of history and geography were established. Later, instruction in these fields was encouraged and promoted by Napoleon. But it was not until 1812, and then as a result of a curious chain of circumstances, that the two existing professorships at the Sorbonne, "history and ancient geography" and "history and modern geography" were transformed into three different professorships, one for geography, one for ancient history, and one for modern history.[8]

In Germany the crucial event which established history as an independent field of study was the foundation of the University of Berlin in 1810.[9] Berlin set a pattern that the other German universities were to adopt. The novel feature in the organization of the University of

---

[6] See Gabriel Monod, "La Chair d'histoire au Collège de France," *Revue historique,* XC (1906), particularly 247 ff. For particulars, see also Louis Liard, *L'Enseignement supérieur en France, 1789-1889* (Paris, 1888), pp. 98 ff.; Charles Jourdain, *Histoire de l'Université de Paris,* vol. II (Paris, 1888), pp. 199 ff. and 382 ff.; Albert Duruy, *L'Instruction publique et la Révolution* (Paris, 1882), pp. 42 ff.; Abel Lefranc, *Histoire du Collège de France* (Paris, 1893), p. 310.

[7] Ernest Allain, *L'Oeuvre scolaire de la Révolution* (Paris, 1891), p. 125, and Alphonse Aulard, *Napoléon Ier et le monopole universitaire* (Paris, 1911), pp. 24 ff.

[8] See Albert Guigue, *La Faculté des Lettres de l'Université de Paris* (Paris, 1935), pp. 16-18.

[9] For a recent discussion, see Eberhard Kessel's "Wilhelm von Humboldt und die deutsche Universitaet," *Studium generale,* VIII (1955), 409-25, and "Zur Geschichte der philosophischen Fakultät," *Studium generale,* XVI (1963), 118-24.

Berlin was the pre-eminent position of the philosophical faculty. For the most part, the older German universities had retained the medieval mode of organization: an arts faculty served as a preparatory school and its requirements had to be met before students could embark on studies in the higher faculties of law, theology, or medicine. Humboldt, the organizer of the University of Berlin, disregarded this hierarchical order of the faculties. In his scheme the philosophical faculty of the University of Berlin was of equal rank to the other faculties; ideally, it was even meant to be "the first and the mistress of all others." [10] While the other faculties trained people for practical professions, study in the philosophical faculty served to educate men; this end was not achieved by indoctrinating students in abstract philosophical systems but by making each student a participant in the exploration of the nature of man and the universe. It was assumed that the study of particular aspects of nature and of social life would imply an increased understanding of the general context of human existence and would result in the acquisition of "true" philosophical insight. Thus each field taught within the framework of the philosophical faculty in the University of Berlin gave particular knowledge as well as a general philosophical education; all fields were equal but independent. Thus history became an autonomous field entrusted to a professor specializing in the teaching of this field, the professor of history.

The creation of historical chairs at the universities represented only one institutional prerequisite for the professionalization of history; the establishment of a close connection between research and teaching was another. For this development, again, the increased functions of the state resulting from the changes of the revolutionary period were decisive. Of course, great historical research enterprises had existed in Europe long before the nineteenth century.[11] In 1607 Rosweyde sent out a prospectus which evolved in the series of the *Acta Sanctorum,* zealously continued by the Bollandists until 1794. Then there were the manifold enterprises of the Maurists who could

---

[10] According to Schleiermacher, quoted by Josef Engel, *op. cit.,* p. 296.

[11] See David Knowles's *Great Historical Enterprises* (London, 1963), pp. 3-32 (The Bollandists), 35-62 (The Maurists), 65-97 (The *Monumenta Germaniae Historica*), 101-34 (The Rolls Series). For eighteenth century research publications, see also Gabriel Monod's "Du Progrès des sciences historiques," *Revue historique,* I (1876), 15-24, and, for a recent description and analysis, Mario Toscano's *Lezioni di storia dei trattati e politica internazionale* (Torino, 1958).

count not only Mabillon, Martène, and Montfaucon among their workers, but who, with Bouquet's *Recueil,* can claim to have been the ancestor of all national collections of medieval documents. And there were Muratori and Rymer and Martens; a great variety of research enterprises flourished in the period before the French Revolution. But those who worked in collecting and editing these materials had no connection with teaching or with universities. Some were librarians of a prince or a great lord; some were members of academies; almost all of them were members of religious orders: Jesuits as were the Bollandists, Benedictines as were the Maurists. These enterprises were tied up with the *ancien régime* and disappeared with its collapse.

It was fitting that historical research enterprises were extinguished in a period in which men believed they had overcome the past and were entering an entirely new era, the final age. But it was equally fitting and inevitable that the age of revolution was followed by the age of historical preoccupation. Attention was directed again to the work that had been accomplished in previous centuries. But the men and the organizations which had undertaken these researches no longer existed. The only agent large enough and strong enough to reassume the abandoned tasks of the previous centuries were the governments. "The government alone possesses the resources which such a large enterprise demands," wrote Guizot, Minister of Education, to King Louis Philippe, in justification of government subsidies for the project to edit unpublished materials on the history of France.[12]

The first great step in direction of government support for historical research enterprises was the foundation of the École des Chartes in 1821.[13] Plans for the establishment of the École des Chartes had been discussed for years before its foundation. It had been decided that its main function was to continue the work of the Maurists, but it was also to serve to train paleographers, archivists, and librarians; moreover, the lectures of the professors of the École des Chartes were to be open to all interested students. Despite the recognition of the need in France for such an institution, the final impetus for its foundation was given by the news that arrived from Germany: that there

[12] "Le gouvernement seul possède les ressources de tout genre qu'exige cette vaste entreprise"; published in François Guizot's *Mémoires pour servir à l'histoire de mon temps,* vol. III (Paris, 1860), p. 395.
[13] See École Nationale des Chartes, *Livre du Centenaire* (*1821-1921*), vol. I: *L'École—son histoire—son oeuvre* (Paris, 1921).

a society had been founded for collecting and editing the sources of medieval German history.

The meeting which represented the starting point for the work of the *Monumenta Germaniae Historica* had taken place in January 1819. At the beginning it had been thought that the enterprise could be financed by voluntary contributions. But soon government support had to be sought and it was secured; from 1834 the financing of the *Monumenta Germaniae Historica* was provided by the German federal governments.

Thus the trend of government support for historical research enterprises was well underway when in 1832, a historian, Guizot, became Minister of Education in France.[14] Guizot's ministerial activities deserve attention because they resulted in assigning to the government a very extended and active role in promoting historical scholarship, and they set a pattern which in the course of the nineteenth century was adopted in most European countries. Guizot's plans were not limited to the collecting and editing of documents and chronicles of the Middle Ages; he envisaged a series of publications in which the unpublished sources of the entire history of France would be printed. The Société de l'Histoire de France, which was founded for this purpose and for which Guizot attained large public funds, has since 1834 produced more than four hundred volumes. But Guizot was aware that the accomplishment of such a plan required researches throughout the whole country. When, in earlier times, research enterprises had been sponsored by religious orders, the members who were assigned to these research tasks had enjoyed freedom from other duties; moreover, the work of the researchers had been immensely facilitated by using the contacts that the orders had in the various parts of the country. But now some secular organization had to replace the net of communications the orders had possessed. Guizot used the governmental machinery to mobilize support for the plans of the Société de l'Histoire de France.[15] The various local officials were ordered to seek out individuals who might act as agents and representatives of the Société. Moreover, these individuals received frequently through government channels instruc-

14 See Guizot, *op. cit.*, vol. III.
15 See Xavier Charmes, *Le Comité des travaux historiques et scientifiques*, vol. II (Paris, 1886), particularly the "Rapport relatif à la réorganisation du Comité des travaux historiques et scientifiques," pp. 303-19, but also the documents printed on pp. 69-97.

tions about the material they ought to collect and the procedure they ought to follow. Thus, through government intervention, local interests and activities were infused with a scientific spirit and subordinated to the enterprises directed by leading scholars. Now the local societies of antiquarians assumed a somewhat different character. With government interest and support the aims and conduct of these local societies became more scholarly and more closely linked to the officials who directed libraries and archives. This development was not limited to France; indeed local historical societies all over Europe assumed new functions. In Germany throughout the nineteenth century there was a steady increase in the number of regional historical societies that were favored and even initiated by the various governments.[16] In Italy, unification brought about the establishment of commissions, one for each province, which were charged to supervise and coordinate the activities of the various local societies.[17] In all these countries the work of the local historical societies was centered around the local archives, and the archivists frequently served as intermediaries between the government and the interested citizens.

Before the French Revolution historical research had been undertaken by men who were not professors and had nothing to do with the universities; the changes which took place in the nineteenth century and which resulted in the professionalization of history were not merely modifications in the organization of historical studies. The most decisive innovation in the nineteenth century was the establishment of a close connection between research in history and the teaching of history in universities. This link was partly the result of institutional arrangements: the research institutes that the governments created and supported were incorporated in the universities; for instance, the École des Chartes became a part of the Sorbonne; the Institute for Austrian Historical Research belonged to the University of Vienna.[18] But the close connection between research and teaching was also the almost inevitable consequence of the dependence of both universities and research enterprises on government financing.

---

[16] See Hermann Heimpel, *Geschichtsvereine Einst und Jetzt* (Goettingen, 1963), particularly pp. 9 ff.

[17] See L' *"Archivio storico italiano"* e *l'opera cinquantenaria della R. Deputazione Toscana di storia patria* (Bologna, 1916), particularly pp. 263 ff. and the report on the first congress of the various regional historical societies in *Archivio storico napoletano*, IV (1879), 601-803.

[18] See Lhotsky, *op. cit.*, p. 29.

It was natural that in selecting men to conduct research projects the governments turned to those men who were their employees as university teachers or archivists. Thus Michelet, who filled Guizot's place at the Sorbonne, reported to the Société de l'Histoire de France about collections of manuscripts,[19] and Mignet, who directed the archives of the French Foreign Ministry, edited for the Société the volumes containing the negotiations about the Spanish Succession. The tendency of delegating to one person the two functions of university professor and director of research enterprises grew stronger. The Historische Kommission at the Bavarian Academy in 1858, the year of its foundation, was almost exclusively composed of the professors of history at the leading German universities—Berlin, Munich, Heidelberg, Jena, Koenigsberg, Goettingen, Wuerzburg, and Erlangen.[20] And one need only to mention the names of Mommsen, Langlois, and Stubbs to indicate to what extent by the end of the nineteenth century participation in research and direction of research enterprises had become a function of the professor of history.

So far, I have discussed the change in historical teaching and research that took place in the nineteenth century. This development also had bearing on the writing of history. It became an axiom that historical writing must be based on research, and that presupposed knowledge of original sources and of methods for the critical evaluation of sources. Political interest or literary talent was no longer enough for the writing of history; it required specialized training. The university professor occupied a key position in which he dominated teaching, writing, and research in history.

I have characterized the nature of the innovations that occurred in the nineteenth century as consisting in a "professionalization of history." Acquisition of particular skills—the ability to handle the critical method—by means of a training directed exclusively toward the education of historians was the essence of the new stage in the history of historiography in the nineteenth century. But we can also notice a development of the tendencies that usually accompany professionalization: specialization and bureaucratization.

Historians, proud of the independence which their field of interest had attained, were eager to have their own outlets for their publica-

---

[19] See Charmes, *op. cit.,* vol. II, p. 45, and Monod, *Michelet,* pp. 357 ff.
[20] See *Die Historische Kommission bei der bayerischen Akademie der Wissenschaften, 1858-1958* (Goettingen, 1958), p. 207.

tions. In 1859 the German *Historische Zeitschrift* was founded, in 1876 the French *Revue historique,* in 1884 the *Rivista storica italiana,* and in 1886 the *English Historical Review.* But they soon seemed insufficient. New periodicals were created for particular aspects of history or for special periods. Moreover, distinct geographical regions established their own historical periodicals and they formed the rallying point of local historical societies.[21] The editors were frequently the directors of the main archives of the region and many of the articles published in these periodicals were results of work done in the local archives. In the nineteenth century most European governments effected a thorough and systematic organization of their archives and created the office of a central director. The new critical method, which called for greater use of documentary sources, had its part in effecting this reform of archival administration. But the rise of a complex system of archival administration also created new fields of activities for historically trained scholars. They might become archivists for their lifetimes; they might work in archives at the beginning of their careers before gaining posts in a university; or—as the examples of Sybel, Maury, Langlois, or Koser show—they might become, after a career in teaching, directors of the archives of the entire country. Because research workers, archivists, and professors all served in government financed enterprises they were all civil servants and therefore they could easily move from one position to another. Thus the professionalization of history engendered a variety of activities for which the training in history was useful and necessary: full-time researchers, archivists, librarians, and most of all, teachers of history at high schools (Gymnasiums and lycées) for which, with the rapid increase in population, the need increased.

A steadily growing absorption of manpower has always been considered as an integral element of bureaucratization; but the development of historical scholarship also revealed features of another tendency typical of a bureaucratic structure: the profession became hierarchically organized. At the top of the pyramid was the professor of history who trained future historians and controlled the research enterprises and their personnel; perhaps even among these university professors there was a hierarchical differentiation in the sense that usually the professor at the most prestigious university, frequently

[21] See Hermann Heimpel, *"Aus der Geschichte der deutschen Geschichtsvereine,"* Neue Sammlung, vol. I (1961), pp. 297 ff.

that of the capital, had the largest empire of enterprises at his disposal, attracted the greatest number of students, and formed the dominating "school." Below the professors there were the various directors of archives, the archivists, the research associates and assistants. And then there were the high school teachers of whom a certain number continued to do scholarly work with the hope of eventually becoming university professors. The heights of the professorships could be attained only by a slow and gradual ascent. At the beginning of the twentieth century a few perceptive minds began to notice that the brilliant and imposing development of European historical scholarship in the nineteenth century was not without drawbacks and dangers. In the obituary on a young German historian, Theodor Ludwig, who had died before he had come into his own, Meinecke, perhaps thinking of the beginnings of his own career, wrote:

We must be aware of the inner difficulties with which a rising historian has to struggle today. At first, he will have to concentrate on studies in a very narrow and isolated area. He is confronted by tasks and problems of a professional character and he must tackle them in a prescribed manner. Editions and specialized documentary studies—usually not chosen by himself but assigned to him or recommended to him—will usually absorb the first decade of his scholarly life. Today scholarship, having become an organized large-scale enterprise, presses most heavily on the individual scholar in the most susceptible years of his development.[22]

Nevertheless, the European attitude toward history contained certain traditional ideas and assumptions which acted, and still act, as built-in counterforces against a total surrender to specialization.

---

[22] "Man muss einmal an die inneren Schwierigkeiten erinnern, mit denen heute ein aufstrebender Historiker zu kaempfen hat. Er muss heute beinahe notwendig damit beginnen, sich zu konzentrieren und isolieren in engbegrenzten Studien. Es treten bestimmte Aufgaben und Fragestellungen der zuenftigen Wissenschaft an ihn heran, denen er zunaechst mit gebundener Marschroute folgen muss. Editionen und spezialisierte Aktenstudien—in der Regel nicht selbstgewaehlte, sondern uebertragene oder anempfohlene Arbeiten—absorbieren gewoehnlich die ersten beiden Lustren der eigenen Forschertaetigkeit. Die Wissenschaft, zur Arbeitsorganisation und zum Grossbetriebe geworden, lastet heute auf dem einzelnen Forscher gerade in seinen frischesten Enwicklungsjahren am staerksten." Friedrich Meinecke, "Theodor Ludwig," *Preussen und Deutschland* (Muenchen/Berlin, 1918), p. 449.

Even after the teaching of history was separated from moral philosophy the view remained that the study of history should strengthen man in his moral attitude and convictions; it might be enough to refer to Burckhardt and Acton as examples of nineteenth century historians who, though trained in critical historical methods, maintained the view that the study of history had moral value.[23] Moreover, the acceptance of history as an independent field of study was founded on the assumption that the study of the past was a path to the understanding of life; such a view implied that no one period of the past was more important than another and that the meaning of history would reveal itself only if the process of history was regarded as a unit, and single events and periods were seen in relation to the whole. Thus, when chairs designated exclusively for the teaching of history were established, the holders of these chairs were entrusted with the teaching of history in general and not with instruction in a special field of history.

At the Continental universities the concept that the professor of history was responsible for the entire field of history, its various periods, its various areas, and its various aspects, was maintained throughout the entire nineteenth century.[24] Because of the practical impossibility of handling the entire course of history, some chronological divisions were soon adopted. First, ancient history was separated from the rest of the historical field. Then, in a later part of the nineteenth century, the postclassical period was usually entrusted to two professors, one for medieval and one for modern history. But this division was chiefly indicative of the work in which the holder of the chair was particularly interested. Neither of the two professors was restricted to the teaching of medieval or modern history. When, in 1891, a chair for the history of the French Revolution was founded in Paris, it was the first French professorship strictly limited to one particular period of history.[25] In Germany and Italy such

23 For Acton, see Gertrude Himmelfarb's *Lord Acton: A Study in Conscience and Politics* (Chicago, 1952); for Burckhardt, the great biography by Werner Kaegi (so far 3 volumes).

24 See Josef Engel, *op. cit.,* p. 351.

25 See Guigue, *op. cit.,* p. 21. Aulard had been charged with lectures on the history of the French Revolution since 1886; see Georges Belloni's *Aulard: Historien de la Révolution Française* (Paris, 1949), p. 16. Under Aulard, this professorship, which had been endowed by the Paris Municipal Government, differed from other professorships; Aulard represented modern and radical trends in scholarship and politics.

specialized professorships did not exist in the nineteenth century and even today they are rather rare. However, the professor of history was in practice much less universal than his title permitted him and required him to be. The prevailing concern of the history teachers at the European universities was the investigation of the past of their own nation. This emphasis grew naturally out of the alliance which historical scholarship and nationalism had formed in the nineteenth century. But the tendency to concentrate on the history of one's own nation was reinforced by the adoption of the critical method. Since the account of the past was to be based as far as possible on documentary sources, it was natural to concentrate on problems for which documentary sources were most easily accessible, namely, on the history of one's own nation. The archives of one's own country also provided the great bulk of the material for the research enterprises that the government supported and the professors of history were directing. In all European countries the central theme of teaching and research was national history.

The necessity of combining a universal approach to history with belief in the development of nationalism and a national state as the true content of history determined both the direction which European historical scholarship took and the concepts which were used in explaining the course of history. Actually the tension between emphasis on universal history and emphasis on national history was less great in the nineteenth century than it appears to us in the second half of the twentieth century, when our horizon, immensely widened, encompasses the entire globe.

In the nineteenth century the area in which historical developments took place was regarded as limited to Europe and the Near East. The general histories written in this period presume that the course of universal history began in the Near East and Egypt, that it led over Palestine to the Greeks and Romans, and then shifted its center to middle and western Europe. In the stage of world history after the fall of the Roman Empire, the possibility of one world-state disappeared, and the various nations emerged as the moving forces in history. Thus it was taken for granted that the nineteenth century idea of the national state had its roots in the Middle Ages and that the study of the medieval period was a necessary and integral part of national history. There was never any doubt about the significance and relevance of the great enterprises concerned with the publication of the sources of medieval history, and throughout the nineteenth century it was assumed that all young historians, even those who wanted ultimately to work in modern history, would write their first work of independent research—their thesis—in an earlier period.[26] Even after this was no longer required, it was still considered a matter of course that the historian would receive training in medieval as well as modern history.

In focusing attention on the line of development that led from indistinct common beginnings to the existence of national states, historical scholars were impelled to emphasize those factors that contributed to the process of separation. Wars and foreign policy, which since classical times had been regarded as the most important and most legitimate historical subjects, remained the central themes of history, though perhaps they became more elaborate and refined. It is certainly true that historians of the nineteenth century did not overlook the great variety of factors working in history; nevertheless their main concern was political and diplomatic history.

Even if the recognition of the absolute value of the national state brought a teleological element into the consideration of the past, the rise of national states did not necessarily demand—or reinforce—the assumption of an organic evolution or a progressive development. The investigation of national entities showed not only continuity but revealed also discontinuity as an important historical fact. The development of political societies could be stultified and suppressed; the limits of the expansion of a nation depended on power relations, on struggles with other nations; the weight which the nations of Europe could exert in the various periods of history varied. There was no European nation that had not undergone a crisis in its development. And this crisis had frequently determined the form and the character of the nation. In the historical analyses of nineteenth century scholars the concept of crisis was of crucial importance.[27] Ranke's national histories of Germany, France, and England were always centered on those moments in the histories of these

---

[26] For examples, see Louis Halphen, *op. cit.*, pp. 157 ff., or Guigue, *op. cit.*, pp. 57 ff. ("Liste des thèses de doctorat ès Lettres").

[27] The most famous discussion of this concept is that by Jacob Burckhardt in his *Weltgeschichtliche Betrachtungen;* an entire section of this work is entitled "Die geschichtlichen Krisen."

countries—the Reformation, religious wars, civil strife—which, in Ranke's opinion, represented a fundamental crisis from which the national society emerged in its definite character. But quite in general, the periods of crisis in which the existence of a nation was threatened, and out of which the character of this nation emerged more sharply delineated, formed the focal points of interest to nineteenth century historical scholars; it is almost astonishing to see how the works of the most prominent historians of the nineteenth century, of Burckhardt, of Thiers, of Taine, of Sybel or Michelet, are directed to a few great and critical periods of European history, to the Renaissance and Reformation, the French Revolution, the fall of the German medieval empire, etc. As much as the development of historical scholarship in the nineteenth century seemed to tap inexhaustible sources and open new horizons, the emphasis on political and diplomatic history, the view of the national state as the main goal of history, and the conceptions of continuity, crisis, and discontinuity as determinants in history created a rather definite and rigid framework for historical work.

My remarks have chiefly been concerned with the professionalization of history on the European continent in the nineteenth century. And for reasons previously stated, I have made little reference to the development of British historical scholarship. It might be enough to remark here that although developments similar to those on the Continent took place in Great Britain, they were later and more gradual. Only in 1857 did Lord Romilly, the Master of the Rolls, aware that England "alone amongst Governments of modern civilized nations" had "taken no steps to produce her historical treasures," obtain a regular subvention from the Treasury for the editing of historical sources.[28] Stubbs and Seeley are regarded as the first serious historical scholars who became Regius Professors of History at Oxford and Cambridge. And their appointments were in 1866 and 1869, respectively. The Historical Tripos, which established the rights of undergraduates to have history as a subject of concentration and examination, was introduced in 1875, but still in 1891 there was among the sixty Fellows of Trinity College in Cambridge not one historian.[29] It is also characteristic that the *English Historical* Re-

[28] See Knowles, *op. cit.*, p. 107.
[29] See G. P. Gooch, *Under Six Reigns* (London, 1958), p. 17.

*view* was founded as the last of the great national historical periodicals.[30]

A reason for the halfhearted and hesitant manner in which English historians accepted the professionalization of history was that England lacked the stimulus to historical studies which Continental governments provided. In England education was not a monopoly of the state as it had been on the Continent since the time of the French Revolution. The acceptance of critical methods and scholarly standards in England did not arise from a need to adjust the universities to the requirements of a changed political structure but rather from a feeling that if they were not adopted England would lag behind. Thus in England the acceptance was one of imitation and therefore incomplete. Evidently in opposition to the dominating role which scholarly research played at Continental, particularly German universities, Oman, in his Oxford inaugural lecture on the study of history in 1906, emphasized that "this university is a place of education as well as a place of research."[31] Among English dons the idea that "Clio was a Muse" never lost defenders;[32] for many, historical writings ought to be works of literature rather than contributions to scholarship. The value of historical studies was to educate, particularly to educate statesmen.

But even those Englishmen who were inclined toward the Continental conception of historical scholarship and wanted to be professional historians rather than literary men or educators did not embark on their work with the same concepts and outlook as their Continental colleagues. Liberal Victorian England seemed to have overcome the conflicts that in the first half of the nineteenth century provoked a revolutionary crisis on the European continent; England appeared to have advanced steadily and securely to the realization of a free society. Undisturbed by external foes, England had been able to develop its institutions in harmony with the ideals of individual freedom. The English historian saw the movements of history di-

30 "It has long been a matter of observation and regret that in England, alone among the great countries of Europe, there does not exist any periodical organ dedicated to the study of history"; this the first sentence of the prefatory note to the first issue of the *English Historical Review,* 1886.

31 Charles Oman, "Inaugural Lecture on the Study of History," *Oxford Lectures* (Oxford, 1906), p. 18.

32 "Clio: A Muse" was the title of an essay by George Macaulay Trevelyan, directed against Bury's "scientific history," first published in 1903 in the *Independent Review.*

rected toward progress; and the themes on which he focused to reveal this development were of an institutional and administrative character.

If Britain's distance from Europe created the differences in outlook and institutions that distinguished the historical work in Britain from that on the Continent, the distance between European and American historical scholarship was still greater. The fate of Jameson's plans and activities is a case in point.[33] In planning a central institute for historical research, Jameson intended to give to historical studies in the United States a foundation similar to that which they had in most European countries. But the failure of Jameson's projects reveals that the presuppositions of the developments in European historiography were lacking in the United States. To historians in the United States there was no immediate connection as there was in Europe between events in the history of their country and those of the general history of Europe, between national and world history. In the nineteenth century the United States lived in isolation from the rest of the world. Thus any attempt to write an American history that would regard relations with the outside world as crucial factors in the formation of the national society had little meaning; the emphasis in Europe on diplomatic history was inappropriate for the history of the United States. But European historical concepts were inapplicable to American history not only because of the geographical separation of America from Europe; the historians' perspective varied also because of the differences in length of time of the history with which American and European historians had to deal. Because American history was short, in the sense that hardly more than a century had passed since the establishment of American independence, American historians in the nineteenth century did not need to be concerned with the problems of discontinuity or crisis. They had no difficulty in combining a critical historical method with a continued belief in the idea of progress. Bancroft's *History of the United States* shows that in the United States adoption of the new critical methods of history was not contradictory to the maintenance of a Hegelian scheme of immanent historical logic. Moreover, the training of historians and the nature of historical scholarship in the United States differed from that of Europe because in Europe the historical profession was decisively shaped by interest in medieval origins. In Europe,

[33] See above, pp. 20 ff.

medieval history was an integral element of national history and therefore of historical education, and European historians received their methodical training in medieval history. The oldest and most important research enterprises were concerned with documents dating from the Middle Ages. The mere fact that medieval source materials were neither existent nor needed for writing the history of the United States prevented the establishment of large research enterprises equal to those in Europe; moreover, it made a large staff of archivists and research workers unnecessary.

As influential as was the pattern of European historiography for the development of American historical scholarship, European concepts, methods, and themes could not simply be taken over. They had to be adapted to the American social scene. Without the necessary adjustment, the historian might treat issues that, in contrast to the importance they might have in Europe, would have little bearing on American developments; and it must be said that some of the works produced by American historians have been irrelevant despite their up-to-date scholarship. But it can also be pointed out that, as Turner's frontier thesis shows, some American historians have been aware of the necessity for using scholarly methods as well as of the necessity for placing their results in a conceptual framework fitted to the American experience. Moreover, American life contains antidotes against irrelevancy in historical scholarship.

The decisive factors that produced the differences between European and American scholarly life are of an institutional nature. A significant feature of continental Europe, the direction of education on all levels by the governments, does not exist in the United States. This has wrought certain disadvantages for the development of historical scholarship in the United States: there are few, if any, research enterprises in the United States that have existed over many decades, that have maintained strict standards for scholarly work, and that have bequeathed a scholarly tradition from one generation to another. Moreover, the principal aim of the European historian was to make a contribution to scholarship. First of all, he wrote for the great number of those who were themselves involved in historical work. Certainly he also aimed for a wider public but this wider public was (in terms of total population) the small educated group who had gone to the university, obtained advanced degrees, and absorbed professional standards of judgment. Thus the final judges of a European historian's work were his professional colleagues. And the yardstick by which they judged was primarily that of scholarship. In the United States the standards of judgment were not purely professional. Among the colleges and universities, numerous and widely dispersed over the country, there was no definite and recognized hierarchy that gave to one or to a few historical scholars a decisive and authoritative voice. Moreover, because general education was the basic aim of college attendance, the reputation of a historian or the standards for judging his work were not dependent on scholarly qualities alone, but on literary qualities, on political timeliness, on the influence he exerted on all educated people, etc., etc. Neither was scholarly production the only standard of judgment nor was the historian entirely dependent on the views of his professional colleagues.

Despite the awe with which European historical scholarship was regarded in the United States the connection between history and literature remained much more close in America than in continental Europe. It is certainly true that in the United States as well as in Europe the main responsibility for the progress of historical studies was placed on the professor of history. But whereas in Europe the acceptance of the critical historical method and of the professionalization of history had the result that the professor considered the training of historians as his foremost obligation, in the United States the professor of history, as well as he might be trained in the new European methods and sympathetic to their aims, continued to regard the teaching of history as his chief purpose.

# THE PROFESSIONAL HISTORIAN IN
# TWENTIETH CENTURY INDUSTRIAL SOCIETY

After the nineteenth century—the Golden Age of History—there followed what was, at best, a Silver Age: thus did one of the leading historians of the first half of the twentieth century judge the value of the contribution which his generation made to the general development of historiography.[1] And he was not alone in his belief; the view that a decline had set in after the great achievements of the nineteenth century historians was general and not without reason.

In the later part of the nineteenth century and the beginning of the twentieth century, European life and society were thoroughly altered. Industrialization spread rapidly throughout the European continent. Ambitious and energetic sons of the middle classes turned to careers in industry, banking, and commerce. These developments had a great impact on the universities. Because industrial growth and development was dependent on discoveries in chemistry, physics, etc., and on the availability of a scientifically trained personnel, the natural sciences gained importance and support in academic life. In addition, there was an increasing interest in fields which were connected with the problems of industrial society and which could be expected to help its understanding: economics, sociology, psychology. History could no longer be regarded as the only field of scholarship concerned with investigation of the forces determining the structure of the social world and its development. Although no objective measure for such phenomena exists, the conclusion can hardly be avoided that at the end of the nineteenth century the number of outstanding talents attracted to the study of history decreased.

The challenge which the rise of industrialization and of the natural and social sciences offered to historical studies aroused a varied and contradictory response among historians. Some of them thought it necessary to take a new look at what historical scholarship could

---

[1] "Dem goldenen Zeitalter der deutschen Historie ist ein silbernes Zeitalter gefolgt." Friedrich Meinecke, "Johann Gustav Droysen," in *Staat und Persoenlichkeit* (Berlin, 1933), p. 99.

do and achieve. Others—and it ought to be said immediately that these were the great majority of historians—were inclined to stick more firmly to the methods and the approach which had been developed in the nineteenth century. The minority, namely, those who were dissatisfied with historical scholarship in its accepted form, believed that if historical studies were to remain of significance in the modern world the historian must be able to produce conclusions and results as definite as those obtained by the scientists: thus, a rightly conceived study of history ought to reveal the laws underlying the developments of history. The views and methods of nineteenth century historical scholarship had been formed in opposition to philosophies of history like those of Hegel; and nobody intended to return to such a priori constructions of the process of world history. But although Hegel's method, through which he had deduced the stages of historical development from what he considered their necessary correspondence to the logical processes of the human mind, was regarded to be false, Hegel was thought to have been right in assuming that there existed a necessary causal connection in world history and that it was possible to discover and formulate laws of historical development. But no deductive method could produce valid results. The establishment of these laws required a strictly scientific, purely inductive procedure.

In France in 1900 there appeared the first volume of the *Revue de synthèse historique*. Henri Berr, the founder and editor of this periodical, felt sure that if historians, in their researches, used the results of modern scientific endeavors in all other fields of knowledge, they would be able to show the pattern of the evolution of the human mind since the beginnings of civilization.[2] Berr's periodical was intended to encourage work of such a synthesis and to publish it. In Germany, the protagonist of a scientific history was Karl Lamprecht.[3] In order to distinguish the new emphasis he wanted to give to historical studies from traditional political history, Lamprecht called the history he advocated cultural history; accordingly the periodical he

[2] See Henri Berr, *La Synthèse en histoire* (Paris, 1911; enlarged ed., 1953) and *L'Histoire traditionelle et la synthèse historique* (Paris, 1935); the program of Berr's *Revue de synthèse historique* is now available in English translation in *The Varieties of History*, ed. Fritz Stern (New York, 1956), pp. 250-55.
[3] For the most recent literature on Lamprecht, see Herbert Schoenebaum's "Karl Lamprecht und Ernst Bernheim," *Archiv für Kulturgeschichte*, XLIII (1961), 217-39.

founded as the mouthpiece for his views was named the *Archiv für Kulturgeschichte*. Under the influence of the psychologist Wilhelm Wundt, who was his colleague and friend at the University of Leipzig, Lamprecht suggested that the new field of science from which historical studies might reap the greatest benefit was social psychology. Lamprecht expected that the laws of psychology might explain the progress in historical development. Each period of history had a peculiar collective psychology, but a necessary causal connection led from the state of mind of one period to that of the succeeding one. Lamprecht enjoyed a great reputation in the wider scientific world and he attracted numbers of young Americans to study under him at Leipzig. But in the German historical profession Lamprecht had few adherents. And his views evoked a vehement debate which became bitter and even unfair: Lamprecht became almost ostracized by his German colleagues; none of his students ever achieved an influential position in German academic life. But historians of other countries were no less opposed to the idea of a search for the laws of history than German historians. Berr was treated with greater respect than Lamprecht but he also remained an outsider frequently involved in polemics with the *historiens historisants* as he called his opponents, the political historians.[4] Berr began to make his impact on French historical scholarship only after World War I when the first volumes of the series "L'Évolution de l'Humanité," which he had planned and sponsored, appeared.

But this dissatisfaction with the state of historical scholarship was not limited to those who wanted to adjust history to the requirements of the natural sciences and worked to establish laws of history. A number of historians, although they did not want to go so far as Berr and Lamprecht, were equally impressed by the work done in the natural and social sciences, and they believed it desirable and necessary to widen the field of history and to take account of aspects of history that previously had been neglected or left aside.

The interest in social psychology contributed to the fame which Burckhardt's *Civilization of the Renaissance in Italy* achieved. Almost neglected at the time of its appearance in 1861, the book gained steadily in popularity from the last decades of the nineteenth century as "a pattern for the treatment of cultural history."[5] Be-

4 See Berr, *L'Histoire traditionelle*, p. 17.
5 See Werner Kaegi, *Jacob Burckhardt*, vol. III (Basel/Stuttgart, 1956), p. 750.

cause of its masterly analysis and description of the mind of an entire epoch, the book was regarded as a successful example of the application of social psychology to historical writing. It is hardly surprising that Huizinga, who might be regarded as Burckhardt's intellectual heir, was deeply interested in problems of social psychology and anthropology in his student years.[6]

With the more general recognition of the importance and usefulness of economics, historians became aware of the role of the economic factor in the past and gave increasing attention to its elucidation. A reflection of this new interest was apparent at the earliest International Historical Congresses, those of Berlin in 1908 and of London in 1913, where Pirenne was a dominating figure; his presentation of theses about the origin of towns and about the relation between early capitalism and the development of centralized administration were high points.[7] Although before World War I few academic historians had more than a superficial acquaintance with Marx, if any acquaintance at all, Marx gave indirectly a stimulus to investigations of previously unexplored areas and causal connections because of the influence he had exerted on sociologists like Durkheim, Pareto, Sombart, Max Weber, whose writings were much debated. Religious developments as well as the history of law, if viewed in their relation to social and economic factors, became historically determined forces rather than absolute values or ideas. In particular, Italian scholars were interested in revealing the social and economic factors and tensions behind political changes and legal developments. Using the experiences of their own time to throw new light on the history of the Italian communes, Anzilotti, Salvemini, and Volpe "reestablished the bond between history and contemporary political experience." [8]

The origin of many of the new approaches which changed historical scholarship and patterned its development after the two World Wars can be traced to the end of the nineteenth and the be-

[6] See Johan Huizinga, *Mein Weg zur Geschichte* (Basel, 1947), pp. 27 ff., and Rosalie L. Colie, "Johan Huizinga and the Task of Cultural History," *AHR*, LXIX (1964), 607 ff.

[7] See Haskins' report on the Congress in Berlin, *AHR*, XIV (1908-09), 6, and Jameson's report on the Congress in London, *AHR*, XVIII (1912-13), 685.

[8] ". . . viene ristabilito il nesso tra storia ed esperienza politica del presente." Benedetto Croce, *Storia della storiografia italiana nel secolo decimonono*, vol. II (Bari, 1930), p. 144.

ginning of the twentieth century. But it is misleading to look upon the years before World War I with the wisdom of hindsight and to focus on those historical writings that historians of later generations have found particularly exciting and that have had an influence on the formation of our own historical outlook. Within historical scholarship as a whole the innovators who wanted to enhance history by making use of the experiences of the modern world and the discoveries of modern science were outsiders; the scholarly scene before World War I was dominated by those historians who followed the paths of traditional political history. Not Pirenne nor Sée, nor Mathiez, Gothein, Huizinga, or Meinecke were the acknowledged leaders of the profession, but rather Lenz and Marcks, Seignobos, Hanotaux, and Lavisse.[9] When at the International Historical Congress in Berlin in 1908, Kurt Breysig suggested a new scheme of universal history that would integrate intellectual, economic, and political developments, the report in the *Revue historique* characterized his ideas as "very dangerous from the scholarly point of view. It is almost unavoidable that today such work is premature and superficial. As a disciple of Nietzsche, Breysig should be very careful that his imagination does not dominate his scholarship and become a substitute for research."[10]

The great majority of academic historians saw no reason to alter the nineteenth century views about the methods and contents of history. The hold that the traditional view had is shown by the most ambitious collective historical enterprise of the years before World War I, *The Cambridge Modern History*.[11] Its collaborators came from many countries of Europe. They were easily assimilated into a team because it was assumed that they were all in agreement about the

[9] See Heinrich Ritter von Srbik, *Geist und Geschichte vom deutschen Humanismus bis zur Gegenwart*, vol. II (Muenchen, 1951), pp. 7 ff. and 18 ff., and Hans-Heinz Krill, *Die Ranke Renaissance Max Lenz und Erich Marcks*, Veroeffentlichungen der Berliner Historischen Kommission, vol. III (Berlin, 1962); or Marc Bloch, *The Historian's Craft* (New York, 1953), pp. 14-17, and Lucien Febvre, *Combats pour l'histoire* (Paris, 1953), particularly pp. 61 ff.

[10] In the report on the Congress in Berlin published in *Revue historique*, XCIX (1908), 304, it is said that Breysig's ideas are "fort dangereux au point de vue scientifique. . . . Il est bien difficile que des oeuvres pareilles no soient pas aujourd'hui très prématurées et superficielles. Un disciple de Nietzsche comme M. Breysig devrait être plus soucieux de ne pas laisser l'imagination guider la science et s'y substituer."

[11] Lord Acton's "Letter to the Contributors to the Cambridge Modern History" is now reprinted in *The Varieties of History*, ed. Fritz Stern, pp. 247-49.

subject matter they were to treat in their contributions; it was taken for granted that politics, foreign policy, and domestic affairs, as well as the relation of foreign and domestic policy to the accepted conceptions of the modern world—Renaissance, Reformation, Enlightenment, etc.—would be pervading themes of the various chapters and volumes. Because what the various authors would emphasize was taken as a matter of course, the main problem was to find the most expert contributor for each period or topic. It is frequently said that *The New Modern Cambridge History,* whose volumes are now being published, is inferior to its older brother, and there are some good reasons for this judgment. But it ought not to be overlooked that *The New Modern Cambridge History* is much more comprehensive because it represents an attempt to embrace history in all its various aspects. The first *Cambridge Modern History* did not advance into new and unexplored territories; it was mainly a codification of views about history that had been formed in the nineteenth century and that were regarded as authoritative and valid by the great majority of historians.

Thus, in the years of the twentieth century before the outbreak of World War I the great majority of historians followed paths that had been previously staked out. Consequently, the tendencies toward specialization and organization that had accompanied the professionalization of history in the nineteenth century not only continued but gained increasing momentum. It became almost a fetish to believe that a historical work had value only if all the available sources on that topic had been exhausted; moreover it was strictly enjoined that most of the sources ought to be new, i.e., not previously used or published. Aulard opened his classes at the beginning of each academic year with the statement. "Let the research be long and the results short." [12] One can probably say that most historians followed his advice to make the research long but few made the results short. Dissertations which previously had been primarily short proofs of ability to do independent work became extended books. The trend toward lengthy dissertations was related to the increasing competitiveness of academic life; the aspiring young scholar wanted to direct attention to himself by producing as his dissertation a real piece of scholarship. But the principal reason for the growing length in dis-

[12] Quoted in James L. Godfrey's "Alphonse Aulard," in *Some Historians of Modern Europe,* ed. Bernadotte Schmitt (Chicago, 1942), p. 50.

sertations was the view that true historical scholarship demanded that any study of worth ought to be based on new sources and had to be as exhaustive as possible. The natural result was that the books became longer but the subjects treated in these books narrower. Seignobos justified the choice of the subject of his doctoral thesis—"Le Régime féodal en Bourgogne jusque en 1360"—by stating that it was "a region small enough to be studied thoroughly, was typical of the feudal regime as a whole, and there were abundant sources in the archives of Dijon." [13]

The emphasis on specialized research and the steadily growing amount of sources and literature becoming available for each period of history made it increasingly difficult for any historian to maintain a knowledge of recent scholarship in a wide historical area. In his student days a young scholar had to decide whether he wanted to become an ancient, a medieval, or a modern historian, and although even a modern historian was expected to have done some work in medieval history, his training became concentrated in one of these fields. Similar developments took place on the teaching level. In Germany, the title of Professor of History remained unchanged and therefore formally the idea was kept alive that the entire field of history was his domain. But actually there were at least three historical chairs, and at larger universities even more professorships of history were established. It was assumed that a division of labor would take place among the holders of these chairs so that each of them would be chiefly concerned with either ancient, medieval, or modern history. In France, at the Sorbonne, specialization on every level of historical studies was frankly acknowledged as the command of the hour. In 1904 a number of new professorships were established. The professorship of ancient history was divided into chairs for Greek and for Roman history. Professorships for the Institutions of the Middle Ages and for Political and Diplomatic History were established. In 1906 and 1907 professorships for auxiliary sciences, for historical method, and for Byzantine history were created.[14]

"L'histoire se fait avec des documents"—thus begins the first chapter of the famous *Introduction aux études historiques* by Langlois

[13] Quoted in Gordon H. McNeil's "Charles Seignobos," in *Some Historians of Modern Europe*, p. 481.
[14] See Albert Guigue, *La Faculté des Lettres de l'Université de Paris* (Paris, 1935), pp. 20-24.

and Seignobos. And the paragraph ends with the same assertion: "Rien ne supplée aux documents: pas de documents, pas d'histoire." [15] If the demand for exclusive reliance on documentary sources led to specialization, it had also the complementary result of reinforcing the trend toward organization in historical scholarship. As scholars bored deeper and deeper into the archives the publication of their finds required new outlets; there was a steady increase in the series of editions of documentary sources. Usually the professor of history whose research interests were most closely concerned organized and directed these publications and he distributed the work on single sections among his students, some of whom might compose their dissertations on the basis of the material they were charged to collect. The editing and publishing of documentary sources became not only part of the historian's training, but participation in the organization of collective research became an integral part of his scholarly activities throughout his entire life. In the evaluation of a historian the amount and importance of the editorial work he was doing and organizing began to count heavily. It remained the rule that the historian was expected to present the results of his researches in literary form in a book addressed to a wide public. But there were an increasing number of cases of historians who never published a narrative or interpretative historical work but who attained a university chair exclusively on the basis of editing source materials.[16] For those who have ever become involved in organized activities, the appeal of extending and widening them seems irresistible. It is no accident that in the years before World War I the first international congresses assembled; they were a positive result of this tendency toward organizational expansion.[17] It seems less comprehensible that in the later years of World War I, when the future began to look very uncertain, German historians met to organize an ambitious enterprise to explore and publish systematically the sources of modern Ger-

[15] Langlois et Seignobos, *Introduction aux études historiques,* Livre I, 1897.
[16] See the remarks on Paul Kehr in Friedrich Meinecke's *Ausgewaehlter Briefwechsel* (*Werke,* vol. VI; Stuttgart, 1962), pp. 29, 63 ff., 78.
[17] The International Historical Congress held at Berlin in August 1908 is usually considered to have been the first of the international historical congresses, which now meet every five years. However, the Berlin Congress was preceded by an International Congress held in Rome in 1903, which is sometimes not "counted" because the Rome Congress was not limited strictly to historians. Smaller international meetings of historians had taken place in The Hague in 1898 and in Paris in 1900.

man history; it was intended to be for more recent centuries what the *Monumenta* was for the Middle Ages.[18]

Since history had become professionalized in the nineteenth century historical scholarship was a going concern which, with the passing of time, gathered increasing momentum. With the intensification of the study of sources new enterprises, new source editions, and more specialized periodicals accumulated; all these various undertakings required more research assistants, more archivists, and more editors. The demand for trained historians increased continuously. History might absorb a smaller percentage of the entire student body than in the previous century; historical scholarship might attract a smaller number of the most gifted young students. But if so, these changes were hardly noticeable because, with the general rise in population, the number of history students steadily rose. Although some thoughtful and perceptive historians might question whether historical scholarship had taken the right path, outwardly history did not give the impression of a declining field of knowledge. On the contrary, all external signs—quantity of students, of publications, of institutes, and of research enterprises—indicated a flourishing state of affairs. It is not astonishing that pride in what was achieved rather than recognition of the need to change and that self-complacency rather than doubts were the prevailing mood among historians.

There was reason for this general attitude of satisfaction and self-congratulation because even critics of the prevailing traditionalism in historical scholarship cannot deny that a great amount of valuable historical work was done in the period before World War I. The administrative history of France and England in the Middle Ages, the rise of the French monarchy and of the English Parliament, the policy of the medieval German emperors, the clash of religious, political, and social forces in the revolt of the Netherlands, the historical significance of the English civil war, the nature of Prussian absolutism, the internal and external aspects of the French Revolution, the forces affecting German and Italian unification—these developments were studied in detail and with great thoroughness. Their treatment was placed on secure documentary foundations; they were divested of myth and legend and presented with practical common sense in a so-

---

[18] See Peter Rassow, "Deutsche Geschichtsquellen des 19. und 20. Jahrhunderts," *Die Historische Kommission bei der Bayerischen Akademie der Wissenschaften* (Goettingen, 1958), pp. 181-89.

ber light. The amount of new material which was found and published in this period was truly impressive and has formed the basis for all further research. Moreover, in all the studies by professional historians high standards of techniques were maintained; indeed techniques and methods were even refined. Nevertheless, the fact remains that the historians who in the twentieth century before the outbreak of World War I were regarded to be the leaders in their fields and who dominated the scholarly scene did not produce works that contained new interpretations or that made the past meaningful to the present.[19]

Thus, the great bulk of historical work done in the first years of the twentieth century shows that the concepts and views of the previous century were maintained and rigidified. Historical scholarship did not become broader; if anything it became narrower. To a certain extent this development was also a sign of the impact of the rise of the natural and social sciences. If a few historians felt that historical scholarship ought to learn from these new sciences and that it ought to have as its aim the discovery of scientific laws, the majority believed that it was necessary to keep history separate from the natural sciences and that historical scholarship had its own aims and methods. History should be maintained, therefore, in the forms in which it had been established in the nineteenth century. Advocates of this traditionalism could draw support from discussions on the theory of history that went on among the philosophers.

To philosophers, the position of history in the system of scientific endeavors represented a crucial problem. Although the subordination of history to moral philosophy had ended with the nineteenth century, history and philosophy remained connected in the sense that both were regarded as means by which man could achieve awareness of his nature as well as of his responsibility. Thus the rise of a positivistic outlook which subjected all phenomena—whether those of the physical nature or those of the mind—to laws of causality was a threat to the prevailing concepts of both philosophy and historical scholarship. In asserting that history had its own method, different from that of the natural sciences, the philosophers were also defending the position of philosophy, at least of that manner of philosophy in which they had grown up. The two philosophers in whose work

[19] Even favorably disposed scholars now make this point; see McNeil, *op. cit.,* or Krill, *op. cit.*

the maintenance of history as a science *sui generis* was a central issue were Dilthey and Croce.[20]

To Dilthey, man could grasp the reality of life and form a world view in three different ways: through his will, his feeling, and his thinking. In every world view elements of each of these three types of human attitudes could be found. But one prevailed—will, feeling, or thinking—and shaped the entire outlook of an individual or of a historical period. The result was the appearance in the course of history of a great variety of world views. Periods of history could be distinguished from each other because each of them had a different world view which was usually rationalized and reflected in a system of values. Dilthey's views opened the door to historical relativism. He did not believe that any of the possible types of attitudes to life was intrinsically better than the other. Neither did he share Hegel's or Comte's view that the various periods of history were tied together in a progressive development, nor did he think that psychology provided any explanation of the manner in which the periods of history succeeded each other. The demonstration of such necessary causal connections or of laws determining the historical process was not in the power of the historian nor was it his peculiar task. Because the mind of every individual had the potential of all possible attitudes to life, the historian was able to understand periods when different systems of values prevailed. And that was the historian's particular function. The method of history was that of understanding. The aim of the concerns of the historian was to increase awareness of the full potentialities of man.

Croce's concern was with social and political action rather than with Dilthey's interest in broadening man's knowledge of his own potentialities. Croce rejected the view that the historian could recreate the past and show "how it really happened." To Croce, a study of the past meant analysis of the forces working in the contemporary world. The past was always viewed through the mirror of the present. Thus, the consideration of the past raised man's awareness of his own position to the highest level of consciousness. In becoming aware of

[20] Among the many studies on Dilthey and Croce, I have found the treatment of Dilthey by Carlo Antoni, *Dallo storicismo alla sociologia* (Firenze, 1940) and the treatment of Croce by H. Stuart Hughes, *Consciousness and Society* (New York, 1958), particularly helpful; a study of Dilthey's historical theory is that by Hajo Holborn, "Dilthey and the Critique of Historical Reason," *Journal of the History of Ideas,* XI (1950), 93-118.

the aims and values which were adopted in the past, man learned that he could exert an active part in forming the future. Man should realize that his actions are not determined by forces outside his control; man could and should set the values to which the use of technical and material factors should be subordinated. Like Hegel, Croce regarded history as the realization of freedom. But in contrast to Hegel, who thought that the course of history followed a logical evolution with consciousness of freedom at its end, Croce believed that by viewing the events of the past in terms of means and ends—revealing the dualism of a world of given laws and causal connections on one hand and of consciously accepted values on the other—man gained the freedom to regulate the outside forces according to the ethical aims which they ought to serve.

Both Dilthey and Croce, despite the differences in their approaches, tried to show that history had its own aims and methods and, therefore, had the right to be called a science even if its methods and results did not come up to the specifications of the exact sciences. Historians became fully aware of the theories of Dilthey and Croce only after World War I. And then their views exerted a very strong influence on the direction of historical studies. In the years before World War I, however, probably the exact nature of these theories remained to the historians of limited interest. It was enough for historians to know that they could rely on the support of philosophy if they remained impervious to demands for adjusting history to the concepts of the natural sciences.[21] However, it can be suggested that even if the traditionalism in historical scholarship had lacked philosophical defenders, it would not have been overcome.

Political and social circumstances at the beginning of the twentieth century contributed decisively to the continued dependence on narrow and rigid concepts in historical studies. The time of the alliance between historical scholarship and progressive political forces had passed. Industrialization had split society into two hostile camps. On the one side there was the bourgeois society and state as they had come into existence in the nineteenth century. On the other side, there was the proletariat which had been organized and guided by Marx and his followers. Living politically and intellectually outside

[21] In the pre-World War I period, Heinrich Rickert, and his distinction between "Kulturwissenschaft" and "Naturwissenschaft" was probably better known than the much more important theories of Dilthey and Croce; see above, p. 108.

the bourgeois world, the proletariat aimed at the overthrow of the ruling group. The workers stood in strong opposition to the forces supporting the existing society and state. In the nineteenth century, many historians had been protagonists of the rising forces of nationalism and liberalism and they had played an active role in creating the state and the society which was under attack by the socialists. Moreover, as civil servants, as members of an educational system supported by and dependent on the state, the professors of history were expected to be defenders of the existing system and its natural advocates. If in Italy university professors of history were somewhat more enterprising than elsewhere, if they were more concerned with social issues and if they were more aware of economic factors as historical determinants, a reason might well be that in Italy the bourgeois revolution was not yet completed but was still being fought in the contest between the industrialized North and the feudal South. Thus the government, representing the industrial forces of the North, and in opposition to the reactionary South, was inclined to encourage a certain amount of social criticism. But in most other countries on the European continent historians had been transformed from advocates of progressive movements into defenders of the status quo.[22] And this development took place in such a way that historians did not have to change their basic concepts. If in the nineteenth century historians had been adherents of the national idea and had focused their work on the origins and the development of the national state, they were still expected in the early twentieth century to extoll the same idea, to consider the national state as the final political unit ethically superior to all other social formations—one that required a higher and fuller loyalty than personal bonds, political parties, social groupings, or intellectual movements. But whereas in the nineteenth century the insistence on the importance of the national idea had been an appeal for reform and change, in the twentieth century it meant an acknowledgment of the perfection of the existing social order and a defense of its ruling group. The prevailing traditionalism in historical scholarship becomes easier to understand if one realizes

[22] For a careful analysis of the German situation, see Krill, *op cit.;* for France see Pieter Geyl, *Napoleon For and Against* (New Haven, 1949), pp. 351 ff.; Guigue, *op. cit.;* and Georges Belloni, *Aulard: Historien de la Révolution Française* (Paris, 1949).

that the question of revising historical concepts and methods was not just an intellectual issue but that it did react upon the position that historians and historical scholarship had acquired in social life.

I began this chapter with a quotation in which at the beginning of the twentieth century Meinecke stated his belief that historical scholarship was declining from the heights of the nineteenth century. If this quotation is placed in its full context it emerges that Meinecke regarded the changed relation of history to political life as the crucial reason for this decline. "Whatever you may think about the achievements and the outlook of the last generation of German historical scholars," he wrote, "it is undeniable that they lacked a certain element of strength which the generations from Ranke to Treitschke possessed: they lacked that peculiar vitamin which had been produced by a symbiosis of scholarship and politics and which was no longer nourished by the political atmosphere after 1871. To express it crudely, history began to taste of the laboratory. The cultivation of traditional and fulfilled political ideas and ideals, even if carried out with loyal and warm sentiments, threatens to become pure convention; and the increasing rigidity of methods, which is now stressed, is not favorable to the production of new ideas." [23]

In the two or three decades before World War I the relation between European and American historical scholarship assumed a new character. With the professionalization of history personal contacts, which had constituted the bond between European and American scholars in the previous century, were augmented by contacts through organizations and institutions. Not infrequently the training of an American historian was completed by study in a European university. The exploration of European archives for sources relating to American history was systematically organized. American historians,

[23] "Wie man aber auch die Leistungen und Aussichten der letzten Generationen deutscher Geschichtswissenschaft einschaetzen moege, es bleibt dabei, dass sie ein gewisses starkes Etwas nicht gehabt haben, was den Generationen von Ranke bis Treitschke eigen war, jenes eigentuemliche Vitamin, das durch die Symbiose von Wissenschaft und Politik erzeugt wurde und in der politischen Luft seit 1871 nicht mehr voll gedieh. Um es etwas krass auszudruecken, es begann Laboratoriumsgeschmack anzunehmen. Denn die blosse Pflege ueberlieferter und erfuellter politischer Ideale, mochte sie in noch so treuer und warmer Gesinnung erfolgen, drohte zur Konvention herabzusinken, und die strengere Methodik, die sich jetzt verbreitete, konnte aus sich heraus neue Ideen nicht erzeugen." Meinecke, "Johan Gustav Droysen," *Staat und Persoenlichkeit*, p. 99.

although still in small numbers, made their appearances at the International Historical Congresses of Berlin in 1908 and London in 1912 and they took part in presenting papers.[24] This was the period in which American historians were most deeply impressed by the amount and the quality of the historical work done in Europe, and Americans looked upon the European procedure in historical training and research as a pattern closely to be imitated. Haskins' report about the Berlin International Congress reflects the view that American historical scholarship had still far to go to equal the European achievements. Haskins noted that the meeting had shown a "distinctly higher level than is reached in most of our American meetings."[25]

Despite the strength of these feelings of inferiority and discipleship toward European historical scholarship, differences arising from divergent social conditions not only continued but became even more pronounced. In America as in Europe the increasing attraction and importance of the natural sciences and the social sciences—of economics, sociology, and psychology—had its bearing upon the position of historical scholarship. But in contrast to Europe where, as we have seen, history was regarded as having its own methods and aims which were thought to be different from those of other fields of knowledge, in the United States the view that history was one of the social sciences and ought to contribute to the discovery of laws of human development had a much stronger appeal. The concept of scientific history that reflected this tendency of joining history to the social sciences was advanced at this time and gained great influence. The advocates of scientific history in America believed that they were elaborating on the ideas implied in the works of European historians. American historians believed in the possibility of an approach to history that combined the method of Ranke and the laws of Lamprecht. The refinements in historical method which Ranke had introduced were considered to have made historical research scientific, and the discovery of laws of development which Lamprecht demanded were believed to be the necessary consequence of the application of Ranke's scientific procedure. But no German historian, in-

[24] See the reports about these Congresses by Haskins, *op cit.*, and by Jameson, *op. cit.*; apparently about twenty American historians attended these Congresses.
[25] Haskins, *op. cit.*, p. 7.

deed, no European historian, would have accepted the notion that Ranke's concept of the individuality of each historical period could ever be compatible with Lamprecht's laws of causality. Scientific history was an American creation.[26]

There are historical reasons for the fact that concepts of history concerned with the laws of social development exerted an attraction in the United States which they did not have to the same extent in Europe. In Europe the various academic fields of knowledge had emerged from a common context, a system of philosophy that justified the division of the search for truth into single branches of scholarship; each discipline had its place and rank in the hierarchy of knowledge. When in Europe issues like those of the true character of history were debated, it was natural to discuss them on the basis of theoretical and philosophical considerations. In American educational institutions the consideration of philosophical connections had less influence, and usefulness provided the criterion for determining the place given to a field of knowledge. It was almost inevitable that in the course of developments this tendency of placing practical considerations above theoretical ones continued and even became stronger. Because the aim of American colleges was to give their students a general education that would fit them into any kind of activity rather than training them for a specialized profession, those fields of knowledge that were helpful in understanding and mastering the outside world seemed particularly valuable. In addition, colleges and universities were dependent on private support. It is not difficult to understand that the argument of immediate practical results and of direct usefulness far outweighed other considerations. If, at the beginning of the twentieth century, the position of history in the curriculum of American colleges and universities was to be maintained, historians had to assert that history was one of the social sciences, and that like other social sciences, it could provide practical knowledge by revealing the underlying pattern in the movement of social life. Although external circumstances furthered in America the conception of history as a social science, the hold which this view had over a great number of American historians would not have been so

26 See above, pp. 98ff.; of particular interest for these questions is the article by Georg Iggers, "The Image of Ranke in American and German Historical Thought," *History and Theory,* II (1962), 17-40.

firm had not the image of a progressive historical pattern corresponded to deeply felt beliefs rooted in the American experience of history. Nothing that had happened since the second half of the nineteenth century was sufficient to shake the conviction of American historians that their history represented an unbroken advance. Even the Civil War appeared not as a social crisis but rather as a significant step on the road to further progress. Industrialization did not produce a rigidification of the class structure not a separation of society in two hostile groups. It had not frightened the wealthier classes into political reaction. The ideas of democracy and liberalism remained unquestioned. Thus the break between historical scholarship and political progressivism that occurred in Europe did not take place in the United States. Through their knowledge of the pattern of the past American historians could have few doubts that their works served to build a better future.[27]

Because many American historians regarded history as a branch of the social sciences—and as such, as an instrument for social improvement—they were eager to apply to the interpretation of the past all the tools that the social sciences used: the past was not only formed by what happened in the political sphere, but also determined by economic factors, psychological attitudes, etc. The result was a revision of the traditional views of American history. By showing the impact of the struggle with the wilderness on the formation of social concepts, Turner revealed the uniqueness of American history; by investigating the connection between economic interests and political actions, Beard reduced the Founding Fathers to human proportions. A point of great practical importance was that some American historians demonstrated the need for further social and political progress by showing that the foundations of the American past were due to particular interests and unique circumstances, and that they could have for later generations no absolute value or binding character. The permanent validity of their historical theses might be questionable, but the direction toward the future gave to the work of American historians on American history a political interest and vitality that the work of their European contemporaries no longer had.

But this freshness and irreverence did not extend to the work American historians did in the field of European history. Probably

[27] For details, see above, pp. 171 ff.

the awe that European historiography inspired impeded attempts to embark on new interpretations and to underline or broaden the scheme within which the European historians were working. The few significant contributions to European history by American historians—for instance those of Haskins—were strictly within the framework which European historical scholarship had set and they show historical views and concepts entirely compatible with those of European historians.[28]

For American work on European history, a new era began only with World War I. It almost appears that the political importance the United States had gained in World War I was reflected in the greater intellectual independence of the American historians toward the problems of European history. Like European historians, American historians also made the causes of the outbreak of World War I a central theme of their studies in modern history. They explored Wilson's pronouncements that the outbreak of World War I revealed the corruptness and bankruptcy of European diplomacy and their writings demonstrated a breadth that European studies lacked. American historians treated the outbreak of the war not from the point of view of a single nation. To them, the European scene was a single unit and therefore every action was evaluated with respect to its repercussions on the policy of all other nations. American historians were eager to study the working of the history of the European state system rather than the policy of an individual nation. This approach gave to the works of Fay and Schmitt on the origins of World War I a comprehensiveness and authenticity that none of the European historical works on this subject could claim. The independence from European patterns that American historians of European history gained after World War I gave them the courage to apply some of the social science concepts that had proved their usefulness in American history to the European scene as well as to broaden the investigation of diplomatic events by exploring the extent to which they were determined by public opinion, economic interests, and the social structure of a society. Although in the early twentieth century European writers had named the contemporary period the age of imperialism, American historians after World War I gave to this concept a reality and concreteness; the diplomacy of imperialism appeared as a

28 For details, see above, pp. 38 ff. and 256 ff.

clearly distinct, unique period in the history of diplomacy. But these American studies were undertaken at the time[29] when the European historiographical scene had been changed under the impact of World War I.

[29] The first edition of William L. Langer's *The Diplomacy of Imperialism* appeared in 1935.

## ๏ 3 ๏

# THREE TWENTIETH CENTURY HISTORIANS:
# MEINECKE, BLOCH, CHABOD

World War I has been the great divide that sets the world in which we live—with its global policy, its rise of non-European nations, its transformation of life through science and technical advances, its rapid changes of customs and habits, and its new forms of social organization—apart from all previous centuries.

The impact of these changes on all aspects of intellectual life and therefore also on the development of historical scholarship is undeniable. Nevertheless, although a new chapter in historical studies begins in this period, historiography was not set suddenly on a new course with the end of World War I; the development was gradual rather than sudden and abrupt. New historiographical tendencies that became strong and dominant after the war had their roots in previous developments. Moreover, there were a number of factors that had an almost retarding effect on the development of historiography and contributed to the maintenance of traditional attitudes.

Strangely enough, one of the retarding factors was the attention given to a new complex of problems raised by the war: the war-guilt question. Because the question of the causes of World War I was couched in terms of moral responsibility and guilt, it was almost unavoidable that European historians, in contrast to those of the United States, treated this question with a national bias—from the point of view of their own country. Thus the war-guilt question, with which historians in all European countries became intensively concerned, reinforced the traditional tendency of thinking about historical events in a national framework. Moreover, in order to refute the thesis of Germany's exclusive responsibility for the war, the German government opened the archives of the German Foreign Office and arranged for a publication of the chief diplomatic documents from the foundation of the Empire in 1871 to the outbreak of World War I in 1914.[1] Most of the other European governments, some hesitantly

---

[1] For the origin of the various documentary publications connected with the outbreak of World War I, see Mario Toscano's *Lezioni di storia dei trattati e politica internazionale* (Torino, 1958).

and slowly, felt that they were forced to follow the German example. The overwhelming amount of sensational diplomatic source material that became available in the Twenties encouraged students of modern history to continue work in the channels of traditional diplomatic history.

Moreover, there was a significant time lag between World War I and the full realization of the impact of this event: that it meant the end of an epoch in history and the beginning of a new one. For some time it appeared that the outbreak of the war had confirmed the validity of the political concepts and ideas of the nineteenth century; the vitality of the ideas of parliamentary democracy, on which the political systems of England and France were built, seemed to have been proved. Moreover, the most striking political change brought about by the war was the extension of the principle of national self-determination toward eastern Europe. The conjunction of liberalism and nationalism which had favored the rise of historical studies in the nineteenth century formed the justification for the political existence of those new independent states which emerged from the collapse of the Austrian, Russian and Ottoman Empires. As long as the peoples of these new national states had been under foreign rule, historical studies had played their part in keeping alive among them the feeling of nationality and of belonging to a separate political entity. Now, after they had achieved independence, historical scholarship was to serve the purpose of strengthening the coherence of these states. If in the first half of the nineteenth century western European governments had promoted historical scholarship in order to widen and control civic education, the same policy was pursued in the new national states of eastern Europe. Historical studies were encouraged but they developed strictly in the national framework of nineteenth century historical scholarship. The development of the nation and of its road to political independence were the central themes of the historical work done in the newly founded states.

In order to commemorate fifty years of the *Revue historique* its editors issued two volumes of essays in which historians described the status of historical scholarship in the different countries of the world.[2] The articles dealing with those countries created after World War I show that historical scholarship there was organized almost strictly

[2] Bibliothèque de la *Revue historique, Histoire et historiens depuis cinquante ans,* 2 vols. (Paris, 1927).

according to the pattern that German, French, and Italian historians had set in the nineteenth century. The picture given of the activities of historical scholars all over the world is striking. In each country long series of editions of sources were underway. Several scholarly historical periodicals were published and a great number of historical societies flourished. But despite the fact that these two volumes give the impression of the steady expansion of historical scholarship, the reader is left with mixed feelings. The organization of activities, the collecting of facts, the editing of sources seems to overshadow the search for new interpretations, new concepts, or new ideas. It was probably unavoidable that these commemorative volumes leave an impression of sterility because their intention was to point out the tangible results and achievements of the past rather than the still uncertain prospects of the future.

Actually when the commemorative volumes of the *Revue historique* appeared in 1927, it was already apparent that many historians wanted to strike out in new directions. The country where the need for a revision of history was earliest and most strongly felt was Germany. There a questioning of traditional attitudes was the almost necessary result of a defeat that had revealed the weaknesses of the political system established in 1871 and the shallowness of the values it embodied. But when in the political and social unrest of the Twenties and Thirties the hope of a return to the stability of the prewar world diminished and finally disappeared, an awareness of the limitations and confinements of the traditional conceptual framework of history spread to other countries. There was widespread recognition that the traditional framework ought to be changed and enlarged. Certainly this did not mean that the soundness of the critical method adopted in the nineteenth century was questioned, nor did it mean that recognized historical procedures were to be abandoned. But it was felt that an exclusive concentration on political history was rather misleading, that the conduct of politics and the nature of political events were dependent on a wider context formed by a great variety of factors. History was much more than past politics; in order to understand an epoch the historian had to analyze its religious beliefs and intellectual values and movements, the economic conditions, and the structure of social life. Certainly such views about the task of the historian were not original, but it was significant that in the period after World War I the advocates of such a broadened concept of history became the acknowledged leaders of historical scholarship. No historian of the twentieth century ever acquired that public esteem which the prominent historians of the nineteenth century had enjoyed. Nevertheless, there were now a number of historians who have been recognized generally as masters in their field and they deserve the name of great historians. Meinecke in Germany, Bloch in France, and Chabod in Italy exerted decisive influence upon the development of historical scholarship in their countries as well as throughout Europe. If historical studies became wider and extended to new fields, it is greatly due to the influence these men exerted through their teaching and their works. It might be well to describe, therefore, the evolution of historical scholarship in the twentieth century in terms of the ideas these men brought to the writing of history.

Although all three—Meinecke, Bloch, Chabod—were convinced of the need for a broadening of the outlook of the historian and a revitalization of historical scholarship, the differences among them were great. Almost inevitably their views about the course which historical studies ought to take were built on the particular traditions of historical scholarship in their respective countries. Above all, Meinecke, Bloch, and Chabod belonged to different generations. Meinecke, born in 1862, was twenty-four years older than Bloch, and although Meinecke's work began to achieve wider recognition and influence only after World War I, he had, when the war began, already been the editor of the *Historische Zeitschrift* for twenty years, he had published the first of his three great works, and in 1914, he had been called to the most prestigious historical chair in Germany, that of the University of Berlin. Marc Bloch and Chabod were separated by a shorter span—sixteen years. But this span is the more significant because these were crucial years; their intellectual development took place in two very different political and intellectual milieus. Thus, Bloch and Chabod were men of different generations. Marc Bloch's training was just completed in 1914. His maturity and achievements belong entirely to the interwar years: *Les Rois thaumaturges* appeared in 1924, *Les Caractères originaux de l'histoire rurale française* in 1931, and, in 1939, the first volume of his great book on *La Société féodale*. The *Annales* of which Bloch was a founder and editor and in which many of his most seminal ideas were originally stated appeared first in 1929.[3] Chabod published some distinguished work in the interwar years, but he was recognized as the leading figure in the world of Italian historical scholarship only after World War II. From 1947, he was simultaneously Professor of History at the University of Rome, Director of the Historical Institute in Naples,[4] and editor of the *Rivista storica italiana.* In 1951 there finally appeared the work in which he realized his ideas about the historian's task: the first volume of his *Storia della politica estera italiana dal 1870 al 1896.*[5]

Throughout Meinecke's entire life[6] a determining factor in his historical thinking was the close connection between philosophy and history which had been maintained in Germany even after history had become an independent subject. Meinecke grew up in surroundings that were still very similar to the Biedermeier of the beginning of the nineteenth century: a modest, almost sparse manner of living, but a material security that made the acceptance of the values of religion and of an idealist philosophy easy as well as firm. In the decisive years of Meinecke's intellectual development there occurred a rapid, almost frightening social change in all ways of life: the rush of the German Empire into industrialization. The contrast between the social still-life of earlier times with its freedom for the development of an individual's personality and the restlessness of a highly competitive society in which the individual became a cog in a wheel was an underlying problem in all of Meinecke's works. The first of Meinecke's three great historical books, *Welbürgertum und Nationalstaat,* published in 1907, viewed intellectual and political devel-

---

[3] When the *Annales d'histoire économique et sociale* appeared, the *Revue de synthèse historique,* which Berr edited and to which Bloch and Febvre had frequently contributed, was transformed into the *Revue de synthèse.*

[4] Istituto Italiano per gli Studi Storici.

[5] The subtitle of this first volume is *Le Premesse;* no other volume has appeared.

[6] Meinecke has published two volumes of memoirs: *Erlebtes 1862-1901* (Leipzig, 1941) and *Strassburg, Freiburg, Berlin 1901-1919* (Stuttgart, 1949). Since his death, Hans Herzfeld, Carl Hinrichs, and Walther Hofer have edited his works; between 1958 and 1962, six volumes have appeared. My quotations will refer to this edition, but since this edition is not complete, it is sometimes necessary to refer to earlier editions and collections. The *Werke* have long introductions that contain bibliographical references. An English treatment of Meinecke's ideas is Richard W. Sterling's *Ethics in a World of Power: The Political Ideas of Friedrich Meinecke* (Princeton, 1958); this book contains a bibliography of Meinecke's works and of works on him.

opments in nineteenth century Germany as an interrelated process. The achievement of national unity and of a national state represented a necessary historical event, the attainment of an absolute and final value. But a German national state was necessary not only because it provided material advantages: protection against other powers and greater room for the development of economic life. The national idea was also the result of an intellectual process: the individual accepted the necessity of a national state because he had realized that his intellectual and spiritual potentialities could be fully developed only in the context of a united nation. Meinecke was convinced of a harmony existing between idea and form, freedom and order, intellectual life and politics. Meinecke expected that by reaching out toward intellectual history historical scholarship would regain the intellectual impact it had once possessed. "German historical scholarship must reestablish contact with the great forces of political and cultural life. It must throw itself more courageously into philosophy and politics; only then will it be able to develop its own essence of being universal and national at the same time." [7] Although in its emphasis on intellectual history *Weltbürgertum und Nationalstaat* was new, it was still tied to the concept of national development as the central subject and final aim of history. But for Meinecke this was not only a political but also a cultural and intellectual process. The well-being of a people, he believed, was based on the harmony of intellectual and political forces, and his book was aimed at effecting a more intimate collaboration between the life of the mind and the life of politics. But Meinecke's pre-World War I optimism that this harmony could be achieved was broken by the war's outcome. The dualism between the world of material interests and forces, the world of causation, and the world of ethical norms and ideals, the world of values, he came to regard as irreconcilable. The work of the historian became now more limited in its aims; it served less the world of action and more the world of thought. Historical insight was to deepen man's awareness of this irreconcilable dualism and of the responsi-

[7] ". . . dass die deutsche Geschichtsforschung, ohne auf die wertvollen Ueberlieferungen ihres methodischen Betriebes zu verzichten, doch wiederum zu freier Regung und Fuehlung mit den grossen Maechtem des Staats- und Kulturlebens sich erheben muesse, dass sie, ohne Schaden zu nehmen an ihrem eigenen Wesen und Zwecke, mutiger baden duerfe in Philosophie wie in Politik, ja dass sie erst dadurch ihr eigenstes Wesen entwickeln koenne, universal und national zugleich zu sein." Meinecke, *Weltbürgertum und Nationalstaat* (*Werke,* vol. V), pp. 1-2.

bility which man carried with his decisions. That is fundamentally the theme of the *Idee der Staatsräson*,[8] Meinecke's next great work, which appeared in 1924. This book is not the presentation of a development that has a beginning and an end and a solution; rather, it is a collection of essays on the conflict between ethics and politics in the various periods of European history since the beginnings of modern times. The last of Meinecke's great works, *Die Entstehung des Historismus,* is the most theoretical and abstract of the three. Meinecke believed that in every human being and in every action and thought of human beings, there is a unique, individual element that distinguishes him and them from all others; the task of the historian is concerned with this element, with individuality and uniqueness. According to Meinecke, the discovery of the existence of individuality was one of the greatest intellectual revolutions that had ever taken place, and his book is devoted to the description of this revolution. The *Entstehung des Historismus* is a very personal book. With it Meinecke seemed to have turned away from the problems of the political and social world and to pursue the origin of his own historical view, to write an *apologia pro vita sua.* It may not be without significance that this work was completed under a totalitarian regime where as soon as a person went beyond the private and isolated sphere of his own intellectual musings he entered a directed and controlled world. Perhaps because the *Entstehung des Historismus* is such a personal book a number of themes that are characteristic of Meinecke's theoretical ideas about history stand out with particular clarity. First of all, in this book Meinecke tried to contribute to the solution of a problem with which Dilthey and Croce in philosophical discussions had been concerned since the beginning of the century. Meinecke's thesis is that because the unique and the individual is the concern of history, the aim and methods of history can have nothing to do with those of the natural sciences. Meinecke also implied that there are no immanent tendencies of development or progress in history; there are no forces which use man as an instrument: the center of history, the object of historical study, is always man in his unique and individual nature. And if this might be considered to lead to a loss of all criteria of judgment, to a relativism of values, Meinecke suggested that this relativism would be restrained by the newly

[8] This work has been translated into English with the somewhat misleading title *Machiavellism,* and with a still more misleading introduction.

gained revelation of the immense and inexhaustible wealth of individual phenomena, by the religious awe that this revelation excites, and by the resulting concern for preserving the integrity of the unique and individual aspects of life.

The fame Meinecke's works have gained can be easily explained: they, particularly the *Weltbürgertum und Nationalstaat* and the *Idee der Staatsräson,* are concerned with issues that are both important and disquieting to every thinking person. In showing the manner in which men of different times took a stand on these problems, Meinecke threw new light on the past and at the same time made history a means for self-examination. The significance of the past for the present was extended far beyond the sphere of political causality. Thus, first of all, Meinecke's influence on the development of historical scholarship worked toward a widening of the material with which the historian deals. Political and social reality were imbedded in a world of ideas, and historical investigation was incomplete without a discussion of the connection between the world of ideas and the world of political and social life. Meinecke's concept of ideas was different from that of Ranke, to whom ideas were "thoughts of God" existing in a sphere above men. In Meinecke's view, the idea, the spiritual element, came to life and existed only through man. Each human being was born into an intellectual atmosphere, a world of ideas which he slowly and gradually absorbed, but because each man was an individual he also brought a new element into this intellectual atmosphere: it was continuously changing. Meinecke was no philosopher nor did he claim to be one.[9] His views about man's relation to the world of ideas were a vision about the working of historical forces rather than a careful defined or definable theory. But the necessary result of his works and influence was to place intellectual history into the center of historical studies. In analyzing and explaining the thought and actions of leading figures of the past, Meinecke demonstrated the fruitfulness of a genetic approach to which he gave great methodical precision. Starting with a general picture of the accepted concepts and ideas of the time, the historian had to show to what extent the individual absorbed them, through his surroundings and through his education; and then, proceeding by careful analysis

[9] The great attention that recent studies have given to Meinecke's essays on theoretical questions is somewhat regrettable; Meinecke's historical works, not his theoretical statements, are important for the development of historiography.

from one written document to the next or, in the case of an intellectual figure, from one of his works to the following, the historian would be able to retrace the process in which an individual adopted or modified the prevailing views and ideas and acquired an individual voice and attitude. For Meinecke and, as we shall see, also for Bloch and Chabod, each period had its own intellectual structure. Man was not merely a maker of political events; his mind was the lens which permitted the historian to view the characteristics of this intellectual structure. But by recognizing the necessity of relating the explanation of individual actions and attitudes to an over-all structure, Meinecke implied that history could not be kept within a national framework. Perhaps the most significant feature of Meinecke's works is the abandonment of the idea of the national state as a permanent value toward which the consideration of the past ought to be oriented. In *Weltbürgertum und Nationalstaat* he wrote that history ought to be "universal and national." Later he might have said purely that history must be universal, although his concept of universal history did not go beyond the European horizon.

While in Germany history and philosophy had been closely allied in the past and remained allied throughout the nineteenth century, in France such a traditional alliance existed between history and geography. The *philosophes,* critical of an educational system that taught exclusively the classics and ethical theories, demanded instruction in useful knowledge, and geography and history were regarded as necessary and crucial in any practical education.[10] Thus history and geography were introduced into the schedule of the colleges after the Revolution; in the course of the nineteenth century, in contrast to the classics, which were identified with conservatism and reaction, history and geography were stressed in educational reforms of all republican governments.

As the son of a distinguished professor of the Sorbonne, Marc Bloch was by birthright a member of the intellectual elite of the Third Republic.[11] But as he himself said, he was also formed by the

---

[10] See note 6 on p. 324. France is still a leading country in geographical studies.

[11] A complete bibliography of Marc Bloch's works will be found in his *Mélanges historiques,* vol. II (Paris, 1963), pp. 1031-1104. The two volumes of *Mélanges* represent a collection of Bloch's scholarly articles; they do not include reviews. Of Bloch's books, three have been translated into English: *L'Étrange défaite* under the title *Strange Defeat* (1949), with an introduction by Sir Maurice

event that stabilized the Third Republic by bringing the political and intellectual leaders together in a common cause and a common struggle: the Dreyfus affair. The Dreyfus affair might have awakened in Bloch awareness and concern for a problem which at this time some of the greatest of his contemporaries—Freud, Max Weber, Pareto—began to investigate and which has remained in the center of the study of the social sciences: the limitations of reason and rationality, the strength of the unconscious, the irrational basis of our structured world. For the Dreyfus affair demonstrated the extent to which traditional, irrational, and emotional factors remained powerful, irremovable, and indestructible. To Bloch, threads from different periods of the past—some rationally based beliefs and convictions, some attitudes and patterns adopted by tradition rather than reason—were woven together in the present. "Le passé command le présent" is one of Bloch's guiding principles. Conditions once formed, beliefs once held, remain realities even when the factors to which they owed their existence have disappeared. That a procedure has lost the rational function to which it owed its origin does not mean that the procedure no longer has a hold over the minds of men or that it is without influence or significance. In his three great works, Bloch touched upon this problem. In *Les Rois thaumaturges* he explained how the belief that the kings of France and England were endowed with healing powers had come about in an almost accidental manner. But Bloch also showed the extent to which this belief became part and parcel of the concept of royalty and an influential element in strengthening the hold that royalty extended over its subjects. The thesis of Bloch's masterpiece is well indicated by its title: *Les Caractères originaux de l'histoire rurale française.* He showed that the forms of French agricultural life have been determined less by legal arrangements, changes in law, and technical innovations than by the

---

Powicke; *Apologie pour l'histoire ou Métier d'historien* under the title *The Historian's Craft* (1953), with an introduction by J. R. Strayer; and *La Société féodale* under the title *Feudalism* (1961). Quotations from these works are given on the basis of these translations. The biographical literature on Marc Bloch is not extensive; next to the introductions of his posthumously published works, see Charles-Edward Perrins, "L'Oeuvre historique de Marc Bloch," *Revue historique,* CXCIX-CC (1948) and the "Souvenirs et témoignages" in *Annales d'histoire sociale,* (1945) and *Mémorial des années 1939-1945,* Publications de la Faculté des Lettres de l'Université de Strasbourg (Paris, 1947).

persistence of the division of land and organization of land tenure established in the earliest times of medieval history. For his analysis of the world of the Middle Ages in his book on *La Société féodale* he made use of an astounding variety of sources—legal documents, narrative accounts, theological writings, literary works, epic poems. His principal interest was to clarify the relation between feudal ideology and economic structure. He showed that they were not only interconnected but that they reinforced each other, helping to maintain and to rigidify the feudal system. Bloch's works are full of details—descriptions of ceremonies and social customs, of legal procedures and administrative practices, of the tools used in the Middle Ages and technical innovations—but his writings are most illuminating when they analyze the sensitive point at which purposeful, rational action is limited by accepted customs and beliefs.

As all of Bloch's writings show, he believed that political and diplomatic histories could not go below the surface of the past because they dealt only with a partial aspect of history. "Rightly or wrongly, it seems clear to me that the old concepts of a rhetorical and political history have ceased to correspond to what people expect from our discipline today. If you want concrete examples: in the developments of the thirteenth century, the prohibition of communion in both kinds to laymen and the general adoption of auricular confession, the minting of large silver coins and the beginnings of the minting of gold constitute more decisive, more significant, and more meaningful facts than the maneuvers of Angevin diplomacy." [12] In his little treatise on the *Métier d'historien,* Bloch postulated a "broadened and deepened history which some of us—more every day—have begun to conceive." [13]

A historical approach that would take account of all aspects of man's concerns and activities and thus reveal human life in its com-

[12] "À tort ou à raison, je puis bien juger que les vieilles perspectives d'une histoire oratoire et politique ont cessé de répondre à ce que les hommes espèrent aujourd'hui de nos disciplines—considérer, si l'on veut, que, dans l'évolution du XIIIe siècle, l'interdiction aux laiques de la communion sous les deux espèces et la généralisation de la confession auriculaire, la frappe des grosses monnaies d'argent et les débuts de le frappe de l'or constituent des faits plus décisifs, plus profonds, plus esplicatifs que les finesses de la diplomatie angevine." Marc Bloch et Lucien Febvre, "Pour le renouveau de l'enseignement historique: Le Problème de l'agrégation," *Annales d'histoire économique et sociale,* IX (1937), 124.
[13] *The Historian's Craft,* p. 18.

pleteness and entirety had been propounded by Henri Berr at the turn of the century. In Berr's *Revue de synthèse historique,* which was hailed as the "Trojan Horse" in the camp of traditional historical scholarship,[14] Bloch's friend Lucien Febvre wrote some of his biting reviews of the works of political and diplomatic historians; and Bloch himself published in this periodical some of his most important articles. In 1929 when the number of scholars working along the lines of a broadened concept of history had considerably increased, Bloch and Lucien Febvre founded the *Annales*[15] so that there would be an organ where the results of researches in every facet of the past could be published. Bloch was not afraid that concern with life in its most varied aspects—food and nourishment, money, techniques of agriculture, techniques of trade, customs, superstitions— would fragment history into a number of different specialized fields so that in the future there would be historians of food, historians of coins and money, historians of science and techniques, etc. To Bloch, this danger was negligible because he believed that since such activities were pursued by man they had to pass through the human mind and therefore they formed the elements that constituted his mental outlook. In assuming a close interaction between social activities and mental processes, Bloch followed the most influential French sociologist of this time, Durkheim. Durkheim maintained that social structures produced a collective consciousness. Thus the concepts of the individual were tied to types of imagery that constituted this collective consciousness. The phenomena of the outside world, the institutions, the regulations, the manners established by man to serve his needs had no immanent, automatic logic but must pass through human consciousness which remains the moving force in social life. Although Bloch was deeply interested in statistical details and technical developments—the development of prices, agricultural tools, etc., etc.—he always viewed such data in their relation to the human mind. Bloch postulated a broadening of factual history because such a widened outlook of the past was necessary for an understanding of the decisive factor in the development of history, the

---

14 So called by Lucien Febvre in *Combats pour l'histoire,* p. 394.

15 Lucien Febvre's two collections of essays and reviews, *Combats pour l'histoire* (Paris, 1953) and *Pour une histoire à part entière* (Paris, 1962) are characteristic for the views of the circle to which Bloch belonged; Bloch and Febvre were close friends. On Febvre, see Palmer A. Throop, "Lucien Febvre," in *Some Twentieth Century Historians,* ed. S. W. Halperin, pp. 277-98.

human element. The subject of history was "man in his social group."[16]

Investigation of the collective psychology of a historical period was not a new or an original idea; that this was the task of the historian had been frequently stated since the beginning of the twentieth century. Bloch was unique in the scientific precision with which he worked to achieve this task. Although he was aware of differences between history and the natural sciences, he belonged to those who were convinced that the historian could learn from the natural scientists. And Bloch was particularly aware that the terminology of the historian was unnecessarily vague and ambiguous; by achieving exactitude in terminology he believed that the results of historical investigations—even if they did not lead to historical laws—might become applicable to the construction of a system of knowledge about the social world. In pursuing this aim Bloch became a powerful influence in introducing the comparative method into history. Bloch himself probably would have said that he was only following in Pirenne's footsteps, but the fact remains that Bloch not only claimed theoretically the need for comparative history in a famous speech at the International Historical Congress in Oslo[17] but he practiced this method in most of his works. He was not interested in comparing similarities that might appear in the developments of different civilizations. His concern was the comparison of institutions that existed in different societies but in the same civilization. Although these institutions might be subsumed under the same general term because they had a common origin and were formed by similar experiences and circumstances, they possessed particularities and showed differences. A striking example of the usefulness of the comparative method was his work on feudalism. Feudalism was a general European phenomenon. But the concept can acquire precise meaning only if the form which feudalism took in England and France is not regarded as a form which possessed *all* the qualities belonging to the meaning of this term. It must be realized that although English or French feudalism had common features they were modified in each country by special circumstances. Because for a historian concerned chiefly or exclusively with national history the feudalism of an

16 See Perrins, "L'Oeuvre historique de Marc Bloch," *op. cit.*, pp. 175 ff.
17 "Pour une histoire comparée des sociétés européennes," now reprinted in Bloch's *Mélanges*, vol. I, pp. 16-40.

individual country becomes almost necessarily identical with the concept itself, it is imperative for the historian to go beyond the framework of national history in order to form terms of general applicabil-
ity. A distinction of the general from the particular, of the basic from
the accidental, can be attained only by confronting the forms of feudalism in one country with those it took in other countries. Such empirical and pragmatic procedure should produce a terminology that is
not only applicable to an individual phenomenon but that permits
statements about society in general. But to Bloch, the primary purpose of the comparative method was not to formulate a general system of social concepts; rather he believed that by distinguishing
sharply between the general and the particular features of social phenomena it was possible to come to a clear view of the individual element. Demonstration of the individual element and the human factor
in the social world remained for Bloch the fundamental goal of history. In the last years of his life when the Nazis had occupied France
and their triumph threatened all rational purposes and human values, he became more aware than ever before of the national roots in
his existence. "I was born in France, I have drunk of the waters of her
culture, I have made her past my own, I breathe freely only in her
climate." [18] Bloch's mind turned to the planning of a work in which
he would evoke the true image of France. But even then he remained faithful to his scientific creed that the image of France could
emerge in all its individuality only through a comparative framework, and the work that he planned was a "history of French society
in the structure of European civilization." [19]

Federico Chabod, the leading figure in Italian historical scholarship in the twentieth century,[20] was closer in years to Bloch than
Bloch was to Meinecke. Nevertheless, in the development of historiography Meinecke and Bloch belong more closely together than
Chabod and Bloch. As different as were Meinecke's and Bloch's
views about theoretical questions of history, for both of them the
common point of departure had been the experience of the rise of
the natural and social sciences. When Chabod began to study history

[18] *Strange Defeat*, p. 3.
[19] *The Historian's Craft*, p. xiv.
[20] After Chabod's death a number of historians evaluated the various aspects of
Chabod's work in the *Rivista storica italiana*, LXXII (December 1950); furthermore, see Gennaro Sasso's *Profilo di Federico Chabod* (Bari, 1961), which contains also an extensive bibliography.

—after World War I—these problems were hardly novel. Chabod's work presupposed the contributions Meinecke and Bloch had made to the development of historiography. Chabod studied with Meinecke in Berlin, and, although he was a great admirer of the work and the person of the German historian, Chabod felt that Meinecke's concept of the role of ideas in history was somewhat romantic, that Meinecke had not entirely freed himself from the eggshells of the Rankean assumption that ideas had a life of their own. Chabod wrote that Meinecke lacked a quality particularly essential for the historian of ideas —precision in distinguishing "that one thing is a fact and another thing is awareness of that fact." [21] When Bloch reviewed Meinecke's *Historismus* he raised rather similar objections.[22] And it has been said that in the later years of his life Chabod moved close to the school of the *Annales*. But if so, Chabod's adherence to the views of Bloch, Lucien Febvre, and their followers was not without reservations. Chabod always stressed that political factors were more decisive than all other factors of history. Moreover, Chabod believed that there were limitations to what technical precision and scientific exactitude could achieve in history; to the historian, intuition was essential and "no logic and no appeal to concepts can ever be a substitute for intuition." [23] Chabod's perceptive awareness of the contemporary trends in historical scholarship, as well as of the independent intellectual position at which he had arrived, is clearly proved in the remarkable article in which he summarized his extensive studies on Milan in the age of Charles V.[24] On one hand, the article reveals Chabod's skepticism about the views of those who ascribe much influence to the working of ideas in history. Chabod recognized the hold which the imperial idea had on the mind of Charles V but he demonstrated that the actual conduct of policy by Charles V was determined by the requirements of the political situation. On the other hand, Chabod's

21 "Manca la chiara precisazione—essenziale proprio per lo storico delle idee— che una cosa è il 'fatto', e altra cosa la 'coscienza' del fatto." Chabod on Meinecke in *Rivista storica italiana*, LVII (1955), 284.
22 See Bloch's review of Meinecke's *Historismus* in *Annales d'Histoire sociale*, I (1939), 429-30.
23 ". . . che è, sempre, il fattore decisivo per lo storico, cioè il suo intuito, che nessuna logica e nessun appello a 'concetti' potranno mai sostituire." Chabod on Meinecke, *op. cit.*, p. 286.
24 Among Chabod's various studies on Milan in the sixteenth century, see particularly the essay "L'Epoca di Carlo V" in the Fondazione Treccani's *Storia di Milano*, vol. IX (Milano, 1961).

article also represented a rejection of the attitude of those who regarded political history as superficial because they believed that political events were moved by other, nonpolitical forces. Chabod made full use of the material about the financing of Spanish policy that Braudel had assembled but Chabod did not assume that bankers were the guiding force behind Charles V's enterprises. Chabod showed that the bankers appeared in Charles V's policy only when they were urgently needed; considerations of financial limitations never entered the emperor's political designs. Moreover, Chabod avoided explanations that referred to inherent or unavoidable trends. His treatment of the reason for Charles V's establishment of a centralized administration for the various Spanish possessions in northern Italy is a case in point. Chabod did not characterize this administrative reform as a victory of the idea of the modern state over obsolete feudal forms of social and economic life. To Chabod, the centralization of administration under the Spaniards was the result of the practical needs of imperial policy.

Toward the theories of history dominant in his own country Chabod exhibited the same intellectual independence he maintained toward the various European "schools" of history. In the first half of the twentieth century almost all Italian intellectuals were under the sway of Croce, and Chabod was no exception. In the final years of the Neapolitan philosopher's life, Chabod was even personally very close to Croce. A sharp distinction between the facts of history and man's consciousness of the facts makes Chabod's lectures on *Storia dell'idea d'Europa* and *L'Idea di Nazione*[25] original and almost novel treatments of somewhat worn-out subjects; and the emphasis Chabod placed on this distinction was certainly due to Croce. But Chabod did not share Croce's liberal optimism. He did not believe in a logic of history in which fuller knowledge would lead to an increasing recognition of the value of freedom. Chabod was distrustful of all theories which asserted that history was determined by abstract forces. "History, at least up to the present, has been made by men and not by automatons, by doctrines or so-called structures that by themselves, from the point of view of historical evaluation, are pure abstractions; they acquire the value of a historical force only when they succeed in dominating the minds of men . . . that means when ideology and social

---

[25] Both books were a series of university lectures, published posthumously by Laterza in Bari, under the editorships of Armando Saitta and Ernesto Sestan.

relations become a moral fact." [26] As much as these sentences express Chabod's awareness of the problems raised in modern discussions on the theory of history, their emphasis on the responsibility of man gives them a somewhat traditional character. Chabod was something of a traditionalist and this attitude contributed to the influence he exerted. For that was what was needed in the situation existing in Europe after World War II when it seemed more important to restore and to maintain old values than to rush after new gods. Moreover, the distortions of the past into which Italian historical scholarship had fallen under Fascism made a return to firm ground, a gaining of continuity and of contact with the traditions of the past, an important and challenging task. Chabod's larger historical works aimed to clarify insufficiently understood facts of the past; elimination of errors about the past was to Chabod quite as important as the placing of the past under a new perspective. Thus Chabod's books are somewhat old-fashioned, at least in the sense that they are consciously formed units in which the attempt is made to exhaust an entire topic. They are concerned with the same subjects as the work of nineteenth century historians: political history, history of religious movements, diplomatic history.

Yet there was a great difference between the work Chabod did in these fields and the work earlier historians had done. An example is Chabod's masterpiece, his *Storia della politica estera italiana dal 1870 al 1896,* which is one of the most important historical books published in the twentieth century. Of course this is a work of diplomatic history, but because Chabod was cognizant of all the most recent trends of historiography and because he acknowledged the need for deepening and widening the study of the past, his book represents a new kind of diplomatic history; it shows the multidimensional background from which actions in foreign policy spring, and it is a model of how diplomatic history ought to be written. For Chabod, foreign policy could not be cleanly separated from domestic policy.

[26] "La storia, almeno fino ad oggi, è stata fatta dagli uomini e non da automi, e dottrine e cosidette strutture, che in sé e per sé dal punto da vista della valutazione storiografica sono pure astrazioni, acquistano valore di forza storica solo quando riescono a infiammare di sè l'animo degli uomini—dei singoli come delle moltitudini—quando diventano una fede, una religione interiore capace anche di creare i martiri; quando cioè ideologie o rapporti sociali diventano un fatto morale. . . ." Chabod in the "Prefazione" of his *Storia della politica estera italiana* (Bari, 1951), p. xii. The entire "prefazione" is characteristic of Chabod's ideas on history.

Certainly the basic source materials of diplomatic history which Chabod used were diplomatic instructions and the reports and the agreements which evolved from them. But the manner in which diplomats reported events was dependent on the concepts with which they viewed and analyzed the forces of social life. An account of diplomatic history required an investigation of the intellectual world in which the policy makers and diplomats lived and acted. What Chabod aimed at and achieved in his book was an analysis of the mentality of the Italian ruling group.

Chabod was well aware of the complex problem involved in the use of this concept. Although Italian policy makers and diplomats might all be members of the same ruling group, they were individuals. The particular nature of their recommendations and actions depended on the individual element. Thus, in the final part of his book Chabod drew a number of biographical sketches that show the refractions of the common outlook in the mind of individual diplomats. Moreover, a closer analysis of the leading personalities showed that the experiences that had formed their outlook frequently were not purely Italian. The intellectual trends that had formed the mind of the Italian ruling group were common to the educated classes of all of Europe. Rome might be the visible focal point of the struggle between Christian tradition and modern skepticism but this debate was fought out in all European countries. What Germans and Frenchmen wrote, what German and French statesmen did, had its bearing on the Italian scene and reinforced the existing divisions in the minds of the Italians, or even created them. Chabod showed with precision and detail that even at the height of nationalism the political life of a single European nation was imbedded in a common European climate; the book is at one and the same time Italian diplomatic history and European intellectual history.

As different as were Meinecke, Bloch, and Chabod—not only as representatives of different intellectual traditions but also as personalities—certain common features apparent in their works opened a new phase in the development of historiography.

All of them extended their historical investigations into aspects of the past that previously had been regarded as of no relevance—or little relevance—for explaining the course of history. Each of them was interested in particular sides of the life of the past; thus their works point to the increasing amounts and kinds of material which the historian must investigate and interpret. Although Meinecke turned to the exploration of intellectual history, although Bloch was concerned with physical, economic, and social factors, and although Chabod emphasized political thought and political ideas, none of them would have claimed—as the political historians had done—that their particular fields of interest were solely important and the only key to the understanding of historical events. All three turned away from monistic explanations; all three recognized the necessity of taking into account a plurality of factors. They thought less in terms of cause and effect than in terms of connections and inter-relationships among the different aspects of life. Such questions and concerns led far beyond the national framework of history that the political historians of the nineteenth century had set and within which they had worked. Meinecke, Bloch, and Chabod all abandoned national history as the central subject of historiography. Whether Meinecke investigated the changing forms which fundamental ethical problems took in modern history, whether Bloch applied comparative methods in order to separate the general European structure of social life from its embodiment in particular national institutions, whether Chabod illuminated the entire European scene by analyzing the problems of Italian diplomacy, all looked upon the single nation from the perspective of a common European society.

In extending the subject matter of history and in widening the historical horizon, all of them tried to restore to history that vital element that to them history seemed to have lost: meaning and relevance to the present. But the course they took to achieve this aim brought into relief the differences among them. Meinecke's solution was "problem history": an issue with which man was confronted could be illuminated by studying the forms which this problem had taken in history or the manner in which man in the past had reacted to its challenge. The true character of the decision man has to make, as well as the full range of his possibilities, will, according to Meinecke, emerge from an attitude to history in which the final aim of an examination of the past is a deepened self-examination. Such an approach to history can have limited impact on the organization of research. Certainly Meinecke aimed to document his works fully, and he certainly regarded as valuable source material areas of history which the political historian had neglected. But the restudy and the reinterpretation of known material was to him no less important than the opening of new sources. Marc Bloch's views, in contrast, gave an impetus to an expansion of research enterprises. Bloch accepted the view that the phenomena of social life could be comprehended and explained in a strictly scientific way. And he believed that one of the essential contributions of history to the present was that historical investigations could assist in the construction of a system of social sciences. Bloch's work focused attention on the importance of all facets of social life; accordingly, in recent years, particularly in France, the collecting and editing of sources extended into new fields: economic statistics, data about prices and money, data about shipping, etc., etc.[27] Bloch believed that history, through its connection with the social sciences, was a part of modern scientific endeavors, but he did not think that history should be absorbed in the social sciences. History had its own independent role. History not only gave account of social development and social facts but its center was man's reaction to these external circumstances, "man in social action."

It might appear meaningless to characterize this stage of historiographical development by stating that it placed man in the center of its considerations because man has always been a subject of history. But it might perhaps be said that with realization of the time-conditioned nature of man's intellectual structure and of the causality determining the social connections in which his existence is placed, the old problem of the role of man in history arose in a new form. Historians of the twentieth century were able to renew the appeal of history because, with full awareness of the limited range of human action, they maintained that the study of history could demonstrate man's responsibility and man's power of decision. It emerged that the connection of history and moral philosophy had not been entirely arbitrary and that even professionalized history could not live without connection with ethics.

History and historians have always been formed by the political climate of their time. One cannot separate the re-examination of historical ideas and concepts since World War I from the rise of forces that denied the value of those achievements of the past to which the historians had been attached. And one notices that the significance of

---

27 See the publications of the École Pratique des Hautes Études, VIe Section: Centre de Recherches Historiques, concerned with *Affaires et Gens d'affaires, Ports-routes-trafics, Monnaie-prix-conjoncture, Les Hommes et la terre.*

the study of history for recognizing man's responsibility was accentuated by the rise of the inhuman forces of totalitarianism and Fascism. Meinecke, Bloch, and Chabod all knew where they stood, and Bloch paid for his convictions with his life.

Since World War I, political events, improved communications, the work of foundations in promoting exchange programs have brought European and American scholars closer together than ever before. The ideas that have been discussed among European historians since the 1920's and the methods and concepts that they introduced quickly became part of the thinking of American scholars. There is evident proof of this in the foundation of a number of periodicals and societies that reflect methodological concerns and the increased interest in intellectual and social history of European historians. In 1940 the first issue of the *Journal of the History of Ideas* was published; in the following year a special *Journal of Economic History* appeared; in 1958 a periodical for *Comparative Studies in Society and History* was founded; in 1961, one for *History and Theory*. But the differences in the organization and structure of educational institutions—which, as I have said, gave to the professionalization of history in America a different form from that it had in Europe—made the impact of the appearance of these new concerns on the development of historical scholarship in the United States rather dissimilar from that in Europe. In Europe, despite the large number of universities, the organization of scholarship was hierarchical and the professors at the most important universities were recognized as the leading figures in their profession. When Meinecke, Bloch, and Chabod were recognized as the outstanding men in their profession, they were appointed to professorships at the greatest universities of their countries, Berlin, Paris, Rome. In these positions they were able to exert a directing influence on the scholarly developments in their countries. Meinecke and Chabod were editors of the most important historical periodicals of Germany and Italy. As directors of seminars and research enterprises, as members of historical commissions, they disposed over patronage, they formed schools, and they could help their students along. But the apparatus had existed and functioned long before they took over its helm; they were continuators and not innovators. If they modified or changed the direction of historical studies, the intention was not to replace one approach by another but to enrich the existing historical thinking and to keep it up to date. The attitude inherent in the existing system was not to break with the past but to amalgamate new concepts and methods with the old, to maintain history as a unified field of scholarship.

In the United States new interests and investigations into unexplored fields were not easily integrated with traditional historical concerns. As I have said, special periodicals were founded for new trends, and the historians interested in these new trends assembled in special meetings and established societies for the promotion of their "cause." Although new fields were added to the existing fields of history, the image of the past did not gain in depth by the addition of another dimension.

Of course, some reasons for this form of procedure were economic. Financial support can be more readily obtained for undertakings for which the claim is made that they represent a new approach. But the possibility of proceeding by adding new fields rather than by modifying old approaches is enhanced by the way in which American educational institutions and their curriculums are formed: by their decentralization and unsystematic openness. There is no single university or single university professor who is so influential that his ideas can influence the entire course of historical scholarship. In addition, the dependence on public support results in giving preference in the curriculum to those fields that have public appeal. And public interest is more aroused by fields that are thought to be modern and capable of throwing new light on the determining factors of social life. Established fields, methods, and approaches—like political and diplomatic history—now represent a vested interest and they will remain. But maintenance or even enlargement of a department in a college or university can be more easily effected by adding specialists working in new, much discussed fields of history than by relying on the appeal of "history in general." For institutions it is prestigious to add specialists working in new fields of knowledge and for individuals it is advantageous to be one. There is a temptation to launch new trends, and sometimes they are not more than short-lived fashions that quickly disappear. But because even those new trends that are rooted in the development of historiography are added as special fields to history rather than integrated with it, they have to compete with other new interests as well as with the established fields. Thus these new trends frequently rigidify in their approach and methods or they are ruled by an exclusive missionary spirit that suggests that they represent not one but the only right approach to history. Some of these historical missionaries seem to live in an intellectual isolation that seems more suited to the Russian "old believers" than to the prophets of a new message.

If the development of European historiography and European historical thinking has given new relevance to the question of what is history, it is characteristic that American historians are continuing to debate whether history belongs to the humanities or to the social sciences. They see history as a scholarly activity that has many uses and therefore also many fields. But they do not see history as an independent and unified way of understanding the world. Because European historiography, despite new methods and developments, is secure in its autonomous position, it has both continuity and a minimum level of standards neither of which American historiography possesses. But it would be wrong to see the differences purely in black and white. American historical scholarship has a sensitivity to new developments that the slowly moving European scholarship does not. It is difficult to decide whether in the situation after World War II the strength of tradition or the ability to make changes is of greater benefit for the development of historical scholarship.

# THE PROBLEMS OF THE PRESENT

World War II and its aftermath placed new tasks before historians. One task was obvious: the events of recent years had to be brought into a historical context; in concrete terms, the developments leading to the outbreak of the war had to be investigated. After World War II, as after World War I, various European countries began to entrust independent scholars with the publication of the documents from the archives of their foreign ministries; again historical studies were directed toward work in diplomatic history looked upon from the point of view of individual nations. However, the situation that developed after World War II was very different from that after World War I. Historical research was not burdened with the moral question of war-guilt. Nobody, with the exception of a few capricious or self-seeking minds, has questioned the responsibility of Hitler and Nazi Germany for the war, and the investigation concentrated on the reasons for the failure of the various governments to take appropriate countermeasures in time. Furthermore, the connection of diplomatic events with military measures, with economic interests, and with social pressures was so evident that the incompleteness of any publication restricted to diplomatic documents and the superficiality of any investigation based purely on foreign office files was generally recognized.[1] But discussion of the interrelationship between foreign affairs and developments in the social, economic, and military spheres could not be contained within the national framework. Even if a study started with the problems faced by one of the European nations, the investigation soon extended beyond such national frontiers. Application of the comparative method and the replacement of the national framework by a European one were regarded almost as presuppositions for explaining the events of recent history. The fluctuations in the fates of the European nations had ac-

[1] For instance, see the discussion at the Tenth International Historical Congress in Rome on Mario Toscano's report on the origins of World War II, Comitato Internazionale di Scienze Storiche, *Atti del X Congresso Internazionale, Roma, 4-11 Settembre 1955* (Roma, 1957), pp. 623-33.

customed European historians to the concept of crisis. With an almost
exaggerated fervor this concept was now used to describe the interrelated complex of recent developments which were viewed as being
rooted in a crisis of European society that affected all European countries, although to a different degree. The symptom of this crisis was
the rise of a phenomenon contradictory to the traditions of European
political and intellectual history: totalitarianism.[2] The manner in
which the most recent period of history was conceived and historically integrated shows clearly the impact of the concepts and methods
that had been evolved in preceding discussions.

But World War II had its bearing not only on developments in
Europe but throughout the whole world. It was a global war and one
of its most decisive consequences has been to change the position of
Europe in the world. Thus, another task forced upon the historian
in consequence of the war was to explain the shift in power away
from Europe toward other parts of the world and to consider those
non-European peoples who now emerged as determining factors in
history but on which, because of the Europe-centered tradition of
historical scholarship, little had been done in the past. Now they had
to be viewed as products of history, as entities formed by their own
traditions. The practical consequence was the promotion of studies
in Chinese and Arabic history, African, Latin American, and even
Russian history. Such enlargement of historical subject matter could
more easily be achieved in the United States than in Europe.[3] Because
a division of history into different geographic departments or fields—
English history, French history, American history, German history—
had been customary in the United States, new fields could be
smoothly added to the history departments in the larger universities.
But in Europe the professor of history was responsible for the entire
field of history, at least, in either the medieval or modern or ancient
period; the fact that his work was frequently limited to the history
of his own nation was not openly contradictory to this fiction because
the national history of a European nation extended necessarily into a

[2] For instance, see Raymond Aron, *Les Guerres en chaîne* (Paris, 1951; translated as *The Century of Total War*), or Hannah Arendt, *The Origins of Totalitarianism* (New York, 1951), or Ernst Nolte, *Der Faschismus in seiner Epoche*
(Muenchen, 1963).
[3] On the problem of the "Europazentrik" of Continental historical scholarship,
see the colloquium "Wege der Universalgeschichte," *Saeculum*, XIV (1963),
41-59.

European framework, and European history was regarded as "history in general." But the history of non-European countries was clearly outside the competence of the traditional European professor of history and unrelated to what he considered to be the core of universal history. In Europe the establishment of chairs for Latin Americans, Chinese, American, or Russian history did not mean that these fields were easily accessible to students of history. Experts in these fields, in special institutes or seminars, led a rather separate existence from that of the "true historians," i.e., the professors and students working in European history. However, the problems that the change of Europe's world position have raised are not only the formal ones of adding the study of the history of non-European peoples to the historical curriculum; the problems are also—and probably foremost—of an intellectual nature, problems of conceptualization. As long as universal history was regarded as identical with the history of Europe and of European expansion over the world, history could be conceived as an interconnected and unifying process. But with the realization that non-European historical events happened earlier or simultaneously with those of European history, though quite unrelated to them, the entire concept of a unified process of history, of universal history, became open to doubt. Even if historical scholars might have been hesitant to venture beyond well-known paths, their attention would have been directed to these problems by the general interest aroused by works that placed universal history in new patterns. The reawakening of interest in Spengler, whose influence at the beginning of the Thirties had almost disappeared,[4] and most of all, the popularity which Toynbee's *Study of History* has enjoyed since the end of World War II (its first volumes, published in the Thirties, had found only a very limited response), were characteristic of the interest in new concepts of universal history.[5] Although few historical scholars will accept the validity of these patterns, they cannot deny the importance of the question which stimulated these attempts to provide a new structure for universal history.

The state of historical scholarship is not only influenced by problems connected with the outbreak and the results of World War II; the most decisive challenge has been brought about by the scientific

[4] See H. S. Hughes, *Oswald Spengler* (New York, 1952), pp. 137 ff.
[5] For a discussion of the problems raised by Toynbee, see *Entretiens autour de Arnold Toynbee,* ed. Raymond Aron (Paris, 1961).

and technical discoveries and changes that have taken place in the last decades. From the danger of complete annihilation through nuclear war to the reduction of global distances by jets, from the economic possibilities of automation to the scientific possibilities through computers, the face of the world has changed so much that it seems to bear little resemblance to that of former centuries. Although, or perhaps, because historians know about the past, they are very much aware of the great transformation going on in the world today; they realize that the question can be raised whether concern with history has any meaning in a world that is fundamentally changed from the world of the past.[6]

The new factors arising from World War II and its aftermath have influenced the development of historical scholarship in different ways. The number of students of history is not diminishing, but in Europe as well as in the United States a decline of interest in the earlier periods of history and an increasing concentration on most recent history can be noticed. A great part of historical work seems to assume the character of an auxiliary science that serves politics by explaining the background of present-day issues. It can be observed that in order to counteract this trend, studies on purely political happenings of earlier times have become fewer; and questions of intellectual and social history have gained in popularity. In investigating the formation of our values and ideas and in examining the organization of social systems on levels closest to man's physical nature and needs, the permanent elements and challenges which underlie complicated social structures and which continue in spite of changes in form become more evident. The relevance of the past to the present becomes recognizable. Another characteristic of the present situation is the increased use of the comparative method. With the adoption of the concept of civilization to designate the broadest possible factor in the historical process that still represents a distinctive and irreducible unit, the comparative method could now be used to analyze not only phenomena of similar character in different societies of the same civilization but also similar phenomena of different civilizations.

In the organization of historical scholarship in recent years, a new element was introduced by the foundation of institutes in which his-

---

6 For some nostalgic reflections on this point, see Carl Bridenbaugh's "The Great Mutation," *AHR*, LXVIII (1963), 316 ff.

torians, free from teaching obligations and duties, could pursue research. Such institutes, although different in purpose and differently organized, have been established in several countries. In the United States, such institutes were frequently intended to initiate and stimulate research and work in areas outside the Western world which had not previously been subjected to intensive scholarly investigation. The Istituto Italiano per gli Studi Storici in Naples, which Croce founded and Chabod directed was conceived as a postgraduate school. Members of the Max Planck Institut fuer Geschichte in Goettingen can devote their full time to research and writing. Behind all these establishments there is realization that the extension of historical research over wider geographical areas as well as over the most diverse aspects of human life requires the acquisition of special knowledge and acquaintance with methods that cannot be acquired in the course of regular academic training. The exchange with scholars working in similar fields, or with experts in the methods of other disciplines, provide scholars with the equipment that the enlarged tasks of historical study require.[7] It is clear that such institutes are particularly suited for work in comparative history, and, at the Max Planck Institut, for instance, this approach is strongly emphasized.

But one might consider this new emphasis on centers for historical research from another point of view. In the times in which we live, the creation of opportunities which would allow a thorough rethinking of the problems and tasks of history is particularly appropriate. University routine leaves little time for probing the consequences of the great transformation of our century. In American universities, the established set-up, whether in examination requirements, arrangement of seminars, organization of courses, can be altered only with difficulty; the individual scholar is forced to keep strictly to his own specialty. Yet it must be said that the increasing willingness of American colleges and universities to give regular leaves, to free young scholars from summer teaching by financial support, and to administer grants given to individuals by foundations indicates a recognition of the problems involved in the present state of historical scholarship and of scholarship in general.

In this consideration of the history of historiography, the connection between political and social events and the development of his-

---

[7] See Bloch, *The Historian's Craft*, p. 47: "For the only true history, which can advance only through mutual aid, is universal history."

torical concepts and methods has been demonstrated again and again. The events described as determining the state of historical scholarship after World War II have been experienced in the United States as well as in Europe. Thus, despite differences in historical outlook and in the social role of history in the past, younger historians in Europe and in the United States must now struggle with the same issues.

In some respects the situation seems similar to that which existed more than a hundred years ago. Again the question whether history is more than an auxiliary science might be raised, and the problem of the relation that ought to exist between research and teaching has reappeared. The intellectual and institutional bonds which merged through the professionalization of history seem to be dissolved. But the similarity of the present situation with that existing at the beginning of the nineteenth century is deceiving. If we leave aside the particular issues that the changed world constellation has raised for the methods and organization of history at present, the foremost task of the historian is to regain an image of the past in which history emerges as the conceptualization of a unified process. For the existence of history as a profession and as an independent field depends on the conception of the past as a totality. But the need for reconstructing a historical consciousness that integrates the present with the past is much more than the professional interest of the historian. It is rooted in the general need of our time. Because history is the study of man in his social conditions, the establishment of the relation of the past to the present reasserts the role of man in a world that appears to slide out of human control. And justification for the concern with history is the conviction that "there is no future without a past and there is no past without a future."

# INDEX

393